THE PSYCHOLOGY
OF DEPRESSION:

CONTEMPORARY THEORY
AND RESEARCH

THE PSYCHOLOGY OF DEPRESSION:
CONTEMPORARY THEORY AND RESEARCH

EDITED BY RAYMOND J. FRIEDMAN AND MARTIN M. KATZ

DIVISION OF EXTRAMURAL RESEARCH PROGRAMS
NATIONAL INSTITUTE OF MENTAL HEALTH, WASHINGTON, D.C.

 V. H. WINSTON & SONS

1974   Washington, D. C.

A HALSTED PRESS BOOK

JOHN WILEY & SONS
New York   Toronto   London   Sydney

Hemisphere Publishing Corporation
1025 Vermont Ave., N. W.
Washington, D. C. 20005

Distributed solely by Halsted Press Division, John Wiley & Sons, Inc.,
New York.

Library of Congress Cataloging in Publication Data:

Main entry under title:

The Psychology of Depression.

"Proceedings of a workshop, sponsored by the Clinical Research
Branch, Division of Extramural Research Programs, National Insti-
tute of Mental Health, the Airlie House, Airlie, Virginia, Oct. 8-9,
1971."
"A Halsted Press book."
1. Depression, Mental—Congresses. 2. Manic-depressive psychoses—
Congresses. I. Friedman, Raymond J., ed. II. Katz, Martin M.,
ed. III. United States. National Institute of Mental Health.
Clinical Research Branch. [DNLM: 1. Depression—Congresses.
WM207 P947p 1971]
RC537.P74   616.8'528   74-712
ISBN 0-470-28084-0

Printed in the United States of America

CONTENTS

PARTICIPANTS

Aaron T. Beck, M.D., Professor of Psychiatry, University of Pennsylvania School of Medicine, Philadelphia, Pennsylvania.

Paul Chodoff, M.D., Clinical Professor of Psychiatry, George Washington University School of Medicine, Washington, D.C.

Jarl E. Dyrud, M.D., Professor of Psychiatry, The University of Chicago, Chicago, Illinois.

Paul Ekman, Ph.D., Professor of Psychology, Langley Porter Neuropsychiatric Institute, University of California, San Francisco, California.

Charles B. Ferster, Ph.D., Professor and Chairman, Department of Psychology, American University, Washington, D.C.

Raymond J. Friedman, M.D., Clinical Research Branch, Division of Extramural Research Programs, National Institute of Mental Health, Rockville, Maryland.

Frederick Goodwin, M.D., Chief, Clinical Research Unit, Section on Psychiatry, Laboratory of Clinical Science, National Institute of Mental Health, Bethesda, Maryland.

Martin M. Katz, Ph.D., Chief, Clinical Research Branch, Division of Extramural Research Programs, National Institute of Mental Health, Rockville, Maryland.

I. Charles Kaufman, M.D., Professor of Psychiatry, University of Colorado School of Medicine, Denver, Colorado.

Gerald L. Klerman, M.D., Professor of Psychiatry, Harvard Medical School, Boston, Massachusetts.

Julian J. Lasky, Ph.D., Executive Secretary, Clinical Projects Research Review Committee, Clinical Research Branch, Division of Extramural Research Programs, National Institute of Mental Health, Rockville, Maryland.

Peter M. Lewinsohn, Ph.D., Professor of Psychology, University of Oregon, Eugene, Oregon.

John B. McDevitt, M.D., Associate Director of Research, Masters Children's Center, New York, New York.

Morris B. Parloff, Ph.D., Chief, Psychotherapy and Behavioral Intervention Section, Clinical Research Branch, Division of Extramural Research Programs, National Institute of Mental Health, Rockville, Maryland.

Allen Raskin, Ph.D., Research Psychologist, Clinical Studies Unit, Psychopharmacology Research Branch, Division of Extramural Research Programs, National Institute of Mental Health, Rockville, Maryland.

Arthur Schmale, Jr., M.D., Associate Professor of Psychiatry and Medicine, School of Medicine and Dentistry, University of Rochester, Rochester, New York.

Dean Schuyler, M.D., Staff Psychiatrist, Center for Studies of Suicide, National Institute of Mental Health, Rockville, Maryland.

Steven Secunda, M.D., Acting Chief, Depression Section, Clinical Research Branch, Division of Extramural Research Programs, National Institute of Mental Health, Rockville, Maryland.

Martin E. P. Seligman, Ph.D., Associate Visiting Professor of Psychology, University of Pennsylvania, Philadelphia, Pennsylvania.

Melford Spiro, Ph.D., Professor of Anthropology, University of California, San Diego, California.

Norman Tabachnick, M.D., Professor of Psychiatry, University of Southern California, Suicide Prevention Center, Los Angeles, California.

Thomas A. Williams, M.D., Associate Professor of Psychiatry, University of Utah College of Medicine, Salt Lake City, Utah.

INTRODUCTION

In this introduction we hope to place this volume in historical perspective by briefly tracing the progress of psychological and psychiatric theory and research on the clinical condition of depression.

The literature on depression has an old and noble lineage which begins with Job and Saul, whose depressions are chronicled in the Old Testament. Hippocrates rendered the first clinical description of "melancholia." In the second century A.D. Aretaeus, of Cappodocia, delineated the manic-depressive cycle, and from Plutarch to Pinel writers, philosophers, and scientists have produced a long train of incisive phenomenological descriptions. Beck has concluded that "there are few psychiatric syndromes whose clinical descriptions are so constant through successive eras of history." Emil Kraepelin, despite his narrow focus on prognosis as the essential criterion for categorization, was the first to advance beyond 19th century phenomenology by providing the first systematic classificatory scheme.

Meyer and Freud, along with Kraepelin, ushered in the modern era of psychiatry and their respective focuses on the personality profiles and reactive patterns, the unconscious determinants of mental life, and the time course of psychiatric conditions, provided the soil for effective treatment and research. Kraepelin's influence on classification lives today. Meyerian thought culminated in 1952 with the adoption of reaction types by the American Psychiatric Association in its *Manual of Mental Disorders*. And of course the Freudian influence on depression theory and research has been profound and was *the* dominant force during the first half of the 20th century.

In 1958 Meyer Mendelson published the *Psychoanalytic Concepts of Depression*, a book which clearly serves as a major statement of psychodynamic theory, and in which he summarized the results of a progressive era of psychoanalytic inquiry. After reviewing the theoretical contributions of Abraham, Freud, Rado, Fenichel, Bibring, and Jacobson, as well as other psychoanalytic contributions to the diagnosis and treatment of depression, Mendelson concluded, "It would have been pleasing to be able to report that this body of literature represented, in essence, a progress through the years of a Great Investigation. It does so in part. But perhaps even more does it represent a Great Debate, with the rhetorical rather than scientific implications of this word." Mendelson reflected upon this rich and productive era which was "chiefly characterized by boldly speculative theoretical formulations and by insightful clinical studies." It was a time of rapid advance in clinical theory and represented "an era of large-scale conceptualizations and generalizations."

Mendelson concluded: "This era is drawing to a close, the theories and categories which were so characteristic of it are now being subjected to critical reappraisal. There are increasing demands for responsible, sober testing of theories and hypotheses." The new wave of research on the depressive disorders did indeed materialize, not on the psychology of depression as Mendelson had predicted, but rather the 1960's witnessed a proliferation of biological and pharmacological research.

The second major historical influence on our present effort is a book by Aaron T. Beck, who in 1967 reviewed the state of depression theory and research in a volume entitled *Depression*. Beck presented an up-to-date and concise summary of biological, pharmacological, and psychological theories and of research in depression, and this volume probably remains the most authoritative reference in the field. Beck concluded, in striking contrast to Mendelson's prediction 8 years earlier, that *"There has been a dearth of systematic psychological and psychodynamic studies of depression as compared with the biological studies."*

In 1969 the Clinical Research Branch of the National Institute of Mental Health sponsored a conference at Williamsburg, Virginia, to assess the current state of research on the psychobiology of depression. The results of this meeting are chronicled in a volume entitled *Recent Advances in the Psychobiology of Depression* (Williams, Katz, Shield, Jr., 1970). One of the primary conclusions was that in an era of burgeoning interest and research on its biological bases, the field was in need of new and innovative thinking concerning the psychology of depression.

The final cornerstone of this volume is the NIMH 1970 *Special Report on the Depressive Illnesses*, which outlined the enormous public health problem posed by the depressive illnesses and concluded by noting that despite the increasing reliance on somatic treatments, particularly new psychotropic drugs, the task of treating or modifying or rehabilitating the greatest proportion of depressed people still depended on the psycho-social therapeutic modalities.

These four reviews of depression research (the books by Mendelson and Beck, the Williamsburg volume, and the 1970 Special Report) form the backdrop for the Psychology of Depression Workshop.

THE PSYCHOLOGY OF DEPRESSION WORKSHOP

Alerted by statements at the Williamsburg Conference concerning the psychology of depression, and with a growing awareness of the enormous public health problem posed by the depressive disorders, the Clinical Research Branch began in 1971 to explore the current status of research on the psychology of depression. A review of Institute research-grant support revealed several studies using an animal model, but only one project that was concerned with the psychology of depression in human beings. Where was the interest and the research legacy which the "Great Era of Exploration" had offered? Where was the expected confirmation of so many rich hypotheses? Why hadn't research on depression attracted the behaviorists who currently loomed so large on the clinical research scene?

These were some of the questions leading to the development of a Psychology of Depression Workshop held in Airlie, Virginia, in October 1971. The Airlie House Workshop represented a means for the Clinical Research Branch of NIMH to consult the research community and was conceived with the following goals in mind: (1) To assess the present state of theory and research on the psychology of depression. (2) To bring together what appeared to be the nucleus of a research community in this area to allow for exchange and cross-fertilization of ideas between researchers working in various disciplines. (3) To attempt to integrate theoretical ideas and research data and to develop new perspectives. (4) To identify areas requiring research and the means of stimulating this research.

The workshop was divided into three sections. The first was devoted to reviewing contemporary psychological theories of the nature and etiology of depression. The second portion of the workshop consisted of papers describing contemporary research efforts in this field. Detailed discussions (which have been summarized in this volume) followed the presentation of each paper. The third section of the meeting was devoted to critical comments by senior investigators who had been in the field of depression but who had also brought with them perspectives from allied fields. The meeting concluded with a broad-ranging discussion by all of the participants concerning the current state and specific recommendations for the future in this area of research.

This volume is organized in the same manner as the workshop, and every effort has been made to preserve the original flavor of the discussions which followed abbreviated presentations of the papers. Some of the papers have been partially revised and expanded following the workshop, and the discussions have been edited.

Reviews of cognitive, behavioral, and psychoanalytic theory by Aaron T. Beck, Charles Ferster, and Paul Chodoff, respectively, comprise the first section of this volume. As noted previously, Dr. Beck's book *Depression* (1967) was one of the major historical antecedents of this workshop, and in Chapter 1, "The Development of Depression: A Cognitive Model," Dr. Beck presents the current status of his theory and research efforts and portrays the critical elements in the onset and development of a depressive episode. Dr. Charles Ferster was one of the first behaviorists to turn his attention to depression when, in 1966, he presented the first functional analysis of clinical depression to appear in the behavioral literature. In subsequent years Dr. Ferster has developed an increasing interest and sophistication in clinical matters, and in Chapter 2 presents the synthesis of his extensive research background in his emerging clinical interest. Chapter 3, "The Depressive Personality: A Critical Review," by Paul Chodoff, represents a critical assessment of psychoanalytic theory and general personality theory concerning the premorbid characteristics of those predisposed to depression. Dr. Chodoff, by analyzing the research literature, has developed suggestions regarding future research in this area and also presents some new theoretical considerations about the fundamental personality characteristics predisposing to depression.

Part II consists of examples of contemporary research on the psychology of depression. Chapter 4, "Depression and Learned Helplessness," is a summary of an exciting new research methodology and potential model of depression developed by Martin Seligman. Dr. Seligman describes the condition in animals brought about by uncontrollable trauma which strikingly resembles reactive depression in humans. The similarity of this condition to human states is discussed in terms of symptoms, etiology, cure, and prevention. In "Depression and Adaptation," Gerald Klerman has synthesized the results of 10 years of his own research on the psychology of depression and has advanced new theoretical considerations regarding the signal functions and the adaptive significance of depression. In Chapter 6, "A Behavioral Approach to Depression," Peter Lewinsohn offers a comprehensive review of his current research program and a discussion of its theoretical basis. Perhaps Dr. Lewinsohn's unique contribution to the area of the psychology of depression rests on his determined pursuit, in a behavioral framework of empirical clinical data, of research on the home environment of depressed patients, their family interaction styles, and the careful observation of the behavior of depressed persons in groups and other clinical and experimental settings. In Chapter 7, "Depression as an Indicator of Lethality in Suicidal Patients," Carl Wold and Norman Tabachnick attempt to bridge the gap that has existed between depression and suicide research. Drs. Wold and Tabachnick outline evidence indicating that somatic factors are particularly significant prognostic indicators. The concluding chapter, "Non-verbal Behavior and Psychopathology," outlines Ekman and Friesen's new techniques concerning the quantification of nonverbal expressive behavior. The potential application of these techniques to depression research is reviewed.

Part III, entitled "Overview and Perspectives," is an edited discussion divided into two sections. The first is composed of a series of comments by a panel of "experts." These senior clinicians and researchers were each asked to prepare critical comments regarding the presentations and discussions at the workshop based upon their own unique experience in the field. Jarl Dyrud's comments are drawn from his experience as a psychoanalytic researcher and more recently as a synthesizer of psychoanalytic and learning theory. Frederick Goodwin presents a plea for the full integration of psychology and biology, as well as a concise and current review of the major trends in biological research. I. Charles Kaufman comments from the vantage point of a psychoanalyst who has an extensive background in experimental primate research. His research efforts concerning the influence of the social matrix on monkeys' reaction to object loss are presented. Arthur Schmale, a member of the Rochester research team, highlights his own theoretical and research findings and shares his comments about the future. The final panelist is Melford Spiro, an anthropologist, who brings a cross-cultural perspective to bear on depression research.

The second section of Part III is composed of a general discussion engaged in by all of the participants of the workshop. Animal model research, the interface between psychoanalytic, psychodynamic and behavioral models, cross-cultural contributions, childhood depression, the methodological breakthroughs necessary for future research, and new directions in depression research are among the subjects discussed in this section.

USES OF THIS VOLUME

It is rare in these days of overspecialization in psychiatry and psychology to assemble clinicians, theorists, and investigators to seriously examine new developments in research and their role in helping us to understand an intensely complex and enigmatic clinical condition. To those interested in and sophisticated about the area of depression research (and psychiatric research in general), the current volume offers an attempt at clarification of the salient research efforts in this field, examples of new styles of research, and indications about the future needs of this field. New methods of investigation are presented and discussed and older techniques are critically reviewed. Finally, although this is a volume concerned with theory and research, a large segment of the participants in the conference and contributors to the volume are clinicians involved in patient care. Therefore, though the focus of the workshop is on "research," the "clinical" perspective is well represented.

Those of us present at Airlie House considered the workshop a success in providing an exchange of ideas and a cross-fertilization of points of view and in identifying areas in need of research effort. Our hope is that this volume will further stimulate new and imaginative thinking in theory and research regarding the psychology of depression.

Raymond J. Friedman
Martin M. Katz

May 1974

FOREWORD

In the National Institute of Mental Health's recent *Special Report on Depression (1973)*, we note that the clinical condition of depression appears on the increase and is beginning to rival schizophrenia as the nation's number one mental health problem. Some ten percent of the general population will have a significant depressive episode at some time in their lives, and we are aware that of the 22,000 suicides reported annually, upwards of 80 percent can be traced to a precipitating depressive episode. It has been important, therefore, for clinical and basic scientists to turn their attention to this critical public health problem, and the NIMH, through its support program and its intramural laboratories has, over the past several years, encouraged a searching and a broad-ranged investigational attack on the problem. During that period of time we have witnessed interesting changes in our notions of causality and some major shifts in our ways of thinking about the general phenomena of clinical depression. In introducing this volume, it is of some interest to review briefly the background of theory on the problem and to note some of these new directions.

The impact of psychoanalytic or psychodynamic thinking in the Thirties and Forties led most American psychiatrists and psychologists to view the more serious forms of depression as the outcome of pyschological and developmental events; biology plays a secondary role. European psychiatry, on the other hand, has always thought of the psychotic form of this condition as a more strictly biological state, labeled "endogenous," and viewed its milder forms as "reactive" referring to the fact that the latter are primarily the outcome of environmental, not internal forces. The introduction of the psychotropic drugs and the refinements in biochemical methodology in the early Fifties began to have significant effects on theories of psychosis in this country. Since that time, we have witnessed a wave of important creative research on the role of biology in shaping the nature of this pervasive human condition. This shift has led to interest in a very elegant theory of causality which places the role of central nervous system transmitters in the center of investigation and has resulted in a provocative debate which views psychodynamic theory as highly relevant only in the less serious or milder forms of normal and clinical depression.

NIMH staff, aware of the burgeoning productivity of biochemists, biological psychiatrists, and psychophysiologists in this field, and the potential impact that these results might have on its understanding and treatment, convened a major national conference—Recent Advances in the Psychobiology of the Depressive Illnesses in 1969, now referred to as the Williamsburg Conference. In looking back on events up to the early Fifties, one is struck by the distance the field has come from earlier ways of thinking about etiology and nature to this new set of theories. It occurred to the staff of our Clinical Research Branch, who were responsible for that '69 conference, that with the current intense interest and focus on biological hypotheses, we may have begun to neglect what needed to be done in the area of psychology to provide a more comprehensive base for ultimately understanding the interaction of internal and environmental forces in the creation of these states.

The understanding of mental disorder, unlike that of other "medical" illnesses or diseases, requires the application of investigational approaches and the synthesis of knowledge from many disciplines, primarily the biological, psychological, and social sciences. Further, I think it fair to say that there is little possibility of our ever comprehending this most complex of human conditions by adopting a unifaceted approach to the study of its nature and its roots. It became apparent that *psychological* research on depression had lagged considerably over these past 15 years and one had reason to wonder whether we were simply dealing with a plateau, or a decline in the influence of psychodynamic theory, or simply a lack of new important ideas in this sphere. Our staff, in investigating that problem in 1970, were surprised to find that the NIMH was, in fact, supporting very little psychological research on depression. Further, the study revealed that what little research existed was different in quality and content than might be expected from current psychological and psychodynamic theories. Further, despite the scarcity of such work, it was apparent that these new directions were provocative in themselves and showed promise of uncovering wholly different paths to our understanding than had prior investigations in this field.

The editors of this volume identified the most representative theories extant in the field, and the best of contemporary psychological research as a way of initiating the kind of discussion and thought that might lead to a reconsideration of the current state of knowledge and stimulate a more integrated approach to research in this field. Thus, the new volume is intended to provide an overview of what is currently known in this field and is viewed as a worthy "partner" for the "psychobiology" volume in our attempts to resolve critical issues of the etiology of this thoroughly human condition.

Bertram S. Brown
Director, National Institute of Mental Health

ACKNOWLEDGMENTS

The completion of this volume would have been impossible without the enthusiasm of the participants of the Conference. Their hard work and punctuality in meeting a variety of deadlines has speeded the publication of this volume. We wish to extend special thanks to Aaron T. Beck, M.D., for his advice during the planning stages of the Workshop, and to Thomas A. Williams, M.D., and Louis A. Wienckowski, Ph.D., for their consultation in the early phases of the project.

Without the dedication of Mrs. Dona V. Kelly to the tiresome task of transcribing the tapes of the meeting, retyping numerous editions of papers and discussions, and editorial assistance, the early publication of this volume might not have been a reality.

PART I
CONTEMPORARY THEORY

1
THE DEVELOPMENT OF DEPRESSION: A COGNITIVE MODEL[1]

Aaron T. Beck
University of Pennsylvania

DEPRESSION AND THE NATURE OF MAN

1 A scientist, shortly after assuming the presidency of a prestigious scientific group, gradually became morose and confided to a friend that he had an overwhelming urge to leave his career and become a hobo.

2 A devoted mother who had always felt strong love for her children started to neglect them and formulated a serious plan to destroy them and then herself.

3 An epicurean who relished eating beyond all other satisfactions developed an aversion for food and stopped eating.

4 A wealthy businessman publicly proclaimed his guilt over a few minor misdemeanors of some decades before, put on a beggar's clothes and begged for food.

5 A woman, on hearing of the sudden death of a close friend, smiled for the first time in several weeks.

These strange actions, completely inconsistent with the individual's previous behavior and values, are all expressions of the same underlying condition—depression.

By what perversity does depression mock the most hallowed notions of human nature and biology?

The instinct for self-preservation and the maternal instincts appear to vanish. Basic biological drives such as hunger and sexual drive are extinguished. Sleep, the easer of all woes, is thwarted. Social instincts such as attraction to other people, love, and affection evaporate. The "pleasure principle" and "reality

---

[1] This chapter will appear in expanded form in Beck, A. T., *Twisted Thinking: The Cognitive Basis of Emotional Disorders,* in press.

principle," the goals of maximizing pleasure and minimizing pain, are turned around. Not only is the capacity for enjoyment stifled, but the victims of this odd malady appear driven to behave in ways that enhance their suffering. Capacity to respond with mirth to humorous situations or with anger to situations that would ordinarily infuriate seems lost.

At one time, this strange affliction was ascribed to demons that allegedly took possession of the victim. Theories advanced since then have not yet provided a more durable solution to the problem of depression. We are still encumbered by a disorder that seems to discredit the most firmly entrenched concepts of the nature of man. Paradoxically, the anomalies of depression may provide the clues for understanding this mysterious condition.

The complete reversal in the patient's behavior in depression would seem, initially, to defy explanation. During his depression, the patient's personality is far more like that of other depressives than like his previous personality. A close examination of the personality and behavioral changes can illuminate the baffling disorder, however. Feelings of pleasure and joy are replaced by sadness and apathy; the broad range of spontaneous desires and involvement in activities are eclipsed by passivity and desires to escape; hunger and sexual drive are replaced by revulsion toward food and sex; interest and involvement in usual activities are converted into avoidance and withdrawal. Finally, the desire to live is switched off and replaced by the wish to die (see Table 1).

As an initial step in understanding a baffling condition such as depression, we can attempt to arrange the various phenomena into some kind of understandable sequence. At various times, writers have assigned primacy to the intense sadness, wishes to "hibernate," self-destructive wishes, or physiological disturbance.

Is the painful emotion the catalytic agent? Certainly distress or suffering in themselves can hardly be considered the stimulus for the other depressive symptoms. Other unpleasant states such as physical pain, nausea, dizziness, shortness of breath, or anxiety rarely, if ever, lead to typical depressive symptoms such as renunciation of major objectives in life, obliteration of affectionate feelings, or wishes to die. In fact, under the influence of pain, people seem to treasure more than ever those aspects of life that they have found meaningful. Nor does sadness appear to have specific qualities that can account for the self-castigations, the distortions in thinking, or loss of drive for gratifications that typify depression.

Similar difficulties are encountered in assigning primacy to other characteristics of depression. Some writers have seized on the passivity and the withdrawal of attachments to other people as forms of an atavistic wish to hibernate. If the desire to conserve energy is its goal, why does the human organism experience increased suffering and why does it seek and occasionally attain death by suicide? Ascribing the primary role to physiological symptoms such as the disturbances in sleep, appetite, and sexuality poses even greater

TABLE 1
Changes from Normal to Depressed State

| Items | Changes | |
	Normal state	Depressed state
Stimulus	Response	
Loved object	Affection	Loss of feeling, revulsion
Favorite activities	Pleasure	Boredom
New opportunities	Enthusiasm	Indifference
Humor	Amusement	Mirthlessness
Novel stimuli	Curiosity	Lack of interest
Abuse	Anger	Self-criticism, sadness
Goal or drive	Direction	
Gratification	Pleasure	Avoidance
Welfare	Self-care	Self-neglect
Self-preservation	Survival	Suicide
Achievement	Success	Withdrawal
Thinking	Appraisal	
About self	Realistic	Self-devaluating
About future	Hopeful	Hopeless
About environment	Realistic	Overwhelming
Biological and physiological activities	Symptom	
Appetite	Spontaneous hunger	Loss of appetite
Sexuality	Spontaneous desire	Loss of desire
Sleep	Restful	Disturbed
Energy	Spontaneous	Fatigued

difficulties. It is difficult to understand the sequence by which these physiological disturbances can account for such varied phenomena such as self-criticism, negative view of the world, and loss of the anger and mirth responses. Certainly when loss of appetite or sleep occurs as the result of a debilitating physical illness it does not produce the other symptoms of depression.

THE CLUE: THE SENSE OF LOSS

The problem of sorting the phenomena of depression into an understandable sequence may be attacked by simply asking the patient why he feels sad or by encouraging him to express his repetitive ideas. Depressed patients often provide essential information in spontaneous statements such as "I'm sad because I'm worthless," "I have no future," "I've lost everything," "My family is gone—I have nobody," or "Life has nothing for me."

It is relatively easy to detect the dominant theme in the statements of the moderately or severely depressed patient. He regards himself as lacking some element or attribute he considers essential for his happiness: competence in attaining his goals, attractiveness to other people, closeness to family or friends, tangible possessions, good health, or status or position. Such self-appraisals reflect the way the depressed patient perceives his life situation.

Although many nondepressed people experience similar deprivations, the depressed patient differs from them in the way he construes this experience: he either misinterprets or exaggerates the loss, or he attaches overgeneralized or extravagant meanings to the loss. In a long-term study of depressed patients, we found that each of the patients presented distortion and illogical thinking centering on the theme of loss (Beck 1963). These aberrations included selective abstraction, arbitrary inferences, and magnification.

In exploring the theme of loss, we once again find that a psychological disorder revolves around a *cognitive problem;* in the case of the depressed patient, distortions regarding the patient's evaluations of his world, of himself, and of his future.

The content of the distorted evaluations is relevant to the concept of shrinkage of the domain as the stimulus for the arousal of sadness (Beck 1971). The depressive's view of his valued attributes, relationships, and achievements is saturated with the notion of loss—past, present, and future. When he considers his present status, he sees a barren world; he feels pressed to the wall by external demands that cheat him of his meager resources and thwart him from attaining what he wants.

The term "loser" captures the flavor of the depressive's appraisal of himself and his experience. He agonizes over the notion that he has experienced significant losses, such as his friends, his health, or his prized possessions. He also regards himself as a "loser" in the colloquial sense: he is a misfit, an inferior and inadequate being unable to meet his responsibilities and reach his goals. If he undertakes a project or seeks some gratification, he expects to be defeated or disappointed. He finds no respite in his dreams: he is portrayed as a misfit and thwarted in his attempts to achieve his goals.

In considering the concept of loss, we should be sensitive to the crucial importance of meanings and connotations. What represents a painful loss for one person may be trivial to another. It is important to recognize that the depressed patient dwells on "hypothetical losses" and "pseudo-losses." When he thinks about a possible loss, he treats his conjecture as though it were an established fact.

A depressed man, for example, characteristically reacted to his wife's tardiness in meeting him with the thought, "She might have died on the way." He then construed the *hypothesized loss* as an actual event and became forlorn. Pseudo-loss is the incorrect labeling of any event as a loss; for example, a change in status that may actually be a gain. A depressed patient who sold some shares of stock at a large profit experienced a prolonged sense of deprivation over eliminating the securities from his portfolio and ruminated over the notion that the sale had impoverished him.

Granted that the perception of loss produces sadness, how does this sense of loss engender other symptoms of depression such as pessimism, self-criticism, escape-avoidance-giving up, suicidal wishes, and the physiological disorder?

To illuminate this problem, it would be useful to explore the chronology of depression, the onset and full development of symptoms. This sequence is most clearly demonstrated in cases of "reactive depression;" that is, depression in which there is a clearcut precipitating factor.

DEVELOPMENT OF DEPRESSION

In the course of his development, the depression-prone person may become sensitized by certain unfavorable types of life situations such as the loss of a parent or chronic rejection by his peers. Other unfavorable conditions of a more insidious nature may similarly produce vulnerability to depression. These traumatic experiences predispose the individual to overreact to analogous conditions later in life. He has a tendency to make extreme, absolute judgments when such situations occur. A loss is viewed as irrevocable; indifference, as total rejection. Other depression-prone individuals spend their childhood setting rigid, perfectionistic goals for themselves so that their universe collapses when they confront inevitable disappointments later in life (see Beck [1972] for further discussion of predisposition to depression).

The specific stresses responsible for adult depressions impinge on the individual's specific vulnerability. Numerous clinical and research reports agree on the following types of precipitating events: the disruption of a relationship with a person to whom the patient is attached, failure to attain an important goal, loss of a job, financial reverses, unexpected physical disability, and loss of social status or reputation. When such events are construed as a subtraction from the individual's personal domain, they may trigger a depression.

To justify the label "precipitating event," the experience of loss must have substantial significance to the patient. The precipitating factor, however, is not always a discrete event; insidious stresses such as the gradual withdrawal of affection by a spouse or a chronic discrepancy between goals and achievements in valued activities at work or at home may also erode the personal domain enough to produce depression. The individual, for example, may be continually dissatisfied with his or her performance as a parent, housewife, income producer, student, or creative artist. The repetitive recognition of a gap between what a person expects and what he receives from an important interpersonal relationship, from his career, or from other activities may topple him into a depression. In brief, the sense of loss may be the inevitable result of unrealistically high goals and expectations.

The manner in which traumatic circumstances involving a loss lead to the constellation of depressive symptoms may be delineated by an illustrative case: a man whose wife has unexpectedly deserted him.

The effect on the deserted mate cannot necessarily be predicted in advance. Obviously, not every person deserted by a spouse becomes depressed. He may have other sources of satisfaction—other members of his family and friends, as well as other sources of help. In fact, our deserted husband may have led a reasonably happy life before he ever met his wife. If the problem were simply a new hiatus in his life, it would seem plausible that in the course of time he would be able to compensate, at least in part, for the loss without becoming clinically depressed. Nonetheless, we know that certain vulnerable individuals respond to such a loss with the profound psychological disturbance called depression.

The impact of the loss depends in part on the kind and intensity of the meanings attached to the key person. The deserting wife has been the hub of shared experiences, fantasies, and expectations. The deserted husband (in our example) has built a network of associations around his wife, such as "She is part of me," "She is everything to me," "I enjoy life because of her," "She is my mainstay," or "She comforts me when I am down." These positive associations range from the realistic to the extremely unrealistic or imaginary. The more absolute these positive concepts, the greater the damage.

If the damage to the domain is great enough, it sets off a chain reaction. The positive values attached to the wife are totally wiped out. The greater and more absolute these positive associations, the greater the sense of loss. The extinction of "assets" such as "the only person who can make me happy" or "the essence of my existence" magnifies the impact of the loss and generates further sadness. Consequently, our deserted husband makes extreme, negative conclusions that parallel the extreme positive associations to his wife. He interprets the consequences of the loss as: "I am nothing without her," "I can never be happy again," and "I can't go on without her."

The further reverberations of the desertion lead the husband to question his validity and worth: "If I had been a better person, she wouldn't have left me." Further, he foresees other negative consequences of the breakup of the marriage: "All of our friends will go over to her side," "The children will want to live with her, not with me," and "I will go broke trying to maintain two households."

As the chain reaction progresses to a full-blown depression, the husband's self-doubts and gloomy predictions expand into negative generalizations about himself, his world, and his future. He starts to see himself as permanently impoverished both in terms of emotional satisfactions and in money. In addition, he exacerbates his suffering by over-dramatizing the event: "It is too much for a person to bear" or "This is a terrible disaster." Such ideas undermine his ability and motivation to absorb the shock.

The husband—we can now refer to him as a "patient"—divorces himself from activities and goals that formerly gave him satisfaction. He is likely to withdraw from his career goals ("because they are meaningless without my wife"). He is not motivated to work or even to take care of himself ("because it isn't worth the effort"). His distress is aggravated by the physiological concomitants of depression, such as loss of appetite and sleep disturbances. Finally, he thinks of suicide as an escape ("because life is too painful").

Since the chain reaction feeds upon itself, the depression goes into a downward spiral. The various symptoms—sadness, decreased physical activity, sleep disturbance—feed back into the psychological system. Hence, as the patient experiences sadness his pessimism leads him to conclude, "I will always be sad." This leads to more sadness, that is further interpreted in a negative way. Similarly, he thinks, "I will never be able to eat again or to sleep again" and concludes that he is rotting or deteriorating physically. As the patient observes the various manifestations of his disorder (decreased productivity, avoidance of responsibility, withdrawal from other people), he becomes increasingly critical of himself. His self-criticisms lead to deeper sadness and we thus see a continuing vicious cycle.

The same kind of chain reaction may be triggered by other kinds of losses such as failure at school or on a job. More chronic deprivations may also provide triggers: disturbance in key interpersonal relations or failure to attain certain academic goals.

This sketch of the chain reaction may be expanded to provide more complete answers to the following problems: Why does the depressed patient have such low self-esteem? Why is he pervasively pessimistic? Why does he berate himself so viciously? Why does he give up? Why does he believe no one can help him?

LOW SELF-ESTEEM

As the traumatized person reflects about adverse events (such as a separation, rejection, defeat, not achieving his expectations), he wonders what it tells him about himself. The tendency to extract personally relevant meanings from unpleasant situations is particularly characteristic of the depression-prone individual. Moreover, a special impetus to ascribing negative meanings to a loss is produced by the tendency to find some personal explanation for important life events. Usually such determinations of causality are very simplistic and may be quite erroneous.

The depression-prone individual is likely to assign the cause of an adverse event to some shortcoming in himself. The deserted husband concludes, "I have lost her *because* I am unlovable." In reality, this conclusion is only one of a number of possible explanations, such as basic incompatibility of their personalities, the wife's own problems, or her desire for an adventure which may be related more to thrill-seeking than to a change in her feelings for her husband.

When the person attributes the cause of the loss to himself, the rift in his domain becomes a chasm: He suffers not only the loss itself but he "discovers" a deficiency in himself. He tends to view this presumed deficiency in greatly exaggerated terms. A woman reacted to desertion by her lover with the thought, "I'm getting old and ugly and I must be repulsive looking." A man who lost his job due to a general decline in the economy thought, "I'm inept and too weak to make a living."

By erroneously explaining reversals as due to a defect in himself, the person produces additional undesirable effects. His awareness of the presumed defect becomes so intense that it infiltrates every thought about himself. In the course of time, his picture of his negative attributes expands to the point that it completely occupies his concept of himself. When asked to describe himself he can think only of this "bad" trait. He has great difficulty in shifting his attention to his other abilities or achievements and he glosses over or discounts attributes that he may have highly valued in the past.

The patient's preoccupation with his presumed deficiency assumes many forms. He appraises each experience in terms of the deficiency. He interprets ambiguous or slightly negatively toned experiences as evidence of this deficiency. For instance, following an argument with her brother, a mildly depressed woman concluded, "I am incapable of being loved and of giving love," and she felt more depressed. In reality, she had a number of intimate friends and a loving husband and children. When a friend was too busy to chat with her on the phone, she thought, "She doesn't want to talk to me any more." If her husband came home late from the office, she decided that he was staying away to avoid her. When her children were ill natured at dinnertime, she thought, "I have failed them." In reality, there were more plausible explanations for these events but the patient had difficulty in even considering other explanations that did not reflect badly on her.

The tendency to make comparisons with other people further lowers the self-esteem. Every encounter with another person may be turned into some negative evaluation of himself. Thus, when talking to other people the depressed patient thinks, "I'm not a good conversationalist. I'm not as interesting as the other people." As he walks down the street, he thinks: "Those people look attractive, but I am unattractive." "I have bad posture and bad breath." He sees a mother with a child and thinks, "She's a much better parent than I am." He sees another patient working industriously in the hospital and thinks, "He's a hard worker. I'm lazy and helpless."

SELF-REPROACHES AND SELF-CRITICISMS

The harshness and inappropriateness of the self-reproaches in depression have either been ignored by writers or have produced very abstract speculations.

Freud postulated that the bereaved patient has a pool of unconscious hostility toward the deceased "loved object." Since he cannot allow himself to experience this hostility, the patient directs the anger toward himself and accuses himself of faults that appropriately belong to the loved object. The concept of inverted rage has remained firmly entrenched in many theories of depression. Freud's convoluted pathway is so removed from information obtained from patients that it defies empirical validation.

Yet a careful examination of the patient's statements can yield a more parsimonious explanation of the self-reproaches which add insult to the injury inflicted by the loss. A clue to the genesis of the self-criticisms is found in the observation that many depressed patients are critical of a certain attribute that they had previously valued highly. These qualities have often been sources of gratification. For example, a woman who had enjoyed looking at herself in the mirror berated herself with indignities such as "I'm getting old and ugly." Another acutely depressed woman, who had always traded on her personal attractiveness and had enjoyed the resulting attention, castigated herself with the thought, "I have lost my ability to entertain people," and "I cannot even carry on a decent conversation." In both cases, the depression had been precipitated by disruption of an important interpersonal relationship.

In reviewing the history of depressed patients, we often find that the depressed patient has counted on this attribute, which he now debases, for balancing the usual stresses of life, mastering new problems, and attaining important objectives. When he believes that he will not be able to master a serious problem, to reach his goals, or to forestall a loss, he downgrades the asset. As this attribute appears to sour, he comes to the conclusion that he cannot get satisfaction out of life and that all he can expect is pain and suffering. The depressed patient proceeds from disappointment to self-blame to pessimism.

To illustrate the mechanism of self-blame, we might consider the sequence in which the average person blames and punishes somebody else who has offended him. First, he tries to find (or manufactures) some bad trait in the offender to account for his noxious behavior—as insensitivity or selfishness. He then generalizes this character flaw to occupy his global image of the offender—"He's a selfish person. He's bad." After such moral judgment, he may consider ways to punish the offender. He not only downgrades the other individual, but given the opportunity, he will strike out at some quality so as to hurt him. Finally, because the offender has brought him pain, he may want to sever the relationship and reject the other person totally.

The self-castigating depressed patient reacts similarly to his own presumed deficiency, except that he makes himself the target for attack. He regards himself as at fault and deserving of blame. He goes beyond the biblical injunction, "If thine eye offends then pluck it out." His moral condemnation spreads from the particular trait to the totality of his self-concept and is often accompanied by feelings of revulsion for himself. The ultimate of his self-condemnation is total self-rejection—just as though he were rejecting another person.

Consider the effects of self-criticism, self-condemnation, and self-rejection. The patient reacts to these self-instigated onslaughts just as he would if they were directed at him by another person: he feels hurt, sad, humiliated.

Freud and many more-recent writers have held that the sadness is a transformation of anger turned inward. By a kind of "alchemy" the anger is supposedly converted into depressive feelings. A more plausible explanation is that the sadness is the result of the self-instigated lowering of the self-esteem. Suppose I inform a student that his performance is inferior and that he accepts the assessment as fair. Even though I communicate my evaluation without anger and may, in fact, express regret or empathy, he is likely to feel sad. The lowering of his self-esteem by my objective evaluation is sufficient to make him sad—even though I am not angry at him. Similarly, if the student makes a negative evaluation of himself, he feels sad. The depressed patient is like the self-devaluating student; he feels sad because he lowers his sense of worth by his negative evaluations. There is no reason to postulate that he is unconsciously angry at someone else and that his anger is transformed into sadness.

When a depressed patient makes a negative evaluation of himself, he generally does not feel anger at himself; he is, in his frame of reference, simply making an objective judgment. Similarly he reacts with sadness when he believes that somebody else is devaluating him, even though this external devaluation may be devoid of any anger.

PESSIMISM

Pessimism sweeps like a tidal wave over the thought content of depressed patients. To some degree, we all tend to "live in the future." We interpret experience not only in terms of what the event means right now, but also in terms of its possible consequences. A young man who had just received a compliment from his girl friend might look forward to receiving more compliments; he might think "She really likes me," and thus foresee a more intimate relationship with her. Similarly, if he has been disappointed or rejected, he is likely to anticipate a repetition of this type of unpleasant experience.

Depressed patients have a special penchant for expecting future adversities and experiencing them as though they were happening in the present or had already occurred. For example, a man who suffered a mild business reversal began to think of ultimate bankruptcy. As he dwelt on the theme of bankruptcy, he began to regard himself as already bankrupt. Consequently, he started to feel the same degree of sadness he would had he already suffered bankruptcy. In this respect, the depressed patient is different from the anxious patient whose "catastrophes" are always in the future and consequently do not produce a sense of loss in the present.

The predictions of depressed patients tend to be overgeneralized and extreme. Since the patients regard the future as an extension of the present, they expect a deprivation or defeat to continue permanently. If a patient feels miserable now, he assumes he will always feel miserable. The absolute, global pessimism is expressed in statements such as: "Things won't ever work out for me," "Life is meaningless. It's never going to be any different." The depressed patient judges that, since he cannot reach a major goal now, he never will be able to achieve it. Nor can he see the possibility of substituting other rewarding goals. Moreover, if a problem appears insoluble now, he assumes that he will never be able to find a way of working it out or somehow bypassing it.

Another stream leading to pessimism arises from the negative self-concept described previously. As already mentioned, the trauma of a loss is especially damaging because it implies to the patient that he is defective in some way. Moreover, because the deficiency is regarded as an integral part of him he sees it as permanent and enduring. He often regards his "flaw" as becoming progressively worse. Since the defect is within him, nobody else can help him nor can he do anything about it.

Such kinds of pessimism are especially prominent when the individual sees himself as the essential force in reaching important life goals: if he has lost these instrumental abilities, then he is beyond redemption. A mildly depressed writer, for instance, did not receive the degree of acclaim that he expected for one of his works. His failure to live up to his expectations led him to two conclusions: first, that his writing ability was deteriorating; second, since creative ability is intrinsic, his loss could not be salvaged by anybody else. The loss was therefore irreversible.

A similar reaction was reported by a student who was unsuccessful in a competition for an academic award; his reaction was, "I lost because I'm weak and inferior. I'm never going to do well in a competitive situation." Since not winning was tantamount (for him) to complete failure, this meant that his whole life—past, present, and future—was a failure.

Similarly, a woman who developed transitory back trouble and had to be confined to bed for a few weeks became depressed. She concluded from her ailment that she would always be bedridden. She incorrectly regarded her "disease" as permanent and irremediable.

As pessimism envelops the patient's total future orientation, his thinking is dominated by ideas such as: "The game is over—I don't have a second chance." "Life has passed me by. It's too late to do anything about it." His losses are irreparable; his problems are unsolvable.

Pessimism not only engulfs the distant future, but permeates every specific wish and specific task the patient undertakes. A housewife who was listing her domestic duties automatically predicted before starting each new activity that she would be unable to do it. A depressed physician expected, before seeing each new patient, that he would be unable to make a diagnosis. The negative expectancies are so strong that even though the patient may be successful in each specific task (for example, the doctor's making the diagnosis), he expects to fail the very next time. He reacts as though he screened out or failed to integrate any successful experiences.

SNOWBALLING OF SADNESS AND APATHY

Although the onset of depression may be sudden, its full development spreads over a period of days or weeks. The patient experiences a gradual increase in intensity of sadness and of other symptoms until he "hits bottom." Each repetition of the idea of loss constitutes a fresh experience of loss which is added to the previous reservoir of perceived losses. With each successive "loss" further sadness is generated.

As described previously (Beck 1971), any psychopathological condition is characterized by a specific sensitivity to particular types of experiences. The depressed person tends to extract elements suggestive of loss and to gloss over other features that are not consonant with or are contradictory to this interpretation. As a result of such "selective abstraction," the patient over-interprets daily events in terms of loss and is oblivious to more-positive interpretations; he is hypersensitive to stimuli suggestive of loss and is blind to stimuli representing gain. He shows the same type of selectivity in recalling past experiences. He is facile in recalling unpleasant experiences but "draws a blank" when questioned about positive experiences.

As a result of this "tunnel vision," the patient becomes impermeable to stimuli that can arouse pleasant emotions. Although he may be able to acknowledge that certain events are favorable, his attitudes block any happy feelings: "I don't deserve to be happy." "I'm different from other people, and I can't feel happy over the things that make them happy." "How can I be happy when everything else is bad?" Similarly, comical situations do not strike him as funny because of his negative set and his tendency toward self-reference: "There is nothing funny about my life." He has difficulty in experiencing anger, since he views himself as responsible for and deserving of any rude or insulting actions of other people.

The tendency to think in absolute terms contributes to the cumulative arousal of sadness. The patient tends to dwell increasingly on extreme ideas such as "Life is meaningless." "Nobody loves me." "I'm totally inadequate." or "I have nothing left."

By downgrading qualities that are closely linked with gratification, the patient is in effect taking gratification away from himself. In calling herself unattractive, the woman is in effect saying, "I no longer can enjoy my physical appearance, or compliments I receive for it, or friendships that it helped me to form and maintain."

The loss of gratification apparently trips a mechanism leading to the opposite of happiness, namely, sadness. The prevailing wind of pessimism maintains a continual state of sadness. If the usual consequence of loss is sadness, then giving up is followed by apathy. When the depressed patient regards himself as defeated or at least thwarted in his life's major goals, he is apt to experience the emotion that goes with this—indifference or apathy.

MOTIVATIONAL CHANGES

The reversals in major goals and objectives are among the most puzzling characteristics of the seriously depressed patient. He not only desires to avoid experiences that formerly gratified him or represented the mainstream of his life, but he is drawn toward a state of inactivity. He even seeks to withdraw from life completely through suicide.

To understand the link between the changes in motivation and patient's perception of loss, it is valuable to consider the ways in which the patient has "given up." He no longer feels attracted to the kinds of enterprises that ordinarily he would engage in spontaneously. In fact, he finds that he has to force himself into any undertaking. He goes through the motions of attending to his routine affairs because he believes he should, or because he knows it is "the right thing to do," or because others urge him to do it, but not because he wants to. He finds that he has to work against a powerful inner resistance as though he were trying to drive an automobile with the brakes on or to swim upstream.

In the most extreme cases, the patient experiences "paralysis of the will": He is (completely) devoid of any spontaneous desire to do anything except remain in a state of passive inertia. Nor can he mobilize "will power" to force himself to do what he believes he "ought to do."

From this description of the motivational changes, one might surmise that perhaps some physically depleting disease had overwhelmed the patient so that he did not have the strength or resources to make even a minimal exertion. An acute or debilitating illness such as pneumonia or advanced cancer could conceivably reduce a person to such a state of immobility.

However, the physical-depletion notion is contradicted by the patient's own observation that he feels a strong drive to *avoid* constructive or normal activities. His inertia is deceptive in that it derives not only from a desire to be passive, but also from a less obvious desire to shrink from any situation that he regards as unpleasant. He feels repelled by the thought of performing even elementary functions such as getting out of bed, dressing himself, and attending to personal needs. A retarded, depressed woman would rapidly dive under the covers of her bed whenever I entered the room. She would become exceptionally aroused and even energetic in attempting to escape from an activity that she was pressed to engage in.

In contrast to the depressed patient, the physically ill person generally would like to be active and to participate in his usual activities, and it is often necessary to enforce bed rest to keep him from taxing himself.

The depressed patient's desires to avoid activity and escape from his present environment are the consequences of his peculiar constructions—negative view of future, of his environment, and of himself (the cognitive triad).

Everyday experience, as well as a number of well-designed experiments, demonstrate that when a person believes he cannot succeed at a task, he is likely to give up or not even attempt to work at it. He adopts the attitude that "There's no use in trying" and does not feel much spontaneous drive. Moreover, the belief that the task is pointless and that even successful completion is meaningless minimizes his motivation.

An analogous situation is typical of depression. The depressed patient expects negative outcomes, so he does not experience ordinary mobilization of the drive to make an effort. Furthermore, he does not see any point in trying because he believes the goals are meaningless. There is a general tendency for people to avoid situations they expect to be painful. The depressed patient perceives most situations as onerous, boring, or painful. Hence, he desires to avoid even the usual amenities of living. These avoidance desires are powerful enough to override any tendencies toward constructive, goal-directed activity.

The background setting for the patient's powerful desire to seek a passive state is illustrated by this sequence of thoughts: "I'm too fatigued and sad to do anything. If I am active I will only feel worse. But if I lie down, I can conserve my strength and my bad feeling will go away." Unfortunately, his attempt to escape from the unpleasant feeling by being passive does not work; if anything, it enhances the dysphoria. The patient finds that far from getting respite from his unpleasant thoughts and feelings, he becomes more preoccupied by them.

SUICIDAL BEHAVIOR

Suicidal wishes and suicidal attempts may be regarded as an extreme expression of the desire to escape. The depressed patient sees his future as filled with suffering. He cannot visualize any way of improving his lot. He does not believe that he will get better. Under these conditions, suicide seems to be a rational solution. It not only promises an end to his own misery but presumably will relieve his family of a burden. Once the patient regards suicide as a more desirable alternative than living, he feels attracted to this kind of solution. The more hopeless and painful his life seems, the stronger his desire to end that life.

The wish to find surcease through suicide is illustrated in the following quotation from a depressed woman rejected by her lover: "There's no sense in living. There's nothing here for me. I need love and I don't have it any more. I can't be happy without love—only miserable. It will just be the same misery, day in and day out. It's senseless to go on."

The desire to escape from the apparent futility of his existence is illustrated by the statement of another patient: "Life means just going through another day. It doesn't make any sense. There's nothing that can give me any satisfaction. The future isn't there—I just don't want life any more. I want to get out of here. It's stupid just to go on living."

Another premise underlying the suicidal wishes is the patient's belief that everybody would be better off if he were dead. Since he regards himself as worthless and a burden, he considers hollow arguments that his family would be hurt if he died. How can they be injured by losing a burden? One patient envisioned suicide as doing her parents a favor. She would not only end her own pain, but would relieve them of psychological and financial burdens. "I'm just taking money from my parents," she said. "They could use it to better advantage. They wouldn't have to support me. My father wouldn't have to work so hard and they could travel. I'm unhappy taking their money and they could be happy with it."

EXPERIMENTAL STUDIES OF DEPRESSION

We have conducted a series of correlational and experimental studies of the ideational productions and related behaviors of depressed patients which led to or supported the construction of the model of depression that I have presented in this chapter.

Thematic Content of Ideational Material

Beck and Hurvich (1959) reported that depressed patients in psychotherapy showed a higher proportion of masochistic dreams than did a matched control group of nondepressed patients. The specific content of the dream was: The dreamer was portrayed as a "loser," in some way; that is, he suffered deprivation of some tangible object, a loss of self-esteem in an interpersonal relationship, or a loss of a person to whom he was attached. Other themes included the dreamer's being thwarted in attempting to reach a goal or being portrayed as inept, repulsive, or defective.

These findings were supported by a second, more refined study of the most recent dreams of 218 depressed and nondepressed psychiatric patients (Beck & Ward 1961).

Beck (1961) developed a Focused Fantasy Test consisting of a set of cards, each card containing four frames that depicted a continuous sequence of events involving a set of identical twins. The scenario was similar to that observed in dreams of depressed patients, namely, the hero loses something of value and is rejected or punished. Beck found that the depressed patients identified with the loser significantly more frequently than did the nondepressed.

In a clinical study, Beck (1963, 1964) analyzed the verbatim recorded verbal productions of depressed and nondepressed patients in psychotherapy. He noted that depressed patients distorted their experiences in an idiosyncratic way; they misinterpreted events in terms of personal failure, deprivation, or rejection; or they exaggerated or overgeneralized the significance of events that suggested negative evaluations of them. They also persisted in making indiscriminate, negative predictions of the future.

The distorted conceptualizations of the. depressed patients showed a continuity with the thematic content of their dreams. This content centered on one dominant theme, namely, a negative view of the self, the outside world, and the future. This set of idiosyncratic patterns, labeled "the cognitive triad" (Beck 1972), pervaded the conscious experiences of the severely depressed patient and were present, but to a lesser extent, in the ideation of mildly depressed patients.

The studies of the dreams and other ideational productions of depressed patients were conducted to test the hypothesis that retroflected rage is a central ingredient in depression. The results of these studies, however, pointed to a different formulation of depression: the patient experiences sadness, loss of spontaneous motivation, loss of interest, indecisiveness, and suicidal wishes because of his idiosyncratic view of the world, himself, and his future. The disturbances in affect and motivation are the outcome of the negative conceptualizations.

We have conducted a series of correlational studies to test these clinical observations. We found significant correlations between the Depression Inventory and measures of pessimism ($r = 0.56$) and negative self-concept ($r = 0.70$). After recovery from depression, the scores on these measures showed substantial decrements, as expected. In a longitudinal study we found that change scores (between the time of admission and discharge) on the measures of pessimism and negative self-concept correlated 0.49 and 0.53, respectively, with the change scores on the Depression Inventory. These findings lent support to the notion that the state of depression is associated with a negative view of the self and the future. The correlation (0.70) between measures of negative view of the future and of negative view of the self supported the concept of the cognitive triad in depression.

The relationship between hopelessness and suicidal wishes has been supported by a number of studies. Factor analyses of the Beck Depression Inventory have yielded a factor with the heaviest loading on the items of hopelessness and depression (Pichot & Lempérière 1964; Cropley & Weckowicz 1966). We have found that our measure of hopelessness (the Global Expectancies Test) correlates significantly with an index of the severity of suicidal intent (0.47). Statistical analysis revealed that hopelessness is the major variable linking depression to suicide intent (Minkoff, Bergman, Beck & Beck 1973).

Another line of inquiry into the phenomena of depression was the experimental manipulation of the cognitive variables and the assessment of the effects upon other variables relevant to depression. According to our formulation, the depressed patient is characterized by unrealistically low concepts of his capabilities. If this negative orientation can be ameliorated, then the secondary symptoms of depression, such as reduction of constructive motivation, should improve.

We found that patients in a superior performance group (Loeb, Feshbach, Beck, & Wolf 1964) were more self-confident, rated themselves happier, and perceived others as happier than did patients in an inferior performance group. Depressed patients were more sensitive than nondepressed patients to task performance in estimating how they would do in a future task. They also showed greater changes in self-ratings of their mood.

In a subsequent study (Loeb, Beck, & Diggory 1971), we found that depressed outpatients were significantly more pessimistic about their performance than were a matched control group of nondepressed patients. In actuality, the depressed patients performed as well as the control group. On a second task in this manipulation, the previous experience of success or failure had different effects on the actual performance of the two groups: *Success improved the performance of the depressed group,* whereas failure improved the performance of the nondepressed group.

The study of depressed outpatients was replicated in a study of depressed inpatients. In addition to specific measures of self-confidence and expectancies regarding test performance, we included the Global Expectancies Test and the Stuart Self-Evaluation Test. We found that following a successful experience there was not only an improvement in ratings relevant to test performance but a generalized increase in self-esteem and optimism. Thus, the patients made more-positive ratings about their personal attractiveness, ability to communicate, and social interest. They also saw the future as brighter and had higher expectations of achieving their major objectives in life.

Another study of depressed inpatients presented a hierarchy of tasks in a verbal dimension. The patients progressed from a simple task—reading a paragraph aloud—up to the most difficult items in the hierarchy. The final item, which all the patients were able to master, consisted of improvising a short talk on a selected subject and trying to convince the experimenter of their point of view. Again, we found significant improvements in global ratings of self-concept and optimism.

From a therapeutic standpoint, the finding that the depressed patient reacts positively to tangible evidence of successful or superior performance is most important. The interpersonal meaning of the experimental situation, in which the subject receives positive or negative information about himself from the experimenter, obviously has a particularly powerful effect on the depressed patient. This tendency to exaggerate the evaluative aspects of situations and to overgeneralize in a *positive* direction after "success" offers obvious clues to the therapeutic management of depression. By pinpointing the patient's specific cognitive distortions and demonstrating their invalidity to the patient through behavioral or cognitive techniques, the psychotherapist can achieve a rapid improvement in the symptoms of depression.

REFERENCES

Beck, A. T. A systematic investigation of depression. *Comprehensive Psychiatry*, 1961, **2**, 162–170.

Beck, A. T. Thinking and depression. 1. Idiosyncratic content and cognitive distortions. *Archives of General Psychiatry*, 1963, 9, 324 –333.

Beck, A. T. Thinking and depression. 2. Theory and therapy. *Archives of General Psychiatry*, 1964, **10**, 561–571.

Beck, A. T. Cognition, affect, and psychopathology. *Archives of General Psychiatry*, 1971, **24**, 495–500.

Beck, A. T. *Depression: Causes and treatment*. Philadelphia: University of Pennsylvania Press, 1972.

Beck, A. T. & Hurvich, M. S. Psychological correlates of depression. 1. Frequency of "masochistic" dream content in a private practice sample. *Psychosomatic Medicine* 1959. 21, 50-55.

Beck, A. T. & Ward, C. H. Dreams of depressed patients: Characteristic themes in manifest content. *Archives of General Psychiatry*, 1961, 5, 462-467.

Cropley, A. J. & Weckowicz, T. E. The dimensionality of clinical depression. *Australian Journal of Psychology*, 1966, 18, 18-25.

Loeb, A., Beck, A. T., & Diggory, J. C. Differential effects of success and failure on depressed and nondepressed patients. *Journal of Nervous and Mental Disease*, 1971, 152, 106-114.

Loeb, A., Feshbach, S., Beck, A. T., & Wolf, A. Some effects of reward upon the social perception and motivation of psychiatric patients varying in depression. *Journal of Abnormal Psychology*, 1964, 68, 609-616

Pichot, P. & Lempérière, T. Analyse factoriella d'un questionnaire d'autoevaluation des symptomes dépressifs. *Revue de Psychologie Appliquee*, 1964, 14, 15-29.

Minkoff, K., Bergman, E., Beck, A. T., & Beck, R. Hopelessness, Depression, and attempted suicide. *American Journal of Psychiatry*, 1973, 130, 455-459.

DISCUSSION

Dr. Friedman: Dr. Beck, could you elaborate on the role of hostility in depression, especially from a therapeutic standpoint?

Dr. Beck: A frequent clinical finding is that the expression of hostility does seem to ameliorate depressive affect. My own early analytic work with a large number of patients seemed to corroborate this finding, and, in a paper I presented in 1958 before the Philadelphia Psychoanalytic Society, "Problems of Transference and Countertransference," I detailed a host of maneuvers designed to mobilize hostility. However, I do not believe the cathartic effect of the expression of hostility results in improvement, but rather that the mobilization of hostility is effective because it helps to change a person's self-image by giving him a greater sense of control over his environment. I hope that Dr. Seligman will elaborate on the aspect of control. The satisfactory expression of hostility seems to be a very powerful means of increasing a person's subjective feeling of effectiveness, thus increasing his self-esteem and combating the negative cognitions which I hold to be so important in the generation of depression. Incidentally, maneuvers to mobilize hostility are risky and may be detrimental in the more seriously depressed patient. Consequently, I no longer use such techniques.

Dr. Goodwin: I was intrigued by Dr. Beck's statement that clinically most depressed people look quite similar and yet, despite this clinical similarity, some will respond better to drugs and others to psychotherapy. When we begin to move into the area of treatment or into genetic investigations or other physiological studies, we find numerous differences among depressed people.

Dr. Beck: I do not doubt that future research will delineate etiologically distinct subgroups, and perhaps the situation can be likened to clinical anemia, which is produced by several completely different types of deficiencies. The clinical state in each case of anemia may appear the same and each may respond to blood transfusions.

The same could be said of "fevers" about 150 years ago. This clearly suggests that we are at a very early stage in our research; indeed, we are just beginning to break depression down into subcategories. My guess is that eventually we are going to separate out the bipolar depressions, which will constitute a complete and separate group, perhaps based on genetic factors. A second category will be a reactive depression-type group, and a third subdivision may be something like a "catecholamine-depletion depression."

It is important to look again at the analogy of anemia and remember that, just as we can treat all of the anemias with blood transfusion even though they are etiologically different, a similar therapy may produce symptomatic relief in the various types of depression. I hope I have outlined a set of common psychological principles that are applicable to all states of depression and can be used with varying degrees of therapeutic effectiveness across a broad spectrum of disorders.

Dr. Secunda: The cognitive theory seems to account very nicely for the unfolding of a depression once a loss has been defined. But I'm wondering how you can account for the differences among people in their appraisal of a similar loss. For example, one man faced with a loss may say, "This is a terrible loss," and become depressed; while another man may say, "Oh, it's a loss, but not so bad," not become depressed, and go about his business.

Dr. Beck: This brings up the question of predisposition to depression. I would suggest that there are many psychological configurations that predispose a person to react to a loss by becoming depressed. I would like to highlight two which appear commonly. The first type appears in the person who has suffered an irrevocable loss. In our research we have found that 27 percent of depressed patients have lost a parent in childhood and as a result they tend to view later loss, particularly interpersonal loss, as irreversible and shattering. A second type of predisposition encompasses those people who have always been successful and have been generally regarded as "saints" or "prodigies" during their childhood, and as a result have not developed coping techniques to handle serious interpersonal difficulties or failures. They are also particularly predisposed to depression because they tend to appraise situations in extreme terms. For example, the girl who was considered a "goddess" while she was growing up is usually only able to think of one other category when her beauty starts to fade and that is that she is ugly. I have observed this phenomenon in a number of patients. Another example would be the "boy genius" who, as an adult, considers himself a total failure when he encounters a few problems that would ordinarily be considered of minor significance.

Dr. Tabachnick: I am very attracted to the reasonableness of Dr. Beck's theory and I believe it explains many of the phenomena that occur in the depressed state. With all of the different theories that abound, however, I am somewhat at a loss to understand why the cognitive approach is granted such a central position.

Dr. Beck: I do this for two reasons. In the first place, I do not feel that the cognitive approach has been tested enough and so I am attempting to investigate depression to the limits of this particular theory. It has its limitations. For example, I do not really believe that it totally explains those states of depression called "endogenous," but I have successfully treated patients with "bipolar" or "endogenous" depressions using cognitive therapy. This leads into my second reason for emphasizing the role of cognitions—the approach is therapeutically useful. Even if we were artificially to dichotomize biology and psychology and state that some depressions may stem from biological causes, we would still find that these depressive states do have a psychological phenomenology which can be approached psychotherapeutically. My point is that you can get to the emotional disorder through the person's thinking.

Dr. Klerman: I believe that in emphasizing the important role of the cognitive state, Dr. Beck has elucidated what has previously been a neglected area. I agree that calling depression an affective disorder, following Bleuler, has tended to mask the fact that depression is not just a mood but also probably a multiple system disorder which includes both catecholamines or adrenal steroids and also cognitions and self systems and motivations.

I would like to highlight some clinical evidence in support of the cognitive theory that emerges from the field of psychopharmacology research. One intriguing observation by a collaborative group at the University of Pennsylvania and Johns Hopkins University, who were studying meprobamate, was that when patients were symptomatically ill they reported more adverse effects (negative events) occurring to them during a previous week than in an interim period. When their condition improved, as a result of the drug, be it anxiety or depression, they showed a decrease in the number of negative events occurring; that is, they reported fewer occurring to them during a week. Now either you assume that there was indeed some interaction so that the group treated with meprobamate actually had more things occur to them during a week, or you are forced to the conclusion that anxious and depressed patients' perception of their real world is cognitively disturbed. This would agree with Dr. Beck's idea of a feedback between the affective state and the misperceptions.

A second line of investigation that bears on the cognitive theory of depression concerns the issue of response set. I believe it has been demonstrated (Dr. Raskin has some data concerning this) that depressed people have an overwhelming sick set. They tend to exaggerate on self-report measures, at least when these measures are compared to clinical ratings. They clearly overperceive or overreport bodily complaints, a state we call "hypochondriasis" in a more pejorative sense.

Dr. Chodoff: My thoughts turned to Dr. Beck's theory the other day as I was talking to a patient who remarked that a friend of hers had commented, "You always see the negative side of things." And, indeed, this patient is rarely able to derive any pleasure or happiness in life—she is a depressed person. Part of the reason she is that way stems from her considerable guilt. She has a pervasive feeling of guilt and also a magical need to protect herself from others and also from good fortune. For example, if she feels that something good is likely to happen, she also anticipates that something terrible will also happen. I believe that part of the reason she sees the world this way is because she spent a long time in Auschwitz during World War II (as a matter of fact, she is a patient whom I described in a recent paper on concentration camps). One can understand her negative view of the world and her negative cognitive set if he understands her overriding guilt, her need to protect herself and others from the misfortune that has always overcome her, and her past life experience. I can also imagine a number of other paths that could have led this woman to a negative view of the world. Thus, I feel the term "negative cognitive set" simply describes the set of a person that could have been arrived at by many different psychodynamic paths. If one has a negative view of the world, of course, he will see things in a particular way and be more susceptible to depression, but it would seem to me that the important question, in developing an explanatory model and also in terms of therapy, is why the person has developed this negative cognitive view of the world and what dynamic interactions maintain it.

Dr. Beck: The question "why" is often a very speculative one which at best can be answered only by careful exploration of each individual case. In general, however, as a person develops, the negative experiences he encounters leave their imprint on his mind and he may be predisposed to see the world through a negative template which distorts his conception of the real world and causes him to evaluate future experiences in the same negative way. At the same time the person is also building up a more reality-oriented template and this is dominant in his perceptions before he catapults into depression. What I'm proposing is similar to what Freud described as the primary-secondary process distinction. The primary process, in a sense, represents this negative view of the world in depressed patients, and the secondary process is, in a way, the more rational part of the person as we see him when he is not depressed.

In response to stress, and particularly stress relevant to loss or to loss of control over reinforcement contingencies, there is an energizing of this negative view of the self, the negative view of the world, and a negative view of the future. This more primary process template assumes dominance and the secondary process is suspended, at least in certain areas of cognitive functioning.

Dr. Lewinsohn: I usually think of the term "cognitive disorder" as referring to a reduction in a person's capacity to process information. The person is able to process less information and makes more errors as he does so. I have most often thought of this in regard to the schizophrenic impairments, but I suspect it is not what Dr. Beck means at all.

Dr. Beck: Unfortunately, this is a sticky semantic problem which does confuse people and one that I have attempted to clarify. I am not suggesting that the cognitive realm is incapacitated as it is in the schizophrenic disorders or mental retardation. The depressed patient has the *capacity* to process information, unlike the mentally defective person. The capacity remains intact but the depressed patient has, in a sense, shifted over so that he processes information in a tubular way. It has been clearly demonstrated, most recently by Weckowicz in Alberta and previously by Friedman in Philadelphia, that when given cognitive tasks to perform, even the most regressed depressed patients do as well as nondepressed controls. The only possible exception is minimal impairment on short-term memory tasks.

Dr. Ferster: There remains a problem in cognitive theory concerning perception to which both Dr. Lewinsohn and Dr. Beck have referred, and I would like to advance a suggestion which might aid resolution of this matter. The idea that the patient perceives the world he deals with or the idea that information comes from the world to the patient, seems to me to be the major limiting factor in understanding the cognitive interpretations which, incidentally, are very meaningful within my own framework. Suppose you turn the statement around and, rather than saying a person perceives the world, examine how the items of the environment, social or physical, come to control the person's behavior. Then the focus of interest is on the active participation of the person acting on the environment. The enlargement of the perceptual repertoire is then an interactive product of doing something in the world in which what happens when one does something depends upon whether he notices how it gets done. We see this process developing from infancy on. For example, the way one sees (perceives) a couch depends on how he sits on it, how he uses it, and so on. The emphasis is not on the information or inside the person perceiving it, but rather on the interaction, i.e., the behavior that comes from him as he pushes the environment around. The depressed person is blocked in expanding his perception of the world because he does not have the behavior with which to interact actively with the world.

Dr. Beck: Observing the interaction of behavior and environmental events, of course, is important. But to get at the meaning of the behavior and the external stimuli, and to interpret the interaction, we must have access to the patient's thinking, i.e., his conceptions. Interpretations based on observables are going to be at best the experimenter's hunches, i.e., his own cognitions.

Dr. Goodwin: Dr. Beck, are there any sequential studies relating to your basic thesis that the cognitive disturbance precedes the affective change?

Dr. Beck: As you know, this type of study is extremely difficult. I have done a number of longitudinal studies with patients before they are depressed. The results satisfy me but are of course subject to interviewer bias and other forms of contamination. I have followed a number of people subject to recurrent depressions over long periods of time and have noticed that before the onset of a new depressive episode they begin to show distortions in the way they interpret matters. Before the onset of dysphoria and depression it is obvious that they are failing to make the fine distinctions necessary to interpret reality correctly and instead are beginning to misinterpret reality situations through this negative cognitive screen. In a number of cases, I have been able to arrest the onset of depression by pointing out to the person how he is beginning to misinterpret reality.

Dr. Lewinsohn: I believe the research of Schachter and Singer (1962), is relevant to this issue, for it reveals that there are many determinants of how people label their physiological states. They demonstrated that people take cues from any number of stimuli which makes it easy to see how someone could overgeneralize a particular label such as "I am feeling bad" or "I am no good" and then begin to apply this label to a wide range of arousal states.

Dr. Beck: I do not think Schachter's work is completely relevant to this particular question because his experiments leave out a crucial step in the process of emotional arousal as it naturally occurs. His laboratory subjects are in a state of excitation, but he brings about the excitation by giving the subject adrenalin. In nature there is usually something that gets people overexcited, whether it's a loss, a loss of control, or some other environmental stimulus. Once Schachter has the subject overstimulated, he then demonstrates that the person will scan his environment for cues and finally interpret his state of arousal as being due to one of the environmental cues, even though experimentally it obviously is not.

To apply Schachter's thesis to a depressed state would mean that if a person suffers a loss, for example, he would then become emotionally aroused and would scan his environment for cues. Then when he noticed he had suffered a loss he would interpret the loss as the cause of the dysphoria. Clearly this is a circle which reflects only on the limitations of this particular experimental design as it can be applied to a natural state.

Dr. Schuyler: When using cognitive therapy, how do you determine when to intervene with a depressed patient? Is your decision based on information about the current state of depression or on information of a more personal nature such as premorbid personality and character structure?

Dr. Beck: I'm not sure that I can answer your question in a general way without reference to a specific case. But I want to emphasize how careful one must be in the manner of intervention, and I would illustrate it with an anecdote. Perhaps I can partially answer the question by showing what not to do.

A very successful author was referred to me for consultation, and there did not seem to be any obvious precipitating cause coincident with his depression. I believe his depression was related to the fact that his aspirations merely continued to outstrip his actual gains, so that he was continually being disappointed. When I first saw him I tried to establish rapport and commented, "You know, I have admired your writings a great deal." At which point, he started to cry. I inquired about this and he stated, "I want to kill myself, for I see that I have deceived you too." I asked what the trouble was and he said, "Well, I think you're either a fool and I have deceived you, or you are lying to me when you say that I'm a good author." At this point I had to back away from this approach and search for some other area that we could agree upon. Sometimes establishing an area of agreement can only be done in a behavioral sense. For example, I might say to a depressed patient, "I bet that you can write 80 words in two minutes." The patient will generally say, "No, I don't think I can." One might demonstrate to the person that he is able to function better than he thinks, and I often start with something like this to establish a point of agreement, e.g., that he underestimates his ability. It's useless to lock horns with a depressed person about something he believes very strongly in. I believe it is just as useless and harmful to do this as it is with a paranoid patient. Through the use of therapeutic skill, however, the therapist can induce the patient to question his distorted ideation. The next step is to help the patient demonstrate to himself in what way his depressive cognitions are incorrect. Finally, the therapist assists the patient in substituting more realistic appraisals and interpretations.

BIBLIOGRAPHY

Beck, A. T. *Depression.* New York, Harper and Rowe, 1967.

Lipman, S., Covi, L., Derogatis, L. R., Rickels, K., & Uhlenhuth, E. H. Mediation, anxiety reduction and patient report of significant life situation events. *Diseases of the Nervous System,* 1971, **32**, 240-244.

Raskin, A., & McKeon, J. J. Super factors of psychopathology in hospitalized depressed patients. *Journal of Psychiatric Research,* 1971, **9**, 11-19.

Chodoff, P. Depression and guilt among concentration camp survivors. *Existential Psychiatry,* Summer-Fall, 1969.

Weckowicz, T. E., Yonge, K. A., Cropley, A. J., & Muir, W. Objective therapy predictors in depression. Monograph, Supplement No. 31, Brandon, Vermont, Clinical Psychology Publishing Company, 1971.

Friedman, A. S. Minimal effects of severe depression on cognitive functioning. *Journal of Abnormal Psychology*, 1964, **69**, 237-243.

Schachter, S., & Singer, J. E. Cognitive, social, and physiological determinants of emotional state. *Psychological Review,* 1962, **69** (No. 5), 379-399.

Beck, A. T. Cognitive therapy: Nature and relation to behavior therapy. *Behavior Therapy,* 1970, **1**, 184-200.

2
BEHAVIORAL APPROACHES
TO DEPRESSION

Charles B. Ferster
American University

Probably the single most important experience that inclines behavioral psychologists toward clinical psychology and behavior modification is that of controlling the behavior of an animal by means of reinforcement. A dramatic illustration of this control is offered in every course in experimental psychology: the alteration of the conduct of the pigeon by operating a food dispenser with a hand switch. It is reliably found that predictable and immediate changes occur in the frequency of the bird's activity in close, point-to-point correspondence with the experimenter's acts. A person viewing such a demonstration gains the conviction that the behavior of the organism is plastic and unlimited if a properly reactive environment can be arranged. He frequently asks why the same approach could not be extended to resolve the pressing problems found in complex human situations.

The conviction which the experimentalist gains from his success in the laboratory—that human behavior is plastic and unlimited—appears to be as powerful a challenge for the experimental psychologist as it has been for mental health professionals from other fields. Skinner's (1948) *Walden Two* is an early statement of the conviction that human behavior is plastic, as is the following statement by this author (Ferster 1958):

> Many psychiatric patients or potential psychiatric patients may be characterized as having repertoires whose performances are not producing the reinforcements of the world: because too much behavior is being punished; because nearly all of the individual's behavior is maintained by avoiding aversive consequences rather than producing positive effects; because the projections of the environment are so distorted that the individual's performances are emitted inappropriately; or a combination of all of these. A potential reinforcing environment exists for every

29

individual, however, if he will only emit the required performances on the proper occasion. One has merely to paint the picture, give affection artfully and the world will respond in kind with prestige, money, social response and love. Conversely, a repertoire which will make contact with the reinforcements of the world will be subsequently maintained because of the effect of the reinforcement on the performance.

Although such a statement does point to the environment and the details of a person's relation to it, it is basically a clarion call exclaiming that a psychological solution is possible for psychological problems. The task still remains to discover why individuals do not make effective contact with the positive and avoid the aversive aspects of their environment. We still need to know what events in a person's developmental history prevent appropriate interaction with the environment.

A second aspect of the behavioral psychologist's clinical work is the actual skills and procedures used to work with patients, as exemplified by the practitioners of behavior therapy and behavior modification (Ayllon & Azrin 1968; Franks 1969; Lieberman 1970; and Wolpe 1969). These psychologists are practitioners who, either from experience in behavioral animal research or by study of the behavioral literature, have developed a specific point of view on which to base their technique of interaction with the patient. The practices of some behavioral psychologists, like those of psychodynamic practitioners, are sometimes hard to describe because there may be a difference between the language and theory with which the practitioner describes his work and his actual activity with the patient. Presumably the behavioral orientation of the behavior therapist makes his practices more amenable to objective description than those of the psychodynamic therapist, but this is not necessarily the case (Ferster 1972). For some practitioners, the differences between behavioral and psychodynamic therapy may be considerably less than appears from their own descriptions of their practices. The convergence of psychotherapeutic practice despite differences in theoretical approaches is greater when the therapist is controlled by the immediate evidence of his interaction with the patient rather than by a preconceived theory. Thus, the behavior of the therapist, if he is in effective contact with the patient, may come as much from his experience with the patient as from the theory that guides him. The relation between therapist and patient is reminiscent of the operant-conditioning cartoon which appeared in a student newspaper showing one rat in a Skinner Box saying to another, as he pressed the bar, "Boy, have I got this guy conditioned. Every time I press the bar he drops in a pellet."

A third aspect of the behaviorist's work in the clinical field is the use of a functional and experimental analysis of behavior as a language with which the data of clinical practice can be described objectively and communicably. Whatever the theoretical basis of the psychotherapist's activities, the actual interaction with the patient is a natural event. Clinical theory becomes complementary to behavior theory rather than contradictory to it when clinical theory is used to suggest the actual events the therapist is observing. When we see an experienced, dedicated practitioner trying to communicate something, we must assume that an important observable event prompts him to do so. Behavior theory is profitably used as a language and conceptual tool for making the events the therapist is observing objective and communicable without translating them into vague, theoretical terms. By paying attention to the observations that prompt the clinical theorist and his related epistemology, a behavior analyst may discover the critical dimensions of complex human situations which otherwise require long experience and sensitivity to observe. By focusing on objective material and scientific descriptions of normal behavioral process, a functional analysis of behavior may serve as a frame of reference for integrating the mass of clinical insights presently available about clinical depression and make them more communicable. For such an analysis, Skinner's (1957) account of verbal behavior is a crucial tool because so many of the phenomena of psychopathology and psychotherapy are verbal.

A FUNCTIONAL ANALYSIS OF DEPRESSION

Depression as Reduced Frequency of Adjustive Behavior

The most obvious aspect of depression is a marked reduction in the frequency of certain kinds of activity and an increase in the frequency of others, usually avoidance and escape. Such a specification of depression allows us to search for the kinds of behavioral processes that may potentially reduce the frequency of a performance. The clinical definition of depression as "an emotional state with retardation of psychomotor and thought processes, a depressive emotional reaction, feelings of guilt or criticism, and delusions of unworthiness" is a good starting place to uncover the actual forms of conduct that describe the way a depressed person interacts with his environment.

Reduced frequency of many normal activities is the major characteristic we observe in most depressed people. The depressed person may sit silently for long periods, or perhaps even stay in bed all day. The time taken to reply to a question may be longer than usual, and speaking, walking, or carrying out routine tasks will also occur at a slower pace. While he may at a particular time answer questions, ask for something, or even speak freely, his overall frequency of such actions is low. Certain kinds of verbal behavior may seldom occur, such as telling an amusing story, writing a report or a letter, or speaking freely without solicitation. The reduced frequency of activity is referred to clinically as a reduction in gratification (Beck, 1967). There is usually a lack of interest in hobbies and sports, and a lack of concern for emotional attachments to other people. Even eating or sexual activity may no longer be rewarding and hence occur less frequently. The frequency of a performance and its reinforcement are obviously related aspects of the same event. When eating or sexual activity are less reinforcing (possibly because of a loss of the social and verbal components involved in them), the frequency of the performance is reduced.

The depressed person's perception of his own activities and those of people around him may be grossly distorted as indicated, for example, by extreme feelings of self-blame or incompetence and indifference to and rejection by those around him. The connection between these verbal distortions and the amount of normal activity requires extensive comment and will be taken up in a later section.

Despite its diagnostic usefulness, bizarre or irrational behavior confuses the objective description of the depressed person's repertoire because it is so prominent. The frequency of such behavior does not imply that it is a strongly maintained or motivated part of the depressed person's repertoire or even a causal factor of the psychosis or neurosis. Such simple, repetitive acts have at best no useful connection to the ordinary social environment, despite their prominence. Sometimes they serve to annoy a particular person or whomever may be in the vicinity. Despite an overall low rate of speech, a depressed person may talk excessively without regard to a listener, become incoherent, repeat hand gestures, adopt complex rituals, or spend a large part of the day in simple innocuous acts like hand wringing, pacing, doodling, playing with hair, genitals or other parts of the body, or compulsively carrying around some object. Despite the high frequency of these performances, we cannot assume that they have the same functional relationship to the environment or even the same persistence and durability as those in a normal repertoire. The frequency of such behaviors may be high because they operate without competition from other, more significant activities. A high frequency of such activities could occur by default of the rest of the repertoire. If the normal repertoire were better maintained, such trivial activities would occur less often.

Skinner has compared bizarre or irrational symptoms to the erratic patterns on the TV set when it is not working properly. The TV repairman deals with the malfunctioning components of the television set rather than with the details of the aberrant picture. Bizarre, irrational, or nonfunctional behaviors frequently occur with the same relation to the normal repertoire in both undepressed and depressed persons when they are in situations where normal activity is restricted. A conference participant, in the presence of a speaker who does not hold his interest but generates enough anxiety to command at least a nominal show of attention, may repetitively rub a spot on the table, doodle, repeatedly touch his body in a ritualistic way, or have bizarre, unconnected, or irrational thoughts. These performances are not significant in themselves but occur in the absence of performances in which a person might otherwise engage. No other activity is appropriate at the moment and the frequency of the irrational behavior is due to its prepotency over an essentially zero repertoire. Similar symptomatic prominence is common with schizophrenic or autistic children (Ferster 1961). The autistic child will often engage in simple repetitive acts and rituals because there are no other significant behaviors in his repertoire. Whenever the child learns to deal successfully with a normal environment we find that the new repertoire preempts nonfunctional activities.

The depressed person's complaints or requests for help are frequent and prominent almost to the exclusion of positively reinforced behavior. He repeatedly tells how bad he feels, talks about suicide, and complains of the inadequacy of his own conduct, external circumstances, fatigue, and illness. Complaints and other negatively reinforced components of the depressed person's repertoire are sometime accompanied by high frequencies of agitated activities such as hand wringing, pacing, or compulsive talking. These activities serve a function similar to complaints because by prepotency they mask other aversive conditions such as silence, inactivity, or anxiety-producing activities.

All of these performances are, functionally speaking, avoidance and escape behaviors (technically, they are behaviors reinforced by the removal of an aversive stimulus). Suicide is, of course, the ultimate expression of the aversiveness of life's experiences. A complaint ("I can't sleep," for example) is a class of activity that has removed or ameliorated aversive conditions in the past, even though it is incapable of ending the current aversive stimulus. In more common forms, "Please turn down the volume of the radio," for example, is a performance which is commonly reinforced. The frequent reinforcements of complaints in ordinary life account for the extensions of similar but ineffective performances in the face of other aversive situations. In technical jargon (Skinner 1957, pp. 46–48) these are superstitious or extended demands akin to the declaration of a child inside on a rainy day who says, "I wish it would stop raining."

Besides their significance for indicating aversive aspects of the patient's life experiences, these negatively reinforced activities also indicate a low frequency of positive reinforcement. The objective of the depressed person's therapy ultimately has to deal with those behaviors that are missing. The avoidance and "depressed behaviors" that do occur are important insofar as they preempt the normal repertoire or are symptomatic of deficits elsewhere. It is problematical whether a person whose repertoire consisted solely of negatively reinforced performances could survive.

The Repertoire of the Depressed Person Is a Passive One

A passive person can be described by the kind of reinforcers sustaining his activity. Magic, superstitious, or extended escape and avoidance behavior are one kind of passive response to the environment, in this case the internal one. The depressed person also responds to the other person's initiative in social interactions. In a two-person interaction, the behavior the active person emits is reinforced by the effect it has on the passive person. The passive person, on the other hand, in complying with the demands of the active one is largely escaping and avoiding aversive consequences. Thus, one connotation of a passive repetoire is that in which the behaviors that are emitted tend to be negatively reinforced by aversive stimuli applied by other people.

A second aspect of a passive repertoire related to depression is associated with the failure to deal with, avoid, or escape from aversive social consequences. Consider, for example, an event that frequently produces depression in a therapy group. A member of the group, who had been severely criticized during a previous session by a number of other members, fails to attend a particular meeting. The therapist has evidence that there is a depression of all of the members of the group because they assume the blame for having injured the person so much that he did not return. When the therapist prompts the group by noting that one member is missing, the conversation reveals evidence that is incompatible with their blame and the depression lifts. Without the prompting and cues from the therapist, however, the aversive stimuli derived from the sense of responsibility for injuring the missing member might prevail.

Passivity surrounds the nature of the control by the aversive stimulus. When it disrupts the ongoing repertoire its control is that of an emotional effect by an aversive stimulus. When the nature of the aversive stimulus is clarified, the control is that of negative reinforcement—the aversive stimulus increases the frequency of those performances that terminate it. The verbal activity that clarifies the actual events that occurred are negatively reinforced because they alter an aversive situation into one which is not.

Depression Needs To Be Defined Functionally, Rather Than Topographically

The missing performances are usually a part of a depressed person's potential repertoire. On many occasions in the past he probably dressed, traveled to work, completed his job, and engaged in many performances reinforced by their interpersonal effects. The problem is that the current conditions do not support the activities of which he is potentially capable. A topographic description of the depressed person's repertoire does not distinguish it from the normal one. Almost any item of conduct to be observed in a depressed person may be seen at one time or another in an undepressed person. The depressed person is distinguished from one who is not by the relative frequency of occurrence of these performances in the total repertoire. Most persons, at one time or another, sit looking quietly out a window, say "That was a dumb thing for me to do." are sad, unhappy, or dejected, or lose interest in an activity. In any one of these instances it may not be possible to distinguish them from pathologically depressed persons.

Different Meanings of the Term "Behavior"

Contrary to the prejudices of many clinical writers, general behavior theory does not talk about a person's repertoire as a collection of response topographies. The phrase "functional analysis of behavior" implies a systematic description in which the significance of a person's activities is connected with the way it operates on the environment, on both sides of his skin. Thus, one person who talks compulsively and another who leaves the room as soon as an unfamiliar person enters may be acting in identical ways, even though the acts are very different topographically. Skinner (1959) notes that a man walking down the street to mail a letter is engaged in very different behaviors from those of a man walking for exercises, even though the topography of the two activities is virtually identical. Despite the identical topographies of the two performances, in no way could they be considered the same when analyzed functionally because their behavioral significance is intimately connected with the reinforcers maintaining them. A description is behavioral, not because it differs from a clinical interpretation but because the component events of the functional relation between performance and the environment are described objectively, as would be any other natural event.

The distinction is sometimes made clinically between behaviors such as muscular tension, reaction time, handwriting, performance on a pursuit rotor, or written personality tests, and the underlying psychological processes of which the behaviors are symptomatic. Besides the term "behavioral" has such explicit connotations to clinical practitioners it will be useful to distinguish between such symptomatic behavior and a functional analysis of behavior. Beck, for example, distinguishes between self-evaluation by a patient and behavioral tests of the patient (1967, p. 177). A functional analysis of behavior does not necessarily reject the patient's self-evaluation as nonbehavioral. The way a depressed patient talks about himself is an important class of factual information and it becomes nonbehavioral and unobjective only when it is taken as symptomatic of events elsewhere rather than as an activity of importance in itself. A behavioral analysis of the patient's self-evaluation stresses its functional relation to the person the patient is talking with or to whom he is complaining about himself.

THE BASIC BEHAVIORAL PROCESS WHICH CONTRIBUTES TO OR REDUCES THE FREQUENCY OF A PERSON'S CONDUCT

Depressions, certainly those generally characterized as reactive, appear to be a functional rather than a topographically defined category. The common denominator among depressed persons is the decreased frequency of many different kinds of positively reinforced activity. We cannot therefore expect that one cause or a single psychological process will be responsible because the frequency of the items in the depressed person's repertoire is a product of so many different psychological processes. Every process that accounts for the frequency of a person's actions explains part of the pathology of depression.

Schedules of Reinforcement

The schedule of reinforcement of a performance is an important determinant of that performance's frequency, independently of the kind of reinforcer or the associated deprivation.

In general, reinforcement schedules requiring large amounts of behavior to produce the relevant change in the environment (e.g., fixed ratio schedules of reinforcement, Skinner 1938; Ferster & Skinner 1957) are those most susceptible to loss. The critical factor is a fixed and large amount of activity required for each reinforcement. The salesman who needs to call on a large number of persons before he consummates a sale, or the person engaged in studying all semester for a final examination, working on a term paper, writing a novel, persuading someone, carrying out an experiment which requires long and arduous procedures without indication of success before completion, or a difficult therapeutic encounter in which much thought and stress go into small indicators of progress, or a housewife's routine housework which may require a fixed and large amount of repetitive work—all exemplify a schedule of reinforcement that may potentially weaken the behavior severely. The result is frequently seen as an abulia in which the novelist, for example, is unable to work for considerable periods after completing his previous work. The effect of such schedules of reinforcement is hard to observe because they at times generate high, persistent rates of activity, even though the predominant result is long periods of inactivity. The parallel to the manic side of depression comes immediately to mind. The enormous influence of such schedules of reinforcement apart from the reinforcer or the associated deprivation is conveyed by animal experiments in which a pigeon pecking for food on a fixed-ratio schedule, for example, will starve to death because the frequency of the performance is so low. Yet the same bird, when exposed to a variable reinforcement schedule, requiring the same amount of activity per reinforcement, sustains its activity easily.

It is tempting to speculate that this particular schedule of reinforcement exemplifies the middle period of life when most individuals settle down to a routine in which there is a constant steady work requirement as opposed to the variability in quality and amount of work that occurs as one prepares for a career or enters into job experiences that change rapidly. Perhaps relevant here is the classical phenomenon of the highly successful professional who, on reaching the pinnacle of achievement, undergoes a profound depression. The upwardly striving person is one whose schedules of reinforcement are variable, sometimes requiring large amounts of activity for reinforcement and at other times requiring less. Such variable schedules of reinforcement are much less likely to produce strain and low frequencies than the schedules associated with a stable work situation in which day in and day out there is a constant amount of activity associated with the required accomplishment.

Changes in the Environment

Where is an organism's behavior when it is not engaging in it? Where is the patellar reflex when it is not being elicited? Where are the reminiscenses that occur with a close friend when the friend is absent? From a behavioral point of view they are "in the repertoire." There are potential performances that will occur when the necessary collateral circumstances are present. Behaviors, in a person's repertoire but not occurring because the current situation has reduced their frequency to zero, are as unavailable as if they had never occurred before. Most people's conduct occurs appropriately to the circumstances in which it has been and can be reinforced. When the circumstances change too drastically, the result may be depression—a loss of behavior.

The death of a close companion or other radical changes in the physical and social environment may reduce the frequency of significant items in a person's repertoire as markedly as schedules of reinforcement. It is even possible to conceive of sudden changes that may virtually denude an individual of his entire repertoire as, for example, the death of a close companion to a secluded spinster. The seclusion of her life produces a situation in which all her conduct is narrowly under the control of her companion. The companion's sudden death therefore removes the occasions that supported almost all her activity. A case history of an autistic child illustrates the same process. The nearly psychotic mother of a four-year-old girl hired a teenage babysitter to take care of her daughter for almost a year. Although the mother remained in the house during the whole year, during which the babysitter took care of the child, she completely abdicated control to the babysitter by having literally nothing to do with the child. If the child said, "Mom, can I have a cookie?", there would be no answer; if she said, "Janet [the babysitter], could I have a cookie?", Janet said, "Yes," and gave the child the cookie. If the child said, "Let's go outside," the mother did not answer. Janet, on the other hand, might reply, "Okay," and take the child outside.

Such interpersonal interactions are functionally identical to standard pigeon experiments in which the pigeon produces food by pecking a key. When reinforcement depends on the color of the light illuminating the key, the pigeon's pecking is brought under the control of the colors by withholding reinforcement on one occasion and allowing it to occur on the other. When the key is red, pecks do not produce food and hence decrease in frequency. Pecking continues in the green color because those pecks continue to produce food. Such control of the bird's behavior by the environment makes it possible to alter its repertoire rapidly by simply changing the color of the light behind the key. An analogy could be drawn between the mother and the babysitter, and the red and green keys in the pigeon experiment. The babysitter's presence (the red light) defined an occasion during which any kind of verbal request of nonverbal interaction had a normal effect. When the babysitter left the child alone with the mother at the end of the year there was a loss of almost all of the child's repertoire. She became incontinent, could not be kept in the nursery school, and lost speech. There is a similar functional parallel between the behavior of the spinster and its control by the presence of her companion.

The normal processes of growth and development, particularly during middle age, occur when similar important changes in life's circumstances take place which require corresponding changes in a person's repertoire. The physical changes associated with aging and normal development may have a major influence on the kinds of positive reinforcement that are possible. Hormonal changes, and the associated changes in amount of sexual activity including fantasy, are one important area of change. Another area of change lies in overall physical capacity for work and severe physical exertion. Even behaviors reinforced by ingesting food become less available as a rewarding activity because decreased physical activity reduces the metabolic requirements of most middle-aged people. Ironically, a person who can finally afford bountiful, rich, and tempting foods cannot eat them because they would produce obesity. Even important social interactions, which in so many cultures surround food and eating, become stressful or less frequent because of limitations on food ingestion or because of disease or decreased metabolic need.

Disease or other kinds of physical incapacity may reduce the change of performances that are possible for the middle-aged or older person. Retirement may impose a very drastic change in an older person's environment, opposite to the problem facing the adolescent. Just as the adolescent faces a complex world for which he does not yet have an adequate repertoire, the older person also encounters a new environment which needs for its reinforcement an entirely new repertoire. All of the activities previously reinforced by the work environment can no longer be emitted. A successful transition to retirement depends on whether the retired person has a sufficient repertoire to make contact with the environment of retirement. The problem is doubly complex because the repertoire available for the transition was shaped and formed in the work world that is no longer present.

The Relationship of Depression to a Limited Repertoire of Observation

One common characterization of a depressed person's repertoire is a distorted, incomplete, and misleading view of the environment which includes hallucinations and delusions, distortions of body image and physical appearance, distortions of his competence, exaggeration of errors, complete inability to evaluate the way other people see him, a tendency to take blame for events for which there is really no responsibility, and a limited and unhopeful view of the world.

Even though our language and accustomed patterns of thinking stress distortions of the person's perceptions and his view of events, a behavioral analysis requires that we talk about how the environment prompts and otherwise controls a person's activity, rather than the way he perceives his own and the outside world. The event that influences the person is the same, no matter how we choose to talk about it. The behavioral description is more useful than the mentalistic one because we can see the details of how a person comes to act distinctively to the various features of his inside and outside environment. When we can describe the process in detail it will suggest therapeutic procedures which can produce performances that can then act successfully on important environments.

Ideally, if a person's every act occurred under circumstances in which it could be effective, there would be a high frequency of reinforcement. Conversely, if a person cannot observe the environment around him accurately (the environment does not control the performances appropriate to activating it), a large proportion of his behavior will be unsuccessful and go unreinforced. The distortions of the depressed person's perceptions may be seen to reduce the possibility of positive reinforcement because the major component of the distortion is the emission of performances that cannot be reinforced. A failure of control by the characteristics of the environment could therefore cause or contribute substantially to a depression.

The low frequency of positively reinforced behaviors in the depressed person's repertoire might perpetuate the incomplete or distorted perception of the environment because the primary event responsible for acting on the environment selectively is some tendency to influence it. In general, the ability to observe the environment depends on a high enough frequency of interacting with it so that the successful reinforcement of the performance on one occasion and its unsuccesful reinforcement on another occasion eventually tailors it to the environment in which it can be reinforced.

An important way in which we learn to observe the environment is to comment on it and describe it verbally. The low frequency of verbal activity, other than complaints, is a serious impediment to an improvement of the depressed person's view of the world. The depressed person may not be able to emit enough potentially reinforceable behavior to discover the differential reaction of the environment, depending upon the kind of performance that is emitted.

The reader may ask, of course, which came first, the depression in which the person behaves without observing the consequences or effectiveness of his performance, or a lack of sufficient repertoire so that the person could effectively discover the characteristics of the environment in which he operates. From a clinical point of view, three aspects of the patient's repertoire bear on the technical behavioral analysis. The patient has (1) a limited view of the world, (2) a "lousy" view of the world, and (3) an unchanging view of the world.

A limited view of the world refers to the differential control of the social and physical environment. Patients' behaviors are not appropriate to the changing circumstances in the external environment. Thus, for example, a person may pout, complain, or sulk in circumstances in which he had but to interact along the lines needed for assistance. We cannot assume that the depressed person actually sees very many of the features of the social world around him. William James' "bloody, blooming confusion" might be the most apt characterization of the depressed person's view of the world.

The "lousy" view of the world describes the aversive consequences of being unable to see the environment clearly enough to avoid aversive situations. Some of the aversive conditions are the inability to behave appropriately to the environment, and the lack of the repertoire by which one can act effectively and positively without engendering punishment by acting in ways that are aversive to other people.

The unchanging view of the world refers to the processes, probably stemming from the person's developmental history, that prevent the normal exploration of the environment, and the clarification and expansion of the repertoire that comes from such exploration. These developmental arrests seem to be the same as the fixation of personality development described psychoanalytically. There still remains the task, however, of identifying the actual behaviors and the interactions that cause the developmental stoppages. The disparity between the person's repertoire and the environment he is in effective contact with also needs to be described. The circumstances are sufficiently complex so that a separate discussion is warranted.

Factors That Block the Cumulative Development of a Repertoire

Ideally, normal growth and development represent a continuous approximation of a complex repertoire. Should there be a hiatus in development in which the contingencies of reinforcement are not consistent with the person's currently emitted behavior, however, the process becomes negatively autocatalytic. Failure to make contact with the current environment reduces the frequency of behavior and prevents the further development of the repertoire. In the normal process of feeding, whether by breast or bottle, the infant engages in an active interplay with the mother. The child's activities are variously successful or unsuccessful from moment to moment as the child adjusts its conduct. Behavior that successfully meets the characteristics of the mother and the relevant features of the physical environment produces physical contact, food, and other rewarding reactions. The adjustment between the child and mother is a teaching device from which the child's view of the mother and the physical environment evolve. The sight of the approaching nipple, for example, becomes an occasion that prompts the child to open its mouth. It is problematical whether the child would in any case notice the mother or be influenced by her if there were not some activity whose outcome was not influenced by her. Even the simplest act, such as the child's moving its fingers across the mother's arm or touching its blanket, is subject to the same kind of differential reinforcement. The visual characteristics of the blanket or the mother's arm come to control the moment of contact between the hand and blanket or skin. The differential reaction of the mother, such as the way she acts in return, further distinguishes the occasions on which the child acts on the mother and serves to enlarge the child's perceptual capability.

Such normal development of the child's perceptual repertoire may be interrupted if there is a serious interference with or interruption of the reinforcers maintaining the child's activities. For example, a child may experience difficulties in feeding which prevent the "give and take" that normally makes eating a natural result of a continuous interaction with the mother. The mother may not be aware of the flow of milk from the bottle, so that the milk passively pours down the child's throat, or the flow might be so slow and require so much sucking that the movements are not reinforced. A mother who does not react to the tension and relaxation of the child's muscular posture will fail to reinforce the child's movements as it adjusts its posture to produce greater body contact with the mother or to escape discomfort when the mother shows physical strain because she is holding the child like a "sack of potatoes." Not only is there a loss of repertoire that would normally emerge from these interactions, but there is a corresponding lack of perceptual development. The child who does not interact in close correspondence with its mother as she holds him also does not learn to observe the nuances that prompt and cue the interactions.

The large magnitudes of emotional reaction that not only preempt positively reinforced behavior but also become firmly established because they produce an effect on the parent which reinforces and increases their frequency are an equally serious consequence of the nonreinforcement of important (high frequency) activities. The child who does not receive food from its mother satisfactorily enough to satiate the underlying deprivation, or one who experiences collateral aversive effects such as choking or extreme physical constraint, may react emotionally. Such activities in turn generate a reaction in the parent, who may either remove the aversive situation by providing the food or react emotionally in direct response to the child's actions. The result is an increase in frequency of the child's rage and frustration because of their influence on the parent. Not only does a primitive, atavistic mode of dealing with the parent become a prominent part of the child's repertoire, but it blocks the child's perception of his world. The diffuse emotional reaction is prepotent over the smaller magnitude component activities of a normal interaction.

The behaviors involved in such disruptions appear to be the same ones described psychodynamically along the dimensions of primary to secondary process. The shift from primary to secondary process appears to describe the adjustment between the child's current behavior and its progressive adjustment to the complex features of its social environment. The child whose interactions with its mother are primarily associated with its own deprivations, which are reinforced because of their aversiveness to her, is ultimately blocked from developing an adequate perception of other people and hence adequate ways of interacting with them (secondary process). The child who fails to come under the control of the nuances of the mother's behavior is progressively left behind in its development of interpersonal behaviors, and whole sectors of interpersonal reactivity are not available to it as a means of commerce with the external world, much along the lines of the classical connotations of the fixation of a personality at a particular stage of development.

Such failures in the perceptual area may at once suggest causes of some kinds of depression and a means of ameliorating them. Behaviorally, the most general way of increasing the perceptual repertoire is to begin with simple activities whose reinforcement is reliable but not so invariant that there are not some circumstances in which the performance is appropriate and others in which it is not. The reinforcement of the performance on the one occasion and its nonreinforcement on another teaches the person to observe the appropriate features. The most important element, however, is to find a way to increase the person's tendency to act positively on the environment rather than to react passively and emotionally. A useful reinforcement schedule applicable to such a problem is the differential reinforcement of other behavior. The increase in frequency of reinforcement behaviors other than primitive or atavistic activities eventually decreases their frequency by prepotency and nonreinforcement (Ferster and Perrott 1968).

Ideally, a therapeutic interaction with a psychotherapist simulates just such a differential reinforcement of other behavior when the therapist observes and functionally analyzes the current verbal activity. By his reactions and questions he reinforces selected parts of the patient's current interaction. Many of these behaviors constitute the patient's talk about his activity. Although the ultimate goal of therapy is the patient's activity rather than his talk about his activity, this class of verbal behavior also serves an important function. First, it is an increase in general verbal activity which of itself could be of practical use. Second, it becomes a means for the patient to observe his own activity because his speech is a repertoire of performances differentially reinforced (by the therapist) according to its relation to the patient's activity. Third, the patient's descriptions of his own primitive reactions to aversive or thwarting situations may prompt more effective ways to escape or produce positive reinforcers, when he observes the incompatibility between what he is doing and what he can say about it rationally. Such talking about one's own behavior needs to be quite durable and of a high frequency before it can preempt more primitive, less effective forms of conduct.

Anger and Aggressive Acts as Factors in Depression

Clinicians speak of "problems of dealing with anger and aggressive impulses" as a prominent feature of psychopathology. It is obvious that such performances have a high frequency of occurrences in normal human activity and that parental and other communities often punish such activities severely. The pathology stemming from anger and aggression is generally agreed to be a by-product of their punishment and suppression when they affect others adversely.

Anger Turned Inward

To understand the suppression or repression of anger behaviorally we first need to describe anger as an operant performance and second to note the characteristics of punishment as a behavioral process. Aggressive or angry acts are generally those reinforced by the injury they produce to another person, by the actual removal of reinforcers, or by the creation of situations or events that are aversive because they indicate a loss of reinforcers. The class of performances is defined, not by its topography, but by the way the performances influence another person. Aggressive acts are frequently disguised or "softened" because a nakedly aggressive act will produce such a large aversive reaction. Sarcasm exemplifies one kind of softening; aggressive humor is another. Their form may be as unobtrusive as a tendency to comment on the unfavorable aspects of another person's conduct, either by criticism or by especially noting unfortunate lapses.

Since aggressive acts are aversive to others by design, their punishment is the rule rather than the exception. Experimental psychology contributes to our understanding of this problem by creating knowledge of the characteristics of the punishment process. There is some dispute in the psychological literature about whether punishment can directly reduce the frequency of the punished act, as in an algebraic subtraction (Azrin & Holz 1966), or whether the reduced frequency is *always* a temporary suppression. However this dispute is resolved, it is clear that the temporary suppression of punished acts is a frequently observed phenomenon. The process is illustrated by the child, facing a piece of bric-a-brac, who has been punished for playing with it. In the face of a tendency to play with the attractive toy, the child puts his hand behind his back. Or the child provoked to laughter in the classroom bites his lip to the point of pain because the teacher would punish laughter. Both of these performances prevent the punished act because they are incompatible with it. Thus, the smiling and the reaching for the piece of bric-a-brac may remain intact in the repertoire, but with a reduced frequency only because any incipient tendency creates an aversive situation whose removal reinforces and increases the frequency of the incompatible performances such as putting the hands behind the back or biting the lip.

The phenomenon of psychodynamic suppression is a close analogue, except that the performances tend to be verbal. As a word, a phrase, a thought, or an association comes into consciousness (its probability of emission increases), there is an automatic reinforcement of incompatible behavior. The repression, according to this process, is an actual activity or performance which will occur in a dynamic balance with the punished or anxiety-provoking performance. Such activity is in its own right a kind of behavior with a certain persistence and frequency which is a part of the person's repertoire. As a prominent and frequent activity, not serving any useful function in the person's commerce with the external environment, it may be a substantial part of the finite amount of activity of which a person is capable. The metaphor of a fixed amount of energy, which may be apportioned to the repression activity or the external world, seems to convey the sense of the behavioral analysis. The repression of punished behavior appears to be a potentially serious contributor to depression because it commits such a large part of a person's repertoire to activities that do not produce positive reinforcement.

Aggressive Social Acts Imply a
Loss of Important Social Reinforcers

A person who is angry at someone who can potentially or has in the past supplied important reinforcers creates the possibility that he may lose important reinforcers. There is an obvious incompatibility between acting to injure someone and continuing to expect him to interact socially and to provide positive events. For this reason, anger comes to serve what is behaviorally called a preaversive stimulus—a situation that precedes the loss of positive reinforcement. Such preaversive stimuli, in classical animal experiments, markedly reduce the frequency of the ongoing operant behavior in the sense of an emotional change—a state of the organism that has a global effect. It is easy to conjecture vignettes from a child's developmental history in which a parent significantly withdrew from a child, perhaps totally, in the face of its anger. The effect on the child is exacerbated because the withdrawal of reinforcers may increase the child's anger and emotionality, leading to further instances of loss of parental attention, affection, and ordinary items of daily support.

REFERENCES

Ayllon T., & Azrin, N. H., *Token economy; A motivational system for therapy and rehabilitation.* New York: Appleton-Century-Crofts; 1968.

Azrin, N. H., & Holz, W. C., *Punishment in operant behavior: Areas of research and application.* New York: Appleton-Century-Crofts, 1966.

Beck, A. T., *Depression.* Philadelphia: University of Pennsylvania Press, 1967.

Ferster, C. B., Reinforcement and punishment in the control of human behavior by social agencies. *Psychiatric Research Reports*, 1958, 101–118.

Ferster, C. B. Positive reinforcement and behavioral deficits of autistic children. *Child Development*, 1961, **32**, 437–456.

Ferster, C. B. The experimental analysis of clinical phenomena, *The Psychological Record*, 1972, **22**, 1–16.

Ferster, C. B. & Perrott, M. C. *Behavior Principles.* New York: Appleton-Century-Crofts, 1968.

Ferster, C. B. & Skinner, B. F., *Schedules of reinforcement*, New York: Appleton-Century-Crofts, 1957.

Franks, C. M. (Ed.) *Behavior therapy: Appraisal and status*, New York: McGraw Hill, 1969.

Liberman, R. P. A behavioral approach to group dynamics. *Behavior Therapy*, 1970, **1**, 141–175.

Skinner, B. F. *The behavior of organisms*. New York: Appleton-Century-Crofts, 1938.

Skinner, B. F. What is psychotic behavior? *Cumulative Record*, New York: Appleton-Century-Crofts, 1959.

Skinner, B. F. *Walden Two*. New York: MacMillan, 1948.

Skinner, B. F. *Verbal behavior*. New York: Appleton-Century-Crofts, 1957.

Wolpe, J. *The practice of behavior therapy*. New York: Pergamon Press, 1969.

DISCUSSION

Dr. Beck: I would like to present several clinical anecdotes to see how they would be handled within a behavioral model. Dr. Ferster, you have stated that the loss of reinforcement in the environment leads to depression, and yet it seems to me that it is the meaning of the loss which is critically important. For example, a parent whose child leaves for camp may have been reinforced by having the child near him, but he does not become depressed when the child leaves for camp. Still, this same parent will become depressed should the child leave for camp and die there. It would seem in this instance that it is not the absence of the reinforcer but rather the meaning attached to the loss that is the critical element.

Dr. Ferster: The behavior of raising a child has many of the characteristics of a weaning for both the parent and the child. During the early years the close dependency of the child on the parent also requires the parent's immediate attention. The parent's involvement with the child consists of events with immediate consequences, such as watching the child with pleasure, having the child on one's lap, ministering to it, and playing with it. As the child gets older, the contact between parent and child becomes less frequent as each begins to lead an independent life. Ths loss of a child after considerable independence has been achieved still involves considerable loss of positive reinforcement, such as news in the child's letters and periodic visits. It is important to distinguish grief and mourning from depression. If the parent became weaned from the child just as the child became weaned from the parent, we would expect grief and mourning. If too large a proportion of the parent's repertoire as connected with the child or conversely there as little repertoire elsewhere, then we might expect depression.

Dr. Beck: My clinical experience leads me to believe that many depressed patients actually continue on the same reinforcement schedule that existed prior to the depression. Their friends rally round them and provide sympathy and support, but the patient will often say, "It doesn't mean anything to me any more." Previous pleasures no longer bring the person satisfaction. He may say, for example, "Bowling doesn't turn me on any more," etc. It seems that all the reinforcement that was previously there still remains. In fact, it has increased, but the person no longer responds to what was once reinforcing.

Dr. Ferster: We need more data to be sure what the reinforcer for bowling was. Besides the bowling itself, it could consist of collateral social activities, for example. It is also difficult to know how inclined the person was to bowl even before his depression. In a particular case, a person might have bowled regularly because there was little else to do. In another case, the bowling could have been avoidance behavior, reinforced not because of the activity of bowling itself but because it avoids an aversive consequence such as being alone, someone else's pressure to go bowling, or conforming to some more general social pressure, such as might occur in a work-connected bowling league. In another case, it might be the proverbial golfer who says he would adore playing golf if only he had the time, but in fact doesn't play frequently. The depressed person, with his hazy view of the world, often does not report his own activity very accurately.

Dr. Tabachnick: I believe Dr. Ferster's warning to examine what appears to be reinforcing in greater detail is well taken. We have observed something quite similar in suicidal situations. If you remember, one of the first slogans that emerged from the suicide prevention movement was the "cry for help." The impression was that mental health workers should retain the idea that suicidal patients are getting less in life but are looking for more. The picture becomes somewhat blurred when you begin to examine in greater detail exactly what "more" and what "less" actually mean. Although suicidal people are asking for a response from the environment and although they do receive a response, a reinforcement, they also receive at the same time a very negative, or at least negatively tinged, message from those who are responding to them. After all, suicidal people are often hostile, nagging, and irritating individuals who relate to others in an ambivalent fashion. The response they receive is therefore an ambivalent one. It is as though the people in the environment were saying, in effect, "Well, we see that you are asking for something and we would like to give you something, but at the same time, we must tell you that you are an irritating person." Thus, the reinforcement and the message are multifaceted.

When such situations occur with suicidal patients, the Suicide Prevention Center and other helpers can play a pivotal role because hopefully they will not become as irritated at the suicidal individual as have his relatives and friends. Even at the Suicide Prevention Center we find it helpful to have a number of workers deal with any particular individual in order to share the burden and reduce the number of negative messages conveyed to the patient.

Dr. Raskin: Perhaps the notion that there is a high spontaneous remission rate in depression, or the concept that depression has to run its course may ultimately be relegated to folklore. But I would be interested to know how Dr. Ferster incorporates this idea into his theories, since it seems to be such a physiological or biological phenomenon.

Dr. Ferster: Remissions are common in almost all psychopathology, so I do not believe the answer to this question is specific to depression. The occurrence of spontaneous remission in involutional depression, presumably hormonal in origin, must mean that there is a behavior adjustment to the hormonal change or that the hormonal change is only a precipitator or disposing factor which operates in the context of a repertoire susceptible to depression. Thus, I repeat the theme stressed in my presentation: I do not see evidence that depression is a unitary phenomenon; rather, it appears to be a disruption in the normal repertoire which can be caused by a multiplicity of factors operating in infinite combinations. The living organism is in constant dynamic balance with its environment. In pathology we see a preponderance of defenses rather than positive and active interchange with the environment. But a reactive, adjustive reinforcing environment is always present and potentially available. The dynamic balance is particularly prominent in the interaction between punished but reinforced behavior and the incompatible performances that produce the suppression. Despite the repression of aggressive or sexual performances, the person is constantly exhibiting some tendency to behave sexually and aggressively. It is the persistence of this tendency that produces a dynamic interaction from which some adjustment is possible to bring the depressed person into better contact with at least part of the environment potentially available to him. The therapeutic environment can not really be more than an intensification and selective application of events and processes which would equally occur in ordinary social commerce.

Dr. Schuyler: I believe the time-limited course of most depressions can be explained by noting that something does happen to the frequency of reinforcement. A simple hypothesis might be, in the case of a husband who is maintaining his wife's depressed behavior by responding to it, for example, that he gradually begins to reinforce the depressed behavior less and less and this initiates the termination of the depression.

Dr. Beck: The technique of paradoxical intention that stems from the existential school seems similar to Dr. Ferster's theory and stimulates the following idea. Suppose an individual has a negative cognition which, within Dr. Ferster's framework, would be the behavior that is constantly tending to be expressed but instead is suppressed. The depressed person who we hypothesize is depressed because of his negative cognitive set may eventually come out of his depression because he becomes habituated or desensitized to his negative cognitions. It follows that a possible therapeutic approach would be to try to have the patient repeat his negative cognitions over and over again instead of trying to persuade him they are not true or to remove them in a more direct fashion. Perhaps we could pull him out of his depression sooner if we could select those things to which we want to desensitize him.

This reminds me of an anecdote provided by a colleague at St. Elizabeths Hospital, where there was a patient so self-critical that his therapist could no longer cope with the self-abuse he heaped upon himself. Out of desperation the therapist ordered him to criticize himself openly in public as often as he could. For example, he ordered the patient to cross the street and go to the drug store and say, "I'm a jerk," and to keep on doing this. Within a few days the patient had knocked himself out and the self-derogatory behavior had dropped out of his repertoire. Dr. Ferster, is this a reasonable derivative of the principles you were setting forth?

Dr. Ferster: Focusing on the patient's blame and self-criticism could have value. It follows the first principle of clinical treatment as well as that of operant conditioning. If these are the emitted behaviors that constitute the bulk of the patient's activity, then they must be the area of first contact with the patient. Initially, the therapist must in some way reinforce the talk about complaints and blame if he is to listen to or interact with the patient at all. The reinforcement of the patient's initial repertoire by the therapist has value because it is a step toward the strengthening of an "intraverbal repertoire," a potential of talking about his life, which is a first step toward being able to observe it.

I would guess that a patient who could persist in practicing such an exercise was not very depressed. Statements, emitted under the control of the therapist's instructions, are functionally different from statements of self-blame and criticism which are caused by the aversiveness of the patient's immediate condition. The complaints have the quality of "primary process." The exercise prompted by the therapist's instruction has the quality of "secondary process."

The negative practice procedure, to which Dr. Beck refers, is also a way of establishing a potential reinforcer for change in the way the patient talks about himself. If the patient has sufficient intraverbal capability, the incompatibility between the two statements creates an aversive situation which is resolved by editing and altering one or the other.

Dr. Katz: Dr. Ferster, how would you account for the observation that so much of what the depressed person does seems to violate any instinct for survival? What is it that could be reinforcing this perseverative misery?

Dr. Ferster: Much of the depressed person's repertoire is not reinforced by the way it alters external people, places, and things. These are primitive activities akin in quality to spitting a bitter substance out of the mouth. Despite the fact that these activities do not effectively remove the aversive condition, functionally they are still avoidance and escape behaviors whose frequency may partially be explained by the extensive history of getting rid of aversive situations by complaint.

Dr. Dyrud: In our discussions we keep referring to this hypothetical depressed person as a poor fellow who is "unsuccessful," "hazy," and not being "reinforced." But suppose we were to conceptualize the depressed person as someone who has an increased need for certainty. Then we might discover that he is very successful because his predictions are fulfilled within the narrow purview he restricts himself to, and that is a very reinforcing experience for someone who cannot tolerate uncertainty. Continually proving "how right" he is maintains his depressed behavior. Just as he predicted, the environment does get fed up, for he has cued others to reject him.

Dr. Chodoff: Dr. Dyrud's remarks appeal to me because they apprach an examination of the function of the behavior and the motivation underlying the behavior. My clinical observations leave me with the impression that in many instances the self-reproach of a depressed person serves a function, often as a controlling device. If one reproaches himself, he can then do something about it, he can expiate his guilt and bring the situation within his control.

In a sense, what I'm suggesting is that such behavior may operate in a defensive way to protect the person from experiencing the full impact of his depression and also the "senselessness" of the affect. An instance that comes to mind is the fate of parents of leukemic children who often blame themselves or resort to other irrational explanatory devices in an attempt to avoid facing the fact that, for no reason in the world, their child has been afflicted with a fatal disease. This seems to be an effective and perhaps also an adaptive method of keeping oneself from feeling terribly helpless. Such a mechanism may represent, as Dr. Dyrud suggests, some benefit to the depressive who is afloat in a sea of misery.

Dr. Ferster: Self-blame is also an avoidance behavior, but is more complicated because it is essentially a means for avoiding responsibility for one's own repertoire, much in the way that Dr. Chodoff suggests with his example about the parents of leukemic children.

Dr. Dyrud: Recent work on memory reveals that people scan their environment based on how clearly they remember it and how effectively they can predict what they will discover. For example, people who remember and predict poorly tend to scan at a high rate, whereas those who predict with a high degree of accuracy tend to scan at a low rate. I have a hunch that "memory loss" and "indifference" to the environment, as observed in the depressed person, mean that he has narrowed his scan so that his "hit rate" is high. He therefore is successful, even though we as observers say he is "inappropriate" and that he is not responding to his environment. My hunch is that the depressed person is very attuned to particular aspects of his environment.

Dr. Ferster: In extension of my analysis of how the low frequency of activity prevents and limits observation and vice-versa, I would say that the depressed person can sustain neither the observation nor the verbal description that the observation prompts. Hence his behavior is controlled by one small, discrete part of the environment at a time. To observe and talk about more extended segments of the environment requires more activity than the depressed person is capable of. Classical depression and other psychodynamic defenses are the algebraic inverse of objective observation of the environment, whether internal or external.

Dr. Beck: In our studies we have repeatedly found that the depressed person underestimates his performance level. For example, I remember a depressed typist who was asked to type a few pages and then without proofreading to estimate how many errors she had made. She grossly overestimated her errors, though actually her performance was very satisfactory. We have verified by way of systematic, well-controlled studies the observation that depressed patients overestimate the number of mistakes they will make, even though their performance remains as adequate as that of nondepressed patients.

Dr. Dyrud: I agree that objectively performance may not be down and only the person's estimate may be askew, but I would imagine that, if this depressed typist were talking to her supervisor about her typing, she would elicit the response she would have predicted. In other words, her supervisor would have been drawn into her negative cognitive set and would have agreed that her work was falling off.

Dr. Seligman: I do not understand how a low frequency of reinforcement can account for the low rate of behavior noted in depressed states, and I question the applicability of this concept to depression. I can understand how, if reinforcement is reduced to zero, you would get extinction of the repertoire and that you might think that this process was analogous to depression. However, the findings from Skinner's laboratory and also from Dr. Lewinsohn's research concerning partial reinforcement indicate that one of the best ways of obtaining enormous amounts of behavior from an organism is to increase the ratio requirements. So, if you start a person off on a high ratio (where some behavior receives a high rate of reinforcement) and then begin to lower the rate of reinforcement, but not to zero, you would elicit a tremendous amount of behavior. Stoppage would occur only when you began to strain the organism so that the amount of behavior required for reinforcement was just enormous. Thus, lowering the rate of reinforcement should increase the amount of behavior and not decrease it as is the case in depression.

Dr. Ferster: I believe Dr. Seligman's observation is more relevant to extinction phenomena than it is to the concept of maintenance of behavior. Intermittent reinforcement, as you describe it, causes behavior to be more persistent, but that is a very different characteristic of the repertoire than how well behavior is maintained. I know of no exception to the rule that the less often you reinforce a performance, the lower will be its frequency. You do not, in terms of maintenance, strengthen behavior by reinforcing it less frequently. On the other hand, a performance on an intermittent reinforcement schedule will endure failure better, be more persistent, and be more resistant to frustration, but its frequency will be lower. Not completely in jest, I would note that I have been reinforced a lot and I have been reinforced a little—and a lot has always been better.

I would also like to reiterate my contention that depression does not appear to be a single functional category, either in the clinical literature or in terms of the analysis I have proposed. Every process known to learning theory (amount of reinforcement, deprivation, schedule of reinforcement, aversive control, prepotency, stimulus control, differential reinforcement, states of the organism, and the effects of preaversive stimuli) can increase and decrease the frequency of important items in a person's repertoire.

Dr. Lewinsohn: I agree with Dr. Ferster that an individual's inefficiency can lead to depression. However, there are many paths, one of which is exemplified by the person who, while on a very high reinforcement schedule, extinguishes the significant others in the environment who are reinforcing him. An example of this is a man who emits five behaviors after his wife has talked to him 10 times. Clearly he is on a very high schedule of reinforcement, but eventually his wife will give up because she is not receiving enough in return and then his reinforcement drops off significantly. My point is that when anything disrupts the balance between two individuals or between an individual and the significant others in his environment, isolation and depression are likely to result. So, either his own behavior is extinguished or he may extinguish the behavior of others toward him.

In addition to stressing the interpersonal aspect of behavior, I would like to point out that we know very little about what is actually reinforcing for people in a positive sense. We may well discover that obvious common-sense answers are incorrect. For example, we have assumed that it is more reinforcing to be responded to positively than negatively. We find, however, that the only true "negative reinforcer" is being ignored by the significant other. In other words, when someone disagrees with or attacks you, that is not necessarily a negative reinforcer because it may increase the probability of your emitting further behavior. But to be ignored is definitely depressing.

Dr. Klerman: I remain dissatisfied with the explanation that depression can be accounted for solely on the basis of a diminished rate of positive reinforcement. Indeed, it seems that the things which were previously reinforcing for an individual are no longer reinforcing when he is depressed. Food, sex, work, obvious premorbid reinforcers, are now—during the clinical state of depression—no longer reinforcers, and this discontinuity remains one of the hallmarks of depression. The question then is what has happened *within* the individual that has changed the schedule of reinforcement. This issue has not been addressed in the learning theory literature.

Dr. Tabachnick: I believe it is important to remember that there are numerous depressive states, with differing manifestations and causes. Thus far, in trying to understand how we can change this hypothetical depressed patient, we have been saying to ourselves: "Here is this depressed person, sort of down and out. What can we do to stimulate him, to bring him back again, to provide reinforcement for him?" I propose, as has Dr. Dyrud, that we also consider the depressed state from a different standpoint, and realize that some depressed individuals are employing a technique calculated to influence other people.

Dr. Freidman: Before we conclude what has been a very stimulating discussion, I would like Dr. Ferster to have the opportunity for a final comment.

Dr. Ferster: I notice that we tend to talk about the symptoms of depression rather than the causes, and it seems that it is a reversal of roles for the behaviorist to be reminding the clinicians that they are emphasizing the symptoms too much. It does seem to me, however, that we are being drawn away from the question of what is missing from the depressed person's repertoire. We have focused on the symptoms and details of the malady. Yet I think the conceptual formulation as well as the treatment of depression really depend upon focusing on the behaviors the patient is *not* engaged in. We must ask why he is not interacting in a normal fashion with the environment. We need to take note of symptoms and work with behaviors he shows at the moment, but the main goal of therapy focuses on performances that need to be created and strengthened. The symptoms are what we observe in the absence of adequate behavior.

3

THE DEPRESSIVE PERSONALITY: A CRITICAL REVIEW

Paul Chodoff
George Washington University School of Medicine

That individuals prone to develop clinical depressive illnesses display certain distinctive personality characteristics which they bear in common with each other and which distinguish them from those not so predisposed is a view that has received considerable although not universal support in the psychiatric and psychoanalytic literature. An examination of the relevant literature, however, makes it clear that we are very far from consensus about the characteristics of such a putative personality pattern predisposing to depression. The issue is an important one for the understanding and treatment of depressive illness, for two main reasons. First, since an observable personality pattern represents to a large degree the crystallization of underlying psychodynamic processes, agreement on the characteristics of such a pattern or patterns would offer significant aid to efforts to study psychological factors in the genesis of depression. Second, agreement on the existence of such patterns has a bearing on the investigation of genetic and biochemical factors in depression, since their presence would have to be accounted for in any coherent organic theory of etiology.

In this paper I propose to make a representative, although not exhaustive review of the literature on this subject, critically examine the acceptability of the evidence which it offers, and summarize my own understanding of the present state of knowledge on the premorbid personality of depressives. Along the way I will have some comments to make about the development and changes in the psychoanalytic concepts of "orality" and the "oral character". I will organize my discussion around what historically have been considered the three main clinical forms in which depression appears, involutional depression, manic depressive depression, and neurotic depression. I will touch on the recently suggested unipolar-bipolar distinction between individuals subject only to depressions and those who display both depressive and manic attacks. Finally, the paper is not intended as a treatise on psychological factors in depression in general and will concern itself only with the relationship between distinctive premorbid personality patterns and depressive illness.

Involutional depression has had a checkered career since its first hesitant inclusion in the canon by Kraepelin. As pointed out by Rosenthal (1968), there has been relatively little work on this entity in the past thirty years. There has also been a considerable alteration in what was considered the classical clinical symptom picture of involutional depression as it has become more difficult to distinguish endogenous involutional depressions from other depressions occurring in middle life. However, the syndrome has an historical continuity, and many psychiatrists are convinced from their clinical experience that a significant number of depressions that occur for the first time in both sexes in middle life in a more or less severe form, usually can be labeled involutional depressions. There exists a considerable consensus about the type of premorbid personality predisposed to its development. Involutional depression is said to occur principally in individuals of obsessional personality make up, described by Noyes in 1939 as "an inhibited type of individual with a tendency to be quiet, unobtrusive, serious, chronically worrisome, intolerant, reticent, sensitive, scrupulously honest, frugal, even penurious, stubborn, of stern unbending moral code, lacking humor, overconscientious, and given to self punishment. Often his interests have been narrow, his habits stereotyped, he has cared little for diversion, has avoided pleasure and has had but few close friends." Incidentally, an almost identical description is repeated in the most recent edition (Kolb 1968) of this well-known textbook. The evidence for this picture, aside from general clinical impressions, is found when examined, however, to rest on a surprisingly small number of studies done largely in the 1930's, notably those of Titley (1936), and Palmer and Sherman (1938). The apparently corroborative work of Malamud, Sands, & Malamud (1941), has been vigorously criticized by Beck (1967). Later contributions to the declining literature on involutional depression (Barnett & coworkers, 1953, with a few exceptions Kielholz, 1959). tend simply to accept the equation "obsessional-involutional" as if it had been amply confirmed. A recent study (Snaith, McGuire, & Fox, 1971), of 50 consecutive patients with primary depressive illness using personality inventory scales failed to reveal any significant differences between the personality substructures of those with early and late onsets.

Little can be said about the psychoanalytic view of the personality factors predisposing to involutional depression since psychoanalysts have not paid very much attention to it. Fenichel (1945), however, while acknowledging the dearth of psychoanalytic contributions, concurs in the above description. Szalita (1966), speaks of an oral fixation in the involutional but feels that this may express itself in any of a number of different personality styles. Fessler (1950), making a distinction between endogenous and nonendogenous depressions of the climacteric, maintains that the latter group consisted of women with premorbid hysterical characters. This work and that of Lazarus and Klerman (1968), who found a negative relationship between endogenous depressive features and hysterical character in a group of successively hospitalized female depressive patients with a median age of 52 years, suggest that the above-mentioned equation "involutional-obsessional" is not axiomatic, and that it may be more accurate to state that among individuals suffering depressive breakdowns for the first time in middle life there exists a certain well-defined subgroup among men as well as women who display premorbid obsessional personality characteristics. A problem with this formulation, however, is that if the diagnosis of involutional depression is made partly on the basis of premorbid personality characteristics rather than on a specific symptom picture, working backward from the diagnosis to the personality becomes an exercise in petitio principii.

Efforts to tease out of the literature data about the premorbid personality of neurotic depressives are even less productive than is the case with involutionals. In general, nonpsychoanalytic psychiatrists in this country and in Europe who accept the reactive-endogenous distinction and who equate neurotic and reactive depressions seem to hold the view that increased premorbid personality disturbance occurs in depressions of the neurotic as opposed to the endogenous variety. Thus, Winokur, Clayton, & Reich (1969), in a recent monograph state that the diagnosis of reactive rather than endogenous depression could be made on the basis of a poorly adjusted as opposed to a healthy premorbid personality in the former, and Klerman (1971), in setting up propositions to delineate the concept of endogenous depression, contrasts what he considers the relatively stable and nonneurotic premorbid personality of the endogenous sufferer from the maladapted personality patterns of individuals prone to neurotic depressions. Perris (quoted in Lazare & Klerman, *American Journal of Psychiatry*, 1968), comparing a group of bipolar, unipolar, and neurotic depressed patients, found that the bipolar patients scored the lowest and reactive depressions the highest in neuroticism scores derived from the administration of the Maudsley Personality Inventory. Mendelson (1967), refers to a depressive personality occurring in those prone to neurotic depressions, characterized by "chronic pessimism, loneliness, dissatisfaction, unhappiness, guilt or feelings of inadequacy."

Psychoanalytic writers since the early references to neurotic depression by Freud (1946), and Abraham (1948), have paid remarkably little attention to this entity. As Mendelson (1960), points out, however, most psychoanalysts accept the distinction between neurotic and psychotic depressions but surprisingly derive their theories almost entirely from studies of the latter. For psychoanalysts, differences between the two conditions are quantitative rather than qualitative, a more severe symptom picture in the psychotic depressives, and a greater replacement of object relationships by intrapsychic conflicts (Fenichel, 1968, p. 108, Rado, 1968, p. 70) in the psychotic illness. This distinction is similar to that made by Bonime (1966, p. 239) from a culturist psychoanalytic position, although this author is generally less impressed by any distinction between neurotic and psychotic depression. Thus, analysts generally consider psychotic depressives to be sicker people—at least potentially—than neurotic depressives (although they do not always make it clear to what extent this is on a constitutional basis). They hold that the basic personality structure of the neurotic depressive is closer to normality in psychosexual maturation (or in ego strength [Bellak 1952]) than that of the psychotic, a position which is clearly at variance with the nonpsychoanalytic authors quoted above.

What about the so-called hysterical depression? This is a term that certainly is common coin in the psychiatric market place for referring to depressive reactions in individuals with the kind of hysterical personality traits such as are often found among women who make suicidal gestures. This subject has been recently reviewed in the paper of Lazarus and Klerman (1968), in which hysterical personality features were found in 43 percent of 35 hospitalized depressed females. These authors found that the hysterical patients were characterized by certain behavioral patterns during their depressions as opposed to the nonhysterical depressives and also that their depressive features seemed to be less severe than those of the other group, thus confirming Pierre Janet's thesis that hysterical features protect against depression. The authors express no opinion about the role of hysterical features in predisposing to depression but are instead concerned with the ways in which this personality structure modifies depressive manifestations. It should be stated incidentally that this study suffers from one of the most common defects of a great deal of the work in this field, that is, subjects were all studied during their periods of clinical depression rather than during intermorbid periods. Gershon, Cromer, & Klerman, 1968 also found depressed hysterics more likely to display open hostility than depressed obsessionals. Observations such as these emphasize the point made by Foulds (1965), and Metcalfe (1968), among others, about the need to distinguish between an individual's basic personality pattern and his psychiatric symptoms when ill. Thus, the personality structure has a bearing on depressive illness, not only by providing possible predisposing factors but also by coloring the depressive illness itself so that hysterics will have hysterical depressions and obsessionals will have obsessive depressions. To disregard this rather obvious point may lead to difficulties about diagnostic categorization in depressions and may also lead to false inferences about personality predisposition.

I turn now to the manic-depressive depression which has received by far the greatest amount of attention from investigators and researchers, both psychiatric and psychoanalytic. Under this rubric I am including all depressions that can be considered psychotic (operationally, for the most part, on the basis of the criterion that they have been hospitalized), whether single or multiple or whether or not they have occurred in individuals who have also suffered from manic attacks. The emerging unipolar-bipolar differential will hopefully have the effect of improving diagnostic clarity, but of the studies I will be reviewing only the more recent ones take this distinction into account. Concentration on the manic depressive illness as a source of study for descriptions and formulations of the depressive state must be a source of some uneasiness when we consider, as has been pointed out by authorities as different as Cleghorn and Curtis (1959), and Rado (1968, p. 96) the extremely wide range of clinical conditions in which depressive illnesses occur.

The classical description of the prepsychotic and intermorbid personality of manic depressives beginning with Kraepelin and Bleuler (1924), and maintained since is that manic-depressives are cyclothymic or cycloid people. This label refers primarily to a consistent tendency on the part of these individuals to display mood swings of a range and intensity beyond those considered normal, but it also includes persistent personality optimism or gloom. The description of Henderson and Gillespie (1932), may be taken as representative. They characterize manic-depressives as "frank open personalities, either bright, talkative, optimistic, agressive people who make light of the ordinary affairs of life, or else they take a gloomy outlook, bewail the past, make mountains out of molehills; or there is a combination of the above moods rendering the person emotionally unstable." As Kretschmer (1931), puts it, manic-depressives are cyclothymic, hyperthymic, or hypothymic. Descriptions of this kind raise a question as to whether they really refer to predisposing personality attributes or simply to minor and persistent degrees of the manic-depressive illness itself.

At any rate, in a recent article, Perris (1966), reviewed a number of studies since the early 1930's on the premorbid personality of manic-depressives. While cycloid characteristics are still commonly referred to, a number of other rather vague descriptive terms have been used. It seems unnecessary to be more specific about this rather mixed bag of outmoded terms; in general, the studies that Perris (1966), reviews refer to subclinical degrees of mood alteration, undue personality sensitivity or its absence, or a tendency to turn towards or away from people, or they indicate the absence of significant departure from the normal. Some studies find no significant degree of personality abnormality. Thus, Rowe and Daggett (quoted in Kretschmer, 1931) describe intermorbid depressives as "active, intelligent and social," and Gillespie (quoted in Abraham, 1948),–(not included in Perris' review)–reports that prepsychotic endogenous depressives are usually vigorous, ambitious, cheerful, and sociable. Many of the studies cited by Perris are of rather poor quality, the clinical descriptions vague and general, the observations superficial, the diagnostic criteria often not clear, and with possible confusion between illness and personality characteristics not taken into account. The more careful study of Titley (1936), comparing involutionals, manic depressives, and normals, found that manic depressives were more like the normals than like the involutionals.

In recent years there have been a number of studies (Metcalfe, 1968, Perris, 1966, and Coppen, 1966) comparing bipolars and unipolars with regard to certain characteristics including prepsychotic personality factors on the basis of catamnestic data and personality scales such as the Maudsley and the Nyman-Marke. These studies agree in finding rather minor degrees of neuroticism in the unipolars, while the bipolars have been found to be syntonic or normal. Relevant to these general findings are the reports of Leonhard and

Hoffman (as summarized by Cadoret, 1969) on the families of manic-depressive probands. These authors found a tendency for relatives of bipolar probands to display hypomanic personality characteristics, while there are more sub-depressives in unipolar families.

The overall impression gained from a review of the studies cited above is that individuals who suffer from severe depressive illness of the manic-depressive variety, in contrast to recovered schizophrenics, do not show major departures from a loosely defined normality during their symptom-free periods although, especially if within the subgroup of those who also have manic attacks, they may display abnormally wide mood swings and in general be rather emotionally labile people. Klerman (1971), agrees with this formulation when he employs as one of his criteria for the definition of an endogenous depressive psychosis an intermorbid personality pattern which is stable, vigorous, and enterprising. As previously mentioned, Winokur, Clayton, and Reich (1969), employ premorbid normality as a standard for distinguishing endogenous from reactive depressions. However, as an illustration of the complexity of the subject, this view appears to be at variance with studies such as that of Rosenthal and Gudeman (1967), which, using a factor analytic method, found endogenous depressed women likely to be of obsessive personality makeup. The apparent disparity here, however, is more apparent than real since the authors seem to regard a certain degree of obsessiveness in the personality as not particularly abnormal. Incidentally and parenthetically, it should be of interest to sociologists of psychiatry that this is not the only instance in which obsessiveness is regarded as normal and hysterical features as evidence of neuroticism. Rosenthal and Gudeman's 1967 paper may also be criticized as including groups that could be called both manic-depressive and involutional without making it clear whether premorbid obsessiveness clusters only about the latter category of patients. Finally, this paper also suffers from the defect previously mentioned that patients were examined during their depressive illness, thus raising questions about the accuracy of the delineation of the underlying personality structure. To illustrate the potential pitfalls of this practice, Foulds (1965), tested a group of depressives during and after their illness and showed that there was some tendency for obsessive traits seen during the symptomatic period to decrease on recovery.

To what extent the formulations of psychoanalytic theorists of depression on premorbid personality can be considered comparable to the psychiatric descriptions summarized above is a continuing question similar to the one previously alluded to in the discussion of the relative premorbid normality of neurotic and psychotic depressives as seen by psychiatric and psychoanalytic writers. It is difficult to reconcile formulations derived from such differing levels as the rather gross behavioral observations and pencil-and-paper questionnaires of clinical psychiatric writers with the mixture of intense observation of the overt behavior of single individuals in a particular setting and inferences about unconscious psychodynamic mechanisms of psychoanalysts. Results of the latter tendency are illustrated in Arieti's *Manic Depressive Psychosis* (1959), possibly over elaborate division of the pre-psychotic personalities of manic-depressives into three types. Much of the psychoanalytic literature on depression is not distinguished by efforts to bridge this observational gap, although there are exceptions like Jacobson (1953) who speaks of intermorbid manic-depressives as " . . . delightful companions or marital partners . . . In their sexual life they may show a full genital response, and emotionally . . . a touching warmth and unusual affectionate clinging to people they like." This description is comparable to some of the psychiatric pictures previously cited but at the same time it does not prevent her from dealing also with the more subtle characterological defects inherent in these patients. Fenichel's remark (1945) that "the expectation that the cycloid person has an oral character is confirmed by clinical experience" may also be taken as an attempt to bridge this observational gap. Probably the most thorough-going psychoanalytic attempt to relate personality characteristics of differing degrees of visibility to manic-depressive illness is that of Cohen et al. (1954) which will be discussed later.

It is a frustrating and sometimes puzzling task to attempt to relate the well-known psychoanalytic articles on depression to current concepts of depression because (with the exception of Freud [1946] and especially Abraham [1948]) clinical and diagnostic considerations are often ignored. Whereas some of the psychiatric authors previously cited may be criticized for making statements about personality structure based on the study of depressed people during their ill periods, it could at least be ascertained from the articles in question that this was the case while many of the psychoanalytic contributions leave the reader in the dark about the extent to which the patients studied analytically were depressed or depression-free while under treatment. All this having been said, however, it is necessary to add that the descriptions and discussions in the classical psychoanalytic articles on depression represent a much more intensive, penetrating, and sophisticated investigative process than most of the psychiatric studies, and many of the former are at least heuristically persuasive. Rado's description (1968), of the kind of person prone to depression deserves to be read at the very least for its literary merit.

Psychoanalytic writers uniformly have regarded the personalities of depressives as composed of anal (obsessional) and oral elements in varying mixtures and combinations. The history of psychoanalytic thought on the subject records a gradual progression of emphasis from the former to the latter so that Gaylin in the preface to a 1968 collection of psychoanalytic papers on depression can say " . . . there is hardly a theory of depression that does not in some way emphasize orality." The statement that intermorbid depressives resemble obsessionals appears in Abraham's 1911 paper, which is the first real psychoanalytic contribution to depression. It seems to be based not only on observation but also on the theoretical necessity to derive the ambivalence towards objects of depressives from its proper psychosexual slot, the anal phase. In *Mourning and Melancholia*, Freud's only mention of the subject is that a disposition to obsessional neurosis gives a pathological cast to mourning, producing guilty self-reproaches. Both Rado's 1928 and 1950 papers on depression echo Abraham's statement about the obsessive tinge in the character of depressives during the intervals of remission, but Rado is clearly much more concerned with the subjects' oral traits. Later writers either give brief mention to obsessional characteristics or deny their universality in the depressive personality or leave these traits out of the picture entirely.

On the other hand, beginning with Abraham's 1916 (p. 248) and 1924 (p. 418) papers, oral characteristics enter the scene and describe an ascending curve in later psychoanalytic writing until they have come to dominate the psychoanalytic view of the personalities of depressives. By the oral character I refer to a fairly uniform set of personality attributes which, while of course being far from identical as delineated by different writers, are seen to be basically similar. Furthermore, this is true not only of psychoanalysts in the classical Freudian tradition but also of others whose orientation is culturist or adaptational or interpersonal. Thus, elements of the oral character run like a red thread through the writings about depressive personality from Freudians like Abraham (1948), the early Rado (1968), and Fenichel (1968), up to the present-day Bernhard Berliner (1966); of Rado (1968) in his adaptational phase, and of non-Freudians like Bonime (1966), and Bemporad (1971). Some sample quotations are Rado's "despairing cry for love" (in Abraham's Selected Papers on Psychoanalysis, 1948) and Fenichel's description of the depressive as a "love addict" in a perpetual state of greediness (1968). Even Bibring (1968), who did much to alter and broaden psychoanalytic theory about depression, feels that oral dependence is the most frequent type of predisposition. Berliner's 1966 paper describes the depressive as "an extremely manipulative individual who maneuvers people toward the fulfillment of his demands," and Bemporad (1971), emphasizes the depressive's extreme emotional dependency.

A summary and condensation of the description of the oral character by these and most other psychoanalytic workers may be put in the following terms: Depression-prone people are inordinately and almost exclusively dependent on narcissistic supplies derived directly or indirectly from other people for the maintenance of their self-esteem. Their frustration tolerance is low and they employ various techniques—submissive, manipulative, coercive, piteous, demanding, placating—to maintain those desperately needed but essentially ambivalent relationships with the external or internalized objects of their demands.[1]

---

[1] A 1973 study utilizing rating scales derived from semistructured interviews of depressives during and following their illnesses found that submissive dependency was illness-related and disappeared almost completely in postillness interviews. The conclusion, contrary to the work here cited, was that evidence was lacking that dependency was a central and enduring feature predisposing to depression.

The well-known 1954 paper of Cohen represents a distillation of the combined experience of five senior psychoanalysts based on the intensive study of twelve manic-depressive patients. In this paper the adult character of the manic-depressive is seen as "a person who is apparently well adjusted between attacks, although he may show minor mood swings or be chronically over active or chronically mildly depressed. He is conventionally well behaved and frequently successful and he is hard working and conscientious; indeed at times his over conscientiousness and scrupulousness lead to his being called obsessional. He is typically involved in one or more relationships of extreme dependence in which, however, he does not show the obsessional's typical need to control the other person for the sake of power, but instead seeks to control the other person in the sense of swallowing him up." Tendencies towards envy, fear of competition, underselling of the self, and a lack of interest in or ability to deal with interpersonal nuances are other important elements in the character picture. Although one can label some of these personality features as obsessional or oral, the description does not really fit comfortably within such terminology. This paper attempts also, rather uniquely in the psychiatric and psychoanalytic literature, to account for both the apparent surface normality of manic-depressives and their more subtle characterological defects. Unfortunately however, the absence of any clinical description or demographic data about the twelve patients studied makes it difficult to relate the findings reported to current ideas about depression, such as the putative differences between unipolars and bipolars. There have been some attempts to validate the paper's conclusions on larger samples of patients, with some success by Gibson (1958), on patients at Saint Elizabeths Hospital and with equivocal results by Spielberger, Parker & Becker (1963).

I now return to the relationship between the oral personality, which is regarded by many psychoanalysts as the characterological underpinning for predisposition to depression, and the psychoanalytic concept of orality. First enunciated by Freud in *Three Essays on Sexuality* in 1910, the concept of the oral stage was given a new dimension by Abraham in his 1916 paper when he distinguished between the sadistic trends of obsessionals and those of melancholics by attributing the latter to a newly formulated oral aggressive stage, the aim of which is to annihilate the object through swallowing it. For Abraham and Freud in *Mourning and Melancholia*, the orally fixated melancholic is literally oral. He exhibits an undue amount of behavior centered on the mouth and alimentary system derived from a combination of constitutional accentuation of this stage and severe narcissistic disappointments in the relationship to the mother during the pre-Oedipal period. For Abraham (1948), individuals fixated at the oral level have great oral needs, manifested by sucking, eating, and use of the jaws. They display insatiable demands for orally expressed affection and are highly sensitive to oral frustrations. Freud in *Mourning and Melancholia* sees the pathological introjection by the melancholic as representing a regression to an infantile stage in which the infant identifies with the loved object through oral incorporation, by swallowing it.

From this early id- and libido-centered description of orality the changes and development which have taken place in psychoanalytic theory have resulted in a gradual broadening of the concept of orality and a loosening of its biological roots. As described by Mendelson (1960), Rado made the first step in enlarging the concept of orality by including not only pleasurable stimulation of the mouth zone, but also the other pleasurable sensations the infant experiences at his mother's breast as well as general feelings of security, warmth, and nourishment. Gero (1936) and Fenichel (1968) further broadened the interpretation of orality, the latter describing the narcissistic oral character of the depressive as a "person who is fixated on the state where his self-esteem is regulated by external supplies," and thus emphasizing the inordinate dependency of the orally fixated character and his need to be loved and nurtured by his love object. A further step was taken by Bibring (1968), who questioned the universality of the oral character in predisposing to depression in an important contribution which relied more on the newer ego psychology than on the earlier id-oriented concepts.

This trend has continued, so that for many psychoanalysts—and not only those outside of the strict Freudian persuasion—the oral character has come to have lost its moorings in psychosexual and constitutional orality and to have become synonomous with traits expressing excessive dependency and ex- aggerated affectional and supportive needs. Some evidence supporting this interpretation is afforded in a factor analytic study by Gottheil and Stone (1968) on 179 normal adult men which confirmed the existence of an oral trait factor consistent with psychoanalytic descriptions but failed to support preferential association between oral traits and mouth habits. Kardiner (1939) also has expressed doubt about the extent to which dependency arises from oral eroticism. The term, the oral character, however, is well entrenched and though its etymology may have become suspect, it retains a metaphorical usefulness and will no doubt continue to be employed. To make the concept of undue dependency somewhat more operational, I would like to suggest the following definition: interpersonal dependency is measured by the degree to which a person's self-esteem is maintained more or less exclusively by the approval and support of other persons or their surrogates.

The origin of the oral or dependent character is explained by culturist and interpersonal psychoanalysts as being derived entirely from certain varieties of early childhood experience, whereas Freudians continue to believe that a constitutional component is operative. As a utopian speculation, many problems about depression would be solved if such a putative constitutional element could be related genetically to the same factor that seems to produce bipolar affective illness.

Having completed the inquiry phase of this presentation, it is now time to ask what conclusions about the premorbid personalities of depressives can be harvested from the material reviewed. They may be summarized, I believe, in the following statements:

1. There is a widespread clinical opinion that an obsessional personality pattern predisposes to the development of involutional depressions. The data supporting this proposition are sparse and inadequate, consisting mainly of a few papers in the 1930's and 1940's which are usually called upon to document otherwise unsupported clinical impressions. Whether one accepts the proposition that premorbid involutionals are obsessive depends, of course, on whether involutional depression is recognized as a separate entity or whether, on the contrary, middle-life depressions are felt to be nonspecific examples of either endogenous or reactive depressions. If the latter view is held, then it of course makes little sense to speak of a specific premorbid predisposition to involutional depression.

2. Judged by rather gross criteria, individuals predisposed to manic-depressive illness may display consistent mood alterations (either up or down or alternating) during their well periods, but for the most part their appearance and behavior fall within a normal range. Psychoanalysts, however, hold that this surface appearance of normality is deceptive and that these individuals are in fact marked by a deep-seated set of personality alterations best described under the heading of the oral character, which carries within it a potential for developing a severe affective illness, and that the presence of this personality pattern distinguishes these individuals from normals and possibly from those apparently or obviously neurotic individuals who may develop less severe varieties of reactive or neurotic depression. The latter part of this statement relies more on inference and a few suggestions than on explicit formulation since, as has been mentioned, the category of neurotic depression is very much neglected in the psychoanalytic literature.

3. Evidence is beginning to appear that a distinction can be made between the premorbid personality structure of unipolar and bipolar depressives, the former being marked by a greater degree of a rather nonspecific neuroticism than the latter. The relationship between this statement and number two above is possibly contradictory and at least somewhat ambiguous. In part, at least, this is because the category of unipolar depressives used to contrast with the bipolars may include not only individuals suffering from recurrent affective illness but also clinical states that might otherwise be diagnosed as involutional or neurotic depression. Also, the level of observation on which this proposition is based does not rule out in the apparently normal bipolars the kind of more subtle psychopathological patterning included under the oral character label.

It is obvious that these conclusions are tentative, equivocal and hedged with qualifications, and that our current knowledge about whether distinctive premorbid personality characteristics can be associated with clinical depressions leaves a great deal to be desired, a statement concurred in by such eminent investigators of depressions as Beck (1967) and Grinker et al. (1961). There are a number of reasons for this unsatisfactory state of affairs:

1. Of the two sets of variables which we are attempting to associate, the clinical depressive states that comprise the supposedly independent set are actually not at all well defined. Lack of agreement and considerable controversy have been present and continue to exist over the boundaries between these states and even over whether some can be included at all. Furthermore, there is a similar lack of agreement about whether differences between normal depressive moods ("the blues") can be differentiated qualitatively from clinical depressive states, or whether they are only one end of a continuum differing only quantitatively from severe depressions.

2. The other set of variables, the personality types, cannot lay claim to a more secure status since the distinctions between personality types is even less well defined and less universally accepted than is the case with the clinical depressive states to which they are being related. It may be true, although paradoxical, that the more we know about a person the more uncertain we are when we call him an obsessive or a schizoid or a hysteric, whereas these rubrics can be applied with brisk finality when we know relatively little about the individual being pigeonholed. Thus, putting together the first two reasons for the uncertain state of knowledge about the relationship between depression and personality, we might say that the task of confining the multicolored and delicately shaded butterflies of personality within the net of classification is itself difficult enough, but that it becomes even more formidable when the net being used is coarse meshed, patched and repatched, and full of holes.

3. Further to extend the above metaphor, our exercise in butterfly hunting is even more hampered when we are searching in the wrong place or at the wrong time of the year or are trying to accomplish our purpose with one or both eyes closed—in short, when our methodology is inadequate. Certainly the above review reveals grave methodological defects in much of the literature from both psychiatric and psychoanalytic sources in which attempts have been made to relate personality to depressive illness. These methodologic defects have already been alluded to in several places, but at this point it would be helpful to summarize them as follows:

i. Formulations about enduring personality characteristics are too often derived from behavior observed during periods of illness, or the state of illness or health of the patient being observed is not specified.

ii. The level of observation in many of the psychiatric contributions is often quite superficial.

iii. Psychoanalytic observations are far more intensive and searching, but the personality descriptions emanating from them may fail to distinguish between observational and inferred data.

iv. Not all of the psychiatric studies employ control groups. Of those that do, such groups are sometimes inadequately specified or are not clearly differentiated from each other.

v. Although the use of controls is not compatible with psychoanalytic methods of observation, there is no reason for the failure of psychoanalysts to include appropriate demographic and clinical data in their reports.

vi. There is overemphasis by both psychiatrists and psychoanalysts on manic-depressive depression as the source of their formulations, to the neglect of other varieties of depressive illness.

To this list should be added, in the case of the psychoanalytic articles, whatever doubts and reservations one may have about psychoanalysis as a method of investigation and about its ability to generate hypotheses and formulations which can be made operational and replicable. For what it is worth and whatever its significance, it is my impression after completing this survey that psychoanalytic articles on depression from the 1960's on have not been of the scope, caliber or originality of earlier contributions.

If the attempt to define and describe premorbid personality patterns predisposing to depression has produced the equivocal results described above, can this be because we have been wrong in assuming that such a relationship exists? The hypothesis that there is such a relationship rests on the assumption that psychological factors are operative in depression and that one way these manifest themselves is in the form of persistent constellations of traits of behavior which can be identified as personality patterns. This assumption is not necessarily valid—the present situation regarding the question we are examining may be similar to the stage in the evolution of psychosomatic medicine when Franz Alexander (1950) proposed that specific unconscious psychodynamic forces were responsible for vulnerability to certain illnesses rather than the previous unsatisfactory efforts to relate them to specific personality profiles. Similarly, those psychodynamic forces responsible for vulnerability to depressive illness may be genotypal in nature, not producing a standard personality picture but rather giving rise to varying and differing personality phenotypes. If this alternative proposition is accepted, personality patterns in depression would have their chief effect in coloring and altering the symptoms of depressive illnesses rather than in predisposing to them. Or in Davies' words: "Depressive illness is colored into almost innumerable shades by the personality and character of the individual in whom the disease occurs" (1964). As has been mentioned previously in the section on hysterical depression, this way of looking at the relationship between personality and depressive illness has probably not been taken sufficiently into account. The finding, previously mentioned (Lazarus & Klerman, 1968), that hysterical personality makeup is associated with less severe depressive manifestations, and the work of Gittleson (1966) in establishing the interesting correlation that obsessive neurotics when depressed almost never develop manic attacks, are illustrations of the valuable data to be derived from emphasizing how personality structure effects rather than causes depression.

However, despite the appeal of this alternative way of looking at the matter we are discussing and despite the difficulties in the way of establishing that personality patterns predispose to depressive illness, it seems premature to abandon efforts to establish a relationship between unconscious psychodynamic conflictual forces and the more or less visible personality structures into which these crystallize and which constitutes a middle stage, a kind of intervening variable between the former and the depressive illness. In short, if psychological factors play a role in depression, as they assuredly do, then careful scrutiny of persons who become depressedly ill may reveal one or more recognizable patterns of personality which bear an understandable predisposing relationship to those clinical depressive entities that we hope will be carved out from the present rather inchoate body of depressive syndromes. The task for research, then, is to find ways to test present hypotheses about predisposing personality factors or to initiate imaginative investigative forays which will provide new hypotheses. In spite of the obvious and grave methodological weaknesses of psychoanalytic formulations, the exhaustive scrutiny of depressed patients that takes place in psychoanalysis still ought to provide the best source from which such hypotheses can be derived. It is necessary, however, to put these hypotheses into some sort of operational form (as Grinker [1968] did in investigating the Borderline Syndrome), and then to work out methods by which the patients may be studied with a kind of middle intensity of observation which does not seek analytic depth, but which at the same time eschews the relative superficiality of some of the psychiatric studies.

I am well aware of the puzzling features and difficulties, both anticipated and unexpected, that such research entails and that stand in the way of a research design with even modest adherence to scientific standards. Such research is not impossible, however, and certainly the fruits to be anticipated from it are important enough to the understanding of depression to warrant the effort.

REFERENCES

Abraham, K. *Notes on the psychoanalytic investigation and treatment of manic-depressive insanity and allied conditions.* Selected papers on psychoanalysis. London: Hogarth Press, 1948.

Abraham, K. The first pregenital stage of the libido. In selected papers on psychoanalysis. London: Hogarth Press, 1948.

Abraham, K. A short history of the development of the libido, viewed in the light of mental disorders. In Selected papers on psychoanalysis. London: Hogarth Press, 1948. (c)

Alexander, F. *Psychosomatic medicine.* New York: W. W. Norton, 1950.

Arieti, S. Manic-depressive psychosis. In Arieti S. (Ed.), *American handbook of psychiatry,* Vol. 1. New York: Basic Books, 1959.

Barnett, J., Lefford, A., & Pushman, D. Involutional melancholia. *Psychiatric Quarterly* 1953, 27, 654.

Beck, A. T. *Depression.* New York, Evanston, Ill., London: Harper & Row, 1967.

Bellak, L. *Manic-depressive psychosis & allied conditions,* New York: Grune & Stratton, 1952.

Bemporad, J. Vol. 1, *New views on the psychodynamics of the depressive character.* World biennial of psychiatry and psychotherapy, 1971.

Berliner, B. Psychodynamics of the depressive character. *Psychoanalytic Forum*, 1966, **1**, 244.

Bibring, E. The mechanism of depression. In Gaylin, W. (Ed.), *The meaning of despair*. New York: Science House, 1968.

Bleuler, E. *Textbook of psychiatry*. Brill, A. A., (Transl.) New York: Macmillan, 1924.

Bonime, W. The psychodynamics of neurotic depression. S. Arieti (Ed.), American handbook of psychiatry. Vol. 3, New York, London: Basic Books, 1966.

Cadoret, R. J. *Family differences in illness and personality in affective disorder*. Paper presented at the 3rd Annual Conference on Life History Research in Psychopathology, October 1969, Glen Oaks, N. Y.

Cleghorn, R. A. & Curtis, G. C. Depression: Mood, symptom, syndrome. *Documenta Geigy Acta Psychosomatica* (N. America), 1959.

Cohen, M. B., Baker, G., Cohen, R. A., Fromm-Reichmann F., & Weigert, E. V. An intensive study of twelve cases of manic-depressive psychosis. *Psychiatry*, 1954. 17, 103.

Coppen, A. The Marke-Nyman temperament scale: An English translation. *British Journal of Medical Psychology*, 1966, 39, 55.

Davies, E. B. Some varieties of depression and their treatment. In Davies, E. B. (Ed.), *Depression*. Cambridge University Press, 1964.

Fenichel, O. Depression and mania. In W. Gaylin (Ed.), *The meaning of despair*. New York: Science House, 1968.

Fenichel, O. The psychoanalytic theory of neurosis. New York: W. W. Norton, 1945.

Fessler, L. The psychopathology of climacteric depression. *Psychoanalytic Quarterly*, 1950, **19**, 28.

Foulds, G. A.: Personality and Personal Illness. J. B. Lippincott Co. (Phila. & Montreal), 1965.

Freud, S. Three contributions to the theory of sex. Contribution 2. *Basic writings of Sigmund Freud*. New York: Modern Library, 1939.

Freud, S. *Mourning and Melancholia*. Collected papers. Vol. 4, London: Hogarth Press, 1946.

Gaylin, W. The meaning of despair. In Gaylin, W. (Ed.), *The meaning of despair*. New York: Science House, 1968.

Gero, G. The construction of depression. *International Journal of Psychoanalysis*, 1936, **17**, 423-461.

Gibson, R. The family background and early life experience of the manic-depressive patient: A comparison with the schizophrenic patient. *Psychiatry*, 1958, **21**, 71-90.

Gillespie, R. D. *The clinical differentiation of types of depression*. Quoted in Abraham, 1948.

Gittleson, N. Depressive psychosis in the obsessional neurotic. *British Journal of Psychiatry*, 1966, **112**, 883-888.

Gottheil, E., & Stone, G. Factor analytic study of orality and anality. *Journal of Nervous and Mental Diseases*, 1968, **146**, 1-17.

Grinker, R. R., Sr., Miller, J., Sabshin, M., Nunn, R. J., & Nunnally, J. C. The phenomena of depressions, New York: Hoeber, 1961.

Grinker, R. R., Werble, B., & Drye, R. C. The borderline syndrome: A behavioral study of ego functions, New York: Basic Books, 1968.

Henderson, D. K. & Gillespie, R. D. *A textbook of psychiatry*. (3rd Ed.), London: Oxford University Press, 1932.

Jacobson, E. Contribution to the metapsychology of cyclothymic depression. In Greenacre, P. (Ed.), *Affective disorders*. New York: International University Press, 1953.

Kardiner, A. *The individual and his society*. New York: Columbia University Press, 1939.

Kielholz, P. Diagnosis and therapy of the depressive states. *Documenta Geigy Acta Psychosomatica* (N. America), 1959, No. 1, p. 37.

Klerman, G. L. Clinical research in depression. *Archives of General Psychiatry*, 1971. **24,** 305.

Kolb, L. C. *Noyes' modern clinical psychiatry*. Philadelphia, London, Toronto: W. B. Saunders, 1968.

Kretschmer, E. *Physique & Character*. New York: Harcourt, 1931.

Lazarus, A. & Klerman, G. L. Hysteria and depression. *American Journal of Psychiatry* (Suppl), May, 1968, **124,** 48.

Malamud, M., Sands, G. L., & Malamud, I. The involutional psychoses: A socio-psychiatric study. *Psychosomatic Medicine*, 1941, 3 410.

Metcalfe, M. The personality of depressive patients. In Coppen, A. & Walk, A. *Recent Developments in affective disorders*. Ashford, Kent, England: Headley Brothers, 1968.

Mendelson, M. *Psychoanalytic concepts of depression*. Springfield, Ill.: Thomas, 1960.

Mendelson, M. Neurotic depressive reactions. In. Freedman, A. M. & Kaplan, H. I. (Eds.), *Comprehensive textbook of psychiatry*. Baltimore: Wilkins & Williams, 1967.

Noyes, A. P. *Modern clinical psychiatry* (2nd Ed.) Philadelphia: W. B. Saunders, 1939.

Palmer, H. D. & Sherman, S. H. The involutional melancholia process. Archives of Neurology and Psychiatry, 1938, **40,** 762.

Paykel, E. S., & Weissman, M. M. Social Adjustment and Depression, *Archives of General Psychiatry*, 1973, 28, 659.

Perris, C. A study of bipolar (manic-depressive) and unipolar recurrent depressive episodes. *Acta Psychiatrica Scandinavica* [Suppl.] 1966, **194,** 42–45.

Perris, C. quoted in Lazare & Klerman; *American Journal of Psychiatry* (Suppl), 1968, p. 28.

Rado, S. The problem of melancholia. In W. Gaylin (Ed.), *The meaning of despair*. New York: Science House, 1968.

Rado, S. Psychodynamics of depression from the etiologic point of view. Gaylin (Ed.), *The meaning of despair*. New York: Science House, 1968.

Rosenthal, S. H. The involutional depressive syndrome. *American Journal of Psychiatry* (Suppl), 1968, **124** 21.

Rosenthal, S. H. & Gudeman, J. E. The endogenous depressive pattern: An empirical investigation. *Archives of General Psychiatry*, 1967, 16, 241.

Rowe, C. J. & Dagett, B. R. *Prespsychotic personality traits in manic-depressive disease*. Quoted in Kretschmer, 1931.

Snaith, R. P., McGuire, R. J., & Fox, K. Aspects of personality and depression. *Psychosomatic Medicine*, 1971, 1 239–246.

Spielberger, C. D., Parker, J. B., & Becker, J. Conformity and achievement in remitted manic-depressive patients. *Journal of Nervous and Mental Diseases*, 1963. 137, 162–172.

Szalita, A. B. Psychodynamics of disorders of the involutional age. In S. Arieti (Ed.), *American handbook of psychiatry*. Vol. 3, New York, London: Basic Books, 1966.

Titley, W. B. Prepsychotic personality of patients with involutional melancholia. *Archives of Neurology and Psychiatry*, 1936. 36, 19.

Winokur, G., Clayton, P. J., & Reich, T. *Manic-depressive illness*. St. Louis: C. V. Mosby, 1969.

DISCUSSION

Dr. Goodwin: Perhaps Dr. Chodoff will comment on one very interesting finding that did emerge from the Cohen study and that seems to dovetail with a comment by Dr. Ferster regarding the depressed person's "hazy" view of the environment. Notwithstanding some of the methodological problems involved in the Cohen study, such as identification of patients and sample size, I think their description of the "interpersonal opaqueness" of manic-depressive patients when they are not depressed is probably a phenomenon of considerable significance. This may fit in with the hypothesis concerning the way these individuals respond to stimulation, especially subtle psychological and interpersonal stimuli. We have been interested in this not just from the point of view of classification of premorbid personality in depression, but also because we have wanted to examine individuals who have a reduced capacity to get mad.

If one examines the manic population (and in a way this population provides some researchable behaviors which the depressed population does not), he finds various parameters that seem to separate manic patients from those depressed patients who do not have the capacity or characteristic for getting mad. Perhaps interpersonal opaqueness in one parameter that may serve to separate these two groups. This is an early and tentative finding, and Dr. Chodoff, Dr. Friedman, and I have been involved in some preliminary planning of research in this area.

Dr. Friedman: The construction of feasible research regarding hypotheses concerning more subtle psychological phenomena is difficult and the question of measuring such behaviors, either directly or indirectly, is critical.

Dr. Ferster: One of the major problems that has plagued this entire area is the persistent use of tests rather than direct measures of behavior. After all, psychoanalysts, it seems to me, have the major data base, but they do not talk about it very well. Clinicians rarely talk about their data in detail, and when studying such processes as dependency and self-esteem they tend to administer tests instead of directly observe and measure the events they are really interested in. These tests, after all, are very far removed from the process under investigation, much as is the use of litmus paper in measuring the pH of a solution. That may give you a measure, but it really has nothing to do with the hydrogen concentration. What I am suggesting is that we need to look more carefully at the direct and observable events under study, and I wonder if Dr. Lewinsohn's research might not be the best example of work moving in this direction. If we want to investigate "haziness," I think we have to ask what it is that the person really sees.

Dr. Chodoff: Dr. Friedman and Dr. Goodwin and I share the frustration of having attempted to design research to tap into these more subtle processes, such as self-esteem, dependency, interpersonal relationships, and world view.

Dr. Ferster, I believe, has put his finger on a puzzling and rather disturbing contradiction—that for research purposes, clinicians seem to shrink away from their clinical data and take refuge in tests, even though they are aware that tests will probably not satisfactorily answer the clinical questions they are interested in. I suppose the main reason for this is simply the difficulty of using interview data for research purposes—their uncontrollability, the split in roles between being at once a therapist and a researcher, and the very diversity and richness of the material. The fact that the use of clinical data for scientific, public purposes is difficult doesn't necessarily mean that it is impossible, however, and there is no question that it is important. What we need is to develop a methodology of intermediate intensity lying between the bewildering heterogeneity of say, the psychoanalytic interview, and the skimpiness of controllable psychological tests.

Dr. Klerman: I have a number of comments about both Dr. Chodoff's presentation and some of the issues regarding the complexity of measuring parameters such as self-esteem and dependency. Some research I have done with Dr. Lazare touches on this, for we used pencil-and-paper tests and recently have been using such indices as the Maudsley Personality Inventory. Indeed, I would agree with Dr. Chodoff that a source of confusion definitely exists, and I can illustrate this with an example drawn from our work. The British concept of neuroticism is based mainly on Eysenck's work and the Maudsley Personality Inventory which yield two dimensions; a neuroticism dimension and an introversion-extroversion dimension. Paykel will be publishing a paper which indicates that there is correlation between these two dimensions, and that the British view of the neurotic is much more a mixture of dependency and hysterical personality types than is the American view, and consists of overt features similar to those the layman labels "neuroticism." Those whom we would label obsessional score very low on the British neuroticism scale, which may be saying more about the British and American views of what is normal than of what is neurotic. Nevertheless, it certainly illustrates one of the problems involved in tests.

There is another way of trying to assess some of the more complex personality characteristics than the use of simple pencil-and-paper tests, and that is by the employment of relative ratings. Relatives can often be very helpful informants. In our research we have developed a form of the Lazare scale which we have given to relatives and then factor-analyzed. We have found that the same oral hysterical or obsessional clusters emerge in the ratings of a group of patients' relatives as was originally found in the patients' own self-report when it was factor-analyzed. So there is some congruence between the way relatives view the ill family member and the way he appears on pencil-and-paper tests. The relatives' ratings thus serve as an independent validation indicating that some of the dimensions seen on the Maudsley inventory are not spurious. Dr. Katz has also done work using relatives to categorize the premorbid state of patients, and I believe I would add this approach as another method of tapping into the areas Dr. Chodoff expressed interest in.

I would also like to comment on Dr. Chodoff's discussion of some of my work, especially in regard to hysteria. We did find that the presence of hysterical features colored the type of depression and produced depression with less sadness, more somatic complaints, more conversion symptoms, and more overt displays of hostility. Dr. Chodoff raises the objection that the hysterical personality merely influences the clinical picture—the way the depression is tainted—but that it does not truly influence the underlying state of affairs. I believe there is evidence to the contrary in the results of studies done by Guze and coworkers of the St. Louis group. They have found longitudinally that approximately 25 percent of people they label "hysteric" present at some time during a 5-year period with a clearcut depressive episode. Now that is a very high percentage, and it makes one wonder whether their idea of hysteria is way off, whether their idea of depression is quite different, or whether there is not a high correlation between the hysterical personality and depression. While this work supports a limited view of a relation between hysteria and depression, we still cannot say that there is one specific personality pattern that predisposes to depression.

Dr. Chodoff: There is no question that cultural trends strongly influence what is considered neurotic, so that it is not surprising that the stiff-upper-lip British ideal might appear to be neurotically obsessive in other cultural settings but healthy and even admirable in the British. This cultural relativity of neurotic character structure does add another complication, however, to the task of studying premorbid personality in depression. Dr. Klerman's use of the testing of patients' relatives to confirm his findings with the patients themselves seems a good idea and a step toward getting away from sole reliance on tests. However, I believe that interviews with relatives about what kind of person the patient is when he is not depressed might be even more valuable.

Although I do not advocate that personality is related to depression only by giving it a particular coloring, I am afraid that the contrary findings about hysteria of the St. Louis group are of limited value because I don't agree, and I doubt if most of the people here would, with their definition of hysteria. What they are talking about as hysteria, although it may "hang together" as a syndrome, is not what most psychiatrists mean by hysteria. I think that Guze and his collaborators ought to give it a different name, like the "St. Louis Syndrome."

Dr. Katz: Most of the research has focused on ratings of patients when they are depressed, but there has been little research conducted during depression-free intervals. I strongly feel that descriptions of personality obtained during the depressive episode, even from relatives, cannot help but be highly colored by the fact that the person is currently depressed. An example of this is to be found in an analysis of some of Paykel's data on relative ratings. While patients were in a depressed state, researchers asked the relatives to describe the premorbid personality of the patient. They finally came up with a composite picture of a premorbid personality which revealed a person who was hypersensitive, whose feelings were easily hurt, and who in general resembled a mildly depressed person. The conclusion I draw from this is that the relatives were describing the patient as he was at present and not as he normally appeared. What we need are relative ratings and patient measures taken during depression-free intervals.

Dr. Klerman: We have done this in various studies, and usually wait approximately 3 months after the clinical symptoms have subsided to take followup measures, both from the patient and from relatives.

Dr. Chodoff: I agree with Dr. Klerman that information from relatives about the premorbid personality of depressives is of much greater value when gathered some time after the illness has subsided. This is also true and even more important in regard to studies of the patients themselves. I have just finished reading a paper by Perris which discusses this problem very seriously. Perris studied a group of depressed patients with unipolar, bipolar, and neurotic depressions. He administered the Maudsley Personality Inventory during the depression, immediately after the depressed state had cleared 6 months later, and then 3 years later. His findings revealed that those who suffered from neurotic depressions were slightly more neurotic than the unipolars or bipolars on followup and that the bipolar depressives had a higher extroversion-neuroticism ratio than did the unipolars.

The St. Louis group is doing some interesting research with relatives different from that Dr. Klerman and Dr. Katz noted. They are studying the probands of depressed patients and have been able to demonstrate that the probands of bipolar depressives have certain personality characteristics that differentiate them from other groups. The probands of bipolar people tend to evidence more manic and hyperactive behavior, whereas the probands of unipolar depressives tend to evidence more neuroticism.

Dr. Tabachnick: Confusion arises concerning the premorbid personality of depressed patients because of our tendency to assume that personality characteristics fall into fairly stable patterns which remain constant over time. This may be an unwarranted assumption, especially in view of a considerable body of evidence suggesting that people do change from one time to another and from one age to another.

Dr. Friedman: I would agree with Dr. Tabachnick, especially in regard to his second point, since there is considerable "clinical" evidence to suggest that people may be classified as different personality types at various times in their lives and based on different orders of stress which they may be undergoing. I am not aware of any "research" evidence which would corroborate this clinical finding, however. On the other hand, I do have some faith in the categorization of people into rough personality types. It seems that man has always categorized his fellow man and, however unsatisfactory these categorizations may be, they do tend to carry some predictive value and certainly possess immense heuristic value. On that basis alone therefore, I think their study is well worthwhile.

Dr. Beck: I saw a woman 17 years ago who presented as a neurotic depressive and gave a history consistent with a neurotic personality, i.e., unstable, erratic, upset, and so on. She returned recently and presented with an endogenous psychotic depression and responded beautifully to electro-shock treatment. This time, however, she presented as someone who seemed to be a classic obsessional personality. The age factor thus seems to be very pertinent. Indeed, in our control-group studies we have found in the older age groups that the obsessive characteristics seem to be somewhat age-specific and are found in the majority of normals of that age group. In the younger age groups we see characteristics more in line with instability, flighty personalities, and other characteristics associated with neuroticism. The younger people tend to develop neurotic depressions whereas the older people tend to evidence a greater incidence of endogenous depression.

I would like to return to the investigation of clinical material and the problem of "relevance." The question of how to conduct investigations in the area between simple pencil-and-paper tests and more complicated intensive therapeutic situations is perplexing. I think there are possibilities, however, and certainly the area of dreams is one of them. The dream is a fairly tangible unit which can be analyzed, and it was this type of psychoanalytic data that I began studying in the early years of my depression research. Recently I received a communication from a society devoted to the study of sleep and dreams which lists approximately 20 or 30 different scales, each purporting to measure varying personality traits based on dream analysis. Furthermore, there are other types of data that may go beyond the simple pencil-and-paper tests; these include descriptions by family members and by psychiatrists, especially about the intermorbid personality of the patient. Certainly bipolar patients lend themselves to this type of study, and I do not believe that we should abandon attempts to research areas of personality or of parameters such as dependency and self-esteem.

One of the outstanding contributions of the study by Cohen and co-workers is a number of relevant hypotheses important in understanding depression that could prove significant for psychotherapeutic intervention. I refer to such variables as envy, traditional family ties, conformity, rivalry, and the need to be a family favorite which interact with other stresses and precipitate depression. The point I wish to make is that these hypotheses are potentially susceptible to rigorous systematic testing with the appropriate use of controls.

Dr. Friedman: I certainly agree with Dr. Beck that the issues raised about dependency and self-esteem are significant. I also agree that we can begin to investigate these areas in a rough clinical sense. I have serious questions about how rigorous we can ever be, however, not because of the technological problems involved but merely because of the time required to observe (and I want to emphasize the word "observe") in such detail. Let me illustrate by way of clinical example. Several months ago I interviewed a patient on Dr. Goodwin's ward who had lapsed into a severe depression for which there appeared no immediate environmental cause. I distinctly recall nodding in agreement that this was an obvious instance of depression that must have been triggered by some biological event, and that historically there did not seem any evidence that frustration of dependency needs or a drop in self-esteem was involved, at least in any causal way. I later learned from the doctor who worked with him during the following months that this patient was locked into a very intense and dependent relationship with his associate at work and that his depression was related to his associate's ruminations about retiring. Ostensibly though, there was relatively little interaction between the two men and their only business contact was shared offices. Occasionally the patient would consult his partner about certain matters, but one would have to know the patient quite intimately to realize that he was indeed seeking "permission" from his partner and had allocated a great deal of control of his own behavior to him. I am not sure that merely observing his behavior, even if one could have known what interactions to observe him in, would have revealed this much dependency without the contribution of his inner fantasy life. I hope this illustration supports my contention that such issues as dependency are not difficult to observe by way of an intensive relationship, but they are most difficult to measure by any approach of less intensity.

Dr. Lewinsohn: Has any research been done on sex as a moderator variable? Could it be that females who become depressed have different premorbid personality characteristics than males who go on to develop depression?

Dr. Chodoff: Most discussions concerning hysterical personalities and the development of depression are really about a sample composed almost exclusively of females. On the other hand, obsessive premorbid personalities are found in either males or females. I am not sure whether sex differences have been investigated more rigorously than this. There certainly are marked differences in the incidence of depression between males and females, with females having the "hysterical" depressions and certainly accounting for more involutional depressions than males. The incidence of manic-depressive disease is also higher in females, the ratio being approximately 3 to 1.

Dr. Goodwin: Does anybody, especially those among us working within a behavioral orientation, have any suggestions as to how one might put into operation the concept Dr. Chodoff advanced about depressive individuals having an increased need for external feedback to maintain their self-esteem? We ought to be able to translate this hypothesis into operational language which could be tested so that we could learn whether an individual's self-esteem fluctuates with the type of feedback he receives in an experimental situation.

Dr. Seligman: Perhaps the Asch technique involving autokinetic movement which was developed in the 1950's might be of use. This technique and others like it try to quantify how "dependent" an individual is on external input to influence his perceptions. It measures the effect of social pressure on individuals, which in a sense could be related to dependency.

Dr. Beck: Becker also employed the autokinetic technique to gauge conformity in this subjects. There is another approach based on the idea of the inner-directed and outer-directed personality type which seems to be relevant to self-esteem and dependency. Research that attempted to test David Riesman's ideas of inner- and outer-directed personality types revealed that there is continuum and that the anchor points at each end tend to represent pure types. Outer-directed people are hypothesized to be depression-prone to a greater degree than inner-directed people.

Dr. Chodoff: I think an approach such as the one Dr. Beck suggests could serve as a beginning, but it could also become oversimplified if we do not recall that dependency may be expressed by behavior that appears to be the opposite. Dependency may be directly expressed through clinging and demanding behavior, but it may be concealed by a pseudo-independent air. It is common clinical knowledge that a person may appear manifestly independent, and yet when one gets to know him, it is quite obvious that he is a "baby" underneath.

Dr. Ferster: Why is it so necessary to venture outside the therapeutic situation? It seems to me that one of the great advantages of the therapeutic situation is the presence of a keen observer who has watched his patient carefully over a long time. A second advantage is that a behavioral interaction exists between them. If the patient is supposedly a dependent person outside treatment, then certainly this behavior should show up within the therapeutic context. If it does not, something is obviously wrong with either the therapy or the original hypothesis.

Dr. Friedman: Yes, the behavior is usually obvious in therapy, especially if it is intensive and prolonged, but it often is not apparent in the external life of the patient. Several other problems occur when one attempts to use the therapeutic situation as a research tool. The first and to me the most significant of these is that it is very time-consuming and expensive. All our ruminations about shortcuts are indeed attempts at circumventing this long and arduous method of study.

Dr. Tabachnick: A second problem is that the therapist is actually being asked to perform two functions. As the therapist, he is developing a concept of what is going on within the patient, and based on that he tries to change the patient. To ask the therapist to serve as a research observer also may contaminate both therapy and research.

Dr. Ferster: I do not suggest placing such a difficult burden on the therapist. What I am suggesting is that in therapy there are data for potential use even if the therapist himself cannot observe all the details. If he is to be the primary observer, then he might be able to keep records in one way or another. The data are not lacking, but what is missing is a way of communicating. I wish to stress my belief that human behavior is very objective.

Dr. Ekman: The observation and measurement (the mean duration and frequency) of eye contact offer an objective measure of conformity when studying normal people, and I assume that the scales developed in the study of normals could be extrapolated to depressed populations. Measurement of eye contact is relatively easy and cheap through videotaping. Perhaps this is an illustration of the type of measurement to which Dr. Ferster is referring when he discusses the objectivity of behavior.

Dr. Klerman: As I listen to the discussion concerning methodology, I am reminded of a similar discussion we had in psychopharmacology approximately 10 years ago when we were considering whether it was possible to make stable symptom ratings. We realized then that clinicians were "prima donnas" and that we needed interrater agreement, construct validities, and factorial stability. The problem was solved despite all the pitfalls involved, and I have a kind of pragmatic faith that if people persist they will find the means of operationalizing "dependency" and breaking it down into behavioral terms.

The study of hospitalized patients allows us greater depth when studying such parameters as dependency and self-esteem, because we possess a structured environment which allows us to make direct observations of the patient's interaction with a known and constant milieu. A second maneuver that can be performed in a hospital setting, which is almost impossible to do with outpatients, is to establish certain types of structured experimental social situations designed to elicit certain types of behavior, such as dependent or achievement behavior. For example, a nurturing milieu might be employed to bring out dependent behavior.

Dr. Chodoff: All of these suggestions about how to get at dependency in some reproducible and roughly quantifiable form are valuable and clearly point in the direction we have to proceed. I think it is significant, however, that the nonclinicians among us seem more sanguine than the clinicians, who know from experience how sticky and complicated it is to try to characterize human beings in general personality terms or to judge them in relationship to such essentially vague and global concepts as dependency. Whether such maneuvers as length of eye contact, though easy to deal with, are any more informative than psychological tests is a real question; but to rely on some kind of quantitative analysis of interview data is a formidable job. The idea of reviewing the tapes of one or more psychotherapeutic relationships has been thought of and tried, but to my knowledge generally bogs down because of the complexity of the material and probably also because the reviewers get bored.

BIBLIOGRAPHY

Asch, S. E. Effects of group pressure upon the modification and distortion of judgements. In Maccoby, E., Newcomb, T. M., & Hartley, E. L. (Eds.), *Readings in social psychology.* (3rd ed.). New York: Holt, 1958.

Becker, J., Spielberger, C. D. & Parker, J. B. Value achievement and authoritarian attitudes in psychiatric patients. *Journal of Clinical Psychology*, 1963, **19**, 57–61.

Cohen, M. B., Baker, G., Cohen, R. A., Fromm-Reichmann, F., & Weigert, E. V. An intensive study of twelve cases of manic-depressive psychosis. *Psychiatry*, 1954, **17**, 103.

Katz, M. M. On the classification of depression: Normal clinical and ethnocultural variations. In Fieve, R. (Ed.), *Depression in the 1970's.* Amsterdam: Excerpta Medica, 1971.

Lazarus, A. A., & Klerman, G. L. Hysteria and depression: The frequency and significance of hysterical personality features in hospitalized depressed women. *American Journal of Psychiatry*, 1968, **124**, 48–56.

Paykel, E. S., Myers, J. K., Drenelt, M., et al. Life events and depression. *Archives of General Psychiatry*, 1969, **21** 753–760.

Perris, C. A study of bipolar (manic-depressive) and unipolar recurrent depressive psychoses. *Acta Psychiatrica*, Scandinavica [Suppl], 1966, **194**, 15–189.

Riesman, D. *The lonely crowd.* Garden City, N. Y.: Doubleday Anchor Books, 1954.

Robins, E., & Guze, S. B. Classification of affective disorders: The primary-secondary, the endogenous-reactive, and the neurotic-psychotic concepts. In Williams, T. A., Katz, M. M., & Shield, J. A. (Eds.), *Recent advances in the psychobiology of the depressive illnesses*: Proceedings of a workshop. Washington, D. C. G.O.P., 1972.

Winokur, G., Cadoret, R. J., Dorzab, J., & Baker, G. Depressive disease: A genetic study. *Archives of General Psychiatry*, 1971, **24**, 135–144.

PART II
CONTEMPORARY RESEARCH

4
DEPRESSION AND LEARNED HELPLESSNESS[1]

Martin E. P. Seligman
University of Pennsylvania

Two fairly substantial literatures dealing with maladaptive behavior appear to be converging. This paper highlights some commonalities between the phenomenon of learned helplessness in animals and depression in man, and it suggests tentatively that learned helplessness may provide a model for the understanding of reactive depression.

It has happened more than once that investigators have discovered and analyzed dramatic bits of maladaptive behavior in their animals and suggested that they illuminated some form of psychopathology in man. Pavlov (1927) found that conditioned reflexes of dogs disintegrated when the experimenter made discrimination problems increasingly difficult. Liddell (1953) found that restrained sheep given many conditioning trials stopped making conditioned flexion responses to the signals paired with shock. Both Pavlov and Liddell claimed they had demonstrated "experimental neuroses." Masserman (1943) and Wolpe (1958) found that hungry cats would not eat in compartments in which they had been shocked and claimed that they had brought phobias into the laboratory. Maier (1949) found that rats formed response fixations when confronted with insoluble discrimination problems and explained the findings as frustration. The experimental analysis of these phenomena was reasonably thorough, but the argument that they analyzed human psychopathology was usually saltatory, and occasionally downright unconvincing. Worse, the arguments were usually plausibility arguments that did not lend themselves

[1] Partially supported by NIMH Grant MH 19604 to the author. I would like to thank A. T. Beck, J. P. Brady, R. Gelman, F. Irwin, P. Rozin, D. Schuyler, K. Seligman, R. L. Solomon, J. Stinnett, and J. Wolpe for their helpful comments.

readily to refutation. How would one *test* whether Masserman's cats had phobias, anyway? Let us try to state some rules of argument for claiming that an animal phenomenon provides a model of a form of psychopathology in man.

Ground Rules

Four lines of evidence that two phenomena are similar seem relevant to this question: (1) symptoms: behavioral and physiological; (2) etiology; (3) cure; (4) prevention. It is not to be expected that any actual experimental phenomenon will meet all these criteria for any actual form of psychopathology in one fell swoop, but making the form of the argument explicit has two virtues: it makes similarity claims more testable and it can help us to narrow the definition of the clinical phenomenon. As two phenomena converge on one or two of the criteria, investigators can then test the model by looking for similarities predicted along the other criteria. So, for example, if learned helplessness in dogs presents behavior similar to reactive depression in man and the etiology of the two is similar, as we shall argue, and it turns out that the only way to cure learned helplessness is to expose dogs forcibly to responding that produces relief, one has a prediction about cure of depression in man: the recognition that responding is effective in producing reinforcement should be the central issue in successful therapy. If this is tested and confirmed, the model is strengthened. Strengthening such a model empirically is not only a matter of the animal phenomenon suggesting what to look for in the human phenomenon, but is a two-way street: so, if imipramine (a tricyclic drug) helps reactive depression, does it also relieve learned helplessness in animals? (See also McKinney and Bunney [1969] for a discussion of the need for an animal model of depression.)

In addition to enhanced testability, a model can help sharpen the definition of the clinical phenomenon since the laboratory phenomenon is often well defined, while the phenomenon to be modeled is poorly defined. Consider, for example, the question whether learned helplessness and depression show similar behavioral symptoms. Because it is a laboratory phenomenon, helplessness has necessary behaviors which define its presence or absence. Depression, on the other hand, does not have a necessary condition that defines it. Rather, it is a convenient diagnostic label which denotes a constellation of symptoms, no one of which is necessary. The relationship among phenomena called depression is perhaps best described as a family resemblance (see Wittgenstein [1953], paragraphs 66-77, for a general statement of this argument). Thus depressives often report feeling very sad, but this is not necessary for the diagnosis to be depression. If a patient doesn't feel sad, but is verbally and motorically retarded, cries a lot, is anorexic, and the onset of symptoms can be traced to his wife's death, depression is still the appropriate clinical label. But the retardation is also not necessary, as in agitated depression, and feelings of both sadness and retardation together are not necessary; for "depressive equivalents" may show neither, but only disturbed sleep, anorexia, weight loss, and crying. Clinical labels can best be seen as denoting a family, "a complicated network of similarities overlapping and crisscrossing." A well defined laboratory model does not mirror the openendedness of the clinical label; rather it clips it off at the edges by imposing necessary conditions on it. Thus, if a particular model of depression is valid, some phenomena formerly classified as depression may be excluded.

The label "depression" denotes passive individuals with negative cognitive sets about the effects of their own actions, who become depressed upon the loss of an important source of gratification—the perfect case for learned helplessness to model; but it also denotes agitated patients who readily initiate active responses, and who become depressed with no obvious external cause. As we shall see, learned helplessness does not capture the whole spectrum of depressions, but it is rather an attempt to understand depressions in which the individual is slow to initiate responses, believes himself to be powerless and hopeless, and has a negative outlook on the future which had begun as a reaction to having lost his control over relief of suffering and gratification.

Let us now turn to an examination of learned helplessness in animals and depression in man in terms of similarity along the four criteria outlined.

BEHAVIORAL MANIFESTATIONS

Learned Helplessness

When an experimentally naive dog receives escape-avoidance training in a shuttle box, the following behavior typically occurs: at the onset of the first traumatic electric shock, the dog runs frantically about, defecating, urinating, and howling, until it accidentally scrambles over the barrier and so escapes the shock. On the next trial, the dog, running and howling, crosses the barrier more quickly than on the preceding trial. This pattern continues until the dog learns to avoid shock altogether. Overmier and Seligman (1967) and Seligman and Maier (1967) found a striking difference between this pattern of behavior and that exhibited by dogs first given inescapable electric shocks in a Pavlovian hammock. Such a dog's first reactions to shock in the shuttle box are much the same as those of a naive dog. In dramatic contrast to a naive dog, however, a typical dog which has experienced uncontrollable shocks before avoidance training soon stops running and howling and sits or lies, quietly whining, until shock terminates. The dog does not cross the barrier and escape from shock. Rather, it seems to give up and passively accepts the shock. On succeeding trials, the dog continues to fail to make escape movements and takes as much shock as the experimenter chooses to give.

There is another peculiar characteristic of the behavior of dogs that have first experienced inescapable shock. Such dogs occasionally jump the barrier early in training and escape, but then revert to taking the shock; they fail to profit from exposure to the barrier-jumping-shock-termination contingency. In naive dogs a successful escape response is a reliable predictor of future, short-latency escape responses.

The escape-avoidance behavior of over 150 dogs that had received prior inescapable shocks has been studied. Two-thirds of these dogs did not escape; the other third escaped and avoided in normal fashion. It is obvious that failure to escape is highly maladaptive since it means that the dog takes 50 seconds of severe, pulsating shock on each trial. In contrast, only 6 percent of experimentally naive dogs failed to escape in the shuttle box. So any given dog either fails to escape on almost any trial or learns normally. An intermediate outcome is rare.

A typical experimental procedure that produces failures to escape shock is as follows. On the first day, the subject is strapped into a hammock and given 64 unsignalled, inescapable electric shocks, each 5.0 seconds long and 6.0 ma intensity. The shocks occur randomly in time. Twenty-four hours later, the dog is given 10 trials of signalized escape-avoidance training in the shuttle box. The onset of the CS (dimmed illumination) begins each trial, and the CS remains on until the trial ends. The CS-US interval is 10 seconds. If the dog jumps the barrier (set at shoulder height) during this interval, the CS terminates and no shock occurs. Failure to jump during the CS-US interval leads to a 4.5 ma shock which remains until the subject jumps the barrier. If the subject fails to jump the barrier within 60 seconds after the CS onset, the trial automatically terminates and the shuttle box performance which typically results is that the group pretreated with inescapable shocks responds much more slowly than does the group not so pretreated.

We use the term "learned helplessness" to describe the interference with adaptive responding produced by inescapable shock and also as a shorthand to describe the process that we believe underlies the behavior (see *Etiology*). So, learned helplessness in the dog is defined by two behaviors: (1) dogs that have had experience with uncontrollable shock *fail to initiate responses* to escape shock or are slower to make responses than naive dogs, and (2) if the dog does make a response that turns off shock, it has *more trouble learning that responding is effective* than a naive dog.

Learned helplessness is not an isolated phenomenon. Aside from the studies of Overmier and Seligman (1967), and Seligman and Maier (1967), such interference was also reported in dogs by Carlson and Black (1957), Leaf (1964), Seligman, Maier, and Geer (1968), Overmier (1968), Maier (1970), and Seligman and Groves (1970). Nor is it restricted to dogs: deficits in escaping or avoiding shock after experience with uncontrollable shock has been shown in rats, cats, dogs, fish, mice, and men. Using rats, at least 16 studies have shown interference as a consequence of inescapable shock. For example, Mowrer (1940), Dinsmoor and Campbell (1956), and Dinsmoor (1958), all found that rats which had received inescapable shock were retarded in initiating their first barpress-escape response and were slower to acquire the response once it had been emitted. Brown and Jacobs (1949), Mullin and Mogenson (1963), and Weiss, Krieckhaus, and Conte (1968), all found that fear conditioning carried out with inescapable shocks resulted in escape and avoidance decrements. In addition, the more trials of inescapable shock there are, the poorer is the subsequent escape and avoidance performance (Cohen and Looney [1971]). Inescapable shocks imposed on weaning rats produce escape (and sometimes avoidance) decrements when the rats are adults (Brookshire, Littman and Stewart [1961]; Levine, Chevalier and Korchin [1956]; Denenberg and Bell [1960]; Denenberg [1964]). Unlike the dog, however, the rat shows small interference with escape responding. Only Cohen and Looney (1971) find rats who will sit and take shock, as opposed to being merely slower to escape.

Using cats, Seward and Humphrey (1967) reported interference in escape resulting from previous inescapable shocks. Behrend and Bitterman (1963) found that inescapable shocks retarded later Sidman avoidance learning by fish in an aquatic shuttle box, and Pinckney (1967) and Padilla, Padilla, Ketterer, & Giacalone (1970) found that uncontrollable shock retarded later shuttle box avoidance learning in goldfish. Using humans, MacDonald (1946) found that inescapable shocks delivered to the finger retarded the later acquisition of finger-withdrawal avoidance. Thornton and Jacobs (1971) found that after exposure to inescapable shock, human subjects (1) failed to escape the shock and (2) failed to associate responding and reinforcement even after they made successful responses. Hiroto (1974) found that students who had received inescapable loud noise were highly debilitated in learning to shuttle to escape noise, whereas escapable noise and no-noise groups were not debilitated. Interestingly, this effect was larger when subjects were given chance versus skill instruction, and in subjects who perceived reinforcers as determined by outside forces (externals) as opposed to being caused by their own actions (internals). Rascinskas (1971) has also reported such debilitation in humans following inescapable electric shock.

Inability to control trauma not only disrupts shock escape in a variety of species, but also interferes with a range of adaptive behaviors. Powell and Creer (1969) found that rats that had received inescapable shocks initiated less pain-elicited aggression toward other rats. McCulloch and Bruner (1939) reported that rats given inescapable shocks were slower to learn to swim out of a water maze, and Braud, Wepmann and Russo (1969) reported similar findings in mice. Brookshire, Littman, and Stewart (1961) (experiment 6) reported that inescapable shocks given to weanling rats disrupted food-getting behavior in adulthood when the rats were very hungry.

Situations involving uncontrollable USs other than shock can produce effects that may be related to failure to escape shock. Escape deficits can be produced by inescapable tumbling (Anderson & Paden [1966]) and by loud noise (Hiroto [1973]); passivity from defeat in fighting (Kahn [1951]), and sudden death from defeat (Ewing [1967]) or restraint (Richter [1957]). Harlow, Harlow, & Suomi (1971) reported that 45-day-old monkeys made helpless by 45 days of confinement to a narrow pit showed deficits later in locomotion, exploration, and social behavior. Maier, Seligman, & Solomon (1969, pp. 299-343) and Seligman, Maier, & Solomon (1971, pp. 347-400) have reviewed and discussed the generality of the effects of inescapable USs across species and situations at greater length.

Besides passivity and retarded response-relief learning, there are four other characteristics associated with learned helplessness which are relevant to depressive symptomatology in man: the first is that helplessness has a time course. In dogs, inescapable shock produces transient as well as nontransient interference with escape (Overmier and Seligman [1967]) and avoidance (Overmier [1968]): 24 hours after *one* session of inescapable shock, dogs are helpless; but if intervals longer than 48 hours elapse, responding is normal. This is also true of goldfish (Padilla, et al. [1970]). With multiple sessions of inescapable shock, helplessness is not transient (Seligman & Groves [1970], Seligman, Maier, & Geer [1968]). Weiss (1968) found a parallel time course for weight loss in rats given uncontrollable shock, but other than this no such time course has been found in the rat or other species (e.g., Anderson, Cole, & McVaugh [1968]). In spite of the fact that nontransient learned helplessness occurs, one session of inescapable shocks may produce a physiological depletion that is restored with time. Weiss, Stone, & Harrell (1970), and Miller & Weiss (1969, pp. 343-372) speculated that some physiological depletion such as norepinephrine may be partially responsible for the transient form of helplessness.

Three other findings exhaust what little knowledge we now have about the physiology of learned helplessness. As for gross physiology, Weiss (1968) reported that uncontrollable shock retarded weight gain more than controllable shock in rats. Mowrer & Viek (1948), and Lindner (1968) reported more anorexia in rats given inescapable shock than in rats given escapable shock. Weiss, Stone, & Harrell (1970) reported that whole-brain norepinephrine was depleted in the brains of rats that could not control shocks, while rats that could control shocks showed elevated NE. It is unknown at present whether such NE depletion is either a necessary or a sufficient condition for learned helplessness, but it seems to be concomitant in rats. It is of interest, moreover, that Weiss, Stone, & Harrell (1970) undertook these studies because NE depletion has been hypothesized as the cause of depression in man.

In summary, experience with uncontrollable trauma produces six effects related to depression. The two basic effects are: (1) animals become *passive* in the face of trauma, i.e., they are slower to initiate responses to alleviate trauma and may not respond at all; and (2) animals are *retarded at learning* that their responses control trauma, i.e., if the animal makes a response that produces relief, it may have trouble "catching on" to the response-relief contingency. This maladaptive behavior appears in a variety of species including man, and over a range of tasks which require voluntary responding. In addition, this phenomenon (3) *dissipates in time,* and has (4) *anorexia,* (5) *weight loss,* and (6) *whole brain norepinephrine depletion* associated with it at least in the rat.

Depression

Depression is not well-defined and indeed, this is one reason why it needs a model. The clinical "entity" has multifarious symptoms, and for our purposes, I shall focus on those that seem central to the diagnosis *and* that may be related to learned helplessness. We shall concentrate on manifestations of depression: 1. Passivity: the slower response initiation, retardation, and lowered amplitude of behavior seen in depression. 2. Negative expectations: the readiness with which depressed patients construe their actions, even if they succeed, as having failed or being futile. 3. The sense of helplessness, hopelessness, and powerlessness which depressed patients frequently voice.

1. Passivity. The word "depressed" as a behavioral description denotes a reduction or depression in responding. It is, therefore, not surprising that diagnoses of depression often centrally involve the failure or the slowness of the patient to initiate responses. In a systematic study of the symptoms of depression, Grinker, Miller, Sabshin, Nunn, & Nunnally (1961) describe this in a number of ways:

> "Isolated and withdrawn, prefers to remain by himself, stays in bed much of the time" (p. 169).
> "Gait and general behavior slow and retarded. Volume of voice decreased, sits alone very quietly" (p. 170).
> "Feels unable to act, feels unable to make decisions" (p. 166).
> [They] give the appearance of an 'empty' person who has 'given up' (p. 166).

Mendels (1970, p. 7) describes the slowdown in responding associated with depression:

> Loss of interest, decrease in energy, inability to accomplish tasks, difficulty in concentration, and the erosion of motivation and ambition all combine to impair efficient functioning. For many depressives the first signs of the illness are in the area of their increasing inability to cope with their work and responsibilities.

Beck (1967, p. 209) describes "paralysis of the will" as a striking feature of depression:

> In severe cases, there often is complete paralysis of the will. The patient has no desire to do anything, even those things which are essential to life. Consequently, he may be relatively immobile unless prodded or pushed into activity by others. It is sometimes necessary to pull the patient out of bed, wash, dress, and feed him.

Bleuler (1911) included inhibition of action as one of the three traits composing "melancholia."

Two recent studies document the lowered voluntary response initiation of depressives. Lewinsohn (1971) found that depressed patients initiated fewer verbal social actions, and were slower to respond to social initiatives of others. Ekman (1971) examined nonverbal communication in depressed patients. He reported that "illustrators," a class of voluntary hand motions which cohere with the intent of the conversation, were depleted in depressed patients. In contrast, "adaptors," involuntary adjustive hand motions like hand-rubbing, were not depleted. As improvement in depression occurred, the number of illustrators increased and adaptors decreased.

Descriptions of the symptoms of depression thus include—often centrally—passivity, a failure of the patient to initiate responses.

2. Negative expectations. Depressed patients are "set" to interpret their own responses when they do make them as failures or as doomed to failure. Beck (1967) construes this as the first member of the primary triad of depression.

> The depressed patient is peculiarly sensitive to any impediments to his goal-directed activity. An obstacle is regarded as an impossible barrier, difficulty in dealing with a problem is interpreted as a total failure. His cognitive response to a problem or difficulty is likely to be an idea such as "I'm licked," "I'll never be able to do this," or "I'm blocked no matter what I do" .... In achievement-oriented situations depressed patients are particularly prone to react with a sense of failure. As shown in controlled experiments (Loeb, Beck, Diggory, & Tuthill 1967) they tend to underestimate their actual performances" (Beck, [1967] p. 256-7). (See also Mendels 1970, p. 8.)

Indeed, Beck views the passive and retarded behavior of depressed patients as stemming from their negative expectations of their own effectiveness:

> The loss of spontaneous motivation, or paralysis of the will, has been considered a symptom *par excellence* of depression in the classical literature. The loss of motivation may be viewed as the result of the patient's hopelessness and pessimism: as long as he expects a negative outcome from any course of action, he is stripped of any internal stimulation to do anything (Beck 1967, p. 263).

Friedman (1964) found that depressed patients performed more poorly than normals in reaction to a light signal and recognition time for common objects, but even more striking was their subjective estimate of how poorly they thought they would do: "When the examiner would bring the patient into the testing room, the patient would immediately protest that he or she could not possibly take the tests, was unable to do anything, or felt too bad or too tired, was incapable, hopeless, etc .... While performing adequately the patient would occasionally and less frequently reiterate the original protest, saying 'I can't do it, 'I don't know how,' etc." This is a very common experience of experimenters testing depressed patients.

3. Feelings of helplessness, hopelessness, and powerlessness. Although this is a discussion of the behavioral and physiological symptoms of depression, we cannot avoid mentioning the subjective content that is a concomitant of passivity and negative expectations in man. Depressed people say they feel helpless, hopeless, and powerless, and by this they mean that they believe that they are unable to control or influence those aspects of their lives which are significant to them.

Grinker et al (1961) conclude their book by describing the "factor describing characteristics of hopelessness, helplessness, failure, sadness, unworthiness, guilt and internal suffering" as the "essence of depression."

Melges and Bowlby (1969) also characterize depressed patients in this way and Bibring (1953) defines depression "as the emotional expression (indicative) of a state of helplessness and powerlessness of the ego."

There are several other characteristics of depression in man that parallel learned helplessness. Depression seems to have its time courses: Wallace (1957) in discussing the "disaster syndrome," reported that following sudden catastrophes depression occurs for about a day or so and then functioning returns to normal. It seems possible that multiple traumatic events intervening between the initial disaster and recovery might potentiate depression considerably, as we have found with dogs. We should also note that endogenous or process depression is characterized by cyclic fluctuations, between depression and mania, usually on the order of weeks or months. Moreover, it is commonly thought that almost all depressions dissipate in time, although whether the period is more commonly measurable in days, weeks, months, or years is a matter of some dispute (e.g., Paskind [1929, 1930], Lundquist [1945], and Kraines [1957]).

Aside from time course, both weight loss and anorexia are common gross physiological signs of depression. As for pharmacology, there is some evidence that imipramine, a drug which increases the NE available in the central nervous system, possibly by blocking its reuptake, breaks up depression. Klerman & Cole (1965), and Cole (1964) reported positive results of imipramine over placebos. Monoamineoxidase (MAO) inhibitors, which prevent the breakdown of NE, may be useful in relieving depression (Davis [1965] and Cole [1964]). Reserpine, a drug that depletes NE, produces depression in man. The catecholamine hypothesis of affective disorders proposed by Schildkraut (1965) claims that depression in man is associated with the deficiency of NE at receptor sites in the brain, while elation may be associated with its excess.

Commonalities

So there are considerable parallels between the behaviors which define learned helplessness and major symptoms of depression. Helpless animals become passive in the face of later trauma; they do not initiate responses to control trauma and the amplitude of responding is lowered. Depressed patients are characterized by diminished response initiation; their behavioral repertoire is impoverished and in severe cases, almost stuporous (Hoch [1921]). Helpless animals do not benefit from exposure to experiences in which responding now produces relief; rather they often revert to passively accepting shock. Depressed patients have strong negative expectations about the effectiveness of their own responding. They construe even actions that succeed as having failed and underestimate and devalue their own performance. In addition, evidence exists which suggests that both learned helplessness and depression dissipate in time, are associated with weight loss and anorexia, or loss of libido, and norepinephrine depletion.

Finally, it is not an accident that we have used the word "helplessness" to describe the behavior of dogs in our laboratory. Animals that lie down in traumatic shock that could be removed simply by jumping to the other side, and who fail even to make escape movements are readily seen as helpless. Moreover we should not forget that depressed patients commonly describe themselves as helpless, hopeless, and powerless.

Differences

Unfortunately for model-building, there are always a large number of differences between any two phenomena and only a limited number of similarities. Let us focus on those differences that loom large. The biggest single difference is that people talk and can tell you about what they are thinking and feeling, but animals do not. Because people talk about their feelings and thoughts, many of the symptoms that go into a clinical diagnosis of depression are couched in subjective terms: sadness, loss of self esteem, feeling blue, apathy, feeling of being at the end of the rope, loneliness, and feeling worthless. Human-based theorizing readily incorporates such verbal reports. For example, Schmale [1964], and Engel and Schmale [1967] have drawn an important and useful distinction between helplessness and hopelessness among human patients: helplessness is a belief that no one will do anything to aid you and hopelessness a belief that neither you nor anyone else can do anything. It is a limitation of our model that such a distinction cannot be made with animals, and that we must use these terms interchangeably. It should not go unsaid, however, that our helpless dogs look different from normal dogs to us. We do not know the dimension, facial, vocal, or whatever, which leads to our impression, but these dogs look "sad" and "morose" to us. In principle this is a quantifiable impression.

In addition to subjective symptoms, there are behavioral manifestations of depressions which do not have clear infrahuman equivalents; two such are suicide and sobbing. One behavioral manifestation of depression that has parallels in animals is sleep disturbance, but there is no evidence one way or the other of its occurring in learned helplessness.

What occurs in learned helplessness that does not occur in depression? Stomach ulcers (Weiss [1968, 1971]; and Miller & Weiss [1969]) occur more during uncontrollable than controllable shock, but we know of no data correlating ulcers and depression in man. Uncontrollable trauma also produces more stress than controllable shock as measured by behavioral suppression (Mowrer & Viek [1948], Hoffman & Fleshler [1965], and Hearst [1965]), by defecation and conditioned fear (Weiss [1968]), and by subjective report (Lepanto, Moroney, & Zenhausern [1965]). The question of whether depressed people are more anxious than others does not have a clear answer. Beck (1967) reported that while both depression and "anxiety" can be observed in some individuals, only a small positive correlation exists over a population of 606 inpatients. We can speculate that anxiety and depression are related in the following way: When a man or animal is confronted with a threat or a loss, he will respond with fear or anxiety initially. If he learns that it is wholly controllable, anxiety, having served its function, disappears. If he learns or is convinced that the event is utterly uncontrollable, depression replaces anxiety.

Finally, the asymmetry between the sets of evidence should be pointed out. The evidence on learned helplessness is experimental and unselected, while the evidence on the behavioral and physiological manifestations of depression is clinical, anecdotal, and selected. Few experiments have *tested* whether depressed people are slower to initiate voluntary responses to obtain relief or slower to learn that responding produces relief. Such experiments would help test the model.

In summary, there seems to be strong similarity of the defining behaviors of learned helplessness and the most salient manifestations of depression. On the other hand, the subjective attributes of depression, while not inconsistent with learned helplessness, are also not deduced from the theory.

ETIOLOGY

Learned Helplessness

The causes of learned helplessness are reasonably well understood. It is not trauma as such that produces interference with later adaptive responding, *but not having control over trauma*. The distinction between controllable and uncontrollable reinforcement is central to the phenomenon and theory of helplessness, so let us now examine it.

Learning theorists have usually viewed the relations between instrumental responding and outcomes that organisms could learn about as described by a line depicting the conditional probability of a reinforcement following a response $p(RFT/R)$. This line varies from zero to 1. At 1, every response produces a reinforcement (continuous reinforcement). At zero, a response never produces reinforcement (extinction). Intermediate points on the line represent various degrees of partial reinforcement. A simple line, however, does not exhaust relations between response and outcomes to which organisms are sensitive. Rewards or punishments sometimes occur when no specific response has been made. It would be a woefully maladaptive S that could not learn about such a contingency. Rather than representing instrumental learning as occurring along a single dimension, we can better describe it using the two-dimensional space shown in Figure 1. The x-axis ($p(RFT/R)$) represents the traditional dimension, conditional-probability of reinforcement, following a response.

Orthogonal to the conditional probability of reinforcement, given a response, is the conditional probability of reinforcement, given the absence of *that* response. This dimension is represented along the y-axis. We believe that Ss learn

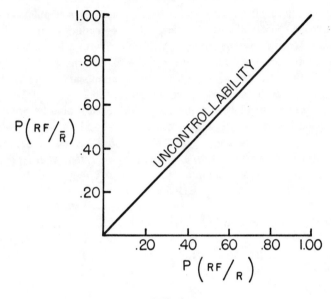

FIG. 1.

about variations along *both* dimensions conjointly. Thus, *S* may learn the extent to which relief occurs when it does not make a specific response at the same time as it learns the extent to which relief occurs when it makes the specific response. Systematic changes in behavior occur with systematic changes along both dimensions.

There is considerable convergence of opinion and evidence among learning theorists today that organisms can learn about the contingencies within this instrumental training space, including the crucial 45° line (e.g., Church [1969]; Gibbon [1970]; Maier, Seligman & Solomon [1969]; Poresky [1970]; Premack [1965]; Rescorla [1967, 1968]; Seligman, Maier & Solomon [1971]; Wagner [1969]; Watson [1967]; and Weiss [1968]).

The traditional training line has been thoroughly explored (e.g., Ferster & Skinner [1957], and Honig [1966]). The points in the training space that are of special concern for helplessness are those that lie along the 45° line, (*x, y*, where *x = y*). Whether or not the organism responds, it still gets the same density of reinforcement. The conditional probability of reinforcement, given a specific response, *does not differ* from the conditional probability of reinforcement in the absence of that response. Responding and reinforcement are independent.

The concept of control is defined within this instrumental training space. Any time there is something the organism can do or refrain from doing that changes what it gets, it has control. Specifically, a response, stands in control of a reinforcer *if and only if*:

$$p\,(RFT/R) \neq p\,(RFT/\bar{R}).$$

That is, the probability of reinforcement given a response is different from the probability of reinforcement in the absence of that response. Furthermore, when a response will not change what S gets, the response and reinforcement are independent. Specifically, when a response is independent of a reinforcer, $p(RFT/R) = p(RFT/\bar{R})$. When this is true of all responses S *cannot control* the reinforcer, the outcome is uncontrollable and nothing the organism does matters.

The passivity of dogs in the face of trauma and their difficulty in benefiting from response-relief contingencies results, we believe, from their having learned that responding and trauma are independent—that trauma is uncontrollable. This is the heart of the learned helplessness hypothesis. The hypothesis states that when shock is inescapable, the organism learns that responding and shock termination are independent (the probability of shock termination given any response doesn't differ from its probability in the absence of that response). Learning that trauma is uncontrollable has three effects: (1) A motivational effect: it reduces the probability that the subject will initiate responses to escape, because part of the incentive for making such responses is the expectation that they will bring relief. If the subject has previously learned that its responses have no effect on trauma, this contravenes the expectation. Thus the organism's motivation to respond is undermined by experience with reinforcers it cannot control. It should be obvious to the reader that this motivational effect is what we believe underlies passivity in learned helplessness, and if the model is valid, in depression. (2) A cognitive effect: learning that responding and shock are independent makes it more difficult to learn that responding *does* produce relief, when the organism makes a response which actually terminates shock. In general, if one has acquired a cognitive set in which A's are irrelevant to B's, it will be harder for one to learn that A's produce B's when they do. By the helplessness hypothesis, this mechanism is responsible for the difficulty that helpless dogs have in learning that responding produces relief, even after they respond and successfully turn off shock. Further, if the model is valid, it is this mechanism that produces the "negative expectations" of depression. (3) An emotional effect: although it does not follow directly from the helplessness hypothesis, we have mentioned that uncontrollable shock also has an emotional impact on animals. Uncontrollable shock produces more conditioned fear, ulcers, weight loss, defecation, and pain than controllable shock. (See Maier, Seligman, & Solomon [1969], and Seligman, Maier, & Solomon [1971] for a more rigorous statement of the helplessness hypothesis and the relevant evidence.)

We have tested and confirmed this hypothesis in several ways. We began by ruling out alternative hypotheses: It is unlikely that our dogs have either become adapted (and therefore not motivated enough to escape shock) or sensitized (and therefore too disorganized to escape shock) by pretreatment with shock; since making the shock very intense or very mild in the shuttle box does not attenuate the phenomenon. Further, it is unlikely that the dogs have learned during inescapable shock by explicit or superstitious reinforcement or punishment, some motor response pattern which competes with barrier jumping in the shuttle box; for interference occurs even if the dogs are paralyzed by curare and can make no overt motor responses during shock. Seligman & Maier (1967) performed a direct test of the hypothesis that learning that shock was uncontrollable, and not shock *per se*, causes helplessness. Three groups of eight dogs were used. An Escape Group was trained in the hammock to press a panel with their noses or heads to turn off shock. A Yoked Group received shocks identical to the shocks delivered to the Escape Group. The Yoked Group differed from the Escape Group only with respect to the degree of instrumental control it had over shock; for pressing the panel in the Yoked Group did not affect the programmed shocks. A Naive Control Group received no shock in the hammock.

Twenty-four hours following the hammock treatment, all three groups received escape/avoidance training in the shuttle box. The Escape Group and the Naive Control Group suffered no impairment in shuttle box performance. In contrast, the Yoked Group showed significantly slower latencies than the Naive Control Group. Six of the eight *S*s in the Yoked Group failed to escape shock. Thus the helplessness hypothesis was supported. It was *not the shock itself*, but not controlling the shock, that produced failure to escape.

Maier (1970) provided more dramatic confirmation of the hypothesis. In response to the criticism that what gets learned during uncontrollable trauma is not a cognitive set as we have proposed, but some motor response which has been reinforced by shock termination that antagonizes barrier jumping, Maier (1970) reinforced the most antagonistic response he could find. One group of ten dogs (Passive-Escape) was tied down in the hammock and had panels pushed to one-quarter inch of the sides and top of their heads. Only by *not* moving their heads, by remaining passive and still, could these dogs terminate shock. Another group of ten (Yoked) received the same shock in the hammock, but it was independent of a responding. A third group received no shock. A response-learning source of helplessness predicts that when the dogs were later tested in the shuttle box, the Passive-Escape group should be the most helpless since they had been explicitly reinforced for not moving during shock. The cognitive-set view makes a different prediction: These dogs could control shock, even though it took a passive response to do it. Some response, even one that competes with barrier jumping, produced relief, and they should not learn response-reinforcement independence. As predicted, the dogs in the Yoked group were predominantly helpless in the shuttle box escape, and the naive controls escaped normally. The Passive-Escape group at first looked for "still" ways of minimizing shock in the shuttle box. Failing to find these, they all began to escape and avoid. Thus it was not trauma *per se* nor interfering motor habits that produced failure to escape, but having learned that no response at all can control trauma.

So learning that responding and reinforcement are independent causes retarded response initiation, but does it also cause a negative cognitive set which interferes with forming later associations? Evidence from four different areas in the recent animal learning literature supports the prediction that independence between events retards later learning that events are correlated: (1) Seligman (1968) reported that when stimulus and shock were presented independently, rats were later retarded in learning that a second stimulus predicted shock. (2) Bresnahan (1969), and Thomas, Freeman, Svinicki, Burr, & Lyons (1970) reported that experience with the value of one stimulus dimension presented independently of food retarded a rat's ability to discriminate along other dimensions (3) MacKintosh (1965) reviewed a substantial discrimination learning literature and concluded that when values along a stimulus dimension are independent of reinforcement, animals are retarded at discrimination learning when values along this dimension are later correlated with reinforcement (see also Kemler & Shepp [1971]). Maier (1949) reviewed a set of related results. (4) Gamzu & Williams (1971) reported that pigeons exposed to independence between a lighted key and grain are retarded in acquiring "autoshaping" when the lighted key later signals grain.

In summary, one cause of laboratory produced helplessness seems to be learning that one cannot control important events. Learning that responding and reinforcement are independent results in a cognitive set which has two basic effects: fewer responses to control reinforcement are initiated, and associating successful responding with reinforcement becomes more difficult.

Depression

The etiology of depression is less clear than its behavioral manifestations. A dichotomy between kinds of depression has been made and will be useful for our purposes: the "exogenous-endogenous" or "process-reactive" distinction (e.g., Kiloh & Garside [1963]; Kraepelin [1913]; and Partridge [1949]). Without endorsing the claim that a dividing line can be well drawn, it appears that depression sometimes occurs cyclically and with no identifiable external event precipitating it (e.g., Kraines [1957]), and that it may cycle regularly between mania and depression. These so-called "endogenous" or "process" depressions and their immediate etiology are presumably biochemical and/or genetic. On the other hand, depression is also sometimes clearly precipitated by environmental events. This form of depression—"reactive" or "exogenous"—is the primary concern of this paper. It is heuristic to regard the process-reactive distinction as a continuum rather than a dichotomy; on the extreme of the reactive side, strong events of the kind discussed below are necessary. In between may lie a continuum of preparedness to become depressed when faced with helplessness-inducing external events, with the most mild events setting off depression at the extreme process end.

Let me enumerate some of the events that typically precipitate depression: failure in work or school; death, loss, rejection or separation from loved ones;

physical disease, and growing old. There are a host of others, but these capture the flavor of the kinds of events that often precipitate depression. What do all these have in common?

Four recent theorists of depression seem to be largely in agreement about the etiology of depression, and what they agree on is the centrality of helplessness and hopelessness. Bibring (1953), arguing from a dynamic viewpoint, sees helplessness as the cause of depression:

> What has been described as the basic mechanism of depression, the ego's shocking awareness of its helplessness in regard to its aspirations, is assumed to represent the core of normal, neurotic, and probably also psychotic depression (p. 39).

Melges & Bowlby (1969) see a similar cause of depression:

> Our thesis is that while a depressed patient's goals remain relatively unchanged his estimate of the likelihood of achieving them and his confidence in the efficacy of his own skilled actions are both diminished ... the depressed person believes that his plans of action are no longer effective in reaching his continuing and long range goals.... From this state of mind is derived, we believe, much depressive symptomology, including indecisiveness, inability to act, making increased demands on others and feelings of worthlessness and of guilt about not discharging duties.

Beck (1967, 1970) sees depression as resulting primarily from a negative cognitive set, largely about the patient's abilities to change his situation:

> A primary factor appears to be the activation of idiosyncratic cognitive patterns which divert the thinking into specific channels that deviate from reality. As a result, the patient perseverates in making negative judgments and misinterpretations. These distortions may be categorized within the triad of negative interpretations of experience; negative evaluations of the self; and negative expectations of the future (Beck, [1967] p. 27).

Lichtenberg (1957) sees hopelessness as the defining characteristic of depression:

> Depression is defined as a manifestation of felt hopelessness regarding the attainment of goals when responsibility for the hopelessness is attributed to one's personal defects. In this context hope is conceived to be a function of the perceived probability of success with respect to goal attainment.

I believe what joins these views and lies at the heart of depression is unitary: The depressed patient has learned or believes that he cannot control those elements of his life that relieve suffering or bring him gratification. In short, he believes he is helpless. Consider a few of the common precipitating events. What is the meaning of job failure or incompetence at school? Frequently it means that all of a person's efforts have been in vain, his responses have failed to bring about the gratification he desires, and he cannot find responses that control reinforcement. When an individual is rejected by someone he loves, he can no longer control this significant source of gratification and support. When a parent or lover dies, the bereaved is in a situation in which he is powerless to produce or influence love from the dead person. Physical disease and growing old are helplessness situations *par excellence*. In these conditions, the person finds his own responses ineffective and is often thrown onto the care of others. Supporting this, Abramowitz (1969) reported a significant correlation between depression and lack of belief in the efficacy of one's own responding as measured by the Rotter Internal-External locus of control scale (Rotter [1966]).

It should be remarked that situations like these may often lead to anxiety as well as depression. Anxiety may occur while the person still hopes and searches for a way out, and it may give way to depression when he finally believes that there is nothing he can do. In summary, I suggest that what depressing situations have in common is that the patient finds himself no longer in control of those aspects of his life that are important to him.

Differences

Both learned helplessness and depression may thus be caused by learning that responding and reinforcement are independent. But this view runs into several problems. It is apparent that depression sometimes results from experiences in which relief is independent of responding. For the aged person forced into an old people's home, no response can relieve the situation. But true independence of responding and reinforcement does not seem to capture other common precipitants of depression. Consider the accountant who is fired from his job because he is incompetent. Here there *are* response contingencies: His own incompetence results in his dismissal and he becomes depressed. This is not response-independence because incompetent responses produced firing, and refraining from incompetent responses would have salvaged the job. So here is a situation in which the person is helpless and becomes depressed but responding and reinforcement are not independent.

This example is difficult for the model and suggests that our operational definition of helplessness may be too restrictive. At one level the patient had control, but at another level he did not. That is, *if he had been able* to make competent responses and refrain from incompetent ones he would not have been fired. But he was not able to and in this sense he was helpless. Mandler (1964), and Mandler & Watson (1966) have discussed helplessness in terms of response unavailability: rats that are placed satiated in a maze where they learned to get food while hungry show highly disrupted behavior. They suggest that the lack of appropriate responses to deal with the new situation is the cause. Obviously if responses and reinforcement are independent, the organism is helpless in this sense of response unavailability, as well as if there are dependencies but the organism cannot make the response. Broadening helplessness to response unavailability, while making the concept somewhat less precise, may help to explain the depression of our incompetent accountant.

Ferster (1966); Kaufman & Rosenblum (1967); McKinney & Bunney (1969); and Liberman & Raskin (1971) have suggested that depression is caused by extinction procedures or the *loss* of reinforcers. There is no contradiction between the learned helplessness and extinction views of depression; helplessness, however, is more general. This is a subtle point and needs some elucidation. Extinction commonly denotes a set of contingencies in which reinforcement is withdrawn from the situation, so that the subjects' responses (as well as lack of responding) no longer produce reinforcement. Loss of reinforcers, as in the case of the death of a loved one, can be viewed as an extinction procedure. In conventional extinction procedures the probability of the reinforcer occurring is zero whether or not the subject responds. It is important to realize that such extinction is a special case of independence between responding and reinforcement. Reinforcement, however, may also be presented with a probability greater than zero, and still be presented independent of responding. This is the typical helplessness paradigm, and such procedures cause responding to decrease in probability (Rescorla & Skucy [1969]). Therefore a view that talks about independence between responding and reinforcement subsumes the extinction view and in addition suggests that situations in which reinforcers still occur, but independent of responding, also will cause depression.

Can depression actually be caused by situations other than extinction, in which reinforcements still occur, but they are not under the individual's control? To put it another way, "Is a net loss of reinforcers necessary for depression, or can depression occur when there is only loss of control without loss of reinforcers?" Would a Casanova who slept with seven new girls every week become depressed if he found out that it was not because of his amatory prowess, but because of his wealth or his fairy godmother? This is a theoretically interesting possibility, and we can only speculate about what would happen. It is appropriate to mention "success" depression in this context. When people finally reach a goal such as becoming APA president or getting a Ph.D. after years of striving, depression often ensues after the goal is reached. This puzzling phenomenon is clearly a problem for a loss view of depression. From a helplessness view, success depression may occur because reinforcers are no longer contingent on present responding. After years of goal directed instrumental activity, one now gets his reinforcers because of who he is rather than what he is doing. The common clinical impression that beautiful women get depressed and attempt suicide frequently also seems relevant; positive reinforcers abound but not because of what she *does* but because of how she looks. Would a generation of children raised with abundant positive reinforcers which they got independently of what they did become clinically depressed?

In the last paragraph, we slipped into talking about uncontrollable "positive" reinforcers as a possible cause of depression, while the laboratory evidence for learned helplessness comes from uncontrollable "aversive" reinforcers. How do organisms react to noncontingent positive reinforcers? Carder & Berkowitz (1970), Jensen (1963), and Neuringer (1969) all reported that animals choose response-contingent food over response-independent food. Receiving positive reinforcers free is not as positive as working for them. Watson (1970) reported that human infants whose own pillow pressing produced the movement of a mobile hung over their cribs smiled and cooed more frequently than a group in which stimulation was response-independent. These studies indicate that response-contingent positive stimulation is more positive than the same stimulation when it is response-independent. We do not know if such response-independent stimulation is actually negative or worse than nothing, and as yet we do not know if noncontingent positive reinforcement retards response initiation and learning of response-reward contingency as does noncontingent aversive stimulation. It seems possible that while response-independent trauma may produce depression and helplessness, response-independent positive reinforcers may merely produce boredom or apathy. To summarize, uncontrollable aversive events produce helplessness in animals and probably depression in man. Uncontrollable positive events are preferred less than controllable ones, and this may be related to success depression in man. But whether uncontrollable positive reinforcement is depression-or helplessness-engendering is unknown.

One final difference concerns the course of acquisition of learned helplessness. Helplessness in the laboratory takes a number of trials to produce. We commonly present 64 electric shocks, and it takes quite a few trials for dogs to learn that responding and relief are independent. Depression, on the other hand, can be produced in one "trial," as when a child dies. There are two responses to this objection: (1) Beck (1967) noted that a series of blows is more effective than one event in producing depression, and (2) the fact that people have language greatly compresses the number of "trials" needed to produce learning. What would take an animal many exposures to learn can be learned by a person when only a few words are spoken. The death of a child literally *tells* a person that its love is now beyond his control.

CURE

Learned Helplessness

We have found only one treatment that cures helplessness in dogs. By the helplessness hypothesis, the dog does not try to escape because he expects that no instrumental response will produce shock termination. By forcibly exposing the dog to the fact that responding produces reinforcement this expectation should be changed. Seligman, Maier, & Geer (1968), moreover, found that forcibly dragging the dog from side to side in the shuttle box, so that the dog's changing compartments terminated shock, cured helplessness. The experimenters pulled three chronically helpless dogs back and forth across the shuttle box with long leashes. This was done during CS and shock, with the barrier removed. After being pulled across the center of the shuttle box (thus terminating shock and CS) 20, 35, and 50 times, respectively, each dog began to respond on his own. Then the barrier was replaced, and the subject continued to escape and avoid. The recovery from helplessness was complete and lasting, and this finding has been replicated with more than two dozen helpless dogs.

The behavior of animals during "leash pulling" was noteworthy. At the beginning of the procedure, a good deal of force had to be exerted to pull the dog across the center of the shuttle box. Less and less force was needed as training progressed. A stage was typically reached in which a slight nudge of the leash would drive the dog into action. Finally, each dog initiated its own response, and thereafter failure to escape was very rare. The initial problem seemed to be one of "getting going."

We first tried other procedures with little success. Merely removing the barrier, calling to the dog from the safe side, dropping food into the safe side, kicking the dangerous side of the box—all failed. Until the correct response occurred repeatedly, the dog was not effectively exposed to the response-relief contingency. It is significant that so many forced exposures were required before the dogs responded on their own. This observation supported the twofold interpretation of the effects of inescapable shock: (1) the motivation to initiate responses during shock was low, and (2) the ability to associate successful responses with relief was impaired.

Depression

We do not know how to cure depression. Left alone, it sometimes dissipates over weeks or months. But there are therapies that are reported to alleviate depression and are consonant with a learned helplessness model. It is important to note that the success of a therapy often has little to do with its theoretical underpinnings, and the following "evidence" should not be regarded as a test of the model. These are merely a set of examples that seem to have exposure to response-produced success as a curative factor for depression. According to the helplessness view, the central theme in successful therapy should be having the patient find out and come to believe that his responses produce the gratifications he desires—that he is, in short, an effective human being. Bibring (1953) saw the matter similarly:

> The same conditions which bring about depression (helplessness) in reverse serve frequently the restitution from depression. Generally one can say that depression subsides either (a) when the narcissistically important goals and objects appear to be again within reach (which is frequently followed by a temporary elation) or (b) when they become sufficiently modified or reduced to become realizable, or (c) when they are altogether relinquished, or (d) when the ego recovers from the narcissistic shock by regaining its self-esteem with the help of various recovery mechanisms (with or without any change of objective or goal). (p. 43)

Beck's (1970) recently developed cognitive therapy for depression is aimed at similar goals. He sees success manipulations as changing the negative cognitive set ("I'm an ineffective person") of the depressed person to a more positive set, and argues that the primary task of the therapist is to change the negative expectational schema of the depressed patient to a more optimistic one.

Melges & Bowlby (1969) also see mitigation of helplessness as the central theme in the treatment of depression:

> If the argument that hopelessness in one or another of its forms is a central dynamic in certain kinds of psychopathology turns out to be valid, treatment measures would need to be evaluated in terms of the degree to which they help the patients to change their attitude toward the future .... A principal aim of insight-oriented therapy is to help a patient recognize some of the archaic and unreachable goals towards which he may still be striving, and some also of the impracticable plans to which he may still be wedded, aims that are especially clear when a patient is suffering from a pathological form of mourning. By psychoanalytic techniques, it is believed, a patient can sometimes be freed from the conditions that led him to become hopeless, and given opportunity both to set himself more reachable goals and to adopt more effective plans. Behavioral techniques also are being explored to see how successful they can be in setting up more positive attitudes in the future.

Other forms of therapy that are reported effective against depression seem to involve inducing the patient to see that he can control important reinforcers by his own actions. The "Tuscaloosa Plan" (Taulbee and Wright [1971]) involves putting severely depressed patients in an "antidepression room." In this room the patient is "abused": He is told to sand a wood block, and then reprimanded because he sanded against the grain. He then sands with the grain and is reprimanded for sanding with the grain. This mistreatment continues until the depressed patient expresses an appropriate amount of hostility. He is then let out of the room. This breaks up depression. From a helplessness view, the patient is *forced* to emit one of the most powerful responses people have for controlling others—anger—and when this response is dragged out of his depleted repertoire, he is powerfully reinforced. Such depressed patients may see that they can be more effective in controlling their environment.

Lazarus (1968) discussed three methods of treatment effective in depression, all of which seem to involve the patient's relearning that he controls reinforcers: (1) Assertive training (Wolpe and Lazarus [1969]), in which the patient rehearses and puts into practice social responses with which he can assert himself and bring about social reinforcers. (2) Affective expression in which the patient merely expresses anger. When this succeeds, it might result from displacement or counterconditioning, but it should not be overlooked that the expression of affect is a response that often has strong effects on the social environment. (3) Morita therapy (Kora [1965]) puts patients in bed for about a week to "sensitize them to reinforcement," and progresses from light to heavy to complicated work. Such gradual exposure to the response-reinforcement contingencies of work resembles Burgess' (1968) therapy aimed at reinforcing active behaviors in depressives. In a graded-task treatment of depression, Burgess first had her patients emit some minimal bit of behavior such as making a telephone call. She emphasized that it is crucial that the patient succeed, rather than just start and give up. The task requirements were then increased, and the patient was reinforced by the attention and interest of the therapist for successfully completing the tasks. Concomitantly, Burgess reduced the secondary gain of the depressed behaviors by ignoring them. Such treatment may be successful because it exposes the patient to the contingencies between his own actions and significant rewards and punishments.

Some comment is in order on the role of "secondary gain" in depression. In order to explain depression, Burgess (1968) and others have relied heavily on the reinforcement that the patient gets for his depressed behaviors. It is tempting to seek to remove these reinforcers during therapy, but caution is in order here. Secondary gain may explain the persistence or maintenance of *some* depressive behaviors, but it does not explain how they began. Helplessness suggests that failure to initiate active responding originates in the perception that the patient cannot control reinforcers. Thus a depressed patient's passivity probably may have two sources: (1) patients who are passive for instrumental reasons, since staying depressed brings them sympathy, love and attention, and (2) patients who are passive because they believe that *no* responses at all will be effective in controlling their environment. In this sense, secondary gain, while a practical hindrance to therapy, may be a hopeful sign in depression—it means that there is at least some response (albeit passive) that the patient believes he can effectively perform. Maier (1970) found that dogs that were reinforced by shock termination for being passive were not nearly as debilitated as dogs for which all responding was independent of shock termination. Similarly, patients who use their depression as a way of controlling reinforcers are less helpless than those who have given up.

Finally, individuals often adopt their own strategies for dealing with their minor depressions. Mine is to force myself to work: sit down and write a paper, read a difficult text or an article from a technical journal, or do a math problem. What better way is there for an intellectual to see that his responses are still effective and bring gratification than to plunge into writing, heavy reading, or problem solving? The problem is getting started.

Commonalities

Learned helplessness can be broken up by forcing the passive dog to see that its responses produce reinforcement. A variety of techniques and theories suggests that therapy aimed at breaking up depression should center on the patient's sense of efficacy. Depression may be directly antagonized when patients come to see that their own responses are effective in alleviating their suffering and producing gratification.

Difficulties

Many therapies, from psychoanalysis to T-groups, claim to be able to cure depression. The evidence presented above is selective: Only those treatments which seem compatible with helplessness were discussed. It is barely possible that when other therapies work it is because they reinstate the patient's sense of efficacy. Less anecdotal and selected evidence, however, is sorely needed on the effective elements of therapy in depression.

PREVENTION

Learned Helplessness

Dramatic successes in medicine have come more frequently from prevention than from treatment, and I would hazard a guess that inoculation and immunization have saved many more lives than cure. Surprisingly, psychotherapy is almost exclusively limited to curative procedures, and preventive procedures rarely play an explicit role. In our studies of dogs we found that behavioral immunization provided an easy and effective means of preventing learned helplessness.

The helplessness viewpoint suggested a way to immunize dogs against inescapable shocks. Initial experience with escapable shocks should do two things: (1) interfere with learning that responding and shock termination are independent, and (2) allow the dog to discriminate between the situation where shocks are escapable and where they are inescapable. The relevant experiment was done by Seligman & Maier (1967). One group of dogs was given ten escape-avoidance trials in the shuttle box before they received inescapable shocks in the hammock. Interference with subsequent escape-avoidance behavior was eliminated. That is, immunized dogs continued to respond normally when placed in the shuttle box 24 hours after inescapable shock treatment in the hammock. Another interesting finding emerged. The dogs that began by learning to escape shock in the shuttle box pressed the panels four times as often in the hammock during the inescapable shocks as did naive dogs, even though pressing panels had no effect on shock. Such panel pressing probably measures the attempts of the dog to control shock. Seligman, Marques, & Radford (in preparation) extended these findings by first letting the dogs escape shock by panel pressing in the hammock. This was followed by inescapable shock in the same place. The experience with control over shock termination prevented the dogs from becoming helpless when they were later tested in a new apparatus, the shuttle box.

Other findings from our laboratory support the idea that experience controlling trauma may protect organisms from the helplessness caused by inescapable trauma. Recall that among dogs of unknown history, helplessness is a statistical effect. Approximately two thirds of dogs given inescapable shock become helpless, while one-third respond normally. About 6 percent of naive dogs are helpless in the shuttle box without any prior experience with inescapable shock. Why do some dogs become helpless and other not? Could it be that those dogs that become helpless even without any inescapable shock have had a prelaboratory history of uncontrollable trauma? Seligman & Groves

(1970) tested this hypothesis by raising dogs singly in cages in the laboratory. Relative to dogs of variegated history, these dogs had very limited experience controlling anything. Cage-reared dogs proved to be more susceptible to helplessness; while it took four sessions of inescapable shock to produce helplessness one week later in dogs of unknown history, only two sessions of inescapable shock in the hammock were needed to cause helplessness in the cage-reared dogs. Lessac & Solomon (1969) also reported that dogs reared in isolation seem prone to interference with escape. Thus dogs that are deprived of natural opportunities to master reinforcers in their developmental history may be more vulnerable to helplessness than naturally immunized dogs.

In this regard, we should mention the dramatic findings of Richter (1957) on sudden death in wild rats. Richter discovered that when wild rats were squeezed in his hand until they stoppped struggling, they suddenly drowned when placed in a water tank from which there was no escape. Unlike unsqueezed rats that swam for 60 hours before drowning, these rats died within 30 minutes. This phenomenon may be related to the findings of Engel & Ader (1967) on enhanced susceptibility to death among hopeless and helpless humans, of Spitz (1946) on the death of children following "anaclitic depression," the common reports of zookeepers on the high mortality rate of captured wild animals, to animal "hypnosis" (Chertok [1968]), and to the findings of Ewing (1967) that submissive cockroaches die mysteriously after defeat by dominant ones. Richter (1957) reported that he could prevent sudden death by a technique which resembles our immunization procedure. If he held the rat, then let it go, held it again and let it go, sudden death did not occur. Further, if, after holding it, he put the rat in the water, took it out, put it in again and rescued it again, sudden death was prevented. These procedures, like our own, may provide the rat with a sense of control over trauma and thereby immunize against sudden death caused by inescapable trauma. Richter (1957) speculated that the critical variable in sudden death was "hopelessness": Being held and squeezed in the hands of a predator seems a dramatic instance of loss of control over its environment for a wild animal.

Depression

Even less is known about the prevention of depression than about its physiology or cure. Almost everyone sometimes loses control over the reinforcements that are significant to him—parents die, loved ones reject. Everyone also becomes at least mildly and transiently depressed in the wake of such events. But why are some people hospitalized for long periods but others resilient? We can only speculate about this, but the data on immunization against helplessness guide our speculations in a definite direction. The life histories of those individuals who are particularly resistant to depression or resilient from depression may have been filled with mastery. These people may have had extensive experience controlling and manipulating the sources of reinforcement in their lives, and may therefore perceive the future optimistically. Those people who are particularly susceptible to depression may have had lives relatively devoid of mastery. Their lives may have been full of situations in which they were helpless to influence their sources of suffering and gratification.

The relationship of depression in adults to loss of parents when young seems relevant. It seems likely that children who lose their parents experience helplessness and may be more vulnerable to later depression. The findings on this topic are mixed but lean toward establishing parental death as a predisposing factor in depression. Birtchnell (1970, a, b) reported that severely depressed patients experienced more parental, particularly maternal, deaths than less depressed patients. He also reported more frequent early parental death or absence in suicide attemptors. Similar findings have been reported by Brown, Epps, & McGlashan (1961), Beck, Sethi, & Tuthill (1963), Forrest, Fraser, & Priest (1965), Dennehy (1966), and Hill & Price (1967), but they conflict as to whether loss of father or mother is the predisposing factor. In addition, the early studies are open to the criticism that the effect is not specific to depression, but may merely reflect a higher incidence of psychiatric disorder. Finally, Munro (1966) did not find a significant difference between depressed patients and controls on early parental loss. So it is possible, although not established, that losing a parent when young may make one more vulnerable to depression.

A caveat is in order here, however. While it seems reasonable that extensive experience controlling reinforcement might make one more resilient from depression, how about the person who has met *only* with success? Is an individual whose responses have always succeeded more susceptible to depression when confronted with situations beyond his control? It seems reasonable that too much experience controlling reinforcers might not allow the development and use of coping responses against failure, just as too little control might prevent the development of coping.

One can also look at successful therapy as preventive. After all, therapy is usually not focused just on undoing past problems. It also should arm the patient against future depressions. Would therapy for depression be more successful if it was explicitly aimed at providing the patient with a wide repertoire of coping responses which he could use in future situations where he found he could not control reinforcement by his usual responses?

Finally, we can speculate about child rearing. What kind of experiences can best protect our children against the debilitating effects of helplessness and depression? A tentative answer follows from the learned helplessness view of depression: A childhood of experiences in which one's own actions are instrumental in bringing about gratification and removing annoyances. To see oneself as an effective human being may require a childhood filled with powerful synchronies between responding and its consequences.

REFERENCES

Abramowitz, S. I. Locus of control and self-reported depression among college students. *Psychological Reports*, 1969, **25**, 149–150.

Anderson, D. C., Cole, J. O., & McVaugh, W. Variations in unsignaled inescapable preshock as determinants of responses to punishment. *Journal of Comparative and Physiological Psychology* [suppl], 1968, **65**, 1–17.

Anderson, D. C., & Paden, P. Passive avoidance response learning as a function of prior tumbling trauma. *Psychonomic Science*, 1966, **4**, 129–130.

Beck, A. T. *Depression*. New York: Hoeber, 1967.

Beck, A. T. Cognitive therapy: Nature and relation to behavior therapy. *Behavior Therapy*, 1970, **1**, 184–200.

Beck, A. T. The phenomena of depression: A synthesis. In Offer, D., & Freedman, D. X. (Eds.), *Clinical research in perspective: Essays in honor of Roy R. Grinker, Sr.* New York: Basic Books, 1970.

Beck, A. T., Sethi, B., & Tuthill, R. Childhood bereavement and adult depression. *Archives of General Psychiatry*, 1963, **9**, 295–302.

Behrend, E. R., & Bitterman, M. E. Sidman avoidance in the fish. *Journal of the Experimental Analysis of Behavior*, 1963, **13**, 229–242.

Bibring, E. The mechanism of depression. In Greenacre, P. (Ed.), *Affective disorders*. New York: International Universities Press, 1953.

Birtchnell, J. Depression in relation to early and recent parent death. *British Journal of Psychiatry*, 1970a, **11**, 299–306.

Birtchnell, J. The relationship between attempted suicide, depression, and parent death. *British Journal of Psychiatry*, 1970b, **116**, 307–313.

Bleuler, E. *Dementia praecox or the group of schizophrenia*. Zinken, J. (Transl.). New York: International Universities Press, 1953 (1911).

Braud, W., Wepmann, B., & Russo, D. Task and species generality of the 'helplessness' phenomenon. *Psychonomic Science*, 1969, **16**, 154–155.

Bresnahan, E. L. Effects of intradimensional and extradimensional equivalence training, and extradimensional discrimination training upon stimulus control. Paper presented at the American Psychological Association, Washington, September 1969.

Brookshire, K. H., Littman, R. A., & Stewart, C. N. Residue of shock trauma in the white rat: A three factor theory. *Psychological Monographs*, 1961, **75** (10, whole number 514).

Brown, F., Epps, P., & McGlashan, A. The remote and immediate effects of orphanhood. *Proceedings of the Third World Congress of Psychiatry*, Montreal, 1961.

Brown, J., & Jacobs, A. The role of fear in the motivation and acquisition of responses. *Journal of Experimental Psychology*, 1949, **39**, 747–759.

Burgess, E. The modification of depressive behavior. In Rubin, R., & Franks, C. (Eds.), *Advances in behavior therapy*. New York: Academic Press, 1968.

Carder, B., & Berkowitz, K. Rats' preference for earned in comparison with free food. *Science*, 1970, **167**, 1273–1274.

Carlson, N. J., & Black, A. H. Traumatic avoidance learning: The effects of preventing escape responses. *Canadian Journal of Psychology*, 1957, **14**, 21–28.

Chertok, L. Animal hypnosis. In Fox, M. W. (Ed.), *Abnormal behavior in animals*. Philadelphia: Saunders, 1968.

Church, R. M. Response suppression. In Campbell, B. A., & Church, R. M. (Eds.), *Punishment and aversive behavior*. New York: Appleton-Century-Crofts, 1969.

Cohen, P. S., & Looney, T. A. Interference effects of noncontingent shocks upon subsequent acquisition of escape responding in a jump-up box. Paper presented at the Eastern Psychological Association, New York, 1971.

Cole, J. O. Therapeutic efficacy of antidepressant drugs. *Journal of the American Medical Association*, 1964, 190, 448–455.

Davis, J. Efficacy of tranquilizing and antidepressant drugs. *Archives of General Psychiatry*, 1965, 13, 552–572.

Dennehy, C. Childhood bereavement and psychiatric illness. *British Journal of Psychiatry*, 1966, 112, 1049–1069.

Denenberg, V. H. Effects of avoidable and unavoidable shock upon mortality in the rat. *Psychological Reports*, 1964, 14, 43–46.

Denenberg, V. H., & Bell, R. Critical periods for the effects of infantile experience on adult learning. *Science*, 1960, 131, 227–228.

Dinsmoor, J. Pulse duration and food deprivation in escape from shock training. *Psychological Reports*, 1958, 4, 531–534.

Dinsmoor, J., & Campbell, S. L. Escape-from-shock training following exposure to inescapable shock. *Psychological Reports*, 1956, 2, 34–49.

Dinsmoor, J., & Campbell, S. L. Level of current and time between sessions as factors in adaptation to shock. *Psychological Reports*, 1956, 2, 441–444.

Ekman, P. Paper presented at a National Institute of Mental Health conference on depression, Airlie House, Virginia, October 1971.

Engel, G. L., & Ader, R. Psychological factors in organic disease. *Mental Health Program Reports.* Public Health Service Publication No. 1568, NIMH, 1967.

Engel, G. L., & Schmale, A. H. Psychoanalytic theory of somatic disorder. *Journal of the American Psychoanalytic Association,* 1967, 15, 344–365.

Ewing, L. S. Fighting and death from stress in a cockroach. *Science*, 1967, 155, 1035–1036.

Ferster, C. B. Animal behavior and mental illness. *Psychological Records*, 1966, 16, 345–346.

Ferster, C. B. & Skinner, B. F. *Schedules of reinforcement.* New York: Appleton-Century-Crofts, 1957.

Forrest, C., Fraser, R., & Priest, R. Environmental factors in depressive illness. *British Journal of Psychiatry*, 1965, 111, 243–253.

Friedman, A. S. Minimal effects of severe depression on cognitive functioning. *Journal of Abnormal Psychology*, 1964, 69, 237–243.

Gamzu, E., & Williams, T. A. Classical conditioning of a complex skeletal response. *Science*, 1971, 171, 923–925.

Gibbon, J. Contingency spaces and random controls in classical and instrumental conditioning. Paper presented at the Eastern Psychological Association, Atlantic City, April 1970.

Grinker, R., Sr., Miller, J., Sabshin, M., Nunn, R. J., & Nunnally, J. C. *The phenomena of depressions.* New York: Hoeber, 1961.

Harlow, H. F., Harlow, M. K., & Suomi, S. J. From thought to therapy: Lessons from a primate laboratory. *American Scientist*, 1971, 59, 538–549.

Hearst, E. Stress induced breakdown of an appetitive discrimination. *Journal of the Experimental Analysis of Behavior*, 1965, 8, 135–146.

Hill, O., & Price, J. Childhood bereavement and adult depression. *British Journal of Psychiatry*, 1967, 113, 743–751.

Hiroto, D. S. The relationship between learned helplessness and locus of control. *Journal of Experimental Psychology*, 1974.

Hoch, A. Benign stupors: A study of a new manic-depressive reaction type. New York: Macmillan, 1921.

Hoffman, H. S., & Fleshler, M. Stimulus aspects of aversive controls: The effects of response-contingent shock. *Journal of the Experimental Analysis of Behavior*, 1965, 8, 89–96.

Honig, W. H. (Ed.) *Operant behavior: Theory and research.* New York: Appleton-Century-Crofts, 1966.

Jensen, G. D. Preference for bar pressing over 'freeloading' as a function of the number of rewarded presses. *Journal of Experimental Psychology*, 1963, 65, 451–454.

Kahn, M. W. The effect of severe defeat at various age levels on the aggressive behavior of mice. *Journal of Genetic Psychology*, 1951, 79, 117–130.

Kaufman, I. C., & Rosenblum, L. A. The reaction to separation in infant monkeys: Anaclitic depression and conservation-withdrawal. *Psychosomatic Medicine*, 1967. 29, 648–675.

Kemler, D., & Shepp, B. The learning and transfer of dimensional relevance and irrelevance in children. *Journal of Experimental Psychology*, 1971, 90, 120–127.

Kiloh, L. G., & Garside, R. F. The independence of neurotic depression and endogenous depression. *British Journal of Psychiatry*, 1963, 109, 451–463.

Klerman, G. L., & Cole, J. O. Clinical pharmacology of imipramine and related antidepressant compounds. *Pharmacological Review*, 1965, 17, 101–141.

Kora, T. Morita therapy. *International Journal of Psychiatry*, 1965, 1, 611–645.

Kraepelin, E. Manic-depressive insanity and paranoia. In *Textbook of psychiatry*. Barclay, R. M. (Transl.). Edinburgh: Livingstone, 1913.

Kraines, S. H. *Mental depressions and their treatment*. New York: Macmillan, 1957.

Lazarus, A. A. Learning theory and the treatment of depression. *Behaviour Research and Therapy*, 1968, 6, 83–89.

Leaf, R. C. Avoidance response evocation as a function of prior discriminative fear conditioning under curare. *Journal of Comparative and Physiological Psychology*, 1964, 58, 446–449.

Lepanto, R., Moroney, W., & Zenhausern, R. The contribution of anxiety to the laboratory investigation of pain. *Psychonomic Science*, 1965, 3, 475–476.

Lessac, M., & Solomon, R. L. Effects of early isolation on the later adaptive behavior of beagles: A methodological demonstration. *Developmental Psychology*, 1969, 1, 14–25.

Levine, S., Chevalier, J., & Korchin, S. The effects of early shock and handling on later avoidance learning. *Journal of Personality*, 1956, 24, 475–493.

Lewinsohn, P. M. Paper presented at a National Institute of Mental Health conference on depression, Airlie House, Virginia, October 1971.

Liberman, R. P., & Raskin, D. E. Depression: A behavioral formulation. *Archives of General Psychiatry*, 1971, 24, 515–523.

Lichtenberg, P. A definition and analysis of depression. *Archives of Neurology and Psychiatry*, 1957, 77, 516–527.

Liddell, H. *Emotional hazards in animals and man*. Springfield, Ill.: Free Press of Glencoe, 1953.

Lindner, M. *Hereditary and environmental influences upon resistance to stress*. Unpublished doctoral dissertation, University of Pennsylvania, 1968.

Loeb, A., Beck, A. T., Diggory, J. C., & Tuthill, R. Expectancy, level of aspiration, performance and self evaluation in depression. *Proceedings of the Annual Convention of the American Psychological Association*, 1967, 2, 193–194.

Lundquist, G. Prognosis and course in manic-depressive psychosis. *Acta Psychiatrica Neurologica* [suppl.], 1945, 35.

MacDonald, A. Effects of adaptation to the unconditioned stimulus upon the formation of conditioned avoidance responses. *Journal of Experimental Psychology*, 1946, 36, 1–12.

MacKintosh, N. J. Selective attention in animal learning. *Psychological Bulletin*, 1965, 64, 124–150.

Maier, N. R. F. *Frustration*. Ann Arbor: University of Michigan Press, 1949.

Maier, S. F. Failure to escape traumatic shock: Incompatible skeletal motor responses or learned helplessness? *Learning and Motivation*, 1970, 1, 157–170.

Maier, S. F., Seligman, M. E. P., & Solomon, R. L. Pavlovian fear conditioning and learned helplessness. In Campbell, B. A., & Church, R. M., *Punishment and aversive behavior*. New York: Appleton-Century-Crofts, 1969.

Mandler, G. The interruption of behavior. In Leving, D. (Ed.), *Nebraska symposium on motivation*. Lincoln, Neb.: University of Nebraska Press, 1964.

Mandler, G., & Watson, D. L. Anxiety and the interruption of behavior. In Spielberger, C. D. (Ed.), *Anxiety and behavior*. New York: Academic Press, 1966.

Masserman, J. H. *Behavior and neurosis*. Chicago: University of Chicago Press, 1943.

McCulloch, T. L., & Bruner, J. S. The effect of electric shock upon subsequent learning in the rat. *Journal of Psychology*, 1939, 7, 333–336.

McKinney, W. T., & Bunney, W. E., Jr. Animal model of depression. Review of evidence: Implications for research. *Archives of General Psychiatry*, 1969, 21, 249–248.

Melges, F. T., & Bowlby, J. Types of hopelessness in psychopathological process. *Archives of General Psychiatry*, 1969, 20, 690–699.

Mendels, J. *Concepts of depression*. New York: Wiley, 1970.

Miller, N., & Weiss, J. M. Effects of somatic or visceral responses to punishment. In Campbell, B. A. & Church, R. M., *Punishment and aversive behavior*. New York: Appleton-Century-Crofts, 1969.

Mowrer, O. H. An experimental analysis of "regression" with incidental observations on "reaction formation." *Journal of Abnormal Psychology*, 1940, 35, 56–87.

Mowrer, O. H., & Viek, P. An experimental analogue of fear from a sense of helplessness. *Journal of Abnormal Psychology*, 1948, 43, 193–200.

Mullin, A. D., & Mogenson, G. J. Effects of fear conditioning on avoidance learning. *Psychological Reports*, 1963, 13, 707–710.

Munro, A. Parental deprivation in depressive patients. *British Journal of Psychiatry*, 1966, 112, 433–457.

Neuringer, A. J. Animals respond for food in the presence of free food. *Science*, 1969, 166, 399–400.

Overmier, J. B. Interference with avoidance behavior: Failure to avoid traumatic shock. *Journal of Experimental Psychology*, 1968, 78, 340–343.

Overmier, J. B., & Seligman, M. E. P. Effects of inescapable shock upon subsequent escape and avoidance learning. *Journal of Comparative and Physiological Psychology*, 1967, 63, 23–33.

Padilla, A. M., Padilla, C., Ketterer, T., & Giacalone, D. Inescapable shocks and subsequent avoidance conditioning in goldfish, *Carrasius auratus*. *Psychonomic Science*, 1970, 20, 295–296.

Partridge, M. Some reflections on the nature of affective disorders arising from the results of prefrontal leucotomy. *Journal of Mental Science*, 1949, 95, 795–825.

Paskind, H. A. Brief attacks of manic-depressive depression. *Archives of Neurology and Psychiatry*, 1929, 22, 123–124.

Paskind, H. A. Manic-depressive psychosis in private practice: Length of attack and length of interval. *Archives of Neurology and Psychiatry*, 1930, 23, 789–794.

Pavlov, I. P. *Conditioned reflexes*. New York: Dover, 1927.

Pinckney, G. Avoidance learning in fish as a function of prior fear conditioning. *Psychological Reports*, 1967, 20, 71–74.

Poresky, R. Noncontingency detection and its effects. Paper presented at the Eastern Psychological Association, Atlantic City, April 1970.

Powell, P. A., & Creer, T. L. Interaction of developmental and environmental variables in shock-elicited aggression. *Journal of Comparative and Physiological Psychology*, 1969, 69, 219–225.

Premack, D. Reinforcement theory. In Jones, M. (Ed.), *Nebraska symposium on motivation*. Lincoln, Nebraska: University of Nebraska Press, 1965.

Racinskas, J. R. *Maladaptive consequences of loss or lack of control over aversive events*. Unpublished doctoral dissertation, Waterloo University, Waterloo, Ont., 1971.

Rescorla, R. A. Pavlovian conditioning and its proper control procedures. *Psychological Review*, 1967, 74, 71–80.

Rescorla, R. A. Probability of shock in the presence and absence of the CS in fear conditioning. *Journal of Comparative and Physiological Psychology*, 1968, **66**, 1–5.

Rescorla, R. A., & Skucy, J. Effect of response independent reinforcers during extinction. *Journal of Comparative and Physiological Psychology*, 1969, **67**, 381–389.

Richter, C. On the phenomenon of sudden death in animals and man. *Psychosomatic Medicine*, 1957, **19**, 191–198.

Rotter, J. Generalized expectancies for internal vs. external control of reinforcement. *Psychological Monographs: General and Applied*, 1966, whole number 609.

Schildkraut, J. J. The catecholamine hypothesis of affective disorders: A review of supporting evidence. *American Journal of Psychiatry*, 1965, **122**, 509–522.

Schmale, A. H. A genetic view of affects. *The Psychoanalytic Study of the Child*, 1964, **19**, 287–310.

Seligman, M. E. P. Chronic fear produced by unpredictable shock. *Journal of Comparative and Physiological Psychology*, 1968, **66**, 402–411.

Seligman, M. E. P., & Groves, D. Non-transient learned helplessness. *Psychonomic Science*, 1970, **19**, 191–192.

Seligman, M. E. P., & Maier, S. F. Failure to escape traumatic shock. *Journal of Experimental Psychology*, 1967, **74**, 1–9.

Seligman, M. E. P., Maier, S. F., & Geer, J. The alleviation of learned helplessness in the dog. *Journal of Abnormal Psychology*, 1968, **73**, 256–262.

Seligman, M. E. P., Maier, S. F., & Solomon, R. L. Unpredictable and uncontrollable aversive events. In Brush, F. R., *Aversive conditioning and learning*. New York: Academic Press, 1971.

Seligman, M. E. P., Marques, D., & Radford, R. Dominance and helplessness in rats. In preparation.

Seward, J., & Humphrey, G. L. Avoidance learning as a function of pretraining in the cat. *Journal of Comparative and Physiological Psychology*, 1967, **63**, 338–341.

Spitz, R. A. Anaclitic depression. *The Psychoanalytic Study of the Child*, 1946, **2**, 313–342.

Taulbee, E. S., & Wright, H. W. A psychosocial-behavioral model for therapeutic intervention. In Spielberger, C. D. (Ed.), *Current topics in clinical and community psychology*, III. New York: Academic Press, 1971.

Thomas, D. R., Freeman, F., Svinicki, J. G., Burr, D. E., & Lyons, J. Effects of extradimensional training on stimulus generalization. *Journal of Experimental Psychology*, 1970, **83**, 1–22.

Thornton, J. W., & Jacobs, P. D. Learned helplessness in human subjects. *Journal of Experimental Psychology*, 1971, **87**, 369–372.

Wagner, A. R. Stimulus selection and a "Modified Continuity Theory." In Bower, G. H., & Spence, J. T. (Eds.), *The psychology of learning and motivation*, III. New York: Academic Press, 1969.

Wallace, A. F. C. Mazeway disintegration: The individual's perception of socio-cultural disorganization. *Human Organization*, 1957, **16**, 23–27.

Watson, J. S. Memory and 'contingency analysis' in infant learning. *Merrill-Palmer Quarterly Behavioral Development*, 1967, **13**, 55–67.

Watson, J. S. Smiling, cooing, and 'the game.' Paper presented at the American Psychological Association, Miami Beach, Florida, 1970.

Weiss, J. M. Effects of coping response on stress. *Journal of Comparative and Physiological Psychology*, 1968, **65**, 251–260.

Weiss, J. M. Effects of coping behavior in different warning signal combinations on stress pathology in rats. *Journal of Comparative and Physiological Psychology*, 1971, **77**, 1–13.

Weiss, J. M., Krieckhaus, E. E., & Conte, R. Effects of fear conditioning on subsequent avoidance behavior. *Journal of Comparative and Physiological Psychology*, 1968, **65**, 413–421.

Weiss, J. M., Stone, E. A., & Harrell, N. Coping behavior and brain norepinephrine level in rats. *Journal of Comparative and Physiological Psychology*, 1970, 72, 153–160.

Wittgenstein, L. *Philosophical investigations.* New York: Macmillan, 1953.

Wolpe, J. *Psychotherapy by reciprocal inhibition.* Stanford, Calif.: Stanford University Press, 1958.

Wolpe, J., & Lazarus, A. A. *Behavior therapy techniques.* Oxford: Pergamon Press, 1969.

DISCUSSION

Dr. Klerman: Dr. Seligman has presented a new and exciting animal model; one which will perhaps complement the fine work of Harlow and Kaufman, who create "depression" by means of separation of infant monkeys from their siblings and mothers. In his 1966 paper, Dr. Ferster speaks of the unsolved problem of creating an animal model. I would be interested in his reaction and the reaction of the other behavioral theorists in the group to these two different animal models. Specifically, do they see any relationship between the separation-loss model and the learned helplessness model?

Dr. Ferster: I do see a relationship between the two models, although it is not a literal one; it is a functional one. I do not see any incompatible behaviors as being relevant in the animals Dr. Seligman is studying. The learned helplessness model reminds me of the case of an autistic boy whom I had a chance to observe many years ago. The child's mother related that she was under the impression that when an infant was feeding he was supposed to be given the entire bottle of milk. This she did. She would hold the child in her arms and keep the bottle in his mouth until all the milk was gone; a feat that sometimes lasted 6 or 7 hours. She was also under the impression that she was not supposed to take the nipple out of the baby's mouth during this entire period, and so would sit with the nipple in place while the child screamed and struggled and tried to eject the nipple. The analogy to learned helplessness is clear of course, because, as much as the infant would attempt to escape, he was completely unsuccessful: the mother only clutched him tighter and held the bottle in place with greater force. I suppose if we had had a chance to observe this interaction, we would have noted a systematic decrease in the frequency of avoidance-escape behavior on the part of the child.

I offer a suggestion of an analogue to Dr. Seligman's work and yet I cannot be certain what the final analysis will reveal. The work with monkeys by Harlow and Kaufman demonstrates that, when one introduces a hiatus into the parent-child relationship, he essentially prevents many behavioral interactions which usually produce a repertoire in the infant. Now when the infant monkey is returned to the parent, it is older and has been away for a while and the parent deals with it as if it were actually older. In a behavioral sense, that is, in terms of its ability to function, however, it is still pretty much at the stage it was at when it was separated. There are many disparities that emerge in the parent-child relationship which I would imagine account for great difficulty between the infant monkey and its parent at the time of reunion.

Dr. Kaufman: I would like to clarify some of the similarities and points of departure among the various primate studies. Harlow, working with Rhesus monkeys, discovered that infants separated from their mothers at about 6 months of age evidence a syndrome very similar to one described by René Spitz in human infants that has been called "anaclitic depression." The state in humans clinically reveals an initial stage of agitation and restlessness followed by depressive behavior and general withdrawal.

My work with the pigtail monkey involves a different social situation, because the animal we are studying has been raised in a group that includes its peers, the mothers of the peers, and the male who has sired all of these infants. Despite the difference in the social milieu of the pigtail when compared to the Rhesus monkey, I have discovered exactly the same response to separation on the part of the pigtail infant. The separated infant becomes depressed even though it has had 4 or 5 months of experience with its mother and has available a host of other animals to interact with during the separation period. The depressive reaction lasts for about one week and then lifts.

I have worked with another species, the bonnet monkey (both the bonnet and the pigtail are macaque monkeys). When the bonnet infant is separated from its mother, it does not show the depressive response. Instead it initially becomes agitated but then gradually approaches other animals and is adopted. This finding seems very relevant to Dr. Seligman's theory that depression may relate to the lack of control over traumatic events because the bonnet, which can exercise some control in the matter, does not become depressed. Another female adopts the separated bonnet infant, which then does not develop the depressive response because it now has the opportunity to carry on its ordinary behaviors with another animal.

Interestingly enough, I have also separated a pigtail from its mother and observed that this particular infant did not show a depressive response. It happened to be the offspring of the dominant female in the group which, because of its mother's status, enjoyed a privileged relationship with the other animals in the group long before the separation occurred. It was able to weather the storm because it had a greater behavioral repertoire available to it; because it had more experience with other animals in the group and had explored its environment far more than the other infants; and because, in general, it had many more coping techniques. So, despite the absence of its mother and the lack of a genuine adoption such as occurs in the bonnet, this animal did not become depressed. I believe the explanation is quite similar to Dr. Seligman's theory about helplessness and the apparent control the organism has over traumatic events.

What is there about the separation procedure that produces the depressive reaction? I would like to describe another experiment completed in my laboratory which indirectly relates to this question and raises some issues not as yet mentioned. We separated two pigtail infants from their mothers at the same time and observed that both infants developed the initial stage of agitation and then entered a depressive phase. However, one infant became mildly depressed while the other developed a severe and incapacitating depression. They both recovered as usual and after recovery we reintroduced the mothers, one at a time inside the cage, in such a way that the infant could see its mother but could not actually get to her. The pigtail infant who had evidenced a mild depressive response ran toward its mother, found that it could not actually get to her, and so stopped trying and went back and started to play with its peers. The infant that had been more severely depressed ran toward its mother and when it realized it could not actually get to her, walked to a corner of the cage, curled up into a ball, which is what it had done when it had been depressed originally, and would not play or respond to the play of others until its mother was removed from the cage, at which time it jumped up and began playing.

This sequence of events was repeated 3 or 4 times a week for 8 weeks. Every time the infant saw its mother, it curled up into a ball until she was removed and then jumped up and started playing again. The only difference between the first response and the subsequent ones was that it no longer even ran toward her, but merely assumed the depressed posture upon seeing her. The same experiment was conducted using two bonnet monkeys. They were both adopted and neither of them showed a depressive response. When the mothers were reintroduced, each infant did exactly the same thing; it took a look at its mother and then ran to its adopted mother.

I believe these are very complicated data and an in-depth study would lead us in many diverse directions. However, I do think there are some conclusions we can draw which are quite relevant to the task at hand. I believe we can say with some certainty that, when the infant is reunited with its mother, the reunion serves as an anxiety-provoking situation for the child. This is clearly seen with the bonnet infant which, when confronted with its mother, runs immediately to its adopted mother. The bonnet's solution to this anxiety-provoking situation is to adopt a technique learned during the mother's absence—a prior anxiety-provoking situation. The pigtail that did not become depressed when it saw its mother after a separation also resorted to the technique it had used to manage her absence, and that was playing with peers. However, the animal that became depressed, that was overcome at the sight of its mother, was again overcome with the incapacitating feeling of helplessness which it had first experienced during the original separation.

Dr. Seligman: I believe that Dr. Kaufman and I, as well as Dr. McKinney and Dr. Harlow, are dealing with a similar phenomenon which could be similarly operationalized. Both the loss of mother and exposure to inescapable shock represent situations in which no response the animal can make will affect the trauma. There is no response the infant monkey can make that will bring its mother back, and there is no response the dog can make that will turn off the shock. I would suggest that this is the crucial variable in both separation and learned helplessness, and this suggestion is testable.

Dr. Friedman: In Dr. Kaufman's experiments the response of the infant monkey to loss is influenced by its place in the social hierarchy. I wonder if in Dr. Seligman's experiments there is variance that can be accounted for in terms of social standing or dominance. A corollary question would be whether the experience of inescapable shock affects the dog's standing within its social milieu.

Dr. Seligman: We have done some experiments on inescapable shock and dominance situations in the rat. There are two major findings. One is that the rat which receives inescapable shock and becomes helpless will later "lose" in competitive situations to the rat that received escapable shock. The second finding is that, if a rat receives escapable shock, its place in the dominance hierarchy actually goes up. Similar findings occur in experiments conducted with a phenomenon called "shock elicited aggression" in rats. If one takes a rat and subjects it to pain in the presence of another rat of the same sex, it responds by attacking the other rat. If an animal is given inescapable shock before being placed in a painful situation with a conspecific, it will not be aggressive toward its peer any longer, but instead it will just lie there. However, if the animal is given escapable shock, shock that it can control by pressing a bar before the experimental situation, it will continue to be aggressive toward its peer. These experiments suggest then, that dominance and aggression are related to the controllability of shock.

Dr. Klerman: I wonder if we're not encouraging premature closure by attempting to squeeze both the separation-loss model and the learned helplessness model into the same explanatory mold. The learned helplessness situation seems to be an example of an extreme type of behavioral response, and I have been trying to imagine what could possibly be comparable in the human being. The only human analogy I feel comfortable with is the concentration camp experience.

Dr. Friedman: Dr. Chodoff has studied and written about the concentration camp experience in great detail and I would be interested in his comments.

Dr. Chodoff: Depression is certainly a prominent symptom of the Concentration Camp Syndrome. Before I proceed though, I would like to address a question to Dr. Seligman. The animal learns that responding does not control reinforcement and becomes helpless, but that dissipates in time, especially when the animal is dragged from the shuttle box. Have you ever taught the animal so well that responding is meaningless, that in effect you are unable to help it, i.e., have you ever produced a permanent condition?

Dr. Seligman: Yes, if you administer multiple shocks, for example giving four 2-hour sessions of inescapable shock spread out over one week, as opposed to one session, you find when you test many days later that the animals are still helpless. We have not as yet tested groups months or years later, but permanence does seem to be a function of how much multiple experience there was with uncontrollability. And so we can say that the more inescapable shock given, the longer will be the persistence of the syndrome.

Dr. Chodoff: The experiments Dr. Seligman describes are quite analogous to the events producing a traumatic neurosis, or for our purposes what we might call a traumatic depression. The concentration camp experience is an example of a stress that is extremely intense and can, especially if experienced at a young and malleable time of life, produce effects that are not appreciable amenable to therapeutic change. These stable and almost permanent effects of a concentration camp experience are anxiety, depression, and a negative view toward life.

There have been a number of instances of naturally occurring traumatic neuroses which have become fixed and most difficult to change, especially when exposure to the stressful situation has been severe and prolonged. The durability of the traumatic neurosis produced in such situations is also interesting because it offers a differing point of view that should influence psychoanalytic theory. Freud held that the creation of a traumatic neurosis was not only dependent upon a traumatic stimulus, but also upon the reawakening of certain infantile constellations in the affected person. The concentration camp data, as well as some inferences we can make about the learned helplessness model, seem to refute Freud's notion, at least in extreme cases.

Dr. Beck: Is the situation in the concentration camp really so qualitatively different from other traumatic life experiences, such as the loss of a parent through death? Certainly the concentration camp is a far more noxious situation, but it seems that underlying the cruelty and trauma there is a strong sense of loss. At the minimum people have lost their freedom, and most probably they have also lost loved ones.

Dr. Chodoff: The loss of relatives was just one particular facet of an extremely noxious situation, the chief characteristic of which was the total lack of control by the concentration camp victim over his environment. The Jew in the concentration camp was abused and tormented simply because of his protoplasm. And this was a truly inescapable experience from which there was no way out and nothing one could do to alter the circumstances. There is a qualitative difference between the experience of losing a loved one and that of existing in a concentration camp. Perhaps the extreme aspect of the concentration camp experience relative to parental loss on the one hand, and the similarity between the concentration camp experience in the human and the severe trauma of the learned helplessness situation which Dr. Seligman produces in the dog may highlight some of the difficulties in drawing analogies between Dr. Seligman's work and the human condition. The concentration camp experience does not seem qualitatively to parallel anything that occurs in "average everyday life."

Dr. Katz: I would like to ask Dr. Seligman about the phenomenon of exhaustion. Is it possible that the dogs that appear depressed and helpless have become exhausted because of repeated exposure to a fearful situation? In other words, could they be worn out instead of helpless, and is this more of a physical phenomenon than a learning phenomenon?

Dr. Seligman: There are two reasons, aside from the appearance of the animal, leading to the conclusion that what we are dealing with is a psychological phenomenon and not a matter of exhaustion. The first is that in all of the experiments we have conducted with animals, we have scrupulously used yoked pairs. This means that one animal received escapable shock while the other was receiving inescapable shock, so that we were dealing with two animals that had the same amount of shock. The one that received escapable shock responded a great deal because escape was contingent on its response. The other animal responded for a while and then ceased to respond because there was no contingency involved. The animal that received the escapable shock did not appear "helpless" or "exhausted," and as described before, the animal receiving inescapable shock did appear so. Thus the activity of the animal receiving the escapable shock was greater because it could control shock and so it was quite active physically. If it were exhaustion that we were seeing, we would hypothesize that controllable shock would prove more exhausting than uncontrollable shock. Yet only uncontrollably shocked dogs become helpless.

Another hypothesis in this regard might be that dogs do not jump over the barrier in the shuttle box because they are too exhausted to do so. My second reason for believing this is not an exhaustion phenomenon relates to the fact that the dogs do indeed jump over the barrier. They occasionally jump the barrier between trials and then go back to sitting in the box. At the end of the day, if you open the door to let them out of the shuttle box, they will just jump over the barrier and come out on their own. Their debilitation seems specific to when trauma is on, but "exhaustion" implies that they should be generally unresponsive. I think these two reasons counter the notion that we are dealing with simple exhaustion.

Dr. Goodwin: Does the phenomenon of learned helplessness generalize to other noxious stimuli? And if it does, does it occur immediately?

Dr. Seligman: I am not able to answer the question definitively at this time. There are about half a dozen studies which seem to indicate that helplessness with respect to shock generalizes to cold water, to dominance, and to shock-elicited aggression. We also have some evidence that inescapable tumbling (where an animal is placed in a globe-like apparatus and tumbled) generalizes to shock.

Dr. Goodwin: Once they have learned helplessness from shock, then, they are no longer naive in other situations, for example, they do not even try to escape from cold water? Is it possible that there is some type of an acclimation to the stimulus which, in fact, may account for these observations? In other words, after a while the animal becomes acclimated and perceives the stimulus as less painful than it actually is.

Dr. Seligman: This is an important issue and was one of the questions we were first concerned with in our work. When we saw the dogs lying there receiving shock, it occurred to us that perhaps they were not motivated enough to get over the barrier; that, indeed, they might have adapted to the shock. We were also interested in the converse hypothesis, which is that sensitization had occurred. It could be argued that inescapable trauma sensitizes the animal to future trauma and that when it is later traumatized, it becomes too disorganized to respond.

One reason we think that it is not adaptation stems from the findings made when the shock level is varied. If one hypothesizes that the animals lie in the shuttle box and passively receive shock because they are adapted to the shock, then he would expect to find they are less adapted as the shock intensity is increased. This is not borne out; however, for when the shock level is increased the animals still lie there passively, although they do vocalize more than when the shock is of lower intensity. If the shock is turned down below its regular intensity, they don't vocalize as much, but the important fact is that they continue to lie there and accept the shock.

Perhaps the most important evidence against adaptation is that animals are yoked and those receiving escapable shock and inescapable shock both receive the same amount of shock physically. The animal exposed to inescapable shock lies passively in a shuttle box and receives shock, while the animal exposed to escapable shock learns to escape. Using an adaptational hypothesis, one is then forced to the uncomfortable conclusion that the animal only adapts to the inescapable shock. Indeed, this comes close to adopting the same premise we have, and that is that animals learn that shock is inescapable and it is because they have learned that they cannot escape from shock that they sit quietly and not because they have adapted to the shock. Also, in going back through the old structuralist literature on adaptation to pain, we were unable to find studies recounting adaptation to severe pain similar to our experiments, so I am inclined to the conclusion that adaptation is not an adequate explanation for our findings.

One final bit of evidence militating against adaptation which impresses me very strongly is that, when one starts dragging the animals back and forth in the shuttle box, they learn and do respond on their own. If they had adapted to shock or were exhausted, why should dragging suddenly make them less adapted?

Dr. Schmale: I believe Dr. Seligman is tapping into a primitive biological mechanism which is more on the level of predepression and prelearned helplessness. This is a phenomenon we have been acquainted with for many years but one that we are just beginning to focus on systematically. We have referred to this phenomenon as "conservation-withdrawal," which describes a biological cutoff point beyond which the organism does not respond to stimulation. It is seen along the entire evolutionary ladder, from the paramecium through the more complicated biological systems.

George Engel's early observations of Monica (1956) revealed this conservation-withdrawal mechanism, which he labeled depression withdrawal. He noted that at times of stress, when one would expect a child to become anxious, Monica instead shut her eyes and went to sleep. There was no secretion of gastric acid associated with this state. We have come to regard this phenomenon as a biological event that protects the animal and serves adaptation, for the animal cuts off and is no longer responsive to the environment when it becomes too adverse. Therefore, I do not think it is just a psychological phenomenon that Dr. Seligman is dealing with, and I would see this state as a precursor to the psychological state of depression.

Dr. Seligman: Dr. Schmale raises a critical question for his theory, my own theory, and the depression theory in general. He asks if the reaction we are seeing is adaptive. I am inclined to believe that, at least in the experiments I have described, the behavior we are seeing is not adaptive. What leads me to this belief has much to do with the phenomenon of sudden death.

Kurt Richter in 1957 did a very important study on rats which unfortunately has not been followed up. Richter took wild rats and held them in his hand until they stopped struggling. He then put them in a bathtub of water and found that they would swim around between 5 and 30 minutes and then dive to the bottom and drown. That is a very interesting finding if one is also aware that had Richter not held the rat in his hand to begin with, it would swim around for between 60 and 80 hours before drowning. The types of deaths seemed to be quite different and Richter claims that the death of the hand-held rat was accompanied by parasympathetic nervous system activity but the death in the long-swimming rat was sympathetic.

Richter labeled this state, death from "hopelessness," partly because he discovered he could immunize rats against it. Immunization was accomplished by holding the rat in the hand and letting it go and repeating this procedure until it stopped struggling. If it was then put into water, it would swim between 60 and 80 hours until it could no longer sustain the activity. Similarly, if the rat was held until it stopped struggling and then put in the water, taken out and held again, then put back in, and so on, it would also swim between 60 and 80 hours. Richter could thus psychologically immunize rats against the development of this state of death from "hopelessness."

We have accomplished similar immunizations in the laboratory with inescapable shock. We can produce the phenomenon of sudden death with inescapable shock given to wild rats and, using a method similar to Richter's, we are able to immunize the rats against this.

The point I wish to make is that my concept of adaptation is strained when the "adaptive" response to stimulation leads to death. If adaptation means anything, it means promoting survival. Otherwise it seems to me that we are using the term too loosely.

Dr. Schmale: I do not believe that just because death ensues, we should assume that the underlying process is not adaptive. Any kind of trauma can so overload the organism that it will be unable to sustain it. I continue to believe that we are discussing a basically adaptive process which in this instance has gone too far.

Dr. Kaufman: I would agree with Dr. Schmale that we are talking about adaptive behaviors. For example, a fowl seeing a hawk flying over will freeze, which is an adaptive response; but it may not work—the hawk may still see the fowl and come down and kill it. The attempt at adaptation would be unsuccessful in this particular instance.

Dr. Klerman: From a strict Darwinian point of view, a behavior is adaptive if it is successful in promoting the survival of the species.

Dr. Schmale: I can only reiterate that behaviors such as hibernation or encystment are all temporary measures designed to protect the animal for a time. If the environment continues to be adverse, then the animal will not survive and what was an adaptive response will not work.

Dr. Friedman: I believe that part of the problem lies in changing the environment on the animal. When this occurs, then behaviors which were adaptive in one environment may no longer be adaptive in the new one. It might well be that Dr. Seligman is creating such a drastic departure from the everyday environment of the animal that he is rendering previously adaptive behavior useless to the animal. The rate of change of the environment is another variable that may be critical.

Dr. Klerman: This type of temporarily maladaptive withdrawal seems to be built into the evolutionary sequence, and there seems to exist a mechanism for eliciting it and also for turning it off, because it is time-limited. The question that emerges is what stimuli or events engage and disengage this mechanism of withdrawal? I would guess that there must be some built-in, behaviorally linked central nervous system mechanisms that turn the phenomenon on and off. Perhaps it is the depletion of norepinephrine or some regeneration of the norepinephrine stores.

From a clinical standpoint, as Dr. Chodoff suggested, we might find a situation analogous to Dr. Seligman's learned helplessness in dogs by examining trauma such as grief reactions or combat neuroses. The return to active duty of men with combat neurosis in the Korean War was much higher than during World War II, and this related to a difference in treatment. World War II soldiers with combat neurosis were evacuated to the rear lines, where various types of hypnotherapy and drug therapy were combined for treatment. In the Korean War, however, they stopped evacuating and kept the men very close to the battalion aid stations, slowly bringing them back into the battlefield milieu. We might look at that as a forced reentry into the traumatic situation with attempts at mastery. It may be stretching the analogy, but it does seem that keeping a person in contact with the traumatic situation and showing him that he can maintain control and develop mastery is similar to Dr. Seligman's treatment of helpless dogs.

Dr. Seligman: Yes, dragging the dog back and forth across the shuttle box so that it comes to see that its responses are effective in turning off the shock cures learned helplessness and seems analogous to being forced back to the battlefield milieu.

Dr. Lewinsohn: I believe that Dr. Seligman has described a very interesting approach, which is clearly empirical and testable, and extremely relevant to depression. However, a distinction should be made between the aversive situation that Dr. Seligman describes and the experimental paradigm in which the individual works for positive reinforcement. With positive reinforcement it is not independence between reinforcement and responding that leads to depression, but rather situations in which the probability of reinforcement for responding is low absolutely. Thus, if a man can earn $1,000 merely by sitting on his chair—if he is reinforced for nonresponding—then I predict that he would become depressed. My underlying theoretical assumption is that depression amounts to the emission of no behavior, whereas not being depressed means emitting behavior. Getting reinforced for not responding leads to not emitting behavior and therefore to depression.

Dr. Seligman: I believe that Dr. Lewinsohn raises a central point, and its resolution will test which of our theories better fits the state of depression. My model states that what elicits depression are situations in which the probability of reinforcement is the same whether or not the response is made. When the individual can increase the probability or reinforcement by doing nothing, this should not lead to depression if everything else is held constant. So in the very hypothetical $1,000 situation, let us contrast a person who gets $1,000 only if he sits in the chair and doesn't do anything, and doesn't get the $1,000 if he gets up out of the chair, with another person who gets the $1,000 whether or not he does anything. The learned helplessness hypothesis says that the person who gets reinforced for just sitting in the chair for $1,000 is not helpless. He has a passive way of controlling the situation. The person who can do nothing, who gets the reinforcement whether or not he does get out of the chair, is helpless. He has no response that controls reinforcement. My whole theoretical thrust is that as long as the organism has a way of controlling the environment, whether it be active or passive, he will be less likely to become depressed. I don't of course believe that depression would necessarily occur in the $1,000 situation, only that controlling the $1,000 should be more pleasant than getting the money uncontrollably.

We don't know whether or not noncontingent positive reinforcement, as opposed to noncontingent negative reinforcement, produces depression. The most I would hypothesize now is that, if we take up Dr. Lewinsohn's suggestion, the person who gets the $1,000 whether or not he gets up out of the chair should be less pleased with that situation (i.e., would find it less positively reinforcing) than the person who gets the $1,000 if, and only if, he sits in the chair.

It is possible that in "success" depression we have another example of a situation which illustrates that it is the lack of contingency between responding and reinforcement which produces the depression. Success depression has remained an enigma for those who hypothesize that depression is related to a loss of reinforcers, ostensibly because of all the reinforcers in the person's environment. An example is the high rate of depression in beautiful women who supposedly get a great deal of reinforcement. The reinforcement the beautiful woman receives is not contingent on what she does, however.

Dr. Ferster: I think Dr. Seligman's findings about learned helplessness are most relevant to the concerns of the field of child development. Avoidance and escape are prominent parts of the infant's repertoire. Perhaps Dr. Seligman's findings may prove to be the link between the Freudian "fixation," that is, the idea of a dynamic fixation at certain developmental stages, and the actual behaviors involved at those stages. There really are very few ways in which one can interfere with the behaviors of an infant. One can interfere with his feeding or with his comfort as he struggles to obtain relief from irritation or pain. Dr. Seligman's work with animals seems to be operating at this level. I think the extrapolations to more complex arrangements, such as depression, are perhaps less useful than the analogies that can more readily be drawn with early childhood development.

Dr. Goodwin: Are there any age differences in the response of dogs to inescapable shock? Are young dogs more susceptible than old dogs? What is the effect on later functioning when inescapable shock is given in childhood?

Dr. Seligman: Due to the long developmental cycle in the dog and the high costs involved, we have only been able to complete one developmental study. The results of this experiment were somewhat surprising because I believed that the effects of childhood events would be significant. We took 12 litters of puppies just after they had been weaned and divided them into three groups: escapable and inescapable yoked shock and no shock. Following the experimental procedure, we waited 12 months and tested them on a variety of tasks. We found that there was no systematic effect on learning and that dominance was the only variable affected by the prior experience of the shock. These results are tentative and inconclusive and we have switched to rats for further work in this area because of the technical and financial problems involved.

I wanted to close with some remarks about the comments of Drs. Ferster, Chodoff, Klerman, and Schmale. Dr. Ferster has suggested that learned helplessness may be an analogue of childhood depression, Dr. Schmale has suggested that it may be an analogue of a more primitive biological mechanism, and Dr. Chodoff and Dr. Klerman have suggested that it may be an analogue of the helplessness induced by war neurosis. Helplessness may play a role in all these phenomena. I am not suggesting that it is only in depression that helplessness has a role. It seems to me that, on the basis of similarity of behavioral symptoms, etiology, prevention, and cure, learned helplessness is a bit closer to depression than to the other pathologies. In closing, I think that helplessness has widespread pathological effects; it seems to be present in a number of disorders, among them the ones that Drs. Schmale, Klerman, Ferster, and Chodoff have mentioned. I have concentrated on its relationship to depression, because it seems to me that it is *central* to this disorder.

BIBLIOGRAPHY

Chodoff, P. Depression and guilt among concentration camp survivors. *Existential Psychiatry*, Summer-Fall, 1969.

Engel, G. L. Anxiety and depression–withdrawal: The primary affects of unpleasure. *International Journal of Psychoanalysis*, 1962, 43, 89.

Engel, G. L., & Reichsman, F. Spontaneous and experimentally induced depression in an infant with gastric fistula. *Journal of the American Psychoanalytic Association*, 1956, 4, 428.

Ferster, C. B. Animal behavior and mental illness. *Psychological Record*, 1966, 16, 345–346.

Harlow, H. F., Suomi, S. J., & McKinney, W. T. Experimental production of depression in monkeys. *Mainly Monkeys* 1970, 1, 6–12.

Kaufman, I. C., & Rosenblum, L. A. The reaction to separation in infant monkeys: Anaclitic depression and conservation withdrawal. *Psychosomatic Medicine*, 1967, 29, 648–675.

Richter, C. On the phenomenon of sudden death in animals and man. *Psychosomatic Medicine*, 1957, 19, 191–198.

Spitz, R. A. Anaclitic depression: An inquiry into the genesis of psychotic conditions in early childhood. *The Psychoanalytic Study of the Child*, 1946, 2, 313.

5
DEPRESSION AND ADAPTATION

Gerald L. Klerman
Harvard Medical School

STATEMENT OF THE PROBLEM

In this paper, I examine clinical depressive states from an adaptational approach. Adaptation, a concept common to biology, ethnology, psychology, and physiology, has relevance to theoretical and therapeutic problems in clinical psychiatry, and also to basic investigations relating behavior to biology (Plutchik 1970; Wilson 1971). Ideally, a concept with such multidisciplinary, theoretical bases should help us to relate the findings from the many areas pertinent to our understanding of the causation and pathophysiology of depression, both as an emotional state and as a clinical disorder. Also, an adaptational approach should help us to reconcile some of the theoretical polarizations in our field, especially the conflicting biological and psychosocial viewpoints.

In this effort, one major theoretical and investigational challenge is to clarify the extent to which clinical depressions may be viewed as part of the adaptive response of the mature human organism to its biological and social environment. More specifically, we need to determine whether the processes involved in the development and perpetuation of the clinical disorder are similar to those operations associated with the normal affective state. Interestingly, one of the unsolved issues is whether psychopathological depressive states are merely quantitative extensions of the normal mood encountered in everyday life or whether they represent conditions that are qualitatively different from the normal mood (Katz 1970).

[1] Supported in part by Research Grant MH 13738 from the Psychopharmacology Research Branch, Division of Extramural Research Programs, National Institute of Mental Health.

I believe we need to develop new concepts for clinical research on depression, particularly in research and theory relating environmental and biological processes. We do not lack sophistication in research design or statistical methods, although the application of existing methodology has not been as widespread as desirable. Our main problems remain at the conceptual and theoretical levels. As I have said in a recent paper on "Clinical Research in Depression," (Klerman 1971) one of our current difficulties has been our retention and perpetuation of outdated concepts and theories. In the past fifty years, the range of depressive illness has been extended, and an increasing variety of clinical problems is being subsumed under the diagnosis of depression. There has been a revival of the debate between the views of depression as an illness, as in the 19th century tradition of disease entities, and depression as a reaction to life events, as formulated in the Meyerian framework.

Following upon the ideas of Adolph Meyer, most clinical teaching and theorizing in the U. S. A. and Western Europe has emphasized the continuities and unities between the normal depressive affect and the clinical disorder. Ideally, this should be purely and simply an empirical problem—that of examining the similarities and differences between normal mood states and clinical aberrations. There has been a lag, however, in applying modern research techniques to this problem. This lag is due, in large part, to the persisting theoretical confusion between concepts of disease entity and of psychobiological reaction type.

The intellectual tensions of earlier decades between the disease concept of depression and the reactive concept of depression have been revived. In Anglo-American psychiatry, the debate over Emil Kraepelin's disease concept and over Richard Gillespie's view of endogenous versus reactive depression appeared settled in 1933 by Aubrey Lewis' (Lewis 1934) monumental research. Lewis applied Adolf Meyer's psychobiological concepts to the existing views of depression, just as Meyer had adapted his idea to Kraepelin's disease concept of *dementia praecox*. In Britain, Western Europe, and the United States, the Meyerian view was predominant from World War I until the early 1960's. Recently, however, there has been a revival of biological theories. New hypotheses propose hereditary and biological causes of depression, and thus support the belief that mood disturbance is a medical condition. The main proponents of this neo-Kraepelinian theory include Coppen, Roth, Kiloh, and their associates in England whose views have become crystallized in the influential British textbook by Mayer-Gross, et al. (Mayer-Gross, Slater, & Roth 1968), and in the U. S. A., of Robins, Guze, Winokur, and their associates in St. Louis (Robins & Guze, in press 1971). Newer somatic therapies strongly support the neo-Kraepelinian view.

It is important to recognize that the new biological theories are far more sophisticated than the late 19th century concepts. The older idea of "disease entity" was derived from clinical pathological correlations at the autopsy table whereas new approaches attempt to integrate the findings from genetics and neuropharmacology. The 19th century concepts of biological causation allowed no role for acquired psychosocial or environmental interactions, whereas modern neurobiology increasingly views CNS structures and functions in terms of their role in mediating and integrating the organism's response to its environments, both internal and external. These new biological approaches have been slow to permeate psychiatric theory in general, although in the field of affective disorders, major findings in neurochemistry have flowed from attempts to understand the role of the biogenic amines, especially as they are involved in modes of actions of newer antidepressant drugs (Kety & Schildkraut 1967; Klerman 1970).

The Meyerian view was basically a *unitary* view. It emphasized the common features among various depressive episodes and stressed the continuity between normal and disease states. The Meyerians, and their English counterparts such as Mapother and Sir Aubrey Lewis, view depression within the range of human experience. They see it as a psychobiological reaction of the human organism to life's vicissitudes. They tend to reject nosologies and to minimize the importance of organic, constitutional, and genetic factors. Most recently, Menninger espoused this general theory in his book, *The Vital Balance* (Menninger 1963). Many American textbooks incorporate this view and emphasize that psychotic depressions differ from neurotic depressions only in severity of symptoms, indications for hospitalization, and legal requirements for commitment or certification. The Meyerians acknowledge gradation from minor to major disturbances, but they claim that the distinctions between neurosis and psychosis, or between endogenous and reactive are unsubstantiated.

In the history of psychiatric ideas in the U. S. A., it is interesting to reconstruct the steps leading to such a strong emphasis on continuity and similarities. The Meyerian psychobiological approach (Meyer 1948) was an explicit reaction against Kraepelin's synthesis of the 19th century continental tradition (Kraepelin 1921) which emphasized biological causation and therapeutic pessimism. Meyer rejected the rigid, mechanistic concept of biology which relegated life experience, personality, and emotions to secondary or tertiary roles in human mental illness.

This reaction had particular importance in the United States in the first half of the 20th century. After the Civil War, dominant American concepts of the causation and treatment of mental illnesses were embodied in the Social Darwinian theory which claimed that the mentally ill were, by hereditary or social position, "unfit to survive in the new industrial order." As elucidated by historians of 19th century psychiatry, particularly Bockoven (Bovkoven 1963), psychiatrists adopted these views to justify "scientifically" their therapeutic pessimism as well as a rigid, mechanistic application of the biological causation of mental illness. Social Darwinism served as a moral vindication of the existing social order. It justified the treatment of the mentally ill as failures to be relegated to the large public mental hospitals which were created in the second half of the 19th century.

Socially, there was the pressing need to educate the public so as to reduce its fears about mental illness. Both the Meyerian and Freudian approaches have broadened the base of psychiatric thinking by emphasizing the significance of both individual psychological development and the social environment. Thus, a theoretical approach which emphasizes the similarities between clinical disorders and normal states and which blurs the distinctions between normal and abnormal conditions, has promoted a humanistic movement in clinical psychiatry which has supported the mental health efforts among public groups.

Though immensely successful in educating the public and the mental health professions, however, the Meyerian approach to depression has lost intellectual and scientific momentum. In its zeal to establish psychology and sociology as legitimate sciences cognate to clinical psychiatry, the Meyerian and psychodynamic schools appeared to pay only hollow lip service to brain and biology and in theory and practice came to espouse exclusively environmentalist positions. Recent discoveries in biology—especially in neuropharmacology, the study of animal behavior, and molecular biology—have posed new challenges which clinical theory must incorporate. The biology of the 20th century is not that of the late 19th century. The 19th century debate between mechanism and vitalism no longer is meaningful. We need approaches to the psychology of depression that utilize concepts more consonant with modern biology than are the theories of libido and death instinct, which were rooted in the 19th century concepts of psychic energy, and we need biological theories more modern than the 19th century concepts of "degenerative diseases" and "constitution" which dominated the continental somaticism of the French and German schools.

Involved in these debates is a major unresolved issue as to the place of depression in man's evolution. What are the functional roles of emotional expression and medical illness in the individual, as well as in the species? Are depressions adaptive or maladaptive? Are they diseases or reactions to the environment? Dennis Hill summarized the current dilemma in his Adolf Meyer lecture of 1968 (Hill 1968). By acknowledging the clinical utility of the distinction between endogenous and psychogenic or reactive, and between psychotic and neurotic forms of depression, he straddled the theoretical polarities. He proposed that depression can be viewed both as a biological illness and as a posture of interpersonal communication. Like the modern physicist who views the electron as both a particle and an electromagnetic wave phenomena, Hill took an eclectic point of view.

An adaptational approach, such as I assume in this paper, examines the possible "function" of depression. It should also inquire into the neuro-anatomical structure and neurochemical mechanism which through natural selection, genetic mutation, and environmental conditioning and learning serve to mediate the impact of environmental change and to initiate, organize, and integrate the affective, metabolic, and goal-directed activities of the organism both in its "normal" moods of depression and in clinical depressive states. From Darwin's theory of the evolution of emotions, the question arises about the adaptive significance of family and for the bond between parent and child. Bowlby (Bowlby, 1969) and others have demonstrated that the genesis of emotion in a child is related to the vicissitudes of the child's relationships to mothering figures. Human infants, with their prolonged state of dependency, are vulnerable to feelings of separation and helplessness. The infant's emotional signal of depression mobilizes his inner resources and alerts the social group to his need for nurturing, assistance, and succor. This generalization is true for the child, but what of the adult living in a modern industrial society? Is civilized man's depression merely the continuation of earlier evolutionary responses? If so, is depression an adaptive response or a maladaptive perpetuation of what was adaptive in a previous developmental stage? These questions bring us to the areas common to clinical biological investigation and theoretical speculation.

SOME THEORETICAL ISSUES AS TO THE FUNCTIONS OF AFFECTS

The concept of adaptation derives mainly from the Darwinian theory of evolution. According to the strictest criterion of evolutionary theory, a trait or behavior is adaptive from the phylogenetic viewpoint if it promotes survival of the species. Moreover, from the ontogenetic stance, a trait is adaptive if it promotes the growth and survival of individual members of the species. Darwin himself pioneered the application of the evolutionary approach to behavior, and especially to emotional responses. As Plutchik has said (Plutchik 1970), Darwin's theory of evolution implies that there exists an evolution not only of morphological structures but also of "mental and expressive capacities." Darwin (1965) collected material to document the phylogenetic continuity of emotional expressions in lower animals as well as in primates and humans, but most of his observations lay dormant for many decades. Since World War II, however, there has been a remarkable upsurge of interest in the comparative biology of emotional states. Based upon studies of mammals, and particularly of primate mother-child development, there has emerged a significant convergence of findings from neurobiology, ethology, and comparative psychology. Likewise, studies of infant development, particularly following psychodynamic theories, have paralleled this research.

It is now widely accepted that all mammals inherit complex behavioral systems that promote the mother-infant attachment and facilitate the formation of social bonds. These behavioral systems are profoundly adaptive for the species and for the individual; they facilitate biological survival of infant mammals during the long period of extrauterine development before biological self-sufficiency is achieved. Moreover, these systems encourage social learning, which is highly significant from an evolutionary standpoint. Mammals, unlike lower species, learn responses that enable them to react appropriately to changes produced by the environment (Scott 1970; Senay 1970).

The field studies of ethologists, the experimental studies of comparative psychologists, and the clinical studies of child behaviorists have yielded convergent findings (Bowlby 1969; Harlow 1959). Animal reactions to separation and loss are so similar to human sadness that few observers doubt the essential continuity between the animal and human infant experiences (Kaufman & Rosenbaum 1967). When the mammal mother-infant bond is broken by separation or loss, typical behavioral patterns emerge. The initial stage is characterized by anxiety, agitation, and "protest," which are followed by withdrawal, lessened social participation, and decreased motor activity. Studies have shown that these characteristics of depression are within the realm of a normal emotional state.

Thus, depression as an affect serves a signal function. It alerts the mother and/or other members of the social group that one of its helpless members, the infant, is in potential danger. This is true especially during the phase of rapid central nervous system maturation and during the acquisition of cognitive, perceptual, motor, and social skills. Alerted protectors can rally resources for nurturance, support, and protection, and thus they promote biological survival.

Multiple Adaptive Functions of Affects

This brief discussion of the significance of separation and loss in infants leads to the opportunity to delineate a general schema of the adaptive role of affects. I have found it increasingly useful to regard affects as having "signal" functions in multiple domains. A signal function approach aids in the integration of findings from multiple disciplines and helps in understanding the adaptive functions of affects. This approach promotes the search for mechanisms and structures by which these functions are fulfilled (Engel 1962; Plutchik 1970).

We can identify four adaptive functions of affects:

(1) Social communication
(2) Physiological arousal
(3) Subjective awareness
(4) Psychodynamic defensive

Let us review each of these briefly from the adaptive view, with special attention to depressive states.

Social communication: the relevance of animal models. The adaptive role of depressive affect as social communication has been elucidated by recent animal studies (Scott 1970; Senay 1970), especially in primates (Harlow, et al., 1971; Kaufman & Rosenbaum 1967), and by studies of human infancy (Bowlby 1969). The mechanisms underlying these activities—crying, facial expression, posture, touch, smell—have been studied experimentally. Perhaps of greatest significance for understanding the adult depression are the recent developments of animal models of depression based on the separation-loss paradigm (Harlow, et al. 1971; Kaufman & Rosenblum 1967). Until very recently, the nearest approximation of animal models was the amine-depleted animal (Klerman 1971) using a reserpine or benzoquinoline derivative. While this model proved very useful for screening new antidepressant drugs and for investigation of neuro-pharmacologic actions of biogenic amines, it has been deficient as a behavioral model. The newer model, based on separation-loss paradigm, has behavioral validity. Not only have these animal experiments replicated the clinical syndrome of anaclitic depression observed in human infants, they provide means of testing hypotheses about late behavioral, cognitive, and social consequences of early separations, data which would have high relevance for the many clinical theories relating vulnerability of certain adults to depression to developmental experiences in infancy and childhood. Moreover, biochemical and electro-physiological investigations of monkeys experiencing separation-loss seem a logical next step (Harlow 1971), which brings us to the second function of affect—physiological arousal.

Physiological arousal. Clinical observation and animal experimentation have established the relationship of separation-loss to infant depressive affect and clarify the role of depressive affect as a social communicational signal for the maturing infant. The question now arises as to the neuroanatomic, electro-physiological, and neurochemical mechanisms whereby these affective behaviors are initiated, perpetuated, and terminated.

These questions have been well-investigated for anxiety-fear, an affect closely related clinically and developmentally to depression. Following upon the research of Cannon, it is accepted that anxiety-fear serve to arouse the organism in preparation for "fight or flight" (Cannon 1932). This function is achieved via the complex neuroendocrine system, especially involving hypothalamic and adrenergic structures and the release of epinephrine.

When we attempt a similar analysis of the functions and mechanisms involved in depression, less agreement is evident, especially since the findings from experimental studies are inconclusive. An initial answer to defining the physiological adaptive function of depression has been offered by Engel and Schmale and their associates at the University of Rochester (Engel 1962; Schmale 1970). They postulate that the depressed state involves "conservation-withdrawal," with reduced psychomotor activity, lowered metabolism, and increased parasympathic activity. This is an intriguing hypothesis for which experimental verification is required. While the hypothesis may be consistent with infantile states, the clinical adult state appears to be associated in many instances with increased adrenal cortical activity and signs of anxiety and tension, presumably due to heightened adrenergic activity. These aspects seem inconsistent with the "conservation-withdrawal" formulation. One explanation for the discrepancies is to assume that the clinical depression of adults involves failure of mechanisms operative in normal and/or infantile states. Obviously, further efforts in this area are required and these efforts must take into account the impressive research on biogenic amines, particularly the indoleamines and catecholamines. Although the evidence derives from neuropharmacological studies more than from direct correlations in man, the patterns and trends increasingly support a role for biogenic amines in mediation of affective responses, especially depression (Kety & Schildkraut 1967). Many of these efforts have arisen from the need to understand the modes of actions of antidepressant drugs, especially the amine oxidase inhibitors and the tricyclic derivatives of imipramine (Klerman 1970).

Subjective awareness. The subjective aspect of affect has been emphasized by most clinical research and thinking and probably is specific to human experience. The subjective function of affect has been very controversial, particularly since the popularization of the James-Lange thesis that conscious awareness follows upon the physiologic reaction so that "we do not run because we are afraid but rather that we are afraid because we run" (Plutchik 1970). Accordingly, the affective state as a conscious awareness is an epiphenomenon; that is, it arises primarily from visceral and skeletal muscular sensations. Since physiologic arousal precedes conscious awareness, this concept contradicts the usual psychological theory that psychological stimuli initiate physiological awareness. Thus, there is a debate over the sequence of events relating stimulus, perception, subjective awareness of "feeling," and the psychophysiological changes.

Whatever the outcome of this debate, the subjective component of human emotion plays important functions in reflection, goal setting, and monitoring of current states and ongoing activities against criteria of internalized values and goals. The capacity to utilize affects to fulfill these self-regulating functions depends upon the species' achievement of language and rational thought—evolutionary attainments of great significance.

Psychodynamic defensive. The fourth aspect of *arousal of defenses* is related directly to clinical practice and particularly to research based upon the *psychodynamic* tradition. Originally, Freud viewed emotions as "archaic discharge syndromes." He maintained a strong biological view which derived human emotional capacities from the instinctual drives. Also, he emphasized the continuity between adult and infant behavior. Thus, psychodynamic theory stimulated interest in the developmental aspects of emotions, and particularly in the role of early childhood experiences as predeterminants of adult psychopathology. Psychodynamic thinking also stressed the important, if not crucial, role of emotional experience that is not directly within the awareness of the conscious self but which is potentially recoverable by reconstruction, free association, dreams, projective tests, or hypnosis.

The specifically psychodynamic function of affect, in addition to drive-discharge, is to stimulate defense mechanisms. Following Freud's writing about anxiety in the mid-1920's, psychodynamic theorists emphasized the defensive functions of affects in the course of their studies of ego psychology. George Engel (1962), whose views on the functions of differentiated affects have strongly influenced my beliefs, stated,

Intropsychically, affects provide information concerning the status of the self per se and of the self in relation to objects, and they indicate the level of drive tensions. In the adult, such intropsychic activities are ego functions having motivational and warning properties. As signals, affects anticipate, on the basis of past experience, intropsychic changes, thereby permitting the ego to initiate psychic processes or behavior to maintain the psychic balance.

Interestingly, while psychodynamic theory has reinterpreted anxiety in light of Cannon's findings of adrenergic mechanisms and Freud's view of this affect as signal to initiate defenses, similar formulations of depression have been slow to appear (Schmale 1970). Ego psychological approaches (Hartmann 1958) have only recently been applied to depression by Bibring and Rapaport. In a later section of this paper, their ideas about depression will be related to current investigations.

SOME EMPIRICAL FINDINGS FROM RESEARCH ON CLINICAL DEPRESSIONS

Viewed by these criteria, the affective state of depression is clearly adaptive, especially for the infant primates, including man. However, in what sense (or senses) can adult clinical depressions be regarded as adaptive? As reviewed in previous sections of this paper, the evidence points to the role of the depressive affect in infants of all mammal species, but particularly in infants of primates and humans, as an important signal of distress and helplessness that mobilizes the responses of the mother and others. Thus, the depressive affect furthers the growth and adaptation of the infant, aids in the regulation of the mother-infant and peer group relations, and facilitates the infant's social, cognitive, and motor development. But what of adult depressive states? Are they similarly adaptive?

It is often held that adult depressive patterns represent persistence into adulthood of behavior and psychic patterns which, while adaptive to the helplessness and immaturity of the infant and child, are inappropriate and maladaptive to adult behavior (Rado 1929). In a parallel situation of neurotic processes, some patterns that are learned and adaptive for one developmental stage are carried into situations for which they are no longer appropriate. This constitutes one of the most useful clinical theories of predisposition—namely that the vulnerability to adult psychopathology is determined by personality conflicts around dependency with attendant features of orality, immaturity, passivity, and helplessness (Chodoff 1970).

This developmental view can offer only a partial answer, however. While it proposes one source of the vulnerability or predisposition to psychopathology, it does not answer completely the questions about the adaptive function of the adult reaction per se. For these, we need empirical data as to the biological and social environmental conditions to which depression may be an adaptive response, and data that relate to the adequacy or inadequacy of the responses. Let me now turn to some research findings pertinent to these issues.

In this section of this paper, I shall review four areas of empirical research in which I have been engaged over the past decade. These are related to (1) the relative independence of depression from hostility and other affective components, (2) loss and separation as precipitating events in acute depressive episodes in adulthood, (3) the relationship between adaptation and an etiological classification of depression, and (4) failures of the social communicative function among adult depressives.

The Independence of Depression from Hostility and Other Affects

A major obstacle in developing a comprehensive adaptive view of depression arises from the theory of the primacy of hostility in clinical depression. Until recently, the dominant clinical teaching stressed that "depression is nothing but hostility turned against itself." In many clinical settings this oversimplification became the practical distillate of the classic psychodynamic theory initially proposed by Abraham and Freud during the period 1908–1921.

In this view, the clinical features of the manifest adult depression result from retroflexion onto the self of the hostility directed at the lost object. In this process, through incorporation, the self is identified with the lost object. The self is defended against the trauma of the loss, and thus avoids its psychic consequences. In depression, predisposition to this mechanism is postulated to have been determined by libidinal fixations in the late oral and/or early anal stages of development. Crucial to this formulation is the central role given to aggressive drives aroused by the ambivalence and dependency characteristic of the depressed person in his interpersonal and object relations (Cohen 1954; Rado 1929). In the period between manifest episodes, the depressed individual functions frequently at the obsessive-compulsive level, in which, as Abraham initially observed, his behavior is often characterized by orderliness, stability, constricted affect, denial, and lack of psychological mindedness.

I propose that there are two reasons why this theory proves a hindrance: first, the trend of findings from recent empirical studies attempting to test this formulation is clearly against the view that depression and hostility are identical during clinical depressive states; second, from a theoretical point of view, the classic version of the dynamic theory fails to classify depression as a primary affective state in its own right, but rather relegates depression to a transmutation or transformation of another affect, in this case hostility. As Bibring, Rappaport, and Chodoff have elucidated (Bibring 1953; Chodoff 1970; Rappaport 1967), this classical theory derives from an exclusively instinctual basis of the genesis of emotions and from insufficient attention to modern means of ego functions. Moreover, it is not in accord with recent clinical findings.

It is of interest that Freud used a "transformation" model to explain three clinical phenomena: conversion hysteria, anxiety, and depression. In Freud's earliest conception of the conversion mechanism in hysteria, developed about 1895, he postulated that in the process of symptom formation, psychic energy which was not discharged was "converted" into a physical symptom of hysterical nature, such as paralysis of limb or loss of vision. He proposed a similar transformation explanation in his early "toxicological theory" of anxiety, and for many years he held that anxiety neurosis was one of the "actual" neuroses based on biological causes, rather than a psychoneurosis arising from conflict. His initial hypothesis was that anxiety was the psychological manifestation of undischarged sexual libido, and it was not until 1923 that he formulated his signal theory of anxiety in which he designated the role of anxiety as the initiator of defense processes. Lastly, his concept of depression as the transformation (retroflexion) of aggressive drives deriving from oral fixations persists into the present. This persistence is in spite of the fact that ego psychology as applied to anxiety has led to major advances in the signal theory of other affects. Based upon Bibring's earlier paper, Rappaport explicated the implicit signal function of depression as a basic ego state. He viewed depression as a primary ego state, not as a secondary transformation of some other instinct or emotion.

In recent years, I have been involved in three studies directly investigating the relation between depression and hostility (Gershon, et al., 1968; Klerman & Gershon 1970; Weissman, et al., 1971). The findings from these studies have confirmed the independence of depression from hostility. The conclusions are consistent with the desirability of rejecting the "hostility turned against self" mechanism as universally necessary and primary in the pathogenesis of depression. The data show alternative patterns; there exist both high and low intensities of manifest depression, depending upon the patient's personality patterns and nature of his social relationship.

Empirical evidence contradicts other features of the classical theory. The capacity to become depressed is almost universal and not restricted to any one personality type (Lazarus & Klerman 1968). A number of investigators have found significant proportions of depressed patients without guilt or shame (Amdur & Harrow, in press 1971; Harrow & Amdur 1971; Harrow, et al., 1966; Rosenthal & Gudeman 1967). Moreover, while the depressive mood is almost universal in acute depressive states, there are ample numbers of patients who are without manifest sadness, as in the so-called "smiling" or "masked" depressions. Thus, the clinical depressive state is comprised of multiple affective components, including anxiety, guilt, hostility, and irritability.

These findings support the Bibring-Rappaport theory that depression as a primary ego state is characterized by signal functions. This theory runs counter to the classic formulation of depression as a derivative of oral and/or aggressive drives. Regarding depression as an independent affect within a primarily ego psychological framework places a new focus on the investigational design. We can now ask questions such as: to what environmental events are adult depressive states responding? how adequate are these responses? what biological mechanisms—genetic or acquired—mediate and/or modify the organism's affective responses?

Loss and Separation as Precipitating Events

An extensive literature has developed concerning the relationship between life events and depression. Most papers have attempted to describe the events that occur before the onset of the clinical depression and are therefore presumed to serve as precipitating events. The greatest emphasis has been placed upon life events as part of the general Meyerian approach to the development of experiential and environmental causations of the pathogenesis of depression. In spite of this deep concern and the general clinical folklore surrounding loss and depression, there has been relatively little systematic research.

A review of the literature reveals about a half-dozen studies of environmental events and depression that utilize systematic control or comparison groups (Paykel 1970). In the study undertaken by our research group in New Haven, a sample of controls derived from a random household sample was compared with a sample of 185 depressed patients. A modification of the Holmes-Rahe schedule of recent life events was used in assessing the significance of loss and separation and other environmental events preceding the onset of the clinical depression. Search for the life events preceding, and possibly precipitating, clinical disorders is clearly derived from the Meyerian approach. It is uncertain, however, if the aim of such research has been to establish an exclusively environmentalist view of causation. The advantage of an adaptational approach is its simultaneous examination of environmental factors and factors concerning the nature of the organisms' responses. The Holmes-Rahe schedule allows quantification of the environmental events variable and thus opens the way to study of interactions with other variables.

Overall, depressed patients reported nearly three times as many life events on the modified Holmes-Rahe Schedule during the 6 months before the onset of the clinical depressive episodes as did the normal subjects. Although many of the differences did not obtain statistical significance because of a low frequency of individual events, the overall pattern was significant. Of particular interest for an adaptive approach to depression were attempts at various clusterings. The form of clustering that proved most successful was once suggested by Jerome Myers of the sociology department of Yale (Myers, et al. 1968). It involves the categorization of events on the basis of entrance or exit of significant persons from the patient's social field. Previous studies showed that in the survey population from which the present control was taken, exits rather than entrances from the social field were followed more frequently by aggravation of symptoms, both of a psychiatric and well as medical nature. For the most part, the present findings complement these earlier findings by Myers and collaborators and indicate that exits from the social field are far more likely to be associated with clinical depression requiring treatment. The concept of the exit from the social field coincides with the psychiatric concept of separation and loss, and supports the role of these events in clinical depression.

A number of major qualifications are required in interpreting these findings, however. At best, the separation and loss category of events accounts for only 25 percent of the total sample of depressed patients. Thus, while they are more significant as precipitating events in the depressive population as compared to normal controls, or schizophrenics, they cannot account for the total variance (Beck & Worthen, unpublished). In fact, Paykel has argued conversely that if one assumes a frequency of such events in the general population as about 5 percent per 6-month period, only about 10 to 20 percent of individuals experiencing these losses or separations as stimuli for adaptation do in fact develop clinical depression (Paykel 1970). Similar findings emerge from the followup studies by Clayton and coworkers in St. Louis on reactions to bereavement (Clayton et al. 1968). Only 2 percent of their followup patients felt sufficiently distressed to seek professional help during the period of bereavement.

Thus, we are forced into the situation in which (1) loss and separation are not universal in all depressions, (2) not all individuals who experience loss and separation will develop depressions, and (3) loss and depression are not specific to clinical depression but rather may serve as precipitating events for a wide variety of clinical conditions that are not only psychiatric, but also general medical (Holmes & Rahe 1967).

This forces us to the consideration that the clinical depressive episode, though it may follow a change in life circumstance and call for response by the individual, represents some failure of adaptation. If my extrapolation from these studies is correct, only about 10 to 20 percent of individuals confronted with loss and separation do in fact develop a clinical syndrome. Most individuals, therefore, have adequate coping techniques or are enmeshed in social environments that support and nourish them in the period of adaptation.

Bibring proposes that the adult depression is a reactivation of the childhood experience of helplessness. There are a number of important questions to be answered before accepting this formulation as complete. The relationship of helplessness in the adult state to the normal childhood affect is unclear, as are the circumstances under which the adult experiences helplessness (Schmale 1970). Moreover, Bibring stated that in adult depressions, helplessness does not occur except when accompanied by a fall in self-esteem (Bibring 1953). Thus, we must explore the relationship of depression to the individual's self-structure and the vicissitudes of self-esteem in its interaction with subjective feelings of helplessness on one hand and changes in the environment on the other (Beck 1967). My current view is that the depressive episode may be initiated as a response to helplessness and fallen self-esteem, and thus may serve as the signal for the individual that there has been a discrepancy within the self system between ideal expectations and practical reality. There is now increasing evidence, however, that the depressive episode per se, while initiated as an attempt at adaptation, in response to environmental change, must be regarded as an index of failure and having maladaptive consequences.

Relations of Adaptation to an Etiological
Classification of Depression

These investigations have brought me back to one of the classic themes in modern clinical psychiatry—the relative roles of predisposition and of environmental events in the precipitation of the overt clinical depressive state. This is a problem that has confronted clinical psychiatry since the observations of Kraepelin on manic depressive disease (Kraepelin 1921), and the distinction between endogenous and reactive depression recently developed by Gillespie in the 1920's (Gillespie 1929). In recent years, there has been a renewed interest in the distinction between endogenous and reactive depression. This interest seems to be the result of two historical trends. First, the advent of effective antidepressant drugs has led to research on differential response to them. One of the major trends emerging from this research is that the characteristics of patients responding to tricyclic drugs is similar to the descriptions of endogenous depression developed in the 1920's (Kiloh & Garside 1964; Klerman 1971). The second trend is the awareness of the changing clinical pictures of depression, with the result that increasing proportions of depression patients are not hospitalized, are not held psychotic, and are younger (Rosenthal 1966).

The problem now arises of how to relate modern research techniques for assessing stress and personality to the concept of the endogenous-reactive depressive continuum, particularly since one of the crucial hypotheses is that a characteristic symptomatic syndrome will occur when there is no manifest stress involved in the events preceding the onset of depression. Thus, the classic formulation of the endogenous depressive complex contains within it an empirical hypothesis, namely that a certain symptom complex (insomnia, retardation, guilt, autonomous course) will be less likely associated with a recent precipitating event, whereas in the case of reactive patterns, the precipitating event will be manifest and readily reconstructed. Whatever objections one may have to the implied biological and constitutional causation implied in the term "endogenous," it is still necessary to review the empirical evidence as to whether or not these hypothesized correlations exist.

Following upon our research, in which we used the Holmes-Rahe schedule for quantifying recent life events, Paykel, Prusoff, and I undertook an analysis of symptom complexes of samples of depressives to ascertain whether different symptom features were associated with those clinical depressions of patients for whom recent life events were clearly identified in the months before the onset of acute symptoms (Paykel, et al. 1971). There are low correlations between recent life events and predicted symptoms. However, when factor analysis, a more powerful multivariate statistical technique is used, a clearer relationship emerges. A factor emerges that includes loadings from life events ratings as well as the symptoms usually regarded as endogenous—retardation, guilt, and insomnia—and ratings of severity of illness. There is a correlational relationship between the presence of stress, or more particularly the absence of manifest stress and certain clinical pictures. These findings confirm the earlier observations of Kiloh and Garside (Hamilton 1960; Mendels and Cochran 1968).

Before we can clearly identify a specific type, however, it is necessary to examine the nature of the distribution. In a number of different studies, attempts have been made to ascertain whether or not the distribution of patients on an endogenous-reactive continuum follows a normal distribution or whether there are distributions indicating separate groupings. The trend from four of five studies is negative in that there is no such bimodal distribution, which indicates the more likely existence of a continuum. We are thus faced with the conclusion that in the current state of empirical research, though a dimension of endogenous-reactive seems readily identifiable, separation into separate groups is not indicated.

Failures of Social Communicative Function Among Adult Depressives

The evidence reviewed thus far supports the view that the adult clinical depressive states are more than affects of depression. The depressive state as a syndrome is composed of a complex of symptoms, bodily dysfunctions, and multiple affects. Although some depressive states represent attempts to cope with loss and separation, most are initiated by environmental or intrapsychic challenges other than loss and separation.

I would now like to present data in further support of the thesis that the clinical states are maladaptive. The data will bear on the social communication function of depression. As reviewed, depressive affect in children and infants communicates the distress. In adults, this communication probably operates also for short affect states, especially grief and bereavement. When the depressive episode persists, however, negative social reactions occur. Most patients withdraw and their sullen, self-depreciating, and complaining interpersonal style no longer draws others to them for nurture, reassurance, and support. Rather, increasing irritation and withdrawal alternate with guilt and pity. The net result is maladaptive—withdrawal and detachment.

Another significant maladaptive consequence is the serious impairment of interpersonal relations experienced by the depressed person in relations with family members. In a recent series of studies with my colleagues in New Haven (Weissman, et al. 1971), techniques were developed for assessing the family dynamics and social adjustment of depressed women by measuring communication, sexual relations, child rearing functions, intimacy with spouse, and degrees of friction in various social contexts. A sample of 40 depressed women was compared on these parameters with a normal sample, matched for age, education, and social class. In almost every area of social adjustment and interpersonal relations, the depressed individual is seriously impaired. Communication is disrupted, friction is increased, and child-rearing functions are severely impaired, with the result that a relatively high proportion of the children of depressed women have difficulties in school and require emotional and psychiatric support. The impact of the depressed mother is felt particularly by the adolescent children. Weissman and collaborators have documented more evidence of acting out, drug addiction, and school difficulty in children of depressed women than in matched normals. Moreover, there is ample evidence of friction, hostility, and impaired communication between parent and child. Thus, whatever may have been the initiating force that the depressive episode set into motion, if allowed to continue for more than a couple of months it has maladaptive consequences, particularly in the affective relations of the depressed woman.

Theoretically, we have followed Parsons' distinction between instrumental and affective role (Parsons 1964), and have found that the depressed woman is far more impaired in her affective role relationships, particularly as a mother and as a spouse, than she is in her instrumental role relationships. It appeared that a moderate percentage of depressed women sought outside employment as a means of providing some gratification or self-esteem or sense of worth, and also often with a conscious desire to create distance between themselves and their loved ones, particularly their children. We often recognize that because of their depression, mood conflicts, and personality difficulties, they were experiencing difficulty in relating to their children. A job, therefore, provided a defensive mode of avoidance and withdrawal from conflictful relationships. In one of the major biological roles of the adult woman, namely mother and spouse, the depressed individual is severely handicapped and is involved in maladaptive patterns which generate a cycle of withdrawal, hostility, frustration, and impaired social performance.

CONCLUSIONS

What implications do these empirical findings have for an adaptational view of depression? As I noted earlier, the evidence supports the view that clinical states vary according to the balance between precipitating external stress and the vulnerability or predisposition of the individual. Even though environmental stress seems to play a role in the timing and precipitation of acute events, these events are not universal or specific to depression. It seems that the most significant factor accounting for the occurrence of depression is the predisposition or vulnerability of the individual. Thus, we have to investigate why certain individuals are able to cope with stressful events while other individuals fail in their coping efforts or even develop clinical symptoms in the absence of apparent life stresses. A number of alternative factors have been proposed to account for this vulnerability, including those familiar to the audience: genetically determined, hereditary predisposition, as postulated in the unipolar-bipolar concept of manic-depressive disease; early life experiences, predisposing the individual to sensitivity to loss and dependency, as proposed in the psychodynamic model; or more recent behaviorists' attempts to regard depression as failures of self-esteem, or feelings of helplessness or worthlessness, as presented in this conference.

Based upon these lines of investigation, my current view is that the adult depressive episode represents an attempt at adaptation that has failed. Perhaps best stated, depressions are maladaptive outcomes of partially successful attempts at adaptation. Though the depressive affect as a pure emotion may be part of human adaptation, especially in the infant, when dealing with adults we are most often seeing maladaptive attempts rather than attempts at adaptation. It is useful at this point to introduce a modification of the homeostasis concept put forth by Nobel laureate D. W. Richards (Richards, 1953) (Richards, 1960) which discusses the concept of homeostasis in physiology; the concept of homeostasis was conceived by Walter Cannon and based upon Claude Bernard's earlier concept of the internal milieu. Richards argues that in studying disease it is necessary to examine the failures of homeostasis as well as to investigate the mechanisms that maintain homeostasis. He proposed the concept of *hyperexes* to refer to those processes that disturb the organism's responses beyond its capacity to maintain homeostasis. Comparable concepts are overdue in theory about the psychodynamics and psychobiology of depression.

In conclusion, I regard the clinical adult depressive state as a composite of the various affects—depression, guilt, hostility, anxiety, and feelings of worthlessness and hopelessness. While the depressive mood itself may be the primary and predominant mood, it is by no means the only one. Various clinical states involve different combinations of these primary affects experienced thoughout human adaptation. We lack information as to what it is that perpetuates the affective mode beyond the period of adaptive value. It would thus appear that though the signal functions of affects may promote adaptation when prolonged and protracted, as in the case of clinical states, maladaptive or hyperexic responses are initiated and a negative feedback cycle is thereby perpetuated, further alienating the patient from social supports, impairing his effectiveness and his instrumental and affective roles, and hindering his biological homeostasis.

REFERENCES

Amdur, M. J., & Harrow, M. Conscience and depressive disorders. *British Journal of Psychiatry*, 1971, in press.

Beck, A. T. Cognition and psychopathology. In Beck, A. T. (Ed.); *Depression: Clinical, experimental and theoretical aspects.* New York: Harper and Row, 1967.

Beck, J. C., & Worthen, K. Precipitating stress, crisis theory and hospitalization in schizophrenia and depression. Unpublished manuscript, Cambridge Hospital and Harvard Medical School, 1971.

Bibring, E. Mechanism of depression. In Greenacre, P. (Ed.); *Affective Disorders.* New York: International Universities Press, 1953.

Bockoven, J. S. *Moral treatment in american psychiatry.* New York: Springer Publishing Co., 1963.

Bowlby, J. *Attachment.* New York: Basic Books, 1969.

Cannon, W. B. *The wisdom of the body.* New York: W. W. Norton, 1932.

Chodoff, P. The core problem in depression: Interpersonal aspects. *Science and Psychoanalysis*, 1970, Vol. 17, (U. S. A.), Grune and Stratton.

Clayton, P. J., & Desmarais, L., & Winokur, G. A study of normal bereavement. *American Journal of Psychiatry*, 1968, 125, 168-178.

Cohen, M. B., Baker, G., Cohen, R. A., et al. An intensive study of twelve cases of manic-depressive psychosis. *Psychiatry*, 1954, 17, 103-137.

Darwin, C. *The expression of the emotions in man and animals.* Chicago: University of Chicago Press, 1965.

Engel, G. L. *Psychological development in health and disease.* Philadelphia: W. B. Saunders, 1962.

Gershon, E. S., Cromer, M., & Klerman, G. L. Hostility and depression. *Psychiatry*, 1968, 31, 224-235.

Gillespie, R. D. The clinical differentiation of types of depression. *Guy's Hospital Report*, 1929, 2, 306-344.

Hamilton, M. A rating scale for depression. *Journal of Neurology, Neurosurgery, and Psychiatry*, 1960, 23, 56-62.

Harlow, H. F. Love in infant monkeys. *Scientific American*, 1959, 200, 68-74.

Harlow, H. F., Harlow, M. K., & Suomi, S. J. From thought to therapy: Lessons from a primate laboratory. *American Scientist*, 1971, 59, 538-549.

Harrow, M., & Amdur, M. J. Guilt and depressive disorders. *Archives of General Psychiatry*, 1971, 25, 240-246.

Harrow, M., Colburt, J., Detre, T., & Bakeman, R. Symptomatology and subjective experiences in current depressive states. *Archives of General Psychiatry*, 1966, 14, 203-212.

Hartmann, E. *Ego psychology and the problems of adaptation.* New York: International Universities Press, 1939 (Translated into English, 1958).

Hill, D. Depression: Disease reaction or posture. *American Journal of Psychiatry*, 1968, 125, 445-457.

Holmes, T. H., & Rahe, R. H. The social readjustment rating scale. *Journal of Psychosomatic Research*, 1967, 11, 213-218.

Katz, M. M. On the classification of depression: Normal, clinical, and ethnocultural variations. *Proceedings of a symposium*: In Fieve, R., (Ed.), Depression Excerpta Medica, 1970, in press.

Kaufman, I. C., & Rosenblum, L. A. The reaction to separation in infant monkeys. Anaclitic depression and conservation-withdrawal. *Psychosomatic Medicine*, 1967, 29, 648-675.

Kety, S., & Schildkraut, J. J. Biogenic amines and emotion. *Science*, 1967, 156, 21-30.

Kiloh, L. G., & Garside, R. F. Independence of neurotic depression and endogenous depression. *British Journal of Psychiatry*, 1964, 110, 53-55.

Klerman, G. L. Chemotherapy of depression. In (Ho, B. T. & McIsaac, W. M., Ed.), *Brain Chemistry and Mental Disease.* New York: Plenum Publishing Corp., 1971.

Klerman, G. L. Clinical research in depression. *Archives of General Psychiatry*, 1971, 24, 305-319.

Klerman, G. L. Pharmacological aspects of depression. Presented at the American Association for the Advancement of Science meeting, Chicago, December 27, 1970. To be published in proceedings of symposium.

Klerman, G. L., & Gershon, E. S. Imipramine effects upon hostility in depression. *Journal of Nervous and Mental Disease*, 1970, 150, 127-132.

Kraepelin, E. *Manic depressive insanity and paranoia.* Translated by Barclay, M., Edinburgh: E. and S. Livingston, 1921.

Lazarus, A. A., & Klerman, G. L. Hysteria and depression: The frequency and significance of hysterical personality features in hospitalized depressed women. *American Journal of Psychiatry*, 1968, 124, 48-56.

Lewis, A. J. Melancholia: Clinical survey of depressive states. *Journal of Mental Science*, 1934, 80, 277.

Mayer-Gross, W., Slater, E., & Roth, M. *Clinical Psychiatry*. Baltimore: Williams and Wilkins, 1968.

Mendels, J. & Cochran, C. The nosology of depression: The endogenous-reactive concept. *American Journal of Psychiatry*, 1968, 124, 1–11.

Menninger, K. *The vital balance*, New York: Viking Press, 1963.

Meyer, A. In Lief, A. (Ed.), *The commonsense psychiatry of Dr. Adolf Meyer*. New York: McGraw-Hill, 1948.

Myers, J. K., Lindenthal, J. J., & Pepper, M. P. Life crises, health status, and role performance. Delivered at the meeting of the American Psychiatric Association, Boston, May 1968.

Parsons, T. *Social structure and personality*. Springfield, Ill.: Free Press of Glencoe, 1964.

Paykel, E. S. Life events and acute depression. Presented at the American Association for the Advancement of Science meeting, Chicago, December 1970.

Paykel, E. S., Prusoff, B., & Klerman, G. L. The endogenous-neurotic dimension in depression: Rater independence and factor distributions. *Journal of Psychiatric Research*, 1971, 8, 73–90.

Plutchik, R. Emotions, evolution, and adaptive processes. *Feelings and Emotions*, New York: Academic Press, 1970.

Rado, S. The problem of melancholia. *International Journal of Psychoanalysis*, 1929, 9, 420–438.

Rappaport, D. Edward Bibring's theory of depression. In Gill, M. (Ed.), *Collected Papers of David Rappaport*. New York: Basic Books, 1967.

Richards, D. W. Homeostasis: its dislocations and perturbations. *Perspectives in Biology and Medicine*, 1960, 3, 238–251.

Richards, D. W. Homeostasis versus hyperexis: Or St. George and the dragon. *Scientific Monthly*, 1953, 77, 289.

Robins, E., & Guze, S. B. Classification of affective disorders: The primary-secondary, the endogenous-reactive, and the neurotic-psychotic concepts. In Williams, T. A., Katz, M. M., & Shield, J. A., Jr., (Ed.), *Recent advances in the psychobiology of the depressive illnesses, Proceedings of a workshop sponsored by NIMH*. Washington: D.C., Government Printing Office, 1972.

Robins, E., Munoz, R. A., Marten, S., & Gentry, K. A. *Primary and Secondary Affective Disorders: A classification for description, research, and management of mood disorders; preliminary report of 314 patients seen in an emergency room*. American Psychopathologic Association, 1971, proceedings in press.

Rosenthal, S. H. Changes in a population of hospitalized patients with affective disorders, 1945–1965. *American Journal of Psychiatry*, 1966, 123, 671–681.

Rosenthal, S. H., & Gudeman, J. E. The endogenous depressive pattern: An empirical investigation. *Archives of General Psychiatry*, 1967, 16, 241–244.

Scott, J. P. Separation in infant dogs: Emotional and motivational aspects. Presented at the American Association for the Advancement of Science meeting December 1970, Chicago. To be published in symposium proceedings.

Senay, E. C. A theory of depression: Summary and overview. Presented at the American Association for the Advancement of Science meeting, December 1970, Chicago. To be published in symposium proceedings.

Schmale, A. H. The role of depression in health and disease. Presented at the American Association for the Advancement of Science meeting, December 1970, Chicago. To be published in symposium proceedings.

Weissman, M. M., Klerman, G. L., & Paykel, E. S. Clinical assessment of hostility in depression. *American Journal of Psychiatry*, 1971, 128, 261–266.

Wilson, E. O. The prospects for a unified sociobiology. *American Scientist*, 1971, 59, 400–403.

DISCUSSION

Dr. Chodoff: Dr. Klerman, how have you defined "hostility-in" in your studies?

Dr. Klerman: "Hostility-in" is manifested for our purposes by self-depreciatory statements and other evidence of self-derogatory and self-condemning behavior.

Dr. Chodoff: I continue to experience difficulty with this concept of "hostility-in." There have been times when I have felt angry at myself and have even wanted to punish myself. There have been other times when I believed I was "no good" and really a terrible person. I assume we have all had such feelings to some extent. It does not seem to me that my being angry at myself is really the same as feeling that I am not a good person. I fail to see what evidence there is that these two states are related.

Dr. Klerman: Dr. Chodoff's remarks are well spoken. Ideally, in research, we would like to have available a measure that would differentiate between self-depreciation, or lowered self-esteem, and anger directed against the self. In our research, Gershon and I used the scales developed by Gottschalk and Glaser. Their justification for combining self-depreciation and hostility in the same scale was derived from their interpretation of psychoanalytic theory as holding that self-reproach is a derivative of unconscious anger against the self. A sounder methodology would be to separate these two variables and to test them to see if, in fact, they are related. I agree with Dr. Chodoff and hope that a similar study could be repeated utilizing a modification of the Gottschalk technique, or another technique that would allow the separation of these two constructs.

Dr. Beck: I have spent about ten years struggling with this same question, and I believe I have derived a satisfactory conclusion, at least one which satisfies me.

I think it is important to realize that we are dealing with a tautology when we consider Freud's formulation that self-criticism and low self-esteem are expressions of hostility turned in. If you agree with the Freudian notion, then, indeed, any time you have a scale which is made up of self-criticisms, by virtue of this tautology you have a "hostility-in" scale. By his definition, self-criticism is hostility turned inward, so there is no need to carry the matter further unless you disagree with his basic premise.

Early in my research career I assumed the task of proving Freud's formulation and I collected a series of dreams from depressed and nondepressed patients and analyzed their content. I demonstrated that depressed patients, by and large, portray themselves in their dreams in a very negative way. A typical depressed patient sees himself as a "born loser," as a person who has lost something of value, as I have detailed elsewhere (Chapter 1). This finding seemed to me to be a partial confirmation of Freud's hypothesis, because depressed patients did view themselves as frustrated, thwarted, deserted, rejected, and inept, all of which seemed to fit the "hostility-in" hypothesis to some degree, though, not fully.

Since I was not completely sanguine about the dream content analysis data, I attempted a verbal conditioning experiment. My reasoning was as follows: if the depressed person had a need to suffer (another translation of the "hostility-in" hypothesis), and were punished whenever he emitted certain responses, the punishment should increase the frequency of these responses. More precisely, my hypothesis was that for the depressed person, punishment should be a positive reinforcer.

However logical and persuasive this hypothesis may be, my research not only disconfirmed it but revealed the opposite, for I found that the depressed patient was extremely sensitive to any negative cue in his environment and would attempt to shun every such cue presented to him.

In a final attempt to test the anger-in hypothesis, I reasoned that if a depressed patient is so hostile toward himself, he really should be quite frustrated by success. I constructed an experimental situation in which depressed patients were given tasks to perform and were apprised of their achievements. However, I told them they were successful even when they were not and discovered, contrary to my expectations, that following a "success" depressed patients perform even better on subsequent tasks than do nondepressed patients. Depressed patients are actually "spurred on" by success. If a person is hostile toward himself, he should try and make himself fail, and success should be so cognitively dissonant that following a successful experience he should go to pieces and break down. I would like to emphasize again that among depressed people nothing succeeds like success.

The most parsimonious explanation for the data I have presented is that the depressed person's negative view of himself, evidenced by such statements as "I am no good" or "I am a flop and a loser," is simply the way he actually portrays himself and is not related to hostility.

Dr. Klerman: I would have to acknowledge that our main focus in this research was on the hostility-out variable. We did not pay much attention to the distinction which Dr. Beck raises between hostility directed against the self and a negative self-image. It would be worthwhile to undertake a research study again using some rating scale or other technique that separates these two aspects.

Both Dr. Chodoff and Dr. Beck present further evidence for a point of view which I find most congenial, the separation of hostility from depression. Similar ideas have been formulated by Bibring, who proposed that depression is linked to the issue of self-esteem and to feelings about one's self, independent of the vicissitudes of hostile drives, whether these drives are directed outwardly or against the self. Furthermore, it is more internally consistent to regard the affects of hostility and depression as separate.

Hostility, sadness, and anxiety are best treated as independent affects. To speak of one affect as being changed into the other represents alchemistic transformation and blurs important distinctions. Moreover, one misses opportunities to examine the contingencies under which one or another affect is predominant in one patient or another, and how the affects might relate to what is essentially a perceptual, cognitive variable—self-esteem. As I understand it, the thrust of both Dr. Chodoff's and Dr. Beck's criticisms is on our research design grouping a cognitive variable—self-esteem—with the drive variable—hostility. Since the emphasis of my argument was on breaking the linkage between hostility and depression, I would agree with Drs. Chodoff and Beck. I believe, however, that their criticism of our methodology further strengthens the conclusion that hostility and depression are separate affects.

Dr. Friedman: To ignore the rule of inwardly directed hostility seems to ignore also a large body of common-sense knowledge and clinical experience. Most lay people will acknowledge that they become sad, down, or depressed when they are unable to express anger or feelings of frustration. Dr. Klerman, would it be more parsimonious to say that hostility directed inward is not a relevant factor in the clinical state of depression, whereas it may be highly significant in the genesis of the depression affect?

Dr. Klerman: I do not propose that we ignore the role of hostility. I am stating two things. First, that hostility against the self is not theoretically necessary in developing a psychology of depression. Second, that in the psychotherapy it is not always necessary or even desirable to attempt to uncover hostility. Close examination of the interpersonal relations of the patient indicates that he is often involved in frustrating, irritating, and nonproductive relationships. In my view, anger or hostility is often there, but is a secondary complication of clinical state. I feel that rather than being primary, it is evoked as a response to frustration. Once initiated, it contributes to a negative cycle of interpersonal relations. It is far better to discover the frustrated wish and the maladaptive pattern of interpersonal relations than to abreact the hostility. Abreaction in itself is of limited therapeutic value.

Dr. Beck: Dr. Klerman has joined an illustrative circle of theoreticians who have also abandoned this particular Freudian hypothesis. Among the most prominent members of this group are Willard Gaylin, Edith Jacobson, Edward Bibring, and Mabel Blake Cohen. The analogy with alchemy is an elegant one which I will treasure for future use.

Dr. Seligman: Personally, and by virtue of my own work, I agree with Dr. Klerman and believe that depression and helplessness are maladaptive for the individual. Depression is an expression of the loss of or the failure of coping techniques. However, I believe we must proceed to ask the even harder question of how depression might be adaptive for the species. In other words, since this phenomenon is there, it might quite possibly have some adaptive significance for the species as a whole. There has been one argument advanced which I find interesting, particularly in the light of the Rochester group's data and some of the Holmes and Rahe findings, which indicate that loss which cannot be coped with produces an increased susceptibility to illness and even an increased incidence of death. Death most definitely removes an individual from the gene pool. Thus, those individuals who are "dumb" enough or unfortunate enough to encounter losses and traumas that they cannot deal with are removed from the gene pool.

Dr. Ekman: Since the highest rate for suicide is in the over 55 years old population, depression would seem of minimal adaptive significance, since the people who become depressed and either die or are ill have already passed their reproductive years and have left their genes behind them.

Dr. Friedman: I have had persistent difficulty with such broad generalizations about the adaptive significance of certain pathological states. Clearly there are cogent arguments on both sides of the issue, and I would like to ask Dr. Klerman if he might comment further about the nature of the maladaptive aspects of depression for the individual. Are we seeing a failure in coping or are we seeing a vulnerability in certain people or both?

Dr. Klerman: This question occurs repeatedly throughout the history of psychiatry. I have identified two main factors as explanations of why people fail to cope and become depressed. These two points of view are embodied in the endogenous-reactive distinction. The endogenous point of view proposes that the predisposition to depression is constitutionally determined, usually on a hereditary basis, and genetically transmitted. The endogenous viewpoint has been recently revived and modified into the new bipolar-unipolar distinction within manic-depressive disease. Support for the genetic view comes from the familial studies done by George Winokur of the St. Louis group (Winokur is now at Iowa), and by similar research groups in Switzerland and England. While I am skeptical about certain aspects of the bipolar-unipolar concept, it does represent an important distinction based upon those patients who have become manic at some point in their lives. There is no single genetic model, however, that fits the data from family studies. Moreover, the research thus far has demonstrated mainly familial association, and there is a big jump between demonstrating familial association and establishing a genetic mode of transmission for depression.

In contrast to the endogenous point of view, the reactive point of view has been most widely held in the United States and United Kingdom. It proposes that the personality constellation of the individual renders him relatively less effective in coping with stresses, such as loss. It is usually held that the determinants of these personality constellations stem from early childhood experiences. Dr. Chodoff, in his paper on the personality of depressives, indicated that this personality constellation usually involves excessive dependency, low self-esteem, and undue reliance on oral ambivalent interpersonal relationships. In the research in which I have been involved, we have demonstrated that there are two different groups, within each of which there are clear statistical correlations. There are indications that patients who experience manifest loss have more neurotic or reactive types of depressions. Those patients who report an absence of stress seem to be "more endogenous," and are characterized by increased retardation, greater sleep disturbance, and an increased likelihood of psychotic components.

The endogenous group seems to be comprised of better responders to tricyclic drugs, and prediction of drug response seems to correspond to the endogenous factor based on criteria of symptomatology and phenomenology. If one looks carefully at the characteristics of patients studied on metabolic research wards, he discovers that they are close to the endogenous type. It may be that some of the discrepancies in the research project reports result from sampling of different groups within the heterogenous "gamisch" called clinical depression.

Perhaps Dr. Raskin can comment on the endogenous factors as predictors of drug response from his research in the NIH drug trials.

Dr. Raskin: In our research, we are still trying to decide just what endogenous is. There appear to be two primary determinants of the endogenous clinical picture. The first is a severity-of-illness dimension which includes items such as depression, guilt, cognitive disturbances, and a global rating. The second endogenous factor is the age dimension. Statistically, we can compress these two dimensions into one bipolar factor—a composite of age and severity of illness. Using this one factor in an inverse factor analysis, the following four depressive subgroups emerge: (1) old, severely ill people who in typical clinical parlance are referred to as "endogenous," and who are usually psychotic and likely to respond to antidepressants; (2) old, moderately ill people who are nagging and hypochondriacal; (3) young, severely ill depressed schizophrenic patients; and (4) young, moderately ill individuals who are primarily neurotic.

My general conclusion is that while it is meaningful to talk about age and severity of illness (and these factors lend themselves to research manipulation), the traditional endogenous-reactive (neurotic) dichotomy, because of its surplus meaning, has limited research value.

Dr. Goodwin: I would like to expand upon Dr. Raskin's point that a continuum based on age and severity may more clearly fit clinical data than does the old reactive endogenous distinction. One aspect of the reactive endogenous distinction centers on the presence or absence of precipitating events. The theory holds that reactive depressions have precipitating events whereas endogenous depressions do not. Some research done at NIH by Dr. William Bunney and others raises questions about the absence of precipitating events in endogenous depression. They studied a group of very sick "endogenous" depressed patients who were hospitalized at NIH and compared them with a group of neurotically depressed patients who were fairly sick (at least enough to be hospitalized), but who did not have the so-called endogenous pattern. They were unable to discover any difference in either the frequency or the type of precipitating events between these two groups, and they found a large number of precipitating events in both groups.

At NIH we generally kept patients for a minimum of 4 months and often for 6 or 8 months, depending on the nature of the study being undertaken and the requirements of the patient. Within the endogenous group, precipitating events were often uncovered only by longitudinal interviews, and it occasionally took as long as 2 or 3 months to unearth the precipitant in some of the more severely endogenously depressed people. Traditionally, the British have strongly supported the reactive-endogenous dichotomy, perhaps because the definition of the reactive group was based on outpatients in psychotherapy. Due to the stability of the outpatient clinic, they were able to gather a considerable number of psychological longitudinal data. On the other hand, the endogenous group was drawn from patients admitted to hospitals. There patients were predominantly treated with ECT and the maximum number of interviews was only three. Now if the NIH research team had stopped at three interviews, they would have found the same thing the British did, namely, that less severely depressed people had more precipitants, and that more severely depressed patients seemed to become depressed "out of the blue." The NIH team went on, however, and interviewed all patients longitudinally, talked to their families, and collected data from every conceivable source. In the final analysis, the supposedly endogenous group had as many precipitants as did the reactive group.

Dr. Chodoff: Are these events gross and obvious or are they more subtle?

Dr. Goodwin: I'm not sure I can definitively answer that since there were certainly subtle losses of self-esteem which it took many months to map out completely, though, on the other hand, there were a number of rather gross events that were clearly very distinct and that were not unearthed until after months of intensive psychotherapy. For example, one woman had a stillbirth four months before admission. Mention of the subject was taboo within her family, so that the issue did not come up until she had been in treatment for many months. She was so retarded when she was admitted that no one could ever have found out about her stillbirth. There were a number of similar instances in the study where rather gross events did not emerge until the patient began to recover from the severe retardation.

Dr. Ekman: I would like to ask Dr. Klerman about the failure of the signal functions of depression. Does the clinical state of depression represent the failure of all four signal functions or can it arise from the failure of just one?

Dr. Klerman: It is unclear whether the clinical state of depression represents the failure of all four signal functions, or can arise from the failure of just one. It may well be that there are alternative pathways in pathogenesis.

The primary data I have presented here concern the social role or communication function of depression. Among the women we studied, depression was clearly maladaptive as a social communication signal. We observed that the depressed woman is often impaired in mothering. Instead of communicating to her children and her spouse the message "please come closer," she often drives them away.

A second signal function of depression which has been studied widely is that of intrapsychic defense. Dr. Schmale's work presents observations concerning the breakdown of defenses, which he has interpreted from a psychoanalytic point of view as being partially maladaptive.

In regard to the other signal functions of depression, considerable work is being done on neurophysiology and neurochemistry. Today, norepinephrine is implicated as the possible neurotransmitter in the central nervous system that mediates the affect of depression.

The subjective signals of lowered self-esteem and feelings of helplessness are currently under investigation at many centers using social psychological techniques. Dr. Beck himself has done considerable work on this aspect of depression and indicates ways in which the depressed person misperceives his own performance and fails adequately to judge his performance relative to his aspirations and other standards.

Dr. Ekman: We have completed some pilot work in which we tried to examine the ways in which people respond to witnessing distress or suffering in others. We find that there is a division between empathic responses in which fear, pain, anger, and sadness are seen on the face of the viewer versus a nonempathic response to the suffering person in which disgust is noted on the viewer's face. We are beginning to wonder whether there are different ways of evidencing distress, so that certain people who are suffering may elicit in those about them a more empathic response whereas others when suffering may promote a disgust reaction. One hypothesis which stems from this work is that depressed people have a defect in their ability to display sadness as an effective social communicative affect. Instead they ultimately elicit a disgust reaction.

Dr. Klerman: Such observations are consistent with my point of view. In the normal situation, sadness brings forth sympathy and serves a highly effective function in social communication by bringing people closer to the sad individual. In contrast, the clinically depressed person has the opposite effect on those around him. Somehow, instead of communicating, "I want you to come closer," he elicits a negative response through his tone of voice, posture, or facial expression, and people withdraw and further isolate him. This only increases the depressed person's anxiety, and he correspondingly increases his demanding behavior, which further aggravates the negative social reaction.

Dr. Katz: What are the main areas of research that a signal function theory for depression suggests?

Dr. Klerman: Within each of the four signal functions of depression, areas of research are underway. Many people, such as Dr. Ekman, are studying nonverbal aspects of communication or voice patterns. One can also look for content analysis of dreams, as has been done by Beck and others. Neurophysiological and neuropharmacological researchers are attempting to discover the possible role of catecholamines in mediating the CNS processes of affect. The concept of coping and adaptation leads to the design of prospective studies that follow individuals exposed to various kinds of stresses or loss to determine the characteristics both of those individuals who succeed in adapting by coping, and of those who develop clinical symptoms.

Dr. Schuyler: What are the treatment implications of the signal affect theory of depression which you propose? If we accept that hostility turned against the self is not critical in depression, what therapeutic implications are posed?

Dr. Klerman: One consequence of the signal theory of depression is to reject the theory of alchemy, which holds that depression is "nothing but hostility turned against the self." This oversimplification of the relationship between hostility and depression has led many therapists to attempt to prod or stimulate their patients into angry hostile expressions towards their loved ones. This only leads to increased guilt, confusion, and feelings of frustration. A signal theory holds that depression is a communication to the individual that he is in a situation in which he feels helpless and unable to cope. Usually it is in response to a disruption of an important relationship. The signal should alert him to the need of realigning his interpersonal relations and reviewing his sources of satisfaction.

Dr. Tabachnick: Dr. Klerman, how do you differentiate between states of sadness in which there is depression but only the affect of depression and the clinical state of depression, which you claim is a more complex issue?

Dr. Klerman: My criteria for distinguishing between sadness and clinical depression are based on the concept that in the clinical state, there is a mosaic or composite of affects, bodily disturbances, and cognitive disturbances. I do not believe there is a sharp demarcation between the clinical state of depression and the everyday normal state of sadness; these two states form poles of a continuum. It is unclear how much overlapping exists between these two ends of the continuum; or, more precisely, how many cases would be clustered in the center of this continuum. Perhaps there would be a multimodal distribution. I do not think that we have adequate instruments as yet for differentiating normal states of sadness from the more complex clinical states of depression, but this is an area that merits further research. We have developed various criteria based on intensity, duration, and quality, but these have not yet been operationalized into quantitative techniques.

Dr. Martin Katz has recently reported findings indicating that in comparing a normal population to a clinically diagnosed population, there was as much depressed affect in the normal population as in the clinically diagnosed one. It was not affective level that distinguished the patient population from the normals, but rather the presence of somatic symptoms, cognitive problems, and impaired social functioning in the clinical group. I think we still have a great deal of research to undertake concerning the differentiation of normal states from psychopathological states.

Dr. Chodoff: Dr. Klerman, are you not going back to the position that Freud took in *Mourning and Melancholia*, in which in a sense he distinguished between depression as an affect and depression as a clinical state?

Dr. Klerman: Dr. Chodoff is correct; on the descriptive level there is a similarity to the point of view Freud first enunciated. The criteria Freud used to make the distinction between mourning and melancholia do not hold up under empirical research, however. For example, he postulated that the presence of guilt was characteristic of melancholia, and furthermore that melancholic patients were unaware of what they had lost. These criteria do not holdup in clinical research. Recent studies indicate, for instance, that a significant percentage of depressed people do not experience guilty feelings.

Dr. Friedman: Dr. Klerman, in addition to the two categories of depression you delineate—namely, depression that refers to everyday sadness and perhaps grief on the one hand, and the clinical state of depression on the other—I wonder if you would comment on the concept of the "depressive personality." I refer to a growing body of literature by such authors as Walter Bonime, Jules Bemporad, Kurt Adler, and Silvano Arieti purporting that there exists a group of people who are in and out of depressions and who use their depression to manipulate others. This category is different from Dr. Chodoff's distinction of the premorbid personality, for I am referring to an ongoing characterlogical state called the "depressive personality."

Dr. Klerman: As I read the literature about the depressive character, I noticed some ambiguity. In some papers the term depression is used to refer to the premorbid personality of individuals who are prone to depression. Dr. Chodoff's paper (Chapter 3) identifies many of these characteristics. The other use of "depressive character" refers to persistent personality types who seem to utilize their depression as an ongoing way of life. This use of the term merits further discussion. The distinction is often made between symptom and character. Symptoms are usually ego-alien and discontinuous, whereas character is continuous and ego-syntonic. My own view is that the so-called depressive character represents chronic depressions in whom the persistent symptoms have become part of their way of life. These individuals usually have persistent bodily complaints, feelings of low self-esteem, demanding and manipulative styles of interpersonal relations, and passive and dependent relationships. I believe they have developed a chronic state of depression which is not severe enough to require hospitalization, and which is only partially responsive to treatment. Depression has come to dominate their existence and has been molded into a persistent life style. These people often fluctuate on the borderline between normality and mild chronic depressions, and they represent a condition analogous to the borderline state of schizophrenia. Thus, the depressive character is to clinical depression as the borderline state is to schizophrenia.

I have some doubt whether there is any one single personality type predisposing to depression. My viewpoint is similar to Bibring's, who stresses that the predisposition to depression is almost universal, and that the personality type colors the clinical picture and perhaps determines the type of stress to which the individual will respond.

Dr. Friedman: The "depressive personality" is a term used to describe a person whose character structure is designed to ward off intense depression. In a sense, this character structure is adaptive (as are neurotic compromises), for without it the person would experience greater pain. Is this use of the concept of adaptation compatible with your own?

Dr. Klerman: My concept of adaptation is derived primarily from the Darwinian view, and also from the ideas of Hartmann and other ego-psychologists. The criteria for successful adaptation are ultimately biological; and include whatever promotes the survival of the species and the individual. The ego-psychology level of adaptation means the capacity to meet the demands of the "average expectable environment." Part of the difficulty with the concept of adaptation when it is discussed with psychodynamic data is that many investigators contend that the symptom formation of depression represents a compromise in an attempt at internal equilibrium. I think this is a useful way to look at the intrapsychic process in symptom formation, but to call this adaptiveness blurs the historical meaning this term has come to possess in both biology and ego-psychology. The depressive personality or depressive character who has developed a life style of "warding off" or defending against depressive feelings by certain ways of relating to people has established a certain equilibrium. Yet, I do not think this is adaptive since the person pays a "price" for this innerstate of balance. The price he pays is of impaired social relations and limited capacity to meet his own potential. Thus it leaves a distinction between the intrapsychic equilibrium and the external adjustment. The classic meaning of adaptation refers to the relationship of the organism to his external environment.

Dr. Schuyler: Dr. Klerman, would you consider any clinical state, e.g., schizophrenia or neurosis to be adaptive? Ronald Laing argues for an adaptive model of schizophrenia which holds that the schizophrenic process is the *only* solution available. Based on duration, can you determine whether a depressive response is adaptive, much as we do with grief, which is considered abnormal after a certain number of weeks?

Dr. Klerman: Once again, we come to the concept of adaptation. I cannot accept Laing's thesis that schizophrenia represents an adaptive solution to a problem. Schizophrenics withdraw and this withdrawal may be regarded as a solution to a problem, but in my opinion it is a maladaptive solution. The individual withdraws to maintain some inner equilibrium, but does so at the expense of normal, expected social role performance.

The criteria for adaptation, I repeat, are derived from the concepts of Hartmann and Darwin. In ego-psychology terms explicated by Hartmann, the ultimate criterion is response to the socially expected average environment. Grief is a good example. Almost all societies have a timetable for grief responses. If this timetable is prolonged, or if the intensity or quality goes beyond certain accepted criteria, the grief is considered abnormal and usually represents maladaptation.

BIBLIOGRAPHY

Amdur, M. J., & Harrow, M. Conscience and depressive disorders. *British Journal of Psychiatry*, 1971, in press.

Bibring, E. Mechanism of depression. In Greenacre, P. (Ed.), *Affective Disorders*. New York: International Universities Press, 1953.

Darwin, C. *The expression of the emotions in man and animals*. Chicago: University of Chicago Press, 1965.

Hartmann, E. *Ego psychology and the problem of adaptation*. New York: International Universities Press, 1939 (Translated into English, 1958).

Holmes, T. H., & Rahe, R. H. The social readjustment rating scale. *Journal of Psychosomatic research*, 1967, 11, 213–218.

Katz, M. M. The classification of depression: Normal, clinical, and ethnocultural variations. In Fieve, R. R. (Ed.), *Depression in the 70's*, Amsterdam: Excerpta Medica, 1971.

Klerman, G. L., & Gershon, E. S. Imipramine effects upon hostility in depression. *Journal of Nervous and Mental Disease*, 1970, 150, 127–132.

Leff, M. J., Roatch, J. F., & Bunney, W. E., Jr. Environmental factors preceeding the onset of severe depressions. *Psychiatry*, 1970, 33, 293–311.

Raskin, A., Schulterbrandt, J. G., Boothe, H., Reatig, N., & McKeon, J. J. Some suggestions for selecting appropriate depression subgroups for biochemical studies. In Williams, T. A., Katz, M. M., & Shield, J. A., Jr., (Eds.), *Recent advances in the psychobiology of the depressive illnesses*. Washington, D.C.: U. S. Government Printing Office, 1972.

Schmale, A. H. *The role of depression in health and disease*. Presented at an AAAS Symposium, December 1970. To be published in proceedings and to be edited by Senay, E., & Scott, J. P.

Winokur, G., & Clayton, P. J. Family history studies. 1. Two types of affective disorders separated according to genetic and clinical factors. In Wortis, J. (Ed.), *Recent advances in biological psychiatry*, Vol. 9, New York: 1967.

6

A BEHAVIORAL APPROACH TO DEPRESSION[1,2]

Peter M. Lewinsohn
University of Oregon

The purpose of this paper is threefold: (1) to explicate the major theoretical assumptions and premises that have been guiding the design of our research; (2) to present our empirical findings, which are consistent with these assumptions; and (3) to describe studies now in progress that are designed to test hypotheses about the relationship between positive reinforcement and depression. Intervention strategies that have been found useful for the treatment of depressed individuals within a behavioral framework have been presented elsewhere (Lewinsohn, Shaffer, & Libet 1969; Lewinsohn, Weinstein, & Shaw 1969; Lewinsohn & Atwood 1969; Lewinsohn & Shaw 1969; Lewinsohn, Weinstein, & Alper 1970; Lewinsohn & Shaffer 1971; Johannson, Lewinsohn, & Flippo 1969).

Operational Definition of Depression and a Methodological Point

We use the term "depression" to refer to the syndrome of behaviors that have been identified in descriptive studies of depressed individuals (e.g., Grinker, et al., 1961). It includes verbal statements of dysphoria, self-depreciation, guilt, material burden, social isolation, somatic complaints, and a reduced rate of many behaviors. We assume depression to be a continuous variable which can be conceptualized as a "state" which fluctuates over time as well as a "trait" (some

[1] This investigation was supported in part by research grants from the National Institute of Mental Health (MH 17725 & 19784).

[2] The author gratefully acknowledges the helpful suggestions he received from Richard Diller and Douglas MacPhillamy in writing this paper.

157

people are more prone to becoming depressed than others). Being depressed does not exclude other psychopathological conditions such as schizophrenia, psychosis, sexual deviation, or alcoholism. For research purposes a patient (subject) is defined as "depressed" if he meets certain experimental criteria (e.g., Lewinsohn & Libet 1972) based on selected MMPI scales and on the interview factors identified by Grinker (1961).

It would seem important that any study relying on differences between depressed and nondepressed *groups* for its conclusions have a normal control as well as a "psychiatric control" group (i.e. patients for whom anxiety or other neurotic symptoms but not depression constitute the major psychopathology) if any observed group differences are to be attributed to depression (depressed $\neq$ psychiatric control, normal) and not to the deviation hypothesis (depressed, psychiatric control $\neq$ normal control).

The Major Assumptions of the Behavioral Theory of Depression

We make the following three assumptions: (1) A low rate of response-contingent positive reinforcement (resconposre) acts as an eliciting (unconditioned) stimulus for some depressive behaviors, such as feelings of dysphoria, fatigue, and other somatic symptoms. (2) A low rate of resconposre constitutes a sufficient explanation for other parts of the depressive syndrome such as the low rate of behavior. For the latter the depressed person is considered to be on a prolonged extinction schedule. (3) The total amount of resconposre received by an individual is presumed to be a function of three sets of variables: (a) The number of events (including activities) that are potentially reinforcing (PotRe) for the individual. PotRe is assumed to be a variable subject to individual differences, influenced by biological (e.g., sex and age) and experiential variables. (b) The number of potentially reinforcing events that can be provided by the environment, i.e., the availability of reinforcement in the environment (AvaiRe). (c) The instrumental behavior of the individual, i.e., the extent to which he possesses the skills and emits those behaviors that will elicit reinforcement for him from his environment.

A schematic representation of the theory is shown in Figure 1.

The behavioral theory requires that (a) the total amount of resconposre received by depressed persons be less than that received by nondepressed persons, and similarly, it will be less when the individual is depressed than when he is not depressed; (b) the onset of depression be accompanied by a reduction in resconposre; (c) intensity of depression covary with rate of resconposre; and (d) improvement be accompanied by an increase in resconposre. Before proceeding to an examination of relevant empirical studies several additional clarifications and hypotheses are offered.

First, even were such predictions affirmed, further data would be needed to ascertain whether the differences between depressed and non-depressed individuals in regard to resconposre are due to: (a) differences in the number and

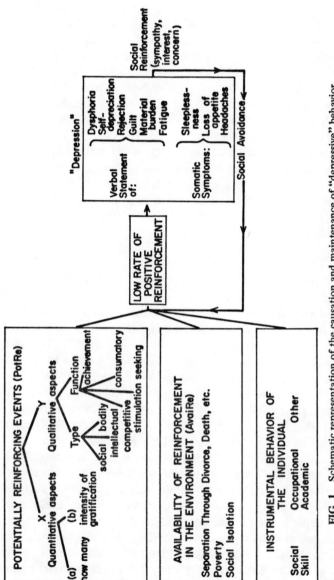

FIG. 1. Schematic representation of the causation and maintenance of "depressive" behavior.

kinds of activities and events which are potentially reinforcing (PotRe); (b) and/or the possibility that depressed individuals may be more likely to be in situations which lack reinforcement for them (AvaiRe); (c) and/or differences between depressed and non-depressed individuals in those skills which are necessary to obtain reinforcement from one's environment.

Second, the degree to which the individual's behavior is maintained (followed) by reinforcement is assumed to be the critical antecedent condition for the occurrence of depression, rather than the total amount of reinforcement received. It is a well-known clinical fact that "giving" (i.e., noncontingently) to depressed individuals does not decrease their depression. We assume that the occurrence of behavior followed by positive reinforcement is vital if depression is to be avoided. We predict depression when the probability is low that the individual's behavior will be followed by reinforcement, and also when the probability is high that the individual will be "reinforced" when he does not emit the behavior (e.g., the retired person receiving his paycheck regardless of what he does). Under both conditions the probability of the individual emitting behavior is reduced.

Behavioral View of Other Aspects of Depression

1. *Low self-esteem, pessimism, feelings of guilt, and other related phenomena.* These cognitive changes are commonly observed in depressed individuals, even though the specific manifestations vary considerably from individual to individual. Thus there are depressed patients who do not have low self-esteem and there are many who lack feelings of guilt. Theorists such as Aaron T. Beck (1967) assign primary causal significance to these cognitive changes. A behavioral theory assumes these to be secondary elaborations of the feeling of dysphoria, which in turn is presumed to be the consequence of a low rate of resconposre. The first thing that happens when an individual becomes depressed is that he is experiencing an unpleasant feeling state (dysphoria). He *is* feeling bad. This feeling state is difficult for the individual to label and a number of alternative "explanations" are available to him including, "I am sick" (somatic symptoms), "I am weak or otherwise inadequate" (low self-esteem), "I am bad" (feelings of guilt), or "I am not likable" (feelings of social isolation). The research of Stanley Schachter (Schachter & Singer 1962) may contain important implications for this aspect of the behavior of depressed individuals and for treatment as well (cognitive relabeling). If the depressed individual can be helped to relabel his emotion (e.g., "I am worthless" into "I am feeling bad because I am lacking something that is important to my welfare"), he may be in a much better position to do something about his predicament.

2. *Relationship between hostility and depression.* The role of hostility which is so central to psychodynamically-oriented theories of depression (i.e., depression is caused by internalized hostility) is hypothesized to be secondary to the low rate of resconposre. In a manner analogous to the way in which aggressive behavior is elicited by an aversive stimulus in Azrin's (1966) studies, aggressive

behavior may be assumed to be elicited by a low rate of resconposre in the depressed individual. When these aggressive responses are expressed, they serve to alienate other people and therefore contribute even further to the social isolation of the depressed individual. He therefore learns to avoid expressing hostile tendencies by suppressing (or repressing) them.

3. *Role of precipitating factors in occurrence of depression.*   In a substantial number of depressed patients, the depression can be shown to have begun after certain environmental events (e.g., Paykel, et al. 1969). Many of these events involve a serious reduction of positive reinforcement in that the event deprives the individual of an important source of reinforcement (e.g., death of spouse) or of an important set of skills (e.g., spinal cord injuries or brain disease). The relationship between the occurrence of such events and depression is consistent with the behavioral theory of depression. There are, however, also instances of depression following "success" experiences (e.g., promotions or professional success). It is also not at all uncommon for an individual to become depressed following the attainment of some important and long-sought goal (e.g., award of Ph.D. degree). The existence of such precipitating factors would seem at first glance to contradict the notion of a relation between a reduction in positive reinforcement and depression. Two considerations would seem relevant: (a) That the individual is judged to be a "success" by external criteria (e.g., is promoted), does not necessarily mean that the number of potentially reinforcing events available to him has increased. Thus, for example, a promotion may *actually* involve a serious reduction in the amount of social reinforcement obtained by the individual. (b) The behavioral theory would predict depression for an individual who attains a goal for which he has worked long and hard *if* the reward (e.g., award of degree) turns out to be a weak reinforcer for him. In that case he has worked hard for little; i.e., his rate of resconposre is low.

EMPIRICAL FINDINGS CONSISTENT WITH THE THEORY AND STUDIES IN PROGRESS

Relationship Between Rate of Positive Reinforcement and Depression

A critical test of the major hypothesis requires a two-step strategy. (1) One must first functionally identify events that act as reinforcement for individuals who may be characterized as either depressed, psychiatric controls, or normal controls, and (2) one must then compute the rate of response contingent reinforcement for these subjects. Holding activity level constant, the theory predicts a lower rate of reinforcement for the depressed individuals. This crucial test has not so far been performed, but a study now in progress with Julian Libet based on home observation and group interaction data will do just that.

Another prediction derived from the theory will be tested in a study being conducted by Douglas MacPhillamy and the author which will compare the total amount of positive reinforcement received by depressed and nondepressed subjects. The operational measure of "total amount of positive reinforcement obtained" for this study will be represented by the sum of the products of the intensity and frequency ratings for each of the 320 items of the Pleasant Events Schedule (MacPhillamy & Lewinsohn 1971). (The Pleasant Events Schedule consists of 320 events and activities which were generated after a very extensive search of the universe of "Pleasant Events." The Ss are asked to rate each item in the schedule on a three-point scale of pleasantness and again on a three-point scale of frequency of occurrence.)

To date the results of several studies are consistent with the major tenet of the behavioral theory of depression, i.e., that there is an association between rate of positive reinforcement and intensity of depression. First, depressed individuals elicit fewer behaviors from other people than control subjects (Shaffer & Lewinsohn 1971; Libet & Lewinsohn 1973). Assuming that it is reinforcing to be the object of attention and interest, this finding suggests that depressed persons receive less social reinforcement. The studies forming the basis for this conclusion are discussed in greater detail below. There is also a significant association between mood and number of "pleasant" activities engaged in (Lewinsohn & Libet 1972).

Three groups of ten subjects (depressed, psychiatric controls, and normal controls) were used. Subjects rated their mood on the Depression Adjective Check List (Lubin 1965) and also indicated the number of "pleasant" activities engaged in each day on a check list over a period of 30 days. The correlation between the mood ratings and the activity scores was computed separately for each subject. The null hypothesis of no association between mood and pleasant activities was strongly rejected ($t = 9.3$, $df = 29$, $p < .001$). There were large individual differences with respect to the magnitude of the correlations between mood and activity, the highest correlation being $-.66$. For 10 of the 30 subjects, however, the correlation was not significantly different from 0. Future research might address itself to the hypothesis that there are important individual difference variables moderating the relationship between mood and activity.

Depressed individuals have a significantly larger number of events associated with their mood (Lewinsohn & Libet 1972). The number of activities negatively correlated (at the .05 level of statistical significance) with mood ratings was counted for each subject. The depressed group had a significantly larger number of mood-related activities than the psychiatric and normal control groups ($F = 7.67$, $df = 2/24$, $p < .05$). Also, the correlation between depression level (as measured by the MMPI D scale) and the number of "related" activities was computed across all subjects ($N = 30$), and was found to be statistically significant at the .01 level ($r = .46$). The finding suggests a greater vulnerability of depressed individuals to the vicissitudes of everyday experiences, a notion that has been central to a great deal of previous theorizing (Fenichel 1945).

Many of the individual activities that are correlated with mood across subjects involve social reinforcement (Lewinsohn & Libet 1972).

The number of subjects for whom each activity was significantly associated with mood was also tabulated. Those items that correlated with mood for four or more subjects are listed in Table 1.

An important qualitative aspect of this list appears to be that many of them involve social interactions.

TABLE 1

Rank Order List of Items Correlating More Than .30 with
DACL Mood Ratings for at Least Four Persons
(From Lewinsohn & Libet 1972)

Items	No. of Ss out of 30
Being with happy people	12
Being relaxed	10
Having spare time	9
Laughing	8
Having people show interest in what you have said	8
Looking at the sky or clouds	7
Saying something clearly	6
Talking about philosophy or religion	6
Meeting someone new (opposite sex)	6
Watching attractive girls or men	6
Reading stories or novels	5
Taking a walk	5
Seeing beautiful scenery	5
Sleeping soundly at night	5
Amusing people	5
Having coffee or a coke with friends	5
Having someone agree with you	4
Petting	4
Being with someone you love	4
Traveling	4
Breathing clean air	4
Having a frank and open conversation	4
Having sexual relations with a partner of the opposite sex	4
Watching people	4

Relation Between PotRe and Depression

Our general hypothesis is that there are qualitative and quantitative differences between depressed and nondepressed groups in regard to the number and kinds of potentially reinforcing events.

Any attempt to study positive reinforcement with human subjects (e.g., determination of the amount of positive reinforcement received by the individual or identification of what are potentially reinforcing events for him) is handicapped by the fact that there is no psychometrically sound instrument for the assessment of responses to potentially reinforcing events. Direct observation of behavior is very expensive and often practically impossible. The closest equivalent, the Reinforcement Survey Schedule (Cautella & Kastenbaum 1967), was primarily designed to assess the valence of reinforcers potentially available for clinical or laboratory manipulation rather than to provide a systematic survey of the events potentially reinforcing for a given individual. The Pleasant Events Schedule (MacPhillamy & Lewinsohn 1971) was constructed to provide quantitative and qualitative information about what is potentially reinforcing for a given individual. Normative data about the instrument and its psychometric properties and dimensional structure are presented elsewhere (MacPhillamy & Lewinsohn 1971).

The design of a study now under way (MacPhillamy & Lewinsohn) is outlined in Table 2. The general expectation is that depressed and nondepressed groups, and the three age groups, can be discriminated by the number and kind of items rated as pleasant, as well as by the frequency with which the person engages in those activities.

In addition to being interested in possible differences between depressed and nondepressed groups as to potentially positively reinforcing events, we have also

TABLE 2

General Design of Study of Relationship of PotRe
with Depression and with Age

Group		Depressed		Nondepressed Psychiatric	Normal Controls
Age	Sex	Endogenous	Reactive		
20-39	M				
	F				
40-59	M				
	F				
60-79	M				
	F				

been interested in collecting data about the hypothesis that depressed individuals are more sensitive to aversive stimuli (i.e., negative reinforcers) than non-depressed subjects.[3] Since most "real-life" situations contain both positive (approach) and negative (avoidance) components, confirmation of the hypothesis would predict greater avoidance by the depressed individual in many situations. The short-term consequence would be greater isolation and the long-term consequence of less skill acquisition for the depressed individual.

Stewart, in a study conducted in our laboratory (Stewart 1969), hypothesized that "the behavior of depressed subjects is more influenced by the quality (positive or negative) of social reinforcement elicited than is the behavior of nondepressed subjects" (p. 2). Stewart found that depressed individuals generally had a longer latency of response (operationally defined as the amount of time between the reaction by another person to the subject's verbalization and a subsequent action by that subject in a group situation). The largest differences between depressed and nondepressed subjects were associated with the occurrence of a negative social reaction (e.g., being ignored, criticized, disagreed with).

We have since tried to expand the hypothesis to the autonomic level. Specifically, a study was conducted (Lewinsohn, Lobitz, & Wilson 1973) to test the following predictions:

H-1: Aversive stimuli elicit a greater autonomic response in depressed subjects.

H-2: Aversive stimuli elicit a greater autonomic anticipatory response in depressed subjects.

H-3: Return to base level following an aversive stimulus is less complete in depressed subjects.

H-4: The autonomic responses of depressed subjects shows less habituation over repeated trials.

The hypotheses about the autonomic reactivity of depressed persons postulate a reaction pattern opposite to that described by Hare (1965) for the psychopath. Psychopaths and depressed individuals are conceptualized as being located at opposite ends of an autonomic response continuum; one is thought to be overresponsive, whereas the other is considered underresponsive to aversive stimuli.

The experimental subjects were classified, using the previously described two-stage selection procedure, into three groups: depressed (D), psychiatric controls (PC), and normal controls (NC). Twelve D, 12 PC, and 12 NC Ss were used, there being an equal number of males and females in each group.

Data were collected during one experimental session which lasted approximately 45 minutes, with the S seated in a comfortable chair. The procedure consisted of the following eight standardized steps: (1) The Depression Adjective Check List (DACL) (Lubin 1965) was administered. (2) The GSR

[3] While this hypothesis is not "discoverable" from the major assumptions of the theory as stated earlier, its affirmation would be consistent with them.

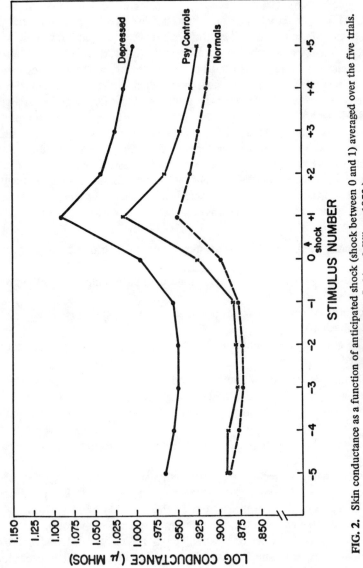

FIG. 2. Skin conductance as a function of anticipated shock (shock between 0 and 1) averaged over the five trials. (From Lewinsohn, Lobitz, & Wilson 1973.)

electrodes were attached. (3) Partially to allow time for hydration, the *S*s were administered the Subjective Interpretation of Reinforcement Scale (Stewart 1968). The statements from the Subjective Interpretation of Reinforcement Scale had been tape-recorded, and the *S*s were asked to rate their reaction to each one on an 11-point scale with +5 indicating the most pleasant and −5 indicating the most negative reaction. (4) The *S*'s threshold for electric shock delivered to the finger was determined. The intensity of the shock was controlled by *E* by a calibrated dial which had 10 positions. The Method of Ascending Limits was used to determine each *S*'s threshold. (5) The shock level for the *S* was set at one arbitrary unit above the threshold. The shock apparatus delivered a shock of short duration (approximately 2 msec.) with a spike of approximately 500 volts. Shock was delivered by means of electrodes attached to the index and ring fingers. (6) The *S*s on this and all subsequent shock administrations rated their reactions on an 11-point scale. The mean shock level and the mean subjective shock ratings for the three groups were comparable. (7) In the next phase the *S* was told that *E* would be counting along with an automatic print-out mechanism which was set to print every three seconds. *S* was told that *E* would start with 5 and count down 4-3-2-1-0 and then count up 1-2-3-4-5 and that the *S* would receive one shock when *E* said "0". This constituted one trial. (8) The procedure was repeated five times.

Skin resistance was measured by passing a constant 7 microamps of current through the *S*'s hand, using zinc zinc-sulphate electrodes. The resistance was measured directly in K-ohms on a digital volt meter and with a print-out occurring every 3 seconds. Following standard psychophysiologic procedure, the scores were converted into log conductance units.

The autonomic data can be thought of as comprising a 36 × 5 × 11 element three-dimensional matrix where one dimension consists of 36 subjects, the second consists of five trials, and the third consists of 11 count-down measures within each trial. The 36 subjects are nested within two orthogonal factors, groups (D, PC, NC) and sex (male, female). The study may be conceptualized as a four-factor experiment with repeated measures on two of the four factors, i.e., trials (T) and countdown measures (M) (Winer 1962).

The entire experiment, using identical procedures and *N*s, was repeated with another group of *S*s (Study No. 2).

Figures 2 and 3 show the groups' mean log skin conductance levels, averaged across all five trials. Points −5 through −2 reflect the anticipatory phase, points −1 through +1 indicate the *S*s' response to the occurrence of the shock, and points +2 through +5 reflect the *S*s' recovery.

Results of the ANOVAs for the two studies are shown in Table 3.

Our first concern is with the effectiveness of the aversive stimulus in producing *change* in skin conductance. The main effect due to *measurements* is highly significant in both studies. There is also a significant decrease in skin conductance level as a function of the repeated administration of the experimental procedure (*trials*). It may thus be concluded that the experimental

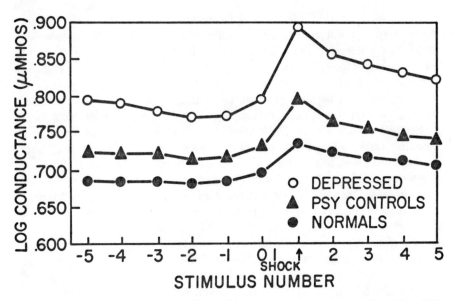

FIG. 3. Skin conductance as a function of anticipated shock (shock between 0 and 1) averaged over the five trials (Study 11). (From Lewinsohn, Lobitz, & Wilson 1973.)

manipulations were successful in eliciting an autonomic response and that adaptation occurred as a function of repeated exposure to the shock.

In both studies the overall skin conductance level is highest (suggesting greater arousal) for the depressed Ss. Due to large differences in conductance level between Ss within the groups, however, the differences between groups do not attain statistical significance.

Hypotheses 1, 2, and 3 demand greater *change* on the part of the depressed group during the anticipatory phase, in response to the shock, and during the recovery phase. The interaction of Groups $\times$ Measurements is statistically significant in both studies. To explicate the basis for this interaction, the three time segments, i.e., anticipatory phase (-5 through -2), response to shock (-1 through $+1$), and recovery phase ($+2$ through $+5$), were subjected to separate ANOVAs. The results suggest that, contrary to H_2, the depressed Ss do not show a greater anticipatory response in Study No. 1 ($F < 1$) and actually decrease slightly in skin conductance during this period in Study No. 2 ($F = 2.7, df = 6$, 90, $p < .02$). Consistent with H_1, depressed Ss show a greater increase in skin conductance in response to the shock ($F = 1.8$, $p < .2$; $F = 2.9$, $p < .05$, for Studies 1 and 2 respectively). Contrary to H_3, there is a slight tendency for the normal control group to show less change in skin conductance during the recovery phase, but the differences between groups do not attain statistical significance.

There was a significant Groups $\times$ Trials interaction in Study No. 1 ($F = 2.3$, $df = 8, 120, p < .05$). However, this interaction is caused by the fact that both the depressed and the psychiatric control groups show less adaptation than the normal control group. The marginally significant Groups X Trials interaction in Study No. 2 is caused by the fact that the psychiatric control group adapts less than the other two groups.

The statistically significant Groups X Sex X Trials interaction in Study No. 1 is also relevant to H_4. Inspection of the data indicates that the female depressed Ss adapt less than the psychiatric and normal control Ss, but this effect is not revealed in the data for males. This triple interaction, however, is not replicated in Study No. 2.

Taken in their totality, the findings provide strong support for H_1. In both studies the depressed group was found to be more responsive to the aversive stimulus. Our results are consistent with those obtained by Zuckerman, Persky, and Curtis (1968), who also found that greater autonomic responsivity to a different aversive situation, namely the Cold Pressor Test, was associated with depression. Within the limits of these experimental manipulations and measurements, the results also suggest that the greater sensitivity of the depressed individual is restricted to the actual occurrence of the aversive stimuli and does not extend backward or forward in time.

TABLE 3

Results of ANOVAS of Skin Conductance Data for
Studies No. 1 and No. 2

Source of Variance	df	F		p	
		Study No. 1	Study No. 2	Study No. 1	Study No. 2
Groups (G)	2	0.5	0.6	NS	NS
Sex (S)	1	0.0	0.1	NS	NS
Trials (T)	4	7.2	23.6	0.01	0.001
Measurements (M)	10	69.5	51.0	0.001	0.001
$G \times S$	2	0.0	0.1	NS	NS
$G \times T$	8	2.3	1.6	0.05	0.20
$S \times T$	4	3.0	8.5	0.05	0.01
$G \times M$	20	1.7	2.2	0.05	0.01
$S \times M$	10	2.4	3.5	0.01	0.01
$T \times M$	40	1.9	2.4	0.01	0.01
$G \times S \times T$	8	3.2	0.6	0.01	NS
$G \times S \times M$	20	0.6	0.4	NS	NS
$G \times T \times M$	80	0.6	0.9	NS	NS
$S \times T \times M$	40	1.3	1.2	NS	NS
$G \times S \times T \times M$	80	0.6	0.8	NS	NS

Even though three out of the four predictions were not confirmed, the fact that the depressed individuals respond more to an aversive stimulus would still lead one to expect them to show a greater tendency to avoid and to withdraw from unpleasant situations. Hence, desensitization to aversive situations may be therapeutically useful with depressed individuals. The findings also suggest the hypothesis that the increased latency of response following the incidence of a negative social reaction from another person found in Stewart's study (1968) may be due to the emotional disruption experienced by the depressed individual in situations involving negative consequences.

Relationship Between Social Skill and Depression

In testing the hypothesis about the instrumental behavior of depressed individuals, we have tended to focus on social skill. The general hypothesis has been that depressed persons as a group are less socially skillful than nondepressed individuals. It is conceivable and not incompatible with the above that depression further reduces the person's social skill.

The first study of the social skill hypothesis was conducted by Rosenberry and coworkers (1968). The hypothesis being tested was that the depressed person's *timing* of social responses is deviant. In the experiment, subjects listened to tape-recorded speeches and responded by pressing a button whenever they would normally say or do something to maintain rapport with the speaker. The depressed subjects, as a group, responded less predictably and less homogenously than did the control group.

Another unpublished study (Lewinsohn, Golding, Johannson, & Stewart 1968) had subjects talking to each other via teletypewriters. Pairs of subjects took turns talking to each other and each subject could say as much or as little as he wanted to before ending his turn. Subjects from two groups, depressed and nondepressed, were randomly assigned to one of three types of dyadic pairings: depressed-depressed; depressed-normal; normal-normal. Each pair of subjects was tested in front of the teletype machines. The subjects were able to communicate with each other via the teletypewriters, which were connected through a wall between the two rooms in which the subjects were seated. There was thus no visual contact between the subjects and they were unable to talk to each other except via the teletypewriters. For all subjects the number of words typed per person increased over the 45-minute session, but for depressed subjects the increase in output was much less than for nondepressed subjects ($F = 3.86$; $df = 1, 26$; $p < .05$ for one-tailed test). The data are graphically shown in Figure 4.

We have since then been concerned with more systematic comparisons between the interpersonal behavior of depressed and nondepressed individuals in small group situations and in the home.

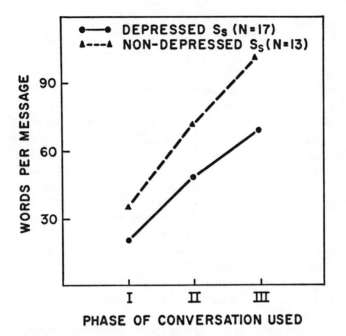

FIG. 4. Mean number of words used for the initial, middle and final two messages by depressed and nondepressed subjects. (From Lewinsohn, Golding, Johansson, & Stewart 1968.)

Operational Measures of Social Skill

Social skill is defined as the ability to emit behaviors that are positively reinforced by others. This definition involves sequences of behavior consisting of actions emitted by an individual together with the reactions he elicits from the social environment. An individual is considered to be skillful to the extent that he elicits positive (and avoids negative) consequences from the social environment. A behavior sequence may elicit positive reactions in situation A but not in situation B. A second behavior sequence may elicit positive reactions in situation B but not in situation A. The socially skillful individual is the one who emits sequence 1 in situation A and sequence 2 in situation B. By definition, lack of social skill is associated with a low rate of positive reinforcement.

As a result of investigating the behavior of depressed and nondepressed persons in group therapy situations (Lewinsohn, Weinstein, & Alper 1970; Libet & Lewinsohn 1973) and in their home environment (Lewinsohn & Shaffer 1971; Shaffer & Lewinsohn 1971), a number of different measures of social skill have evolved. The measures differ in that they focus on various aspects of an individual's interpersonal behavior. Nevertheless, they embody a common rationale. Consistent with the definition of social skill, each measure of social skill is assumed to be related to the amount of positive reinforcement an individual elicits from the environment.

A system for coding the interactional behavior of people serves as an operational basis for the measures of social skill. The system is shown schematically in Figure 5. Behavior interactions are seen as having a "source" and an "object". "Actions" are followed by "reactions" which can be coded as either positive (i.e., expressions of affection, approval, interest) or negative (criticism, disapproval, ignore, etc). A simplified illustration of an interaction involving four people might be as follows: A makes a statement (an action) which is responded to by B (a reaction). B continues talking (an action) and this is followed by a reaction on the part of C, which in turn is followed by some new action on the part of D, etc. Data so generated allow one to focus on any one individual in terms of the actions which he emits and the kinds of reactions he elicits. Two observers code all interactional behaviors. The observers pace themselves with an automatic timer which delivers an auditory and visual signal simultaneously every 30 seconds. Differences between raters are conferenced. Interjudge agreement for the major scoring categories has been quite high, and is shown in Table 4. A manual for the coding system has been developed (Lewinsohn, et al. 1968).

1. *The amount of behavior emitted by the individual.* A very simple but very important aspect of social skill is represented by the activity level of the individual defined as the total number of actions emitted by him (expressed as a rate per hour). We have found (Libet & Lewinsohn 1973; Shaffer & Lewinsohn 1971) that depressed individuals emit interpersonal behaviors at about half the rate of nondepressed control subjects.

2. *Interpersonal efficiency.* One may conceptualize the "efficiency" with which an individual interacts with other people in two different ways. *Interpersonal Efficiency-Actor* is represented by the ratio of the number of behaviors directed toward the individual (return, income), divided by the

TABLE 4

Estimated Spearman-Brown Reliability Coefficients for One
Conferenced Rating Based on 3-way ANOVAS[a]
(10 Persons, Categories, Two Conferenced Ratings)
(From Libet & Lewinsohn 1973)

Source	Actions		Reactions	
	Emit	Elicit	Emit	Elicit
(A) Persons	0.995	0.774	0.956	0.973
(B) Categories	0.800	0.763	0.890	0.893
(AB) Profiles	0.851	0.634	0.956	0.914

[a]Winer (1962, pp. 124-132, 289) discusses the statistical basis of and outlines the computational procedures for estimation of reliability using an analysis of variance model.

Action		Reaction			
Interactional Categories		Positive		Negative	
Psychol. Complaint	Psy C	Affection	Aff	Criticism	Crit
Somatic Complaint	Som C	Approval	App	Disapproval	Disapp
Criticism	Crit.	Agree	Agr	Disagree	Disagree
Praise	Pr	Laughter	L+	Ignore	Ign
Information Request	I-	Interest	Int	Change Topic	Ch T
Information Giving	I+	Continues talking about topic	Con T	Interrupts	Inter
Request for Help	Req H	Physical Affection	Phys Aff	Physical Punishment	Pun
Personal Problem	PP				
+-					
-+					
Instrument Problem	IP				
Other People's Problems	OP < I / E				
Talking about abstract impersonal general, etc.	Ta				

Content—Topics	
School	Sch
Self	X, Y, Z
Other People (group, family)	X, Y, Z
Treatment	Rx
Therapist	T
Sex	Sx

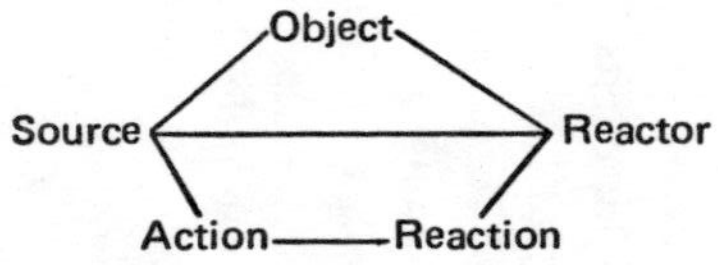

FIG. 5. Behavior rating scale.

number of behaviors he emits towards other people (work, effort). If individuals X and Y each emit 100 actions during a session and X is the object of 80 actions while Y is the object of 120 actions, then Y gets more for what he does than X. Interpersonal Efficiency-Actor looks at the individual's efficiency from the point of view of what he has to do relative to what he gets. A low Interpersonal Efficiency-Actor ratio would imply that the individual is on a low schedule of reinforcement.

Another way of looking at interpersonal efficiency is from the vantage point of the other person, wondering what he "gets" for interacting with our subject (e.g., a depressed individual). For example, if B (the other person) emits 10 actions to A (a nondepressed person) and 10 actions to C (a depressed patient), and if he elicits 20 actions from A but only 5 from C then clearly it is more "efficient" for B to interact with A than it is for him to interact with C. C might be said to be less reciprocal (his *Interpersonal Efficiency-Other* ratio is lower), and holding other things constant, one would over a period of time expect B to reduce his interactions with A and to increase his interactions toward C. We have not been able to find systematic differences between depressed and non-depressed individuals in either Interpersonal Efficiency-Actor or in Interpersonal Efficiency-Other (Libet & Lewinsohn 1973; Shaffer & Lewinsohn 1971).

A post hoc analysis (Shaffer & Lewinsohn 1971) indicated, however, that while it was impossible to predict the direction of lack of reciprocity, the relationships of depressed individuals tended to be less reciprocal overall, i.e., the depressed individual either did much more for the other person than the other person did for him or vice versa. We intend to examine this emergent (or revised) hypothesis again with new data. One might hypothesize that to the extent relationships lack reciprocity, they would tend to be less stable over longer times.

3. *Interpersonal range.* Another aspect of social skill, interpersonal range, concerns the number of individuals with whom a person interacts, i.e., the ones to whom he emits behaviors and from whom he elicits behaviors.

To quantify the degree to which an individual distributes his actions equally to other members, a measure was derived from information theory (Attneave 1959). The interpersonal range measure [Relative Uncertainty Value (R)] varies from 0 to 1. If an individual emits actions to one other group member, $R = 0$, which indicates minimum unpredictability and minimum interpersonal range. Conversely, if a person distributes his actions equally among his peers, $R = 1$, which indicates maximum unpredictability of the targets of his actions or maximum interpersonal range. Procedural details on how to compute R have been provided elsewhere (Libet & Lewinsohn 1973). On the basis of small-group interaction data, the prediction that depressed individuals have a restricted interpersonal range is supported for males but not for females (Libet & Lewinsohn 1973).

4. *Use of positive reactions.* Another aspect of social skill involves reinforcing the behavior of others directed toward the subject. The number of positive

reactions emitted per session (holding activity level constant) is used to measure this aspect of social skill. The depressed subjects emitted a smaller proportion of positive reactions than did the nondepressed persons (Libet & Lewinsohn 1973).

5. *Action latency.* Another operational measure of social skill is represented by action latency, which is defined as the lapse of time between the reaction of another person to the subject's verbalization, and another subsequent action by that subject. In order to maintain the behavior of others, it is not merely sufficient to reinforce their behavior, but this has to be done at the appropriate time, namely, in close temporal proximity to the other person's behavior. Also, the individual who delays (has a long action latency) is more likely to "lose the floor". We have found (Stewart 1968; Libet & Lewinsohn 1973) significant differences that reflect a 3:1 ratio in latency for depressed and nondepressed.

6. *General comments about social skill and depression.* Though the data support the hypothesis that measures of social skill discriminate between depressed and nondepressed groups, there remain many unanswered questions such as, Does the social skill of an individual when he is depressed differ systematically from that when he is not depressed? Clinically, one can find individuals who show extreme manifestations of one or more of the above-mentioned measures of social skill. The advantage of the social skill measures is that they are quantitative and can easily be used to define goals for behavior change (Killian 1971; Lewinsohn, Weinstein, & Alper 1970). New hypotheses that have suggested themselves to us and which can be tested empirically but for which we have as yet no data are as follows:

H-1. The social skill of depressed persons is more adversely affected by size of group than that of nondepressed persons.

H-2. Being unfamiliar to others in the group has a more negative effect on social skill of depressed than of nondepressed persons.

THE RELEVANCE OF THE BEHAVIORAL THEORY OF DEPRESSION TO THE PHENOMENA OF AGING

Within a behavioral framework, depression is conceptualized as an extinction phenomena. On reading the gerontological literature one is struck by the many behavioral similarities between the depressed and the elderly person: (1) One of the most striking features of both old age and depression is a progressive reduction in the rate of behavior. The concept of "disengagement" has been advanced to account for this reduction of behavior. It is assumed to be a natural process which the elderly person accepts and desires, and which is thought to have intrinsic determinants (Cumming & Henry 1961). From a behavioral framework, the elderly person's reduced rate of behavior suggests that his behavior is no longer being reinforced by his environment, i.e., that he, like the depressed person, is on an extinction schedule. (2) Other aspects of the depressive syndrome (feeling rejected, loss of self-esteem, loss of interest, psychophysiological symptoms, etc.) are quite common among the elderly (Wolf 1959). (3) Motivation is a critical problem in the elderly, as it is in the depressed patient. It is hard to find effective reinforcers for either. The number of potentially reinforcing events seems reduced. (4) The elderly person and the depressed person are turned inward, and focus on themselves, their memories, fantasies, and the past. The hypothesis immediately suggests itself that a reduction in the response contingent rate of positive reinforcement is a critical antecedent condition for many of the behavioral changes described in the elderly person.

We are in the process (Lewinsohn & MacPhillamy 1972) of collecting data about the following hypotheses:

H-1. The number of events and activities with reinforcement potential diminishes with age.

H-2. The availability of reinforcement in the elderly individual's environment has diminished because of separation from children, former friends, business associates, and generally those people who have been maintaining the individual's behavior.

H-3. There are systematic differences between groups differing in age on the social skill measures, with increasing age being associated with decreasing social skill.

CONCLUDING REMARKS

The hypotheses and the conclusions that have been presented are meant to be very tentative. Our conceptualization of depression and the kinds of questions we have been asking are in a state of flux. New possibilities suggest themselves continuously and undoubtedly the hypotheses will have to be revised and new ones developed.

We do think that we are developing methods for studying depression. Perhaps this constitutes progress.

REFERENCES

Attneave, F. *Application of information theory to psychology.* New York: Holt, Rinehart, & Winston, 1959.
Azrin, N. H., Hutchinson, R. R., & Hake, D. F. Extinction-induced aggression. *Journal of the Experimental Analysis of Behavior*, 1966, 9, 191-204.
Beck, A. T. *Depression: Clinical, experimental, and theoretical aspects.* New York: Harper & Row, 1967.
Cautela, J., & Kastenbaum, R. A reinforcement survey schedule for use in therapy, training, and research. *Psychological Reports*, 1967, 20, 1115-1130.
Cumming, E., & Henry, W. *Growing old: The process of disengagement.* New York: Basic Books, 1961.
Fenichel, O. The psychoanalytic theory of neurosis. New York: W. W. Norton, 1945.

Grinker, R. R., Sr., Miller, J., Sabshin, M., Nunn, R. J., & Nunnally, J. C. *The phenomena of depression.* New York: Harper & Row, 1961.

Hare, R. D. A conflict and learning theory analysis of psychopathic behavior. *Journal of Research in Crime and Delinquency*, 1965, 2, 12-19.

Johansson, S. L., Lewinsohn, P. M., & Flippo, J. R. *An application of the Premack Principle to the verbal behavior of depressed subjects.* Paper presented at the meeting of the Association for the Advancement of Behavior Therapy, 1969. Mimeo. University of Oregon, 1969.

Killian, D. H. *The effect of instructions and social reinforcement on selected categories of behavior emitted by depressed persons in a small group setting.* Unpublished doctoral dissertation. University of Oregon. 1971.

Lewinsohn, P. M., et al. *Manual of instruction for the behavior rating used for the observation of interpersonal behavior.* Unpublished manuscript. University of Oregon, 1968. Revised, 1971.

Lewinsohn, P. M., & Atwood, G. E. Depression: A clinical-research approach. *Psychotherapy: Theory, Research, & Practice*, 1969, 6, 166-171.

Lewinsohn, P. M., Golding, S. L., Johansson, S. L., & Stewart, R. C. Patterns of communication in depressed and nondepressed subjects. Unpublished data, 1968.

Lewinsohn, P. M., & Libet, J. Pleasant events, activity schedules, and depression. *Journal of Abnormal Psychology*, 1972, 79, 291-295.

Lewinsohn, P. M., Lobitz, C., & Wilson, S. "Sensitivity" of depressed individuals to aversive stimuli. *Journal of Abnormal Psychology*, 1973, 81, 259-263.

Lewinsohn, P. M., Shaffer, M., & Libet, J. *Depression: A clinical-research approach.* Paper presented at the meeting of the Western Psychological Association, 1969; Mimeo, University of Oregon, 1969.

Lewinsohn, P. M., & Shaffer, M. The use of home observations as an integral part of the treatment of depression: Preliminary report and case studies. *Journal of Consulting and Clinical Psychology*, 1971, 37, 87-94.

Lewinsohn, P. M., & Shaw, D. A. Feedback about interpersonal behavior as an agent of behavior change: A case study in the treatment of depression. *Psychotherapy & Psychosomatics.* 1969, 17, 82-88.

Lewinsohn, P. M., Weinstein, M. S., & Shaw, D. A. Depression: A clinical-research approach. In Rubin, R. D., & Frank, C. M. (Eds.) *Advances in Behavior Therapy*, 1968, New York: Academic Press, 1969.

Lewinsohn, P. M., Weinstein, M. S., & Alper, T. A behaviorally oriented approach to the group treatment of depressed persons: A methodological contribution. *Journal of Clinical Psychology*, 1970, 4, 525-532.

Libet, J., & Lewinsohn, P. M. The concept of social skill with special reference to the behavior of depressed persons. *Journal of Consulting and Clinical Psychology*, 1973, 40, 304-312.

Lubin, B. Adjective checklists for the measurement of depression. *Archives of General Psychology*, 1965, 12, 57-62.

MacPhillamy, D. J., & Lewinsohn, P. M. *Pleasant Events Schedule*, 1971.

MacPhillamy, D. J., & Lewinsohn, P. M. The structure of reported reinforcement. In preparation.

Paykel, E. S., Myers, J. K., Dicnett, M. N., Klerman, G. L., Lindenthal, J. J., & Pepper, M. P. *Life events and depression: A controlled study.* Mimeo. Yale University, 1969.

Rosenberry, C., Weiss, R. L., & Lewinsohn, P. M. *Frequency and skill of emitted social reinforcement in depressed and nondepressed subjects.* Paper presented at Meeting of Western Psychological Association, 1969. Mimeo. University of Oregon, 1969.

Schachter, S., & Singer, J. E. Cognitive, social, and physiological determinants of emotional state. *Psychological Review*, 1962, 69, 379-399.

Shaffer, M., & Lewinsohn, P. M. *Interpersonal behaviors in the home of depressed versus nondepressed psychiatric and normal controls: A test of several hypotheses.* Paper presented at meeting of the Western Psychological Association, 1971. Mimeo, University of Oregon, 1971.

Stewart, R. C. *The differential effects of positive and negative social reinforcement upon depressed and nondepressed subjects.* Unpublished Masters thesis. University of Oregon, 1968.

Winer, B. J. *Statistical principles in experimental design.* New York: McGraw-Hill, 1962.

Wolf, K. *The biological, sociological, and physiological aspects of aging.* Springfield, Ill.: Charles Thomas, 1959.

Zimet, C. N., & Schineider, C. Effects of group size on interaction in small groups. *Journal of Social Psychology*, 1969, 77, 177-187.

Zuckerman, M., Persky, S., Curtis, G. C. Relationships among anxiety, depression, hostility, and autonomic variables. *Journal of Nervous and Mental Disease*, 1968, 146, 481–487.

DISCUSSION

Dr. Seligman: I find Dr. Lewinsohn's data very rich and significant, particularly in view of my own research focus. However, I would like to address myself to the theoretical basis and particularly to the hypothesis that a low rate of positive reinforcement explains the findings. I will try to outline the reasons leading me to believe that the hypothesis of a low rate of positive reinforcement does not serve as an adequate explanation for the data at hand.

When one takes a concept such as a low rate of positive reinforcement, which after all emerges from the animal literature, there should be an empirical basis in this literature indicating that a low rate of reinforcement corresponds to his findings. That is, in the animal one should see low activity level and low latency following a decrease in positive reinforcement before any of his clinical findings can be meaningful.

There are three lines of evidence indicating that this correspondence is not to be found in the animal literature. One is that changing the rate of reinforcement from a high to a low rate is the whole basis not of the depression literature but of the frustration literature. Indeed, that is a perfect way to generate more behavior in an animal, at least transiently and occasionally over long periods of time. One might retort in response to this contention that a low rate of reinforcement produces a chronic extinction schedule, but then I would point out that what you are describing is not truly a low rate of reinforcement but is rather intermittent reinforcement. Despite Dr. Ferster's remarks about the maintenance of the repertoire, it simply cannot be denied that animals on an intermittent schedule (or as Dr. Lewinsohn states, a low rate of reinforcement) are emitting absolutely large quantities of behavior and not low rates of behaviors similar to the depressed state. It is a well-known and documented fact that intermittent schedules are very effective in obtaining large quantities of behavior in animals. Note, if one hypothesizes that the depressed person is on an extinction schedule, he generates a paradoxical prediction. If the person were being maintained on an intermittent reinforcement schedule (a low rate of reinforcement), and then were to be experimentally shifted to a real extinction schedule consisting of no reinforcement at all, the hypothesis forces the prediction that a depressed person would persist much longer than a non-depressed person. I suspect one would not be able to verify this experimentally or clinically, because the principles coming from the animal literature clearly tell us that intermittent reinforcement causes greater persistence.

Finally, I would suggest that the hypothesis stating that there is a lack of contingency between responding and reinforcement in the depressed subjects best explains Dr. Lewinsohn's findings.

Dr. Lewinsohn: I would first like to address myself to Dr. Seligman's final point. Of course, it is the temporal relationship between the behavior of a person and positive reinforcement which I assume to be of critical importance for the occurrence of "depression". It is essential that the reinforcement be contingent upon behavior. I think it is a clinical fact that giving (noncontingently) to the depressed person does not reduce his depression; for it is not the absolute amount of attention or other "goodies" received that is critical but the fact that the environment provides consequences sufficient to maintain the individual's behavior. One might say that the depressed person is not getting paid much for what he is doing, and that it is being paid for what one does that is critical and not just being given a check. For example, in the case of the elderly person who receives his Social Security check regardless of what he does, his behavior is not being maintained by that check.

Dr. Lasky: I would appreciate some clarification on the investigation of the interpersonal range of the depressed person, which appears to me to be desirable research. Could you elaborate briefly on your work and the assumptions underlying the experiments you have done?

Dr. Lewinsohn: We define "social skill" in a circular way, i.e., as those behaviors that elicit positive reinforcement from others. We assume there are a wide variety of behaviors used by individuals to elicit positive reinforcement from others, and we have been searching for quantitative measures with which to define social skill operationally. Our major hypothesis is that individuals who are prone to depression are less "skillful" in social, interactional situations. One of our measures (interpersonal range) was generated by the clinical observation that some depressed individuals are clearly overinvolved with one significant person to the exclusion of most other potential relationships. We are collecting data in group therapy situations about this hypothesis and certainly observe depressed individuals with extremely restricted interpersonal ranges. Our observations have also led us to hypothesize that as the size of the group increases, the participation of depressed individuals diminishes. Depressed patients appear to be more comfortable in dyadic relationships, and their behavior begins to drop off when they are in groups of more than three people.

Dr. Lasky: In your research program do you actually set up dyads or do you study dyads within a larger group setting?

Dr. Lewinsohn: Not yet. We plan to manipulate group size. On occasion we have subdivided some of our groups, which typically consist of either eight or twelve individuals, for specific tasks.

Dr. Ekman: Are you measuring verbal behavior only or verbal behavior plus nonverbal behavior?

Dr. Lewinsohn: Our data are based on verbal behavior only.

Dr. Ekman: Do you have any data to suggest that patients who interact primarily with one or two other persons in a group receive less total positive reinforcement than others who spread their interaction around among a larger number of group members?

Dr. Lewinsohn: We have the data but I cannot answer that question at this time.

Dr. Chodoff: Clinically, we know that it is not only depressive patients but almost all psychiatric patients who show deficits in their interpersonal skills and reduced interpersonal fossae. It is also the paranoid as well as the depressive who produces negative reactions in the people in his environment and who has a negative cognitive set which purports that the world is against him.

There are two aspects to Dr. Lewinsohn's research that I would like to question. The first concerns the sample selection. The portion of the sample of "depressed" people that troubles me comes from classrooms where Dr. Lewinsohn has selected those students who scored high on a rating scale which he administered.

I'm not sure that I could clinically consider these people depressed; it seems they are, at the best, mild or borderline depressives. The other portion of the sample is composed of patients who are more obviously depressed, but, again, only mildly so, for none of them are hospitalized and they are all living at home and indeed are clinic patients. I have great difficulty accepting findings based on the college students and also some reservations about the findings based on the depressed outpatient sample as indicative of the more serious "clinical" depressions.

My second question concerns the use of a rating scale as the primary criterion of depression. There are, as you know, many other ways to diagnose depressive illness in addition to the patient's own report and evaluation of his feeling state. Findings such as anorexia, weight loss, and other somatic concerns, as well as clinical judgments, may often be entirely at variance with the mood the patient ascribes to himself.

In addition to the methodological problems, I see a historical redundancy in this approach. Dr. Lewinsohn states that depression is maintained by a lack of contingent positive reinforcement and, although the language is new, at least to me, it seems that he is talking about a phenomenon clinicians, patients, and their families have been aware of for years. This approach also has a long history as a therapeutic device. Depressed patients are told to "get out there and find something you enjoy". Or, "Go out and do it—you are not as bad as you think you are". Depressed patients receive plenty of positive encouragement and they get it until it comes out their ears, but most of them cannot use it! That depressed patients lack and want positive reinforcement is perhaps an assumption that may not be true. Profoundly depressed individuals no longer enjoy doing anything. If you force them to engage in activity, they will tell you they do not derive much satisfaction from it. This seems to be a common-sense approach which everyone takes in dealing with depressed patients, and I might add that it is not just the families of depressed people who try this method. Every psychiatrist, whether he admits it or not, generally tries to get depressed people to engage in activity and to enjoy themselves. It usually does not work very well, however. I conclude that Dr. Lewinsohn is really systematizing, in a rather elaborate way, a type of approach which—at least in my experience—has been tried and has not proved very effective.

Dr. Lewinsohn: Dr. Chodoff focuses on an extremely important methodological point, namely, the selection of subjects in research studies on depression. As we all know, depression rarely exists in "pure" form and different researchers' operational definitions of depression and of depressed patients vary widely. In our research we employ a two-stage selection strategy using an abbreviated MMPI to screen very large samples, and then conduct semistructured interviews with those whose MMPI scores exceed certain critical levels. On the basis of the interview, the subjects are rated on some of the factors identified by Grinker. To be included as a depressed subject, a person has to have an intensity of depression exceeding a certain cut-off score, and depression must constitute his major presenting psychopathology. In absolute terms I would place the depression level of our subjects from mild to moderate.

I would also like to address myself to the other issue raised by Dr. Chodoff, namely, the similarities and the differences between our approach and what might be called the "common sense" approach to the management of the depressed patient. I believe our approach differs in two ways. In the first place we attempt to identify those events and activities likely to be reinforcing (meaningful) for the patient and we do not assume we know beforehand which these might be. For example, we are beginning to use the Pleasant Events Schedule to pinpoint specific activities for individual patients because they are functionally related to his being or not being depressed.

The second point of departure from a strictly common-sense approach is to be found in our systematic efforts to apply reinforcement principles. We are well aware that the depressed patient often receives a great deal of advice and encouragement and that, more often than not, he is unable to use it. In fact, depressed patients are very resistant to suggestions and sensitive about being controlled. We employ a reinforcement paradigm designed to increase the depressed person's activity level. For example, we have been using the amount of time the patient can talk about his depression, as well as the total amount of therapy time, as a reinforcement for becoming more active. Our results confirm

Dr. Beck's research findings that once the person actually begins to engage in activities, he does receive reinforcement and his mood changes. The difficulty is to get the depressed person to begin to engage in activities, even though intellectually he appreciates that he should.

Dr. Friedman: Dr. Lewinsohn, if I understand you correctly you are maintaining that depression is a state of the organism and that you are addressing in your research what we might call depression of affect rather than what some of us have labeled earlier in this conference as the "clinical condition of depression". In other words, you do not see a qualitative difference between the "clinical state" and depression that sometimes occurs in every human being.

Dr. Lewinsohn: We do define depression in our research as a state that can occur in any of us in different degrees or intensities and under given circumstances.

Dr. Goodwin: The theoretical notion that depression exists as a continuum from everyday sadness to the severe "clinical state" is easier to maintain if one refrains from studying hospitalized patients. I find it an appealing construct, but I believe that future research will not bear it out.

Dr. Tabachnick: I would also like to respond to the criticism Dr. Chodoff raises and suggest an alternative way of viewing the situation. I agree with Dr. Chodoff's observation that much of the activity described by Dr. Lewinsohn and other clinicians is precisely what most human beings have been doing to other human beings who are called "depressed" for centuries. However, I think we are hasty in assuming that such activity by concerned friends and relatives is ineffective; after all, depressions do end. Human beings do not live outside a social milieu, and the intervention of that milieu may be one of the factors that brings a depression to a close. Perhaps our assumption that intervention of this type is ineffective is hasty, because we are expecting the results to be direct and obvious instead of indirect and part of a general picture of improvement. Perhaps all of the cajolery and encouragement which the depressed person receives has a cumulative effect and is *the* significant variable in shortening or terminating the depression.

Both Dr. Chodoff's contention and my counter suggestion are only hypotheses at present, and one of the values of Dr. Lewinsohn's research is that it does represent an approach to the problem that may allow us to choose more intelligently between such widely varying explanations.

Dr. Lewinsohn: I could not agree more!

Dr. Chodoff: So far our discourse has been based on hypotheses generated on the basis of behavior only. We really have not taken into account a hypothetical construct of immense value in psychology, namely, the unconscious. In reality we discover that behavior is rather complicated and that superficial explanations are often undermined by more contradictory unconscious determinants. A person may agree that some activity or some input would be reinforcing to him, and yet at a deeper level he may be forced to reject this input because it arouses unconscious conflicts. We do not do the complexity of human nature justice if we cling to the idea of rational man only.

Dr. Lewinsohn: There are obviously many different levels at which one can approach personality. We have found it useful to focus mainly on the depressed person's behavior.

Dr. Beck: Dr. Tabachnick has touched one of the truly positive aspects of Dr. Lewinsohn's research—the fact that it is a systematic application of positive reinforcement. I have research data to corroborate the finding that the systematic application and tailoring of treatment to the individual patient works. We have found improvement in mood after giving depressed patients "positive informational feedback," a form of reinforcement which demonstrates to the patient that he can succeed on a task which he previously predicted would end in failure.

Dr. Friedman: I would like to draw on Dr. Seligman's findings about the control issue. Dr. Seligman has demonstrated that the control of trauma is critical in the etiology of depression, and in a similar vein Dr. Beck explained that the expression of hostility seems to be effective in depressive states because it shows the person that he can exercise control over his environment. From the therapeutic standpoint I believe we all agree that we must *give* the depressed person something, and I hope we can agree that the "quality" of what we give is essential.

I believe Dr. Chodoff is equating positive reinforcement with positive encouragement or with other signs of something "positive". We all know that doesn't do much good, and I believe the strategy advocated by Drs. Lewinsohn and Beck is a tribute to the necessity for showing the depressed person that he can control his world. It is not enough to sit down with the depressed person and determine with him what he thinks he would like. That can only be the first step. The second step is to devise a method to show him that he can obtain what he wants because of the power or ability or control he has. In other words, he can earn it.

Dr. Lewinsohn: Dr. Friedman not only points to some of the underlying similarities between our positions which might otherwise be obscured by semantic differences, but he also focuses on the importance of having the depressed individual learn that he can control his environment by his own actions.

Dr. Klerman: I would like to advance the hypothesis that Dr. Lewinsohn's research sample consists of two groups. One is a group of relatively "normal" people who have a mood fluctuation as part of "normal" life. I believe it is very important to study the depressive mood as part of a person's interaction with his environment. A second group is composed of people who are suffering from an "ambulatory depression". The determinants of the relationship between external events and mood in the latter group probably are determined more by internal factors than they are among the normal people of the first group.

I hypothesize that in the first group, in which the mood seems to follow a behavior or an event, we are dealing with relatively normal people because that is indeed what we consider normal, namely, that contingent positive reinforcement promotes a sense of well-being. The second group, in whom the mood disturbance appears to precede the activity, seems to me to characterize what empathically I feel is the condition we are observing in the clinical state of depression. Earlier I used the label "endogenous" to refer to the second group. I realize this may not be the best descriptive term for this subsample because, historically, "endogenous" has connoted biological or constitutional determination. Perhaps the concept of "depressive character" would be more appropriate than "endogenous", but I must admit that I am uncertain whether the concept of the depressive character actually refers to a specific personality organization in which we see dependency, excessive requirements for reassurance, and low self-esteem, or whether it refers to a person who is perking along at a low grade of clinical depression.

I urge Dr. Lewinsohn to examine his clinical population as admixtures of these groups and admixtures of depression as a normal state and as a clinical entity.

Dr. Dyrud: I am troubled that we are employing what is really a very precise language in a loose way. I believe the study which Dr. Lewinsohn has described represents more of an empirical, Meyerian type of research than it does a Skinnerian study.

I think it might be more appropriate to use the term "response" instead of "reinforcement". The term "reinforcement" has great precision when we are looking at schedules of reinforcement, and I find it part of an interesting and challenging area of research. However, I'm not sure that the clinical field is ready for research which purports to employ the precision of the animal laboratory.

My plea to Dr. Lewinsohn and others is to use terms such as "response" and "pleasant event" instead of "reinforcement" because they are not of the same order. Perhaps when the data are more refined, we can go back and begin to study the phenomena more precisely, using a language consistent with greater precision and control.

7

DEPRESSION AS AN INDICATOR OF LETHALITY IN SUICIDAL PATIENTS[1]

Carl I. Wold and Norman Tabachnick
University of Southern California

In this paper we will detail the differing rates of depression among several characterologic suicidal groups (which we call suicidal subgroups). More specifically, we will contrast the rate of depression between those patients within each characterologic group who actually killed themselves and those who did not.

These data bear on the problem, "Is depression a unitary concept?" We will discuss this issue in one section of the paper.

(This research is a portion of a larger effort, directed by Robert E. Litman and Norman L. Farberow, to develop a mathematical model of suicide. [Litman, et al. 1971]).

SUICIDAL SUBGROUPS

Based on early clinical experiences at the Los Angeles Suicide Prevention Center (SPC), it was clear that suicide could not be viewed as a unitary concept, nor could suicidal people be viewed as a homogeneous group. In 1961, Litman & Farberow, and Tabachnick & Farberow discussed variations in self-destructive potentiality among suicidal people. They observed that variations in age and sex, suicidal history, and the suicidal individual's phenomenology were important factors. During subsequent years, determinants of suicide risk or self-destructive

[1] The research reported here has been supported by #1 R01 MH 17850-02 of the National Institute of Mental Health to the Los Angeles Suicide Prevention Center and the Institute for Studies of Self-Destructive Behavior.

potential have been clarified and made more rigorous by a coordinated research effort (Litman 1970).

In 1965, work was initiated on operationalizing the concept of suicidal syndromes or subgroups. The goal has been to develop phenomenologic subgroups which cut across standard psychiatric nosology. That endeavor had two purposes: (1) with subgroups, we hoped to make better lethality predictions, and (2) intervention would become tied in with the identified characteristics of these subgroups. This makes intuitive sense when one considers the heterogeneity of a group of suicidal people that includes old men who are quite stable and have outlived everyone else in their lives, young adolescent boys, ostensibly stable but covertly depressed, chaotic, and disorganized young women, et al. The focus is on the suicidal situations faced by the people in the subgroup, as well as their life style and personality characteristics.

The development of the subgroup research has been reported by Wold (1971) and is summarized here. Initially the identity and description of the subgroups came from our clinical experience with suicidal patients. In order for the subgroups to be utilized in quantitative research studies, reliable measures of each subgroup were developed. Each subgroup was defined by a series of four to eight items initially formulated in regard to a 1967 sample. Work on refining the subgroups has continued since 1967, however, and in the process some items were changed to increase their reliability. The data presented in this study are the result of the modified series of subgroups developed for the 1970 version of this study.

The entire body of SPC patients about whom the subgroup analysis was made comprised 465 living patients (those cases were randomly selected from the SPC files) and 52 SPC patients who went on to commit suicide after being seen alive at our clinic.[2] We excluded telephone contacts which had resulted in only a single contact.

There is some information about the interval between the last SPC contact and date of death of the 52 people who committed suicide. Forty-four percent died within 1 year of the last SPC contact; by 2 years, 63 percent had died; and by 3 years, 77 percent were dead.

All of the cases were blindly rated, that is, the rater did not know if the case was one of a patient who was still living or one who had committed suicide.

It should be noted that not all SPC patients fell into only one of the subgroup categories, although most did. In the 1970 study, 80 percent of the living patients fell into at least one of the subgroups. 45 percent fell into one and only one subgroup, 25 percent into two subgroups, and the remaining 10 percent were scored in three subgroups. Among the group who committed suicide, 70 percent fell into one or more subgroups, 45 percent were scored in one and only one subgroup, 15 percent in two subgroups, and 10 percent in three.

---

[2] The subgroup data formed a portion of this research. The bulk of the research was carried out by Timothy R. Brown and Daniel J. Lettieri.

DEFINING THE SUBGROUPS

Now we will name and characterize those subgroups that were evaluated in the present study. We refer to one group as *"discarded, unstable."* These are people who have a history of unstable love relationships. They experience suicidal feelings in response to the disruption or break-up of such a relationship. Beside suicidal impulses, other components of the depressive state are strong feelings of worthlessness, shame, and guilt. Instability is in evidence in other areas of their lives, especially employment and residence. Diagnostically, they are seen as neurotic character problems. 17 percent of the general patient population of the Suicide Prevention Center are classified as "discarded, unstable." 12 percent of SPC patients who commit suicide are so classified.

A second, smaller group of suicidal people are referred to as *"discarded, stable."* These people also become suicidal in response to the break-up of a love relationship, but in contrast to the "discarded, unstable" subgroup, this is not a lifelong pattern but an acute situation. The people in this group have developed and sustained a relatively long-lasting relationship that was stable. The suicidal partner has been increasingly dependent, and when the relationship ends, he is left feeling, "I can't live without you." His depression is characterized by feelings of painful incompleteness at the loss of the symbiotic partner. 6 percent of the SPC patient population are classified "discarded, stable," and 6 percent of those SPC patients who go on to commit suicide fall within this category.

A third, fairly large diagnostic group is called *"down and out."* This group accounts for 25 percent of SPC patients and 29 percent of those SPC patients who go on to commit suicide. They are usually middle-aged people for whom life has followed a downhill course in most areas. They have experienced repeated failures in love and work, and they are often either alcoholic or heavy drug users. The suicidal state is less of a crisis than it is a chronic state, and the end product of a gradually increasing sense of hopelessness.

The next subgroup is called *"violence,"* and this accounts for about 20 percent of the SPC patients. 12 percent of the SPC patients who go ahead to commit suicide belong to this subgroup. These are both men and women who experience periodic episodes of violent rage directed at themselves and/or others. These episodes often involve the police on a call of "family disturbance."

The next subgroup is called *"old and stable."* These account for only 2 percent of SPC patients, but 6 percent of committed suicides of the SPC population belong to this group. These are people who have led fairly stable lives and have outlived others with whom they have had significant relationships. They feel their current lives are empty and meaningless, and they feel neither optimism nor strength to generate new relationships.

The final subgroup which we are including in this analysis is designated *"chaotic, psychotic, borderline."* Suicidal states among these people are very strongly intrapsychic and seem unrelated to external stress and interpersonal relationships. Often the suicidal state arises suddenly, and actions are impulsive, indeed, often bizarre and chaotic. 30 percent of SPC patients are classified in this subgroup, and 33 percent of the patients who commit suicide are classified in this group.

THE METHOD FOR
RATING DEPRESSION

Along with a number of other variables, depression ratings were made on all subjects in both study groups (the large group of 465 SPC patients, and the second group of 52 SPC patients who went on to commit suicide). The reliability of the ratings was checked by presenting the same 10 cases to each of 12 different raters and calculating the percentage of agreement for each rated item. The average agreement among all items was over 80 percent. Depression items taken by themselves were highly reliable, since there was over 80 percent agreement among the raters.

The ratings of depression (as well as all other items) were made from case file data, which usually contained the results of extensive therapeutic interviewing, some psychological testing, recorded staff conferences, and follow-up correspondence frequently covering many years. We divided the depression ratings into four areas.

The first was the rating of *somatic depression*. This was judged by the following indicators: sleep disturbances, including early morning waking; major acute fluctuations in weight or appetite; a variety of vague somatic complaints associated with depression.

Affective depression was judged by the feeling states reported by the patient. These included feelings of hopelessness and helplessness, feelings of being frozen or immobilized, painful guilt, and self-depreciation.

Social depression was defined by social isolation, loneliness, and general withdrawal from contacts with other people.

Finally, the rater was asked to judge the *duration* of the patient's depressive state.

THE RESULTS

Table 1 presents the percentages of each rating of depression in the group of nonsuicide SPC patients and the completed-suicide group. In addition, these data are presented for each subgroup.

Table 2 summarizes the statistically *significant* findings of this report. The first horizontal line presents the rates of depression in the four categories for the total suicide sample as compared with the nonsuicide sample. The next six horizontal lines present the same comparison for each of the suicidal subgroups.

An initial prediction with which one might approach these data would be that in each category, when comparing the suicide and nonsuicide groups, there

TABLE 1

Percentages of Each Category of Depression Among the
Study Groups

Study groups	Somatic	Affective	Social	1 yr + duration
Total sample				
SPC patients ($n = 465$)	65	88	49	25
SPC pt-suicides ($n = 52$)	79	87	52	34
Discarded, unstable				
SPC patients ($n = 91$)	68	89	44	34
SPC pt-suicides ($n = 6$)	83	83	50	50
Discarded, stable				
SPC patients ($n = 31$)	33	64	48	9
SPC pt-suicides ($n = 3$)	100	100	67	0
Down and out				
SPC patients ($n = 134$)	75	93	57	38
SPC pt-suicides ($n = 15$)	87	80	67	33
Violence				
SPC patients ($n = 99$)	60	88	35	38
SPC pt-suicides ($n = 6$)	100	83	17	50
Old and stable				
SPC patients ($n = 8$)	50	88	50	28
SPC pt-suicides ($n = 3$)	100	100	100	33
Chaotic-psychotic-borderline				
SPC patients ($n = 159$)	66	90	46	41
SPC pt-suicides ($n = 17$)	82	94	59	56

would be more depression in the former. However, a glance at Table 2 indicates that it is impossible to generalize about the severity and duration of depression when comparing those SPC patients who went on to commit suicide with those who did not. This statement is true for the final three categories of depressive measurements, that is, affective depression, social depression, and duration of depression.

One can make a generalization that is true of all groups when considering somatic depression alone, however. Here we see that when we compare the total

TABLE 2

A Comparison of Depression Ratings Between SPC Patients Who
Committed Suicide ($n = 52$) and a Selected Group of
SPC Patients Who Did Not Kill Themselves
($n = 465$)

Groups	Somatic	Affective	Social	1 yr + duration
SPC suicides compared with other SPC patients	More prevalent	Same	Same	Same
Discarded, unstable suicides vs nonsuicides	More prevalent	Same	Same	Longer
Discarded, stable suicides vs nonsuicides	Much more prevalent (3X)	More prevalent	More prevalent	Same
Down and out suicides vs nonsuicides	More prevalent	Less prevalent	More prevalent	Same
Violence suicides vs nonsuicides	More prevalent	Same	Less prevalent	Same
Old and stable suicides vs nonsuicides	Much more prevalent (2X)	More prevalent	Much more prevalent (2X)	Same
Chaotic-psychotic-borderline suicides vs nonsuicides	More prevalent	Same	More prevalent	Longer

Note:—All indications of change in this table, such as "More prevalent," "Less prevalent," or "Longer," are statistically significant evaluations. Those which did not achieve statistical significance were rated as "Same." Statistical significance was determined using a Chi-square analysis with a 0.05 level as criterion.

group of suicides with the total nonsuicide group, somatic depression was more prevalent among the suicides, and this situation holds for each of the subgroups.

The categories "affective depression" and "social depression" show considerable variation among the subgroups. In evaluating the duration of depression, it is noted that there is no discernible difference between the suicides and nonsuicides in all subgroups, as well as the sample taken as a whole, except in two groups, "discarded, unstable" and "chaotic, psychotic, borderline." In those groups, the committed suicides had a longer duration of depression than those who did not suicide.

Brown and Lettieri have completed separate analyses of these same data. Using discriminate function analysis, Brown isolated about ten variables which maximally discriminate between those SPC patients who went on to commit suicide and those who did not. The ten variables were statistically significant at the 0.10 level or better. Brown found that somatic depression was the tenth variable in rank order of discriminate power. *More somatic depression occurred among those SPC patients who went on to commit suicide.* Affective depression was the 13th variable in order of importance as a discriminant. Affective depression was found to be less frequent among committed suicides. Age and sex proved to be highly discriminant, corroborating the findings of many previous studies. The committed suicides were older and more were men.

Lettieri, accepting the importance of age and sex as determinants of suicide risk, began with four age-sex subgroups. He subdivided both research groups (both the sample of SPC patients who went on to commit suicide and those who did not) into older men, older women, younger men, and younger women. He then performed a discriminate function analysis of each of these four subgroups. On this basis, a depression variable appeared for only one of the four subgroups, the older males. *Somatic depression was more frequent among older male SPC patients who went on to commit suicide.*

CONCLUDING REMARKS

First, some comments in regard to the scope and limitations of this research. We must emphasize that work is progressing at the Suicide Prevention Center on the evaluation of a great number of factors (beside depression) in the suicidal subgroups (Litman et al. 1971). If this research bears fruit in directions that now seem possible, there will be a time when we will add other factors correlated with suicidal lethality to what seems to be the significant factor of somatic aspects of depression.

A point of caution in regard to the evaluation of these data is the relatively small number of suicide cases which were available. The total number was 52. When this total is divided among the six subgroups (although it is true that there is some overlapping, so that the same case of suicide may appear in two or more groups), the number of completed suicides in each subgroup is relatively small.

It should also be stated that the evaluation of these factors is now in a preliminary stage. We will have to relate these findings in a more extensive way to the covariants that assume significance in our larger study.

How generalizable are the data presented in this study? On the one hand, we know that many of the subjects included in the study were in contact with physicians, psychotherapists, and other authoritative helpers during their periods of concern about suicide. However, we already have evidence to suggest that those who come to the Los Angeles Suicide Prevention Center form a group with more proclivity to suicide than exists in the general population (Litman et al. 1971).

Depression has traditionally been linked to suicide. A number of theorists, such as Sigmund Freud and Karl Menninger, have postulated that suicide is one of the usual end points for severe depression. That depressive patients are quite likely to commit suicide is supported by many statistical studies and clinical observations. A few quotations from the recent book, *Depression*, by Beck substantiate this point:

> At the present time, the only important cause of death in depression is suicide [Beck 1967].
>
> Pokorny [1964] investigated the suicide rate among former patients in a psychiatric service of a Texas veterans' hospital over a 15-year period. Using a complex actuarial system, he calculated the suicide rates per 100,000 per year as follows: depression, 566; schizophrenia, 167; neurosis, 119; personality disorder, 130; alcoholism, 133; and organic, 78. The suicide rate for depressed patients, therefore, was 25 times the expected rate and substantially higher than that of other psychiatric patients.

As we stated earlier in this paper, one result of the research at the Suicide Prevention Center has been support for the conception that suicide is not a unitary concept. We have been able to document that many variables differentiate several types of suicidal individuals. We are emphasizing in this paper that as a result of those variations (as well as for other reasons), we have moved toward the formulation of a number of suicidal subgroups which can be distinguished from each other.

Now let us consider an old question in psychiatry. Can depression be conceived of as a unitary entity? Every experienced clinician and theoretician will know that this topic has been debated at great length and with great heat. Indeed, the debate still continues. In his book, *Depression* (1967), Beck, after presenting a scholarly review and critique of the literature as well as some original research, comes to the conclusion that there can be a unitary concept in regard to depression. He finds this concept in the cognitive aspects of depression.

The data we present here seem to speak against a unitary concept of depression. This is our reasoning: If depression is a unitary concept, if the four categorizations of depression which we used in this study can be taken as significant aspects of the total entity, and if suicide is a typical end point of depressive conditions, we could make certain predictions about our data. We would predict that there should be an increase of all four ratings of depression in the suicide subgroups of each characterologic suicidal type. This prediction is not supported by our data, however.

Of course, we realize that the point in itself is hardly conclusive. There are questions as to how highly linked with depression each of our four depressive categories were. There are questions as to how they were categorized and investigated. Many other practical and theoretical issues have to be raised; we acknowledge that our point is only suggestive.

There is a second way in which our data speak against a unitary concept of depression. If depression is a unitary concept and suicide is seen as one of the usual parts in the development of this entity, then one would expect a similar pattern of depressive symptoms to be found in all depressive people moving toward suicide. Our data clearly indicate that the last prediction does not hold true. We find many variations of depressive symptoms in our suicidal subgroups. Thus, in the "discarded, stable" subgroup, we find 64 percent affective depression and 48 percent social depression, whereas in the "violence" subgroup, affective depression is equally high—88 percent— while social withdrawal is 35 percent. Many other comparable variations are seen throughout the data. The research thus supports the idea that there are a number of *different* ways in which the components of the depressive *syndrome* may be put together.

One possible implication of our work is the following: Included in the general concept of depression are many significant events. They are dynamic events, constitutional situations, environmental correlates. In our SPC patients, there are undoubtedly higher rates of depression than there are in the general population. As we try to categorize our patients, however, we find that they fall into particular characterological subgroups and that these subgroups correlate in differing degrees with various aspects of the total depressive situation. Particularly does this differing type of correlation become evident when we look at the differences between those in our subgroups who go on to commit suicide and those who do not. We therefore conclude that some elements of the depressive constellation are of greater significance and more highly correlated with lethality in a particular subgroup than in other subgroups. If suicide is looked upon as a frequent and significantly linked concomitant of depression, depression appears not to be a unitary concept.

Now for a consideration of the therapeutic significance of our finding (concerning somatic depression). If repeated evaluations support it, we would seem to have come across an important new finding for the detection and treatment of suicide. It has already been established that two frequent indicators of suicidal lethality are age (older) and sex (male). To these should now be added somatic depressive signs. These signs are not difficult to elicit once one is prepared to look for them. However, it is our clinical impression that they often are not spontaneously volunteered, and that when patients speak about depression and when clinicians ask about depression, they more often focus on affective symptoms. Also worth noting is that such signs (that is, somatic depression signs) may be very frequent in individuals coming to nonpsychological clinicians (such as internists or general practitioners). Our finding would indicate that when the somatic signs of depression are seen, routine investigation of the suicidal potentiality is important. In addition, the somatic signs seen in older age, and particularly in older-age men, would seem to form a particularly significant lethal triad.

Finally, let us speculate on the possible theoretical significance of our finding. Although it has been known for a long time that older age is significant as an indicator of suicidal lethality, it is not at all clear why this is so. Various factors have been mentioned: the loneliness and isolation of old age, the fact that most old people have become accustomed to death through seeing and experiencing the death of many who are dear to them, a sense of hopelessness accompanying the realization that one's time is running out.

At this time, we do not know what the relationship is between somatic factors and old age in suicide. But the following possibilities exist:

1. As an older individual experiences physical decline, he approaches a state of anxiety and concern over his existence. It may be that he experiences parts of his total self dropping off or disintegrating. This may produce a movement toward suicide.

2. There may be, in the linking of old age and somatic factors, support for the concept of something like a death instinct. As the physical processes fail and as the individual deals psychologically with this failure, there may be manifestations in his personality of a death trend that is linked to the somatic failure. One of these manifestations may be suicide.

REFERENCES

Beck, A. T. *Depression: Clinical, Experimental, and Theoretical Aspects.* New York: Harper and Row, 1967.
Litman, R. E., & Farberow, N.L. Emergency evaluation of self-destructive potentiality. In Farberow & Shneidman (Eds.), *The cry for help.* New York: McGraw-Hill, 1961.
Litman, R. E., *Suicide prevention: Evaluating effectiveness.* Presented at the 123rd Annual Meeting of the American Psychiatric Association. Summarized in *Scientific Proceedings.* Washington: American Psychiatric Association, 1970.
Litman, R. E., Farberow, N. L., Wold, C. I. & Brown, T. R. *Prediction models of suicidal behavior.* Presented at a Workshop on Suicidal Behavior, Philadelphia, October 1971.
Pokorny, A. D. Suicide rates in various psychiatric disorders. *Journal of Nervous and Mental Disease,* 139 1964, 499-506.
Tabachnick, N., & Farberow, N. L. The assessment of self-destructive potentiality. In *The cry for help* Farberow & Schneidman (Eds.), New York: McGraw-Hill, 1961.
Wold, C. I. Sub-groupings of suicidal people. *Omega* 1971, 2, 19-29.

DISCUSSION

Dr. Klerman: I want to comment on the conceptual issue regarding Dr. Tabachnick's data pertaining to the unitary concept of depression. Dr. Tabachnick feels that his data are more consistent with a pluralistic grouping of depressions than a unitary conceptualization of depression such as Dr. Beck puts forward. The usual way this subject is discussed, however, is in terms of subtypes of depression rather than separate clinical states. One can have a unitary view of depression and still recognize subtypes such as unipolar, bipolar, endogenous, reactive, and neurotic. I believe Dr. Tabachnick's data are not directly pertinent to that issue, but rather touch on the question of dimensionality and the whole measurement problem in depression research.

Dr. Tabachnick has four measurements of depressed people: duration, somatic measures, affective measures, and a social withdrawal measure. I would be very interested in knowing how these different dimensions correlate and what happens if they are added into a single score. Would a single score do better in a discriminant function test than each factor alone? I'm not sure I can even guess at an answer, but I think recent findings in this area pose a whole set of interesting questions whose answers would be of immense practical significance to the clinician. Such data would allow him to assess the seriousness of suicidal threats in a patient if he knew the patient's age, sex, and character type and if, in addition, he could determine whether the patient was a somatic complainer or a social withdrawer.

Dr. Beck: We have found that the psyiological symptoms that Dr. Tabachnick calls "somatic" depression seem to occur with increasing frequency as a person is rated more severely ill. In other words, the more ill he was rated, the more likely he was to have somatic symptoms. And also the more likely he was to suicide. Such people seem to be representative of that group previously called "endogenous" but now more identified with those patients studied by the biologists.

Dr. Schuyler: It is commonly accepted that the depressed patient is at risk for suicidal behavior. The vast majority of depressed people, however, do not engage in suicidal behavior. It would be an important contribution to delineate which among the depressed are most likely to attempt suicide or commit suicide. Attempters and completers have been shown to differ in a variety of demographic and diagnostic ways.

In Dr. Tabachnick's sample we are comparing two groups of suicide prevention callers: one group who have died by suicide; the other group composed of those who have lived. Data about suicide attempters are not provided and apparently are not an issue in this paper, but certainly this is an issue for future research.

Dr. Tabachnick: Although I do not have the exact data available about those callers who actually made suicide attempts, my impression is that about one-third of the callers actually did so. As I think about what percentage of suicide callers in each of the subgroups would be suicide attempters, I am unable to make any estimates. I agree that it would be important to utilize suicide attempters as a third group (the other two being nonattempt callers to the Suicide Prevention Center and completed suicides) in the depression evaluations.

Dr. Klerman: The demographic predictors of suicidal risk (for example, older men, divorced or widowed, unemployed and socially isolated), may have validity with depressed as well as with nondepressed groups of patients. To my knowledge, no study has been done that has identified the relevant predictors of suicidal death in a sample of depressed patients.

Dr. Tabachnick: I too am unaware of any previous studies along this line.

Dr. Schuyler: Dr. Tabachnick has identified the somatic factor in his depressed patients as a predictor of suicidal death. If this finding is replicable it would be an important contribution to the identification of those depressed people whose suicidal risk is significant. Does the somatic factor hold as a predictor across all age groups in this study or is it limited to older males only?

Dr. Tabachnick: This factor is limited only to older men.

Dr. Schuyler: I wonder if Dr. Seligman's research on helplessness does not have particular relevance to identifying depressed patients who will commit suicide. It seems logical to me that the suicidal person who feels helpless, who feels he cannot act on his environment to secure gratification, might decide that he can achieve control of his environment by electing the suicidal alternative.

The decision to commit suicide might in a sense relieve the feeling of helplessness. We do know that many suicidal persons do not carefully assess the consequences of their actions. The lifting of a depression after the person has decided to kill himself is an oft-quoted clinical anecdote and might obviously reflect an increased feeling of control. It is almost the "American way" to seize the initiative in a near-hopeless situation. An example might be the man who is in the hospital, has been told that he has a terminal illness, and that he will die within an indeterminant time. Soon after being told, he jumps out of the sixth floor window carrying his i.v. bottle carefully in hand. Now, most people look at this behavior and say, "Well, that's a very logical kind of thing to do—because he's going to die." Such an act might relieve his immediate depression because the control of his life is seemingly his own and is not being imposed from without.

The hypothesis that helplessness makes a depressed person more vulnerable to suicidal behavior would seem testable in a study similar to Dr. Tabachnick's.

Dr. Seligman: Dr. Schuyler's comment is an interesting one and deserves testing. Dr. Schuyler and I once did a reanalysis of some of Dr. Beck's pilot data that are related to this point. We examined the case histories of 40 attempted suicides for instrumentality. Instrumentality meant whether the person was trying to accomplish something like getting revenge on his wife or relieving a burden on his children by his suicide. So "instrumental," in this sense, means trying to have an effect on the world over and above just ending one's life. We rated these cases blind on a 1-3 scale of instrumentality where 3 meant highly instrumental and 1 meant not instrumental at all. We then correlated this with depression as rated by the Beck Depression Inventory. We found a fairly strong inverse correlation; that is to say, people who make suicide attempts for instrumental purposes seem not to be as depressed as people who make suicide attempts merely to end it all. Attempting to exert an influence on one's environment seems here to be antidepressant. It should be noted that these were highly tentative and merely pilot data, but they seem worth pursuing.

Dr. Tabachnick: My own clinical impressions very much support Dr. Seligman's line of thinking. Of the completed suicides I have seen, most strike me as people who are old, alone, infirm, and helpless. The impression I have is that they have nothing left to live for and really no one whom they could impress. Although the "regaining a sense of power" hypothesis is tenable, I have often thought they just wanted to get out of a very bad situation. On further reflection, it seems that the latter motive is not at all incompatible with the desire to feel more powerful.

Dr. Friedman: Dr. Tabachnick, you have identified somatic symptoms as one set of factors predictive of suicide in older males. Do you have any hypotheses about other factors that might be important in other age groups? What research needs to be done along these lines? Could it be that perhaps there is nothing intrinsic to depression that increases the likelihood of suicide and that the clues may instead lie within the premorbid adaptation or "style" of the patient?

Dr. Tabachnick: The question is a provocative one. First, we have to know what we mean by "depression." As Dr. Wold and I (as well as a number of others) have suggested, it may be that the syndrome known as depression is a rather indefinite one. As clinicians and researchers, we have an associated set of images that come to mind when the word "depression" is mentioned, but since the syndrome is indefinite, different impressions may occur to each individual.

Our findings surprised me since, when I think of depression, I usually think first of the affective changes. However, we found somatic symptoms to be more highly correlated with suicide than any others. Our research suggests that a strict and objective definition of symptoms is most valuable in exploring the depression-suicide relationship.

I believe that certain parts of the depressive syndrome are significantly linked to the occurrence of suicide, but more research of the type we are reporting here is necessary to identify the specific "depressive" signs and symptoms. In addition to the "depressive" indicators, there are almost surely other important predictors of suicide, including the premorbid adaptation or style. It may well be that impulsive people will be found to commit more suicide. We already know that schizophrenic people have a high incidence of suicide, which may be linked to their more tenuous contact with usual life-preserving attitudes and their tendency to act on internal fantasy.

Dr. Beck: I would like to digress for a moment to offer one correction about the percentage of depressed patients who go on to commit suicide. There have been about eight studies to the present, most of which have found that between 12 and 14 percent of depressed people eventually die from suicide (in other words, if one follows a depressed group until they have all died, he will find that 12 to 14 percent died from suicide).

These figures have been criticized in the past because of a possible selection bias, i.e., many of these depressed patients were initially picked up in the hospital. Quite recently a study has been completed in Rochester that involved hospitalized patients as well as those from Community Mental Health Centers and other treatment facilities. This study, which should answer the criticism of the earlier studies, shows the same figure—12-14 percent.

Dr. Schuyler: I have done some work on suicidal motivation which may relate to this discussion of the interface between depression and suicide. Understanding a person's "intent," that is, the intensity of his wish to die, has proved complex. Suicidal motivations include a wish for escape or surcease through death, a wish to escape through sleep, with death either not desired or not consicously contemplated, and a wish to influence another's behavior through suicidal actions.

One method of measuring intent once suicidal behavior has occurred is to focus on the circumstances of the behavior and the self-report of the attempter. We have developed an Intent Scale which enables us to systematically question suicide attempters about their motivation. In a 1971 study by Silver, et al., a highly positive correlation was demonstrated between suicidal intent measured with our scale and severity of depression assessed with the Beck Depression Inventory. This suggests that severely depressed patients may be overrepresented in the group of suicide attempters with high intent to die.

Dr. Tabachnick: As Dr. Schuyler points out, understanding a person's suicidal "intent" is a complex matter. For example, intention varies markedly over time, sometimes over very short intervals. The complexity is introduced primarily by ambivalence—an admixture of wishes to die and fantasies of rescue and rebirth. In my judgment, objective measures have not yet been able to identify these complexities.

Dr. Goodwin: I was somewhat surprised that when Dr. Tabachnick separated the group of people who killed themselves from the overall population, the distribution of different diagnostic or characterological subgroups within the two larger groups was the same. In other words, Dr. Tabachnick didn't find that there was any greater likelihood that psychotic people would suicide than nonpsychotic people. Such findings surprise me, and I wonder if I have correctly summarized them.

Dr. Tabachnick: The finding is surprising and I believe Dr. Goodwin raises a valid question.

Dr. Goodwin: In view of this seemingly paradoxical finding, I cannot help but suspect some sampling bias. I wonder if there is something common to all people who come to the suicide prevention center which differentiates them from others who do not seek help at the SPC. I would further suppose that this common denominator is not measured by the various subgroupings and tests employed to study the population. Unless we assume the presence of some other factor, we would expect to find some different character types in the sample in relation to the suicide rate.

Dr. Tabachnick: Contact with the Suicide Prevention Center provides a very important common denominator: almost all these people are suicidal. In effect, the service acts as a primary screen of the general population to identify a group of suicidal people. The risk of suicidal death among this group is one hundred times that of the general population. Thus, those in contact with the center have a suicide risk of clinical magnitude. The research task, which has involved us for some years, is to distinguish among that clinical group of suicidal people those with the greatest likelihood of committing suicide.

Dr. Raskin: Dr. Tabachnick, do you find that a significant number of people come to the Suicide Prevention Center with real somatic problems such as cancer?

Dr. Tabachnick: I do not have any firm figures in mind. Just anecdotally, I think the number is rather small. We don't actually see too many people with terminal cancer, but we do see a number of people who think they have cancer.

Dr. Beck: In response to Dr. Raskin's comment, I am reminded of the recent Buffalo study. This study was done in a general hospital where patients on a terminal cancer ward were studied and compared with a group of depressed patients in the same hospital. The central and outstanding finding of the study was that the suicide rate among depressed patients was about 100 times higher than that among cancer patients.

Dr. Klerman: I think it would also be very important to look at a group of depressed patients and examine causes of death other than suicide. Not only would we be looking for misclassifications of actual suicidal death, but we might also find that some other theoretical notions would be confirmed.

Based on Dr. Schmale's research, we would hypothesize that depressed patients who have the helpless-hopeless point of view are in a biological state that renders them more susceptible to illness in general, whether it is peptic ulcer, leukemia, infectious hepatitis, or suicide. Thus, examining the death rate from all causes in a depressed group of people would provide data relevant to this hypothesis as well as to the suicide issue.

Dr. Schmale: There are really two separate issues involved, one being the increased incidence of mortality associated with depressive illness, and the other that it is the same vulnerability that produces depressive illness and also predisposes to other somatic conditions. Thus, a person might react to a stress or a loss, not by becoming depressed but by developing physical illness. My hypothesis is that the underlying mechanism is one of helplessness-hopelessness.

Dr. Tabachnick: My feeling is that this research has at least two rather important implications. The first is that it is probably erroneous or at least not sufficiently satisfactory to correlate broad entities such as suicide and depression. Suicide, although having numerous ambiguities of its own, can at least be characterized by a type of death that is fairly specific (that is, intentioned, self-inflicted death). But depression is so ambiguous a term that one really needs to specify what signs and symptoms he is thinking of when using the term. By getting more specific and objective about the depressive phenomena we are interested in, we will be able to isolate those factors that correlate more highly with suicide. Of course, looking for such key factors should not be restricted to elements of the depressive syndrome, but should also include phenomena outside the syndrome.

The second important point is the identification of somatic signs of depression as an important predictor of suicidal lethality. If the finding is replicable, then an important and fairly easily elicited clinical manifestation may be added to the relatively small group of factors closely linked with suicide.

Incidentally, the use of the "suicidal" subgroup classification indicates that at least as far as depressive signs and symptoms go (but this would probably be true for other clinical manifestations also), there are important quantitative differences in the distribution among various suicidal subgroups.

BIBLIOGRAPHY

Pederson, A., Barry, D., & Babigian, H. M. Epidemiological Considerations of Psychotic Depression. *Archives of General Psychiatry*, in press.

Plumb, M., Park, S., Holmes, J., Dykstra, L., & Holland, J. *Comparative study of depression in patients facing death by suicide or fatal disease*. Paper presented at the Annual Meeting of the American Association of Suicidology, Washington, D.C., May, 1971. In preparation.

Silver, M. A., Bohnert, M., Beck, A. T., & Marcus, D. Relation of depression of attempted suicide and seriousness of intent. *Archives of General Psychiatry*, 1971, 25, 573-576.

8
NONVERBAL BEHAVIOR AND PSYCHOPATHOLOGY

Paul Ekman and Wallace V. Friesen
Langley Porter Neuropsychiatric Institute
University of California, San Francisco

INTRODUCTION

We believe that the investigation of facial expression and body movement has valuable applications in the study of depression and other forms of psychopathology. The study of nonverbal behavior encompasses the examination of both global categories of activity such as facial mobility, hand movements, and posture, and of a whole array of very specific types of actions such as mutual eye glances, brow raising, hand rubbing, and foot tapping. Both the subject's *encoding* of behavior and his *decoding* of behavior may be measured. That is to say, in an *encoding* study we examine the subject's own nonverbal behavior, measuring some aspect of what the person actually does. In a *decoding* study, we measure the subject's interpretation of the nonverbal behavior of others. Individual differences in either the encoding or decoding of nonverbal behavior may permit interpretation of transient emotion, enduring mood, attitude, or personality. Films or videotapes of the behavior are generally used in both kinds of study.

For investigators doing research on psychopathology, measurement of the nonverbal behavior of patients can provide, we believe, systematic information of use in two aspects of their research.

Nonverbal behavior can be a data source for ascertaining the comparability of patients assigned to different treatment groups within an institution, or the comparability of patients in different institutional settings. One can utilize the

[1] All the research reported here is supported by Research Grant MH 11976 and Career Scientist Award 5-KO-2-MH06092 from the National Institute of Mental Health. The authors are grateful to Patsy Garlan for her editorial assistance.

nonverbal measures of encoding (the patients' actual nonverbal repertoire) or of decoding (the patients' ability to interpret the behavior of others). Both can provide a way to assess patients without having to rely solely upon diagnostic labels or global clinical judgments. The usefulness of measures of nonverbal behavior for this purpose will depend, of course, on evidence of how rich and complex the information is that can be gleaned from the patients' encoding and decoding of behavior, on the relevance of this information to the usual kinds of distinctions made by those studying psychopathology, and the extent to which such information provided by nonverbal measures differs from that which is readily available from other measures.

Nonverbal encoding and decoding measures can also be used in a pre-post design to assess change which occurs with some intervening treatment. The utility of such measures will depend on the extent to which they capture the kind of changes that occur when patients move from an acute to a remitted state.

A third use of the study of nonverbal behavior is more relevant to treatment than to research in psychopathology. Information about the meaning of certain kinds of encoding by a patient, and knowledge of any unusual characteristics in the patient's decoding ability could be useful in the training of psychotherapists. Our concern in this paper, however, is not with that application of our findings.

In recent years, there has been a rapid growth of research into one or another aspect of nonverbal behavior. Most investigators have studied body movements, though some have studied facial expression. Most have conducted encoding studies, though there have been some decoding studies. There have been two methodological approaches to encoding studies. One involves direct measurement of the *components* of the behavior. The other entails the study of observers' *judgment* or interpretation of the facial expression and/or body movement of the patient.

Using the components approach one might, for example, obtain a videotape of the patient's facial expressions during five minutes of an interview and measure the frequency with which the patient looked in the direction of the interviewer, the duration of glances, the frequency of eyebrow raises, of smiles, of lip presses, etc. A judgment approach to the same videotape would be to show it to a group of observers, trained or untrained, with or without coincident speech, and ask them to use their own words or a standard rating instrument to record their impressions about the patient's mood, personality traits, attitudes, etc.

Before discussing our own work, let me briefly note the major lines of research and some of the recent reviews of this literature.

Perhaps the most popular area in recent years has been research on *eye contact*, or *mutual glancing*. In our terminology, these are encoding studies using a components approach, in which the frequency and duration of the mutual glancing is measured. Most of these studies have examined only this variable, though some have also considered distance, but few have considered other aspects of body movement or facial expression as well. Exline (1972) has recently reviewed his own work and that of others on mutual glancing.

A few investigators have looked at different types of hand movements, again conducting encoding studies measuring the hand activities of the subject with the components approach. Some of these investigators have examined other nonverbal variables as well, comparing hand movements with facial behavior, leg movements, etc. Recent work in this field includes that of Dittmann (Dittmann 1962; Dittmann & Llewellyn 1969), Freedman (Freedman & Hoffmann 1967; Freedman, Blass, Rifkin, & Quitkin 1973), and our own research group (Ekman & Friesen 1968, 1969a, 1969b, 1972).

There have been very few studies of the full range of facial expressions in an interpersonal situation. Most have been decoding studies, in which normative data are gathered within and across cultures. Recent work along these lines is that of Izard (1971), Ekman, Friesen, and Ellsworth (1972), Ekman (1972), and Ekman (1973). I will later discuss some of our own studies in progress on differences between face and body in the type of information conveyed and on differences among psychiatric patients in ability to decode particular facial expressions of emotion.

Another line of research on nonverbal behavior, using a *cross-channel comparative method*, falls generally within the definition of the encoding study with a judgment approach. Different groups of observers are exposed to different "channels"; i.e., they read a typescript, or hear filtered speech, or observe a silent film or videotape. Measures are then taken of the agreement or lack of agreement across channels in the information obtained by the observers from these different sources. (Later I will briefly present some of our own findings, which suggest that separating the patient's behavior into the three channels of voice, verbal content, and nonverbal behavior is too simplified a device, missing important distinctions within each channel and obscuring important similarities across channels.) Recent examples of this work are that of Bugental (Bugental, Kaswan, Love, & Fox 1970) and Mehrabian (1972).

Duncan (1969), in his recent review of research on nonverbal behavior, contrasted Birdwhistell's (1970) approach with our own (1967, 1968, 1969a, 1969b) to characterize two divergent lines of study of body movement and facial expression. Other reviews of the field are that of Harrison (1973), Knapp (1972), and Ekman, Friesen and Ellsworth (1972); the last is concerned only with facial expression.

In our own research, to which I will now turn, we have examined both facial expression and body movement, have conducted both encoding and decoding studies, and have employed both the components and the judgment approach. We have studied normal and disturbed persons, children and adults, alone and in interaction, in this culture and in other cultures. I shall present here our studies of interview behavior in this country, conducted with psychiatric patients and normal individuals, because it would appear to be the area of our work most relevant to investigators concerned with depression and other forms of psychopathology. My purpose is twofold: to acquaint you with some promising findings, which I hope will encourage you to include measures of facial expression and body movement in your own research, and to give you some idea of the variety of methods and measurement techniques available to you.

Let me first describe our encoding studies using the judgment approach and then those using the components approach and lastly our decoding studies.

THE JUDGMENT APPROACH TO THE STUDY OF NONVERBAL BEHAVIOR

Global Assessments of Nonverbal Behavior

Some years ago, we conducted a series of encoding studies to demonstrate that facial expression and body movement spontaneously shown in the course of a psychiatric interview provide information about both changes in psychological functioning between admission to and discharge from a mental hospital, and about some of the more subtle distinctions among psychiatric patients suffering from the same general syndrome (e.g., depression) at either admission or discharge.

The methods employed in this research were fairly simple. An eight-minute film of each patient was made during a standardized interview conducted within 48 hours of admission to the hospital and again within a week of the time of discharge. A silent version was shown to a group of untrained observers (college students), who were not told that the person they were viewing was a mental patient. Each group of observers saw either the admission or the discharge film of one of three female patients and recorded their impressions of the person by checking adjectives on Gough's Adjective Check List. The results, reported in detail elsewhere (Ekman & Friesen 1968), need only be summarized here.

1. The nonverbal behavior shown at admission to the hospital conveys quite different information from that shown at discharge. For each patient, a number of adjectives checked by the majority of observers who saw the admission film were not checked by the majority of observers who saw the discharge film. And, conversely, a number of adjectives checked by the majority who saw the discharge film were not checked by the majority who saw the admission film. For example, one patient was judged to be despondent, worried, dissatisfied, fearful, self-pitying, sensitive, unstable, complaining, disorderly, gloomy, and moody by the majority of observers who saw her admission film, while she was described as friendly, talkative, active, impulsive, immature, cheerful, coopera- tive, energetic, feminine, and informal by the majority of the observers who saw her discharge film.

2. The information conveyed appears to have some relevance to the patient's psychological state. This finding, however, is more tentative, because the evidence is sketchy and not entirely consistent. When we compared the observers' judgments of one patient with her own self-ratings and with the

ratings of her made by the ward psychiatrist (both using Gough's list), we found the observers of the film to be more in agreement with the patient than with the psychiatrist at both admission and discharge. However, considering only those adjectives checked by both patient and doctor, we found that at admission all of these adjectives were also checked by the observers of the film, and at discharge all but one.

3. Nonverbal behavior conveys information that distinguishes among patients. Despite the fact that at admission they all shared the status of being acutely disturbed and the diagnosis of depression, and at discharge they were all in a state of remission, some adjectives checked by the majority of observers who saw one patient's admission film were not checked by the majority of those who saw another's, and similarly for the discharge films.

We consider this experiment to have provided a rough assay of the kinds of information that can be gleaned from spontaneous facial expression and movement. It showed that information relevant to psychopathology and changes in psychopathology can be readily obtained by untrained observers. While there is an obvious need to replicate these findings and to extend them to other patients, we believe they are encouraging and do offer a fairly simple means of assessing changes in psychological functioning associated with intervening treatment. Pilot studies conducted subsequently suggest that considerably shorter samples of interview behavior, from two to four minutes, will produce comparable results. Later I shall discuss some of our findings on how specific types of movement vary with changes in psychopathology.

The Face and Body as Sources of Nonverbal Leakage

After presenting in 1967 some of the findings just described to the Third Research and Psychotherapy Conference, sponsored by the American Psychological Association, we became convinced that investigators of psychotherapy outcome were not likely to adopt measures of nonverbal behavior unless we could show that such measures would provide crucial information not more easily obtained from a patient's verbal behavior. This pragmatic need focused our attention on a question fundamental to any theory of interpersonal communication. Are the verbal and nonverbal channels of communication redundant? And if not, what information is particularly conveyed by the nonverbal channel?

A number of situations come to mind in which a person's nonverbal behavior might be expected to provide distinctive information. A person's nonverbal behavior may speak for him when he is not willing to verbalize certain matters, or he cannot be directly asked, or the relevant information is not within his awareness, or there is reason to doubt his verbal statements. Of particular interest to us has been the situation in which there is conflict within the individual, either about the act of communicating or about the topic of communication. In this situation, we have hypothesized, it is likely that the two channels will be discrepant (Ekman & Friesen 1969a). Following this line of thought, we began to develop a descriptive theory about the characteristics of deceptive interactions. We postulated differences among nonverbal behaviors, suggesting that some function to maintain the deception and others either betray the occurrence of deception or reveal the information being withheld. This formulation of *deception clues* and information *leakage* was the basis for research I shall shortly discuss. It suggested that the hypothesis that one channel (verbal or nonverbal) was more reliable than another was too simple. Instead, within each channel or behavior modality there may be some types or classes of events that function to maintain deception and others that escape efforts to control, censor, or disguise communication.

Our theory of nonverbal leakage and deception clues (Ekman & Friesen 1967, 1969a) postulated that the body more than the face escapes efforts to disguise communication, conveying clues to deception or leaking the withheld information. We reasoned that people are generally held more accountable for what they show in the face than what they reveal in the body, and, because of greater feedback and reinforcement, people will monitor their facial behavior more than their bodily activity, committing lies of omission by inhibiting facial muscular movement and lies of commission by simulating feelings they do not have. We further postulated a special class of facial behavior, very brief facial expressions (*micro-expressions*)[2], which would escape censoring and would provide leakage. We believed, however, that most observers would not notice such micro-expressions and would therefore be misled by the more frequent and obvious macro-expressions. Our theory also specified particular types of body movements that would provide leakage or deception clues.

We have tested the general hypothesis that different information is conveyed by the face and the body, both with clinical material of naturally occurring deception and with studies of normal subjects in experimentally arranged, deceptive, and honest interactions. Of 120 filmed interviews with psychiatric inpatients, there were three interviews of which we could be certain, from the patients' later confession, that they had been withholding information from the interviewer and lying about their feelings or thoughts. Separate groups of observers were shown either the face only or the body only during these deceptive interviews. The observers were not told they were viewing psychiatric patients and were required to use an adjective check list to describe their impressions of the person they viewed. For each of the three interviews, a comparison of the adjectives checked most frequently by those who observed the face suggested they were picking up the false message more than the concealed message, while the reverse was true for those who viewed the body.

---

[2] Haggard and Isaacs (1966) were the first to describe micro-expressions; our formulation expands upon but does not disagree with their interpretation of these very quick facial expressions.

We designed an interview procedure for obtaining deceptive and honest behavior, to replicate this finding with a larger sample of subjects, and to obtain materials for testing our more specific hypotheses about particular body movements during deception. We chose first-year student nurses as subjects, because we could ethically justify showing them some extremely unpleasant surgical films, and because we could motivate them to seriously attempt deception by our pointing out that skill in deception was an interpersonal skill relevant to successful nursing.[3] In both the honest and deception interviews the subject first watched a silent motion picture film, while the interviewer sat turned away from both the subject and the film. After a minute of such unobserved film watching, the interviewer turned and faced the subject, asking her about her feelings as she continued to watch the film. After another minute the film ended and the interviewer continued to ask a standard set of questions about the subject's experience. In one session the subject saw a pleasant film and was instructed to describe her feelings frankly. In another session the subject saw a stress-inducing film and was instructed to conceal negative feelings with intent to convince the interviewer that she had pleasant feelings and was seeing a pleasing film. Five of the twenty-one subjects confessed during the experiment, and the videotape of their behavior was not used to test our hypothesis, since they had failed to maintain the deception.[4]

Separate groups of untrained observers saw either the face or the body behavior of the nursing students during the deceptive and honest pleasant interviews. The observers were asked to judge if each person they viewed was being honest (defined as attempting to describe frankly one's feelings about a pleasant film) or deceptive (defined as attempting to conceal negative feelings in response to a stress film and to convince the interviewer that positive emotion about a pleasant film was felt). Our hypothesis that the body more than the face provides leakage and deception clues was supported, in that those who saw the body reached a significant level of accuracy in detecting deception, while those who viewed the face did no better than chance (Ekman & Friesen 1974a).

This experiment has substantiated our hypothesis about a difference between the face and the body in deceptive interactions. Body behavior, more than facial behavior, escapes efforts to disguise communication or conceal information. We expect, in studies now planned, to show parallel differences between the verbal and the vocal channel. Those who judge filtered speech and perceive, thereby, just voice quality should be more accurate in detecting deception than those

[3] We have in fact found that measures of nursing students' nonverbal behavior in our honest and deceptive interaction experiment correlate about 0.60 with their clinical and academic grades one year later.

[4] We are pursuing the question as to why some subjects confessed. We are reasonably convinced that it is unrelated to their understanding of the experiment, their motivation in the experiment, or their motivation to become a nurse and instead is related to a stable interpersonal characteristic.

who read a typescript of the verbal content. And even within the verbal channel, those who are instructed to notice speech disruptions, incomplete words, etc., should be more accurate in detecting deception than those who focus attention on the content of speech.

The relevance of this particular experiment to those interested in studying depression is twofold. First, it shows that when an individual is in conflict, very different information may be obtained from different aspects of his nonverbal behavior. Second, it may be possible to utilize measures of the amount of agreement between judgments of the face and judgments of the body (and perhaps also between judgments of verbal content and voice), as an index of intrapsychic conflict. From inspection of our films of psychiatric patients we would hypothesize, for example, little discrepancy and high redundancy between the face and the body for the retarded or agitated depressive at the time of admission to a mental hospital and considerably more discrepancy towards the middle of hospitalization. We plan to test this hypothesis in the coming years.

THE COMPONENTS APPROACH TO THE STUDY OF NONVERBAL BEHAVIOR

Let me turn now from our encoding studies utilizing a judgment approach to those utilizing a components approach, in which the actual movements shown by the individual are classified and measured. First I shall explain our classificatory system for hand movements, and report results on hand movements during deception and hand movements in relation to psychopathology. Then I shall describe the classification and measurement of facial behavior and report some results with such measures.

Classification of Hand Activity

When we first began to measure body movement, our unit of analysis was the *nonverbal act* (Ekman & Friesen 1966; Ekman & Friesen 1968; Ekman, Friesen, & Taussig 1969). An act was defined as

> ... a movement within any single body area (head, face, shoulders, hands, or feet) or across multiple body areas which has visual integrity and is visually distinct from another act.... Acts which look alike, established by paired comparison procedures, were given the same classification label.... The classification of acts ... is thus based upon what is easily recognizable to any observer. The classificatory scheme is built directly from the acts ... found in the film records, rather than derived from *a priori* notions.... This unit of behavior focuses on the type of nonverbal behavior which may be *potentially* communicative between two interactants. It is geared to the type of cue to which each member of the dyad may be responding (Ekman & Friesen 1968, pp. 193-194).

We found that acts so defined were systematically related to the concomitant verbal behavior, and conveyed specific and distinctive information to observers when judged out of context. While the frequency of particular acts differed markedly between time of admission and time of discharge for particular psychiatric patients, we failed to find similarity across patients in the partcticular acts that characterized their admission and discharge interviews. This failure suggested to us the need to develop a theory for the classification of acts into functional categories. Our theory of the repertoire of nonverbal behavior (Ekman & Friesen 1967, 1969b) proposed five categories of nonverbal behavior defined as to the origin, usage, and coding of nonverbal acts. Each category included a variety of visually distinctive acts which, although differing in their appearance, were similar in their origins, usage, or coding.

Three of these categories are relevant to hand activity: *emblems, illustrators,* and *adaptors.*

Emblems differ from the other two categories of hand activity in their usage, particularly in relationship to verbal behavior, awareness, and intentionality. An emblem can usually be replaced with a word or two, or perhaps a phrase, and is known explicitly by all members of a culture, subculture, or social class. An emblem may repeat, substitute for, or contradict some part of the concomitant verbal behavior. A crucial question in determining whether an act is an emblem is whether it could be replaced with a word or two without changing the information conveyed. Emblems occur most frequently when verbal discourse is prevented by noise, by external circumstance (e.g., while watching a play), by distance (e.g., between hunters), by agreement (e.g., in the game of charades), or by organic impairment. In all of these instances emblematic behavior carries the messages that would otherwise be carried through words. Emblems, of course, also occur during the verbal exchange.

People are usually aware of their use of an emblem. If asked, they can repeat the emblem and usually will take responsibility for having stated the emblematic message. While the use of an emblem is usually intentional and deliberate, occasionally emblems are used with little awareness. There can be emblematic slips, much like slips of the tongue, but these are the exceptions rather than the rule. Emblems can be shown in any area of the body, although most typically they involve the face or the hands. Elsewhere (Ekman & Friesen 1967, 1969b; Ekman 1973), we have discussed the origins and coding of emblems, how they differ across cultures, and their relationship to emotional expression, but these matters are not directly germane to our discussion here.

Illustrators are movements directly tied to speech; they seem to illustrate what is being said verbally. We distinguish eight subclasses: *batons,* movements which accent or emphasize a particular word or phrase; *idiographs,* movements which sketch the path or direction of thought; *deictic movements,* pointing to an object; *spacial movements,* depicting a spatial relationship; *rhythmic movements,* depicting the rhythm or pacing of an event; *kinetographs,* depicting a bodily action; *pictographs,* drawing a picture of the referant; and the use of *emblems* to illustrate verbal statements, either repeating or substituting for a word or phrase. This class of behavior and some of the terminology was first described by Efron (1941, 1972), who proved that the type of illustrator employed varied with ethnic background.

Illustrators are intimately related on a moment-to-moment basis to the phrasing, content, inflection, loudness, etc., of speech. Illustrators can repeat, substitute for, contradict, or augment the information provided verbally. Illustrators are similar to emblems in that they are used with awareness and intentionality. A person may be slightly less aware of his illustrators than of his emblems. Persons differ markedly in their rate and type of illustration. Changes in rate are associated with mood and articulation problems. When demoralized, tired, and unenthusiastic, people drop from their usual rate of illustrator activity. With excitement and enthusiasm about the topic or process of communication, people increase their rate of illustrator activity. When difficulty is experienced in finding adequate words, or when feedback from the listener suggests difficulty in comprehension, illustrator activity increases. In such instances the increase in illustrators may not only function to aid in communicating to the other person, but also may serve a self-priming purpose, helping the person past an awkwardness in his speech. Illustrators are also employed to command renewed attention if the listeners' interest appears to lag.

Adaptors are movements first learned as part of one's adaptive efforts to satisfy self or bodily needs, or to perform bodily actions, or to manage and cope with emotions, or to develop or maintain prototypic interpersonal contacts, or to learn instrumental activities. We have distinguished self-adaptors, alter-adaptors, and object-adaptors, although it is only the first category that concerns us here. Self-adaptors are learned in connection ·with the mastering or management of a variety of problems or needs. Some are relevant to facilitating or blocking sensory input; some are relevant to ingestive or excretive or autoerotic activity; some are relevant to grooming or enhancing the attractiveness of the face and body; and some were first learned to facilitate or block sound-making and speech. When first learned, these self-adaptors were associated with drive states, with particular emotions, with particular interpersonal events, with particular settings. Adults use adaptors *either* as an appropriate adaptive activity or because some aspect of the current situation triggers the adaptive reaction. In the latter instances only a fragment or a reduced version of the adaptor will usually be shown, probably because of later learned inhibitions about performing certain activities in public places.

Self-adaptors are usually performed with little awareness and no intention to communicate. Self-adaptors are not intrinsically related to speech; but they may be triggered by the motives or affects which are being verbalized. Self-adaptors receive little direct attention or comment from others, with the exception of a parent's comments to a child for performing self-adaptors in public. Although self-adaptors may be inhibited in the presence of others, people still do engage in such behavior during conversations; when they do so, they break visual contact with their fellow conversant, who also politely averts his gaze from this behavior.

Persons differ markedly in their rate of self-adaptor activity. Self-adaptors increase with psychological discomfort and anxiety, unless the person becomes immobile and muscularly tense. We believe that specific types of self-adaptors are associated with specific feelings and attitudes. Both the *action* and *location* of the self-adaptor must be considered, in distinguishing its specific meaning. Action refers to the activity of the hand when it contacts some part of the face or body. It may be scratch-pick, rub-massage, squeeze-pinch, hold-support, or cover. Our list of locations is based on both biological and psychological functions associated with different parts of the body. For example, we distinguish the eyes, ears, nose, and mouth, but do not make locational distinctions within the cheek area. While we make no distinctions within the forehead area, we do distinguish the temple because it can symbolize thought. Two examples of the psychological meaning of specific self-adaptors can illustrate our thinking. We have found that the eye cover act is associated with shame and guilt, and the scratch-pick act is associated with hostility.

Hand Movements and Deception

The first major test of the utility of our classification of hand movements into emblems, illustrators, and adaptors was in our research on nonverbal behavior during honest and deceptive interviews. In our theory of nonverbal leakage (Ekman & Friesen 1969a), we hypothesized that when individuals attempt to deceive they will fail to manage their hand activity (and leg activity properly and will instead concentrate on falsifying their facial behavior, speech content, and voice quality. More specifically we predicted that there would be more self-adaptors during a deceptive interaction than during an honest one, and fewer illustrators. The increase in self-adaptors and the decrease in illustrators were expected because subjects might well be less enthusiastic (illustrate less) and more anxious (self-adapt more) when trying to deceive the interviewer. Pilot studies suggested that a specific emblem, hand-shrugs, would occur with greater frequency in the deceptive than in the honest interviews. In other research we have verified that the hand-shrug emblem denotes helplessness and inability. In the deception session this emblem might occur if the person felt frustrated or unable to perpetrate the deception successfully. Though we believe that emblems usually occur intentionally and with awareness, the hand-shrug emblem during deception would be an exception, occurring with little awareness as the nonverbal equivalent of a verbal slip of the tongue.

We tested these hypotheses by analyzing from the videotape all of the observable hand movements in the honest and deceptive interviews of 16 nursing students. Two independent technicians located the beginning and end points of each observable hand act; they classified each movement as an illustrator, hand-shrug emblem, or adaptor. Self-adaptors were further subclassified by nine locations and five actions. As predicted, there were significantly more hand-shrug emblems in the deceptive interview than in the honest interview.

Again, as predicted, there were significantly fewer illustrators in the deceptive interview than in the honest interview. Our prediction that self-adaptors would increase during deception was not supported. When all the different types of adaptors (disregarding differences in location and action) were considered together, there was about the same frequency in the deceptive as in the honest interview.

We had not made predictions about specific subcategories of self-adaptors, but we did find that one such subcategory significantly increased in the deceptive interview. Face-play, an action in which one hand contacts some part of the face and engages in a very small, hard-to-distinguish movement, occurred with greater frequency in deception. We are not certain as to why this one subcategory changed in frequency nor can we easily explain why total self-adaptors failed to show the predicted increase in deception. One possibility, of course, is that our hypothesis that total self-adaptors are related to anxiety is incorrect or at least reflects too simple a view. There are two data sources that are relevant to that question and suggest that we may be correct in our interpretation of self-adaptors. Our prediction could have failed if anxiety was evoked for at least some subjects in both the honest and deceptive interviews. We had taken great pains to motivate the subjects, telling them that their behavior in both the honest and deceptive interviews was indicative of the likelihood of their success in nursing school. Self-report questionnaires administered at the time and some months later suggest the subjects believed us. In that context, conceivably some subjects would be anxious about their performance in both sessions and might show similar rates of self-adaptor activity in both sessions. The fact that the rate of self-adaptor activity in the two sessions was significantly correlated (.54) is consistent with this reasoning. The second bit of evidence consistent with our hypothesis that self-adaptors are related to anxiety comes from examination of how naive observers judge body movement. If you will remember, earlier we described an experiment in which groups of observers viewed videotapes showing only the body and judged whether they thought the person was being honest or deceptive. Even though the rate of self-adaptors did not differ in the two sessions (perhaps because both sessions were anxiety-provoking), if our interpretation of self-adaptors is correct we should expect that observers who view the entire repertoire of body movement might tend to call people deceptive if they showed many self-adaptors (thus appearing anxious, fidgety, nervous) and honest if they did not, regardless of the actual facts of the case. That indeed is what occurred. The rate of self-adaptors was significantly correlated (.75) with observer's judgment of deception.

Our results on illustrators and shrug emblems need to be replicated with another group of subjects and steps must be taken to verify further the meaning of self-adaptors.[5] We consider the findings to date encouraging, however. They suggest that our classification of hand activity into illustrators, adaptors, and

[5] We are also measuring leg movement, posture, gaze direction, and facial behavior.

emblems is useful, and that specific types of hand activity do relate to the occurrence of deception. We shall shortly see that some of the ambiguity about our interpretation of the self-adaptors is clarified by findings on psychiatric patients which are consistent with our interpretation of this class of activity.

I will postpone discussing the relevance of these findings to studies of psychopathology until after describing our findings on hand activity of psychiatric patients.

Hand Activity and Psychopathology

Kiritz (Kiritz 1971; Kiritz, Ekman, & Friesen in preparation) analyzed the hand activity in the admission and discharge films of 31 female psychiatric inpatients, whom we had filmed some years ago. Nine were diagnosed as psychotic depressive, 7 as neurotic depressive, and 15 as schizophrenic. All of the hand movements shown in the admission and discharge interviews of the patients were classified as illustrators or self-adaptors, and the self-adaptors were subclassified in terms of location and action.

On the basis of our theory that illustrators will vary with mood, increasing with enthusiasm and involvement, we predicted an increase in illustrators for the depressives from the admission to the discharge interview. This prediction was confirmed for the psychotic depressives and the trend was in the same direction, although not significant, for the neurotic depressives. We had not expected any change from admission to discharge in illustrator activity for the schizophrenics because there would not necessarily be the same shift in mood in these patients as in the depressives. As expected, there was no difference in illustrator activity in admission and discharge interviews of the schizophrenics. Illustrator activity in psychiatric patients, then, is not simply a function of the shift in the severity of psychopathology, but is related to shift in mood or affect.

Again, on the basis of our postulate that illustrators are related to enthusiasm and to involvement with the communication process, we made predictions about differences among these three patient groups in their illustrator behavior during the admission interview, when they were in their most acutely disturbed state. As hypothesized, the psychotic depressives showed fewer illustrators than either the neurotic depressives or the schizophrenics at admission. There was a trend for the neurotic depressives to use fewer illustrators than the schizophrenics at admission, but the difference did not reach significance.

To determine whether the hand measures were related to finer distinctions among patients than are captured by diagnostic labels, we obtained ratings of the patients on the Overall and Gorham (1962) Brief Psychiatric Rating Scale. The raters, experienced clinicians, first viewed and heard (sound film) the patient's response to the opening question in the admission interview ("How are you feeling today?"). After completing their ratings of the patient based on this sample of behavior at admission, the rater was then shown the same time-slice from the discharge interview and ratings were again made on the Overall and Gorham scales. In addition, the rater used a unipolar scale to judge improvement from admission to discharge. There was reasonably good agreement among three independent raters who used the Overall and Gorham scales, and a measure of their combined ratings was used.

As predicted, a number of the rating scales were significantly correlated with our measures of illustrators or adaptors. The scale *depressive mood* was correlated negatively with amount of illustrating at both admission (−.51) and discharge (−.39). The scale *motor retardation* was negatively correlated with amount of illustrating at admission (−.66) and at discharge (−.36). The scale *emotional withdrawal* was negatively correlated with illustrating at admission (−.56) and at discharge (−.37). The scale *blunted affect* was negatively correlated with illustrating at admission (−.55) and at discharge (−.40). Although not predicted, illustrator activity was also significantly correlated with *conceptual disorganization* (.46) and negatively with *mannerisms* (−.43) and *cooperativeness* (−.46).

It seemed possible that these findings might be spurious, reflecting merely a relationship between rate of illustrating and rate of speaking. An increase in the patients' speech rate as they moved from a disturbed to a remitted state could account for most of the correlations reported. To check on this, we separately measured word rate and, although we found it was correlated with illustrator rate, when we controlled for word rate by using partial correlational techniques, most of the correlations with the clinical rating scales survived. Most of the relationships remained statistically significant, if somewhat lowered, when the influence of rate of speaking was removed.

Another way of using the clinicians' ratings on the Brief Psychiatric Rating Scale was to factor-analyze these ratings at admission and at discharge and examine the correlation of factor scores with hand measures. I will report only the results with the admission factors, as the results were substantially the same with the discharge factors. The scales with the highest loadings on the first factor were *withdrawal* and *motor retardation*. We call this factor "out of it" and it was negatively correlated with illustrators (−.67). The scales with the highest loadings on the second factor were *anxiety* and *guilt feelings*. We labelled this factor "upset," and it was positively correlated with total self-adaptor activity (.38). The scales with the highest loadings on the third factor were *unusual thought* and *concept disorganization*. We called this factor "schizi-ness," and it was unrelated to illustrator output. The scales with the highest loading on the fourth factor were *hostility* and *suspiciousness*. We called this factor "negativism," and it was positively correlated with picking or scratching adaptors (.33).

These results, like the results I have described to you on hand movements and deception, indicate the usefulness of our classification of hand behavior. We have shown that the distinction between illustrators and adaptors does indeed relate to

1. differences in the interview behavior of depressed patients at admission and at discharge;

2. differences between psychotic and neurotic depressives; and

3. clinical descriptions of the characteristics of patients.

Presumably when clinicians evaluate patients making judgments on such characteristics as withdrawal or anxiety, as in the Overall and Gorham rating scales, they utilize a variety of data sources: past history, the words, word usage, word content, voice quality, paralinguistic cues, facial expressions, posture, leg movements, and hand activity. Our study was not designed to determine the extent to which clinicians utilize hand activity as they customarily make their judgments, but to test whether our systematic measure of hand activity would relate to such judgments. That I believe we have achieved. We would expect that as we measure other aspects of nonverbal behavior—leg movements, posture, eye contact, facial muscular movements—we will also obtain correlations with clinical judgments. When we take into account a number of these nonverbal variables, we will perhaps be able to make assignments that will replicate those made on the basis of clinical judgment.

The usefulness of this research for those studying depression or psychopathology is not, however, as a substitute for clinical judgment. Even if measuring hand activity or other kinds of nonverbal behavior could produce the same judgments as a clinician, it would be a rather impractical way of going about matters, since measurements of nonverbal behavior are more laboriously achieved than the usual clinical ratings. Instead, its usefulness is as a different, clinically relevant method of assessing an individual's interpersonal behavior. We need not rely only on the clinicians' inferences about such states as anxiety, but can also directly measure the patient's behavioral repertoire through procedures such as our classification of hand activity. As I pointed out at the beginning of the paper, nonverbal measures can be used either as a way of insuring comparability in the assignment of patients to different groups or insuring the comparability of patients studied across different institutions, or, if taken at different points in time, as a pre- post-measure of treatment outcome.

FACIAL BEHAVIOR: COMPONENTS
AND JUDGMENT APPROACH

For the last seven years a major part of our research on facial expression has been concerned with similarities and differences across cultures (Ekman 1968; Ekman, Sorenson, & Friesen 1969; Ekman & Friesen 1971). Before approaching the question of individual differences in facial expression of emotion, we felt it was necessary to attack the question of universality, which was the central issue in most of the past confusions and contradictions in theory and data about facial expression. The argument has been whether facial expressions of emotion are unique to each culture, learned much like a language (as claimed by Birdwhistell 1963, 1970; Klineberg 1938, 1940; LaBarre 1947), or instead are universal for all men, biologically based in man's evolution (as Darwin 1872, 1965, and recently Tomkins 1962, 1963, have held). Let me acquaint you with our current thinking on this issue by quoting from our most recent integration of the results of our cross-cultural studies (Ekman 1972):

> The evidence is remarkably consistent from four experiments, and, in our evaluation, conclusively proves that there are universal facial expressions of emotion. We have reported data on five literate cultures, four Western and one Eastern, and on two pre-literate cultures from New Guinea. The samples were drawn from six different language groups. . . . The first experiment studied judgments of spontaneous facial expressions in Japan and the United States showing that these facial expressions were judged the same way by members of both cultures. In the second experiment we then showed through measurement that the same facial behaviors . . . characterized the Japanese and American reactions to a stress film. Further evidence of the universality of facial expressions of emotion was obtained in the third experiment which showed that the same facial expression was interpreted as showing the same emotion in five literate cultures.
>
> The possibility that these findings might not reflect the operation of a [common, biologically based] facial affect program, but that facial expressions are pan-cultural only among people who have had sufficient visual contact to learn each other's facial expressions or learn common expressions from mass media models was eliminated in the studies of two visually isolated pre-literate cultures. The same facial expressions were found for the same emotions among these people who had no opportunity to learn Western or Eastern facial expressions from a mass media and who had seen so few Caucasians that it was unlikely that they could have learned a foreign facial language. We believe then that we have isolated and demonstrated the basic set of universal facial expressions of emotion. They are not a language which varies from one place to another; one need not be taught a totally new set of muscular movements and a totally new set of rules for interpreting facial behavior if one travels from one culture to another. . . .
>
> In explaining these results . . . [we have developed a neuro-cultural theory of facial expression which postulates] both universal and culture-specific expressions. . . . Our neuro-cultural theory postulates a facial affect program located within the nervous system of all human beings linking particular facial muscular movements with particular emotions. It offers alternative nonexclusive explanations of the possible origin of the linkages in the affect program between the felt emotion and the movement of the facial muscles. Our theory holds that the elicitors, the particular events which activate the affect program, are in largest part socially learned and culturally variable, and that many of the consequences of an aroused emotion also are culturally variable, but that the facial muscular movement which will occur for a particular emotion (if not interfered with by display rules) is dictated by this affect program and is universal. (pp. 276–279)

We introduced the concept of display rules to describe a learned mechanism which can override the affect program and control facial appearance.

Our theory is *neuro-cultural* because it deals with two quite different sets of determinants of facial expressions, the first responsible for universals and the second for cultural differences. "Neuro" refers to the facial affect program, which determines the relationships between particular emotions and the firing of particular patterns of facial muscles. "Cultural" refers to the second set of determinants, which are most of the events that elicit emotions, the rules about controlling the appearance of emotions (display rules), and the consequences of emotions; these, we hold, are learned and vary with cultures. There is, however, a third set of determinants. These are the psychosocial determinants of facial expressions of emotion, which are responsible for differences within a culture among social classes, age grouping, sex roles, families, and personality.

In the last few years we have been developing theory and conducting experiments on how personality may be manifest in facial behavior. It would be premature to attempt here more than a brief description of our approach to this phenomenon. We believe that some of the individual differences of facial behavior result from idiosyncracies in the learning of display rules. Display rules are social norms regarding facial appearance, probably learned early in life and functioning on a habitual basis. They specify which one of four management techniques is to be applied by whom to which emotion in a given circumstance. The four management techniques are to (1) intensify, (2) deintensify, or (3) neutralize the appearance of a felt emotion, or (4) to mask it with the facial configuration of another emotion. For example, at a United States white middle-class wedding display rules specify that the groom must mask any appearance of distress or fear with a happy countenance, while the bride is not similarly constrained. Another example of a display rule is that, in a patient-physician encounter the patient, no matter what the illness, must in the initial greeting reciprocate the physician's (also required) smile, before facially displaying negative affect relevant to the illness. We believe that psychotic-depressives fail to follow this display rule and, unlike neurotic-depressives, will not as often show the initial greeting smile. We also believe that the later appearance of the greeting smile is correlated with a sign of improvement in mental state. More generally, the psychotic-depressive patient fails to follow the usual display rules regarding the management of negative affect. It is not that psychotic-depressed patients are unique in the facial appearance they show with negative affects, but in their consistently maintained negative affect across situations and their seeming inability to modulate it. Put in other terms, in the depressed patient certain negative affects are *flooded*.

We believe that, as a result of particular display rules learned within the family, individuals may in their adult life show *blocks* in facial affect expression. In the extreme, the person may be poker-faced, never revealing in his face how he feels. A less extreme deviation is the block in expressing a particular emotion; for example, a person may never facially show anger. A lesser deviation is the block in the expression of a particular emotion toward a particular class of people. For example, the person may never show anger towards female authority figures. From a pilot study, it appears that blocks in expression may be manifest in two rather different ways. One is that the person simply doesn't show the facial expression of a felt emotion. In a more complex manifestation, the expression is not blocked, but the feedback is, such that the person is remarkably unaware of having shown the particular expression.

We believe it may also be possible to characterize people in terms of an extraordinary facility for showing emotional expressions in their face. For some, this may be characteristic of all the emotions, and they may get into trouble or at least be known for showing everything in their face. The facility may be more specific to a particular emotion, however, so that the person often looks afraid or angry, etc. A neighboring concept, first described by Silvan Tomkins, is that of the *frozen* affect. The frozen affect is an enduring muscular set of the face; after a particular expression, the face, instead of returning to a neutral countenance, may return to a slight version of one or another affect. Thus, the person always looks just slightly disgusted or amused or melancholy, etc.

Another manifestation of personality may be in affect blends and affect sequences. In an affect blend, the face shows the distinctive characteristics of two emotions simultaneously. While it is possible for any given event to elicit two emotions simultaneously, resulting in a blend expression, individuals may show a blend when only one emotion has been elicited by an external event, if they have an established habit of associating a second feeling with the elicited one. For example, when disgust is aroused, some people may characteristically feel also afraid of being disgusted, others may feel angry, others may feel happy, etc. This affect-about-the-affect will repetitively be manifest in either a blend or a rapid sequence of the two emotions in the face.

It should be clear that what I have said so far about individual differences and facial expressions of emotion is based on either pilot studies or hunch and still enjoys more the status of conjecture than formalized hypothesis. Yet these kinds of phenomena are now amenable to systematic investigation. Research on personality differences and facial behavior has been stymied by the lack of any systematic, quantitative procedure for measuring the spontaneous facial expressions of emotion. In the course of our cross-cultural studies, we have developed a technique for such measurement (Ekman, Friesen, & Tomkins 1971), the Facial Affect Scoring Technique (FAST). This procedure provides the investigator with a tool for quantifying the moment-to-moment changes that may occur in facial behavior. Applied to films or videotapes, it provides frequency and duration data on the occurrence of six emotions (happiness, sadness, anger, fear, surprise, and disgust), blends of these emotions, and sequences. Our major work until now has been normative, as we have attempted to validate this measurement technique. While FAST is far from completely validated, we have achieved success in three validation experiments to date and will be expanding our efforts now to utilize it in studies of the face and personality. (Our most recent work on personality and facial expressions is reported in Ekman and Friesen, 1974b.)

DECODING STUDIES OF NONVERBAL BEHAVIOR

The approach to the study of individual differences discussed so far has entailed the investigation of patients' encoding of nonverbal behavior. It is also possible to study how individuals differ in their decoding of the nonverbal behavior of others. Personality and psychopathology may be manifest, for example, not just in a patient's blocks in the facial expression of certain emotions, but in blocks in his sensitivity to or understanding of the facial expression of others.

We have begun a series of experiments on individual differences in the decoding of facial expression of emotion. We have developed a test which we call the Brief Affect Recognition Test (BART), which measures a person's accuracy in decoding six emotions—happiness, sadness, anger, fear, disgust, and surprise. The test employs still photographs of facial expressions which, when seen for five seconds, elicit very high agreement about the presence of one or another of these emotions. In the test we present these faces in a tachistoscope, with an exposure ranging from 1/100th to 1/25th of a second. Our rationale for such a brief presentation is that it approximates usual interpersonal conditions, in which a single facial expression can easily be missed. The usual facial expression lasts only a second or two, is embedded in preceding and subsequent facial behavior, and competes for attention with body movement, voice quality, and verbal content.

Our hypothesis is not that people will differ in their total performance, that is, in their accurate recognition of all six emotions, but that they will differ in their patterns of accuracy, recognizing three or four emotions and not the others. Two studies have been completed.

One experiment (Shannon 1970; Shannon & Ekman, in preparation) compared medical patients, schizophrenics, and depressives. No difference was found in total accuracy; as predicted, depressives were less accurate on fear, while schizophrenics were less accurate on disgust. In the second experiment (Ekman, Jones, Friesen, & Malmstrom 1970), we found that subjects who had ingested marijuana performed differently from those who had ingested alcohol; moreover, there was a relationship between self-reported mood and accuracy in recognizing particular emotions. We are currently attempting to replicate these findings and standardize the Brief Affect Recognition Test.

CONCLUSION

In summary, then, the facial expressions and body movements both shown by psychiatric patients (encoding) and recognized by them (decoding) can provide information about emotion, attitude, and personality useful to those doing research on psychopathology. To date the promise is far greater than the achievement, but this field of research is now beginning to make rapid progress. Encoding can be studied with a judgment approach and with a components approach. The first approach involves global assessments of encoding; it employs trained or untrained observers, who make judgments based on some sample of nonverbal behavior. The second approach is to measure directly some aspect of the patient's activity. I have described our studies of hand movement and presented some of our conjectures about measurement of facial behavior. In studies of decoding, we investigate differences in how patients interpret the nonverbal behavior of others. I have described our preliminary findings with our Brief Affect Recognition Test of patients' ability to interpret facial expressions of emotion.

At this time such studies of nonverbal behavior are, at best adjuncts to more conventional measurements of individual differences utilized by those who study psychopathology. Evidence about the utility and validity of these techniques for measuring nonverbal behavior is still far from conclusive. We are still at the stage of validating nonverbal measures in relationship to the usual diagnostic distinctions or clinical ratings. Some work has begun on the next stage of research on nonverbal behavior to show that measures of nonverbal behavior provide more reliable data, or more sensitive indices, or qualitatively different information from that which is customarily obtained with more conventional methods of assessing individual behavior. It is the results of such studies that will determine the potential of this growing field of research on facial expression and body movement for those interested in psychopathology.

REFERENCES

Birdwhistell, R. L. The kinesic level in the investigation of emotions. In Knapp, P. H. (Ed.), *Expression of the emotions in man*. New York: International Universities Press, 1963.

Birdwhistell, R. L. *Kinesics and context*. Philadelphia: University of Pennsylvania Press, 1970.

Bugental, D. E., Kaswan, J. W., Love, L. R., & Fox, M. N. Child versus adult perception of evaluative messages in verbal, vocal, and visual channels. *Developmental Psychology*, 1970, 2(3), 367-375.

Cohen, A. A., & Harrison, R. P. Intentionality in the use of illustrators in face-to-face communication situations. *Journal of Personality and Social Psychology*, 1973, 28(2), 276-279.

Darwin, C. *The expression of the emotions in man and animals*. London: John Murray, 1872; (current ed.) Chicago: University of Chicago Press, 1965.

Dittmann, A. T. The relationship between body movements and moods in interviews. *Journal of Consulting Psychology*, 1962, 26, 480.

Dittmann, A. T., & Llewellyn, L. G. Body movement and speech rhythm in social conversation. *Journal of Personality and Social Psychology*, 1969, 11(2), 98-106.

Duncan, S., Jr. Nonverbal communication. *Psychological Bulletin*, 1969, 72(2), 118-137.

Efron, D. *Gesture and environment*. New York: King's Crown, 1941; (current ed.) The Hague: Mouton, 1972.

Ekman, P. *The recognition and display of facial behavior in literate and non-literate cultures*. Paper peresented at the symposium on Universality of Emotions of the American Psychological Association, September, 1968.

Ekman, P. Universals and cultural differences in facial expressions of emotion. In Cole, J. K. (Ed.), *Nebraska symposium on motivation, 1971*. Lincoln, Nebraska: University of Nebraska Press, 1972.

Ekman, P. Cross-cultural studies of facial expression. In Ekman, P. (Ed.), *Darwin and facial expression: A century of research in review*. New York: Academic Press, 1973.

Ekman, P., & Friesen, W. V. *The nonverbal act: A visual unit of nonverbal behavior*. Paper presented at the American Psychological Association Symposium, New York, September, 1966.

Ekman, P., & Friesen, W. V. *Origin, usage, and coding: The basis for five categories of nonverbal behavior.* Paper presented at the Symposium on Communication Theory and Linguistic Models, Buenos Aires, October, 1967.

Ekman, P., & Friesen, W. V. Nonverbal behavior in psychotherapy research. In Shlien, J. (Ed.), *Research in psychotherapy*, Vol. 3. Washington: American Psychological Association, 1968.

Ekman, P., & Friesen, W. V. Nonverbal leakage and clues to deception. *Psychiatry*, 1969, 32(1), 88-105. (a)

Ekman, P., & Friesen, W. V. The repertoire of nonverbal behavior: Categories, origins, usage, and coding. *Semiotica*, 1969, 1(1), 49-98. (b)

Ekman, P., & Friesen, W. V. Constants across cultures in the face and emotion. *Journal of Personality and Social Psychology*, 1971, 17(2), 124-129.

Ekman, P., & Friesen, W. V. Hand movements. *Journal of Communication*, 1972, 22(4).

Ekman, P., & Friesen, W. V. Detecting deception from the face and body. *Journal of Personality and Social Psychology*, 1974, in press. (a)

Ekman, P., & Friesen, W. V. *Unmasking the face.* Englewood Cliffs, New Jersey: Spectrum-Prentice Hall, 1974, in press. (b)

Ekman, P., Friesen, W. V., & Ellsworth, P. *Emotion in the human face: Guidelines for research and an integration of findings.* New York: Pergamon Press, 1972.

Ekman, P., Friesen, W. V., & Taussig, T. VID-R and SCAN: Tools and methods for the automated analysis of visual records. In Gerbner, G., Holsti, O., Krippendorff, K., Paisley, W., & Stone, P. (Eds.), *Content analysis*. New York: Wiley, 1969.

Ekman, P., Friesen, W. V., & Tomkins, S. S. Facial Affect Scoring Technique: A first validity study. *Semiotica*, 1971, 3(1), 37-58.

Ekman, P., Jones, R. T., Friesen, W. V., & Malmstrom, E. J., Jr. *Psychoactive drugs and the recognition of facial expressions of emotion.* Unpublished manuscript, Langley Porter Neuropsychiatric Institute, San Francisco, 1970.

Ekman, P., Sorenson, E. R., & Friesen, W. V. Pan-cultural elements in facial displays of emotion. *Science*, 1969, *164*(3875), 86-88.

Exline, R. V. Visual interaction: The glances of power and preference. In Cole, J. K. (Ed.), *Nebraska symposium on motivation, 1971*. Lincoln, Nebraska: University of Nebraska Press, 1972.

Freedman, N., Blass, T., Rifkin, A., & Quitkin, F. Body movements and verbal encoding of aggressive affect. *Journal of Personality and Social Psychology*, 1973, 26(1), 72–85.

Freedman, N., & Hoffmann, S. P. Kinetic behavior in altered clinical states: Approach to objective analysis of motor behavior during clinical interviews. *Perceptual and Motor Skills*, 1967, 24, 527-539.

Haggard, E. A., & Isaacs, K. S. Micro-momentary facial expressions as indicators of ego mechanisms in psychotherapy. In Gottschalk, L. A., & Auerbach, A. H. (Eds.), *Methods of research in psychotherapy*. New York: Appleton-Century-Crofts, 1966.

Harrison, R. P. Nonverbal communication. In de Solo Pool, I., Schramm, W., Maccoby, N., Fry, F., & Parker, E. (Eds.), *Handbook of Communication*. Chicago: Rand McNally, 1973.

Izard, C. E. *The face of emotion.* New York: Appleton-Century-Crofts, 1971.

Kiritz, S. A. *Hand movements and clinical ratings at admission and discharge for hospitalized psychiatric patients.* Unpublished doctoral dissertation, University of California, San Francisco, 1971.

Kiritz, S. A., Ekman, P., & Friesen, W. V. Hand movements and psychopathology. In preparation.

Klineberg, O. Emotional expression in Chinese literature. *Journal of Abnormal and Social Psychology*, 1938, 33, 517-520.

Klineberg, O. *Social psychology.* New York: Holt, Rinehart & Winston, 1940.

Knapp, M. L. *Nonverbal communication in human interaction.* New York: Holt, Rinehart & Winston, 1972.

LaBarre, W. The cultural basis of emotions and gestures. *Journal of Personality*, 1947, **16**, 49-68.

Mahl, G. F. Gestures and body movements in interviews. In Shlien, J. (Ed.), *Research in psychotherapy*, Vol. 3. Washington: American Psychological Association, 1968.

Mehrabian, A. Nonverbal communication. In Cole, J. K. (Ed.), *Nebraska symposium on motivation, 1971*. Lincoln, Nebraska: University of Nebraska Press, 1972.

Overall, J. E., & Gorham, E. R. The brief psychiatric rating scale. *Psychological Reports*, 1962, **10**, 799-812.

Shannon, A. M. *Differences between depressives and schizophrenics in the recognition of facial expression of emotion.* Unpublished doctoral dissertation, University of California, San Francisco, 1970.

Shannon, A. M., & Ekman, P. Psychopathology and the recognition of facial expression of emotion. In preparation.

Tomkins, S. S. *Affect, imagery, consciousness.* Vol. 1. *The positive affects.* New York: Springer, 1962.

Tomkins, S. S. *Affect, imagery, consciousness.* Vol. 2. *The negative affects.* New York: Springer, 1963.

DISCUSSION

Dr. Friedman: Dr. Ekman, could you give us any more detail on the results of your studies on individual differences in the decoding of facial expression as measured by your Brief Affect Recognition Test?

Dr. Ekman: In one study (Dr. Anna Shannon's doctoral dissertation, 1970), a depressed, a schizophrenic, and a control group of general medical patients at the Palo Alto Veterans Administration Hospital were compared. There was no difference between the three groups in their recognition of sad facial expressions. The depressed and schizophrenic patients were less accurate than the general medical group in the recognition of anger facial expressions. The depressed group did considerably worse than either the schizophrenic or the general medical patients in the recognition of fear facial expressions. The schizophrenics were less accurate than the depressives or general medical patients in the recognition of disgust facial expressions.

In another study (Ekman, Jones, Friesen, & Malmstrom 1970), the Brief Affect Recognition Test was given in a pre-post design to medical students. One-third of the subjects smoked marijuana, another third drank alcohol, and the last third were a placebo group. There was no change in accuracy for the placebo group. The alcohol group became more accurate in recognizing disgust facial expressions and the marijuana group became less accurate in recognizing sadness and fear facial expressions.

We believe that these findings must be considered with great caution. The differences obtained in the drug study were not predicted and only some of the differences obtained in the schizophrenic-depressive study had been predicted. The schizophrenic-depressive study has not yet been replicated. We are in the midst of attempting to replicate the drug study but the data analysis is not complete.

Dr. Schuyler: Dr. Ekman, based on your findings, have you made any inferences about the various clinical entities?

Dr. Ekman: There exists very little theory, experimental data, or clinical observation to guide our research on individual differences in the recognition of specific facial expressions of emotion. The study on psychiatric patients did replicate one finding of Silvan Tomkins' some years ago. He used a different test procedure. Rather than a tachistoscopic presentation, he used a stereoscope to superimpose two photographs of different facial expressions, requiring the subjects to judge the emotion they perceived. He found that the depressives failed to recognize the fear facial expression, and this is consistent with our finding. However, he found depressives differed in their judgments of sadness, a finding we did not obtain. Let me repeat my caution that our results on individual differences in judgment of facial expression should be regarded with skepticism until some replication has been achieved.

Dr. Klerman: There is one aspect of theory which might be tested with this technique, namely, the interpersonal theory of depression advanced by the Mabel Blake-Cohen group (1954). In their classic paper they described the depressed group as consisting of people who are generally insensitive to interpersonal nuances and one component of that skill is thought to be the capacity to sense empathetically the communications of others. Dr. Ekman, I believe, has described a method to test this hypothesis, for we would predict that depressed patients would be impaired in their ability to recognize emotional states in others.

Dr. Ekman: The one finding that has replicated in our various studies of individual differences in the recognition of facial expression with the Brief Affect Recognition Test is that performance is patterned. It is a rare individual who fails to recognize all six emotions accurately when they are briefly presented in the tachistoscope. While some individuals are good in their judgment of facial expression, accurately recognizing all six emotions, almost no one is bad in the sense of failing to recognize the majority of the photographs for all six emotions. Most people, whether psychiatric patients, general medical patients, or intoxicated medical students, show a patterned response, accurate on three or four emotions and inaccurate on one or two. Our findings on the depressive patients are not as you suggest, Dr. Klerman. The patients are *not* impaired in their ability to recognize *all* emotional states but instead are impaired only in the recognition of anger and fear facial expressions.

Dr. Friedman: This work is in its infancy, as you say, and some of the findings might be more specific to Dr. Klerman's suggestion when subsamples of depressed patients are studied. For example, the Mabel Blake-Cohen group described manic-depressive patients and I believe, Dr. Ekman, the studies which you described were done with a variety of depressed patients but not necessarily a pure manic-depressive group. Perhaps more light will be shed on this aspect of interpersonal opaqueness when others begin to study more clearly defined diagnostic entities. I think it would also be exciting to engage in studies that attempted to measure the changes that occur in depressed patients between admission and discharge, i.e., between the height of their depression and remission.

Dr. Ekman: These are excellent suggestions. There is no doubt in my mind that in further work with the Brief Affect Recognition Test we should, as Dr. Friedman suggests, attempt to differentiate types of depressive patients and also determine whether there are changes between admission and discharge from the hospital.

Dr. Goodwin: I believe that Dr. Ekman's studies of the nonverbal behavior of the patient, what he has termed encoding studies, in which the actual facial expression and body movements shown by the patient are examined, are very exciting and potentially useful for depression research. I believe there will be a number of practical applications of this technique to biological studies in depression. One of the most troublesome and confounding variables in all biological research has been the factor of agitation-retardation. Many studies are confounded by the absence or presence of agitation, and clinically people are extremely poor at labeling this variable. I wonder if it would be possible to train a nurse to count hand or other bodily movements without using a TV camera, or is the videotape necessary so that you can go back over the same segments several times?

Dr. Ekman: We have never attempted to train people to count movements without using the videotape, but we have trained some skilled nurses to do so off of the videotape. Since agitation is manifested across the entire body, it would be necessary to look at the hand, the feet, the shoulder, and the head movements all at one time, and this could not be done by a single observer except by using the videotape, with which several passes of the same time segment could be made by replay. Whether a nurse could be trained to obtain the same information without using the TV is an empirical question and could easily be determined.

Dr. Chodoff: Have you done any studies attempting to correlate the various dimensions such as illustrators and adaptors with personality variables such as obsessiveness or hysterical features or schizoid patterns, etc.?

Dr. Ekman: If you will recall, we did find correlations between illustrators and adaptors and clinical ratings on the Overall & Gorham Brief Psychiatric Rating Scale. For example, illustrators were negatively correlated with emotional withdrawal and adaptors were positively correlated with the factor that had to do with anxiety and guilt feelings. In our study of illustrators and adaptors shown by normal subjects in our honest-deception experiment we have also obtained some relationships between hand activity and personality. The frequency that the subject illustrates during the honest session is negatively correlated with the California Personality Inventory (CPI) dominance scale (−.54) and positively correlated with the CPI feminity scale (.61). Another beginning study on individual differences in the encoding of nonverbal behavior and personality also used measures of the subjects' behavior in the honest session. Here we correlated how the subject's facial behavior during the honest session was judged with personality tests. Subjects whose facial behavior during the honest session was judged as honest (and not deceptive) tended to be dominant (.68) and sociable (.55), as measured by the CPI and Machiavellian (.49).

Although I believe these results will replicate, replication studies have not yet been performed, and thus these findings must be considered quite tentative.

Dr. Seligman: I believe that Dr. Ekman presents some very exciting data about the depression model I have put forth. Specifically, I am referring to the finding that between admission and discharge depressed patients show an increase in their illustrator-adaptor ratio. My inference is that they thus change from being an adaptor to being an illustrator. Since I am saying that depression ensues when the person has learned that there is nothing he can do to relieve the situation, I would predict that response initiation would be retarded, but specifically that purposive, voluntary response initiation would be retarded and the involuntary and non-purposive response initiation would not necessarily be impeded. Now as I understand Dr. Ekman's illustrator-adaptor findings, that is exactly what he is showing. Clearly an illustrator is something voluntary and purposive and is decreased in depression, whereas adaptors seem to be unconscious and involuntary and they do not seem to change over the course of the depression.

Dr. Ekman: This is an interesting interpretation of our findings and is consistent with our thinking.

Dr. Beck: Dr. Ekman's data do seem to corroborate Dr. Seligman's theory and also suggest to me an interesting methodology which could be employed in research to differentiate the agitated and the retarded depressions. There is a growing body of evidence that these two subgroups will respond differentially to drugs. Agitated depressions seem to respond better to phenothiazine regimens whereas retarded depressions do best with one of the antidepressant drugs.

Dr. Ekman: I believe Dr. Beck is correct in his suggestion that our measures of individual differences in the encoding of nonverbal behavior could be usefully employed in differentiating agitated from retarded depressives.

Dr. Klerman: Dr. Beck makes a valid point, but I suspect the true value of Dr. Ekman's methodology will rest on the biological studies, as Dr. Goodwin pointed out, rather than as a differential diagnostic tool. I believe the differentiation of agitation and retardation is a specific problem in the United States because American-trained psychiatrists, at least when compared to their British counterparts, have rather low diagnostic acumen around the use of terms such as agitation and retardation. This might well be because we emphasize verbal content in the United States at the expense of nonverbal behavior and, indeed, Dr. Ekman has some data which support this contention.

I believe one of the future uses of this technique which Dr. Ekman has presented to us will be in the area of training, where learning to discern facial and hand movements and especially the various subtypes of nonverbal behavior which Dr. Ekman has discovered will prove to be valuable for the clinician. Another immediate use I can foresee for this technique will be in the training of observers who participate in research experiments. One problem that has plagued clinical research is the training of clinical observers to use rating scales with any degree of reliability. I have often hypothesized that we fail to obtain treatment effects in certain studies because of this high "noise" in the system caused by inadequate observer training.

Dr. Ekman: I certainly agree with Dr. Klerman that one of the future uses of our research is in the area of clinical training. We believe that our approach will go beyond simply bringing this domain of behavior to the attention of the clinical practitioner. Our aim will be to provide more specific instruction about the meaning of particular body movements and facial expression (c.f. Ekman & Friesen 1974) We have begun such training but have not yet attempted to systematically evaluate its usefulness for the practitioner. I had not considered Dr. Klerman's other suggestion, although I think it is a very good one. I believe he is correct in suggesting that some of our materials could be used to improve the training of observers who use rating scales to judge the behavior of psychiatric patients.

Dr. Klerman: I would hypothesize that illustrators serve a communicative function and that adaptors serve to discharge a drive state.

Dr. Ekman: Yes, illustrators and adaptors could serve these functions. We find that people only illustrate when they speak, not when they listen. Consistent with our interpretation and Dr. Klerman's interpretation of illustrators, studies show that if visual contact between speaker and listener is blocked, there is a decrease in the speaker's illustrators (Mahl 1968; Cohen & Harrison 1973). This is not to suggest that in such circumstances there will be a total absence of illustrators. People will illustrate when talking on the phone or when rehearsing a speech, although presumably less than when the listener is visually present. Presumably the maintenance of some illustrator activity, even when the listener is not visually present, is due to habit and/or the self-priming of articulation which illustrators may accomplish.

The increase in adaptors that occurs when a listener is not visually present probably results from the fact that we have been taught to inhibit grooming activity somewhat when we can be seen. Just as some illustrators will still occur when the speaker is alone, some adaptors will still occur when the speaker and listener are in each other's visual presence. People are not nearly as polite as they think; ear-scratching and other self-adaptors still do occur during conversation, although they are slotted in such a way that speaker and listener collusively do not attend to their occurrence.

We believe that most people are aware of their illustrator activity. You can interrupt someone and ask him what movement he was making while he was speaking and if it was an illustrator he can repeat it, but he will be less successful in remembering if it was a self-adaptor which he had just performed. We believe that illustrators are tied to the moment-to-moment verbal flow but that adaptors are not. We are in the midst of a joint study with Allen Dittmann (NIMH Laboratory of Psychology) to test that hypothesis.

Dr. Katz: Dr. Ekman, have you engaged in any cross-cultural studies of illustrators?

Dr. Ekman: Most of our cross-cultural studies have been on facial expression of emotion, not on hand movement. These studies were concerned with the universality of facial expressions of emotion and not with individual differences in relation to personality. Our cross-cultural studies of hand movements did not examine illustrators or adaptors but instead what we call *emblems*, movements that have a precise, almost dictionary-like verbal meaning known by all members of a culture or subculture. As with our study of facial expressions, our investigation of emblems was concerned with universals and cultural differences and not with individual differences within a culture.

It would be very interesting, I think, to study the occurrence of illustrators and self-adaptors in depressed patients from other cultures. It would also be interesting to study the differences between the face and the body and the occurrence of illustrators and self-adaptors in deceptive interactions in examining people from other cultures.

Dr. Kaufman: Dr. Ekman, how do you explain the finding that adaptors increase when a person is alone?

Dr. Ekman: My explanation is simply to note that people have been taught not to engage in some of these behaviors in the presence of others. For example, people learn not to clean their noses or their ears except when alone.

Dr. Kaufman: I would agree that this is probably one determinant. I think another explanation rests on the assumption that adaptors serve more than one function, and that they increase when the person is alone because they serve as a form of sensory input for the individual.

Dr. Dyrud: Dr. Kaufman touches on a very significant area, especially in view of research now being conducted on the organism's need for sensory input and the erection of stimulus barriers to ward off excessive input. For example, one often sees people on Forty-second Street or Eighth Avenue in New York engaging in a great deal of what looks like self-stimulation behavior. They are working with their fingers or blowing their noses or whatever. This intrigues me because I believe that when they leave the city and go to the country or more open spaces, this type of behavior drops off because they need this stimulus barrier less.

Dr. Ekman: Dr. Dyrud and Dr. Kaufman raise intriguing questions for which I wish I had relevant data. So far we have not had an opportunity to study people alone or in situations described by Dr. Dyrud. We have only observed psychiatric patients in the presence of interviewers, and in our studies of normal subjects, they have either been engaged in an interaction or if alone it was when watching a stress film.

Dr. Spiro: You have not mentioned observations of the lower extremities. Do legs and feet serve any illustrative function?

Dr. Ekman: We have a general theory about the difference between the face, the hands, and the feet. We believe that the face is the most explicit communicative tool. Some movements of the face may correspond in a rough way to hand illustrators. The microfacial expressions—the very brief ones—may give the same information obtained from the self-adaptors. The movements in the lower extremities more closely parallel the self-adaptors. We have not observed movement in the lower extremities that we would classify as "illustrator" in the sense that it seems tied to speech rhythm.

We find that if we show people the face and the body separately, we get negative correlations about the impressions they receive from these two sources if the person being observed is in any kind of message conflict. We reported an example of this earlier. In one interview a depressed patient had been concealing that she still had suicidal thoughts. When we showed a videotape segment to observers, those who saw the face picked up the positive message—the lie—and concluded that the person was feeling pretty good. The observers shown the body detected that the individual was upset, however. This finding with the depressed patient is consistent with our findings where we studied normal subjects who were asked to try to deceive an interveiwer about their feelings.

Dr. Klerman: If you can lie better with your face than with your body, then what about the old adage of "looking one straight in the eye" if you're going to tell the truth?

Dr. Ekman: The face-body distinction belies a more complicated state of affairs, for within the face there are subdivisions in terms of efficacy of communication. The facial musculature is sufficiently complex so that different messages can be displayed in different facial areas. We have hypothesized that when someone is lying, the lower facial musculature, far more than the eyelids, is used in the service of the lie. Thus, if somebody is lying to you and you want to pick it up, you are better advised to observe the eyelids than the lower facial musculature. We are just beginning to measure gaze direction. We may be able to verify the clinical adage that patients who are deceptive tend to look away from the interviewer.

Dr. Schmale: When depressed patients misidentify fear, what affective state do they most often confuse it with?

Dr. Ekman: When somebody fails to recognize an emotion on a T-scope, he usually applies the label of the emotion most similar in muscular movement. Thus, surprise is the most common error for a fearful face, disgust for an angry face, and sadness for a face showing disgust.

Dr. Schmale: I would have predicted that people would misidentify in the opposite direction. We have repeatedly observed that seriously depressed patients tend to ignore despairing scenes when they are given pictures to rate. We have shown depressed patients pictures of bleak and stormy scenes, and they have reported that this is a "pleasant country scene." They seem repeatedly and consistently to deny the despair which is about them.

Dr. Ekman: Our evidence on this point is contradictory. In depressed patients, contrary to your expectation and to Tomkins' finding, there was no failure to recognize sad facial expressions accurately. Among the medical students who participated in our marijuana-alcohol study, the relationship that you predict did occur in that there was a negative correlation between self-rated feelings of dysphoria and accuracy in recognizing sad facial expressions. I cannot reconcile these findings. We are dealing with very different people; in one case those with an enduring affect disorder and in the other those with a transient drug-induced mood.

Let me emphasize once again that our findings on individual differences in the judgment of facial expression are tentative and at best hopeful. I would recommend that they be considered as not more than a possibility. In contrast, I have more confidence in our findings on the differences between the face and the body and in the relationships between the occurrence of illustrators and self-adaptors and psychopathology or the occurrence of deception. In these studies of individual differences in the encoding of nonverbal behavior our research has been guided by theory, and consistent findings have been obtained across very diverse samples of people (psychiatric inpatients and nursing students) and settings (standard psychiatric interviews and experimentally arranged honest/deceptive interactions).

BIBLIOGRAPHY

Cohen, M. B., Baker, G., Cohen, R. A., Fromm-Reichmann, F., & Weigert, E. V. An intensive study of twelve cases of manic-depressive psychosis. *Psychiatry*, 17, May 1954, 103.

Cohen, A. A., & Harrison, R. P. Intentionality in the use of illustrators in face-to-face communication situations. *Journal of Personality and Social Psychology*, 1973, 28(2), 276–279.

Ekman, P., & Friesen, W. V. *Unmasking the face*. Englewood Cliffs, New Jersey: Spectrum-Prentice Hall, 1974, in press.

Ekman, P., Jones, R. T., Friesen, W. V., & Malmstrom, E. J., Jr. *Psychoactive drugs and the recognition of facial expressions of emotion*. Unpublished manuscript, Langley Porter Neuropsychiatric Institute, San Francisco, 1970.

Mahl, G. F. Gestures and body movements in interviews. In Shlien, J. (Ed.), *Research in psychotherapy*, Vol. 3. Washington: American Psychological Association, 1968.

Shannon, A. M., *Differences between depressives and schizophrenics in the recognition of facial expression of emotion*. Unpublished Doctoral Dissertation, University of California, San Francisco, 1970.

Tomkins, S. S. *Affect, imagery, consciousness*. Vol. 1. *The positive affects*. New York: Springer, 1963.

Tomkins, S. S. *Affect, imagery, consciousness*. Vol. 2. *The negative affects*. New York: Springer, 1963.

PART III
OVERVIEW AND PERSPECTIVES

SECTION 1 PANEL DISCUSSION

M. M. Katz, Chairman: Introduction
Jarl Dyrud: On translating concepts across disciplines
Frederick Goodwin: On the biology of depression
I. C. Kaufman: On animal models
Arthur Schmale: On development and the conservation-withdrawal reaction
Melford Spiro: On meaning and expression in other cultures

SECTION 2 GENERAL DISCUSSION

SECTION 1
PANEL DISCUSSION

Martin M. Katz, Chairman

INTRODUCTION

Dr. Katz:

Throughout the planning stages of this workshop the role of the panel of "experts" has remained an important one for us. We look toward the panel and also toward the general discussion which will follow for reflections about the material that has been presented over the past day and a half, as well as for thoughts and considerations regarding future directions in this area of research. We are especially interested in specific recommendations and suggestions. So, we are interested in your long-term thinking as well the kinds of reflections that have been stimulated by the material presented at the workshop so far. Many considerations were involved in the selection of panelists, but one central criterion, one principle under which we were operating, was the selection of men who have had experience in attempting to integrate thinking from two different fields, men who have worked across two theoretical systems or with two or more species.

Dr. Dyrud spans the two systems of psychoanalysis and behavior theory, the two ways of looking at human psychological functioning, systems that have provided major foci of discussion throughout this workshop.

Dr. Goodwin is our "resident biologist," a veteran of the psychobiology meeting held at Williamsburg in 1969. We look forward to his comments about the material presented as well as other issues concerning the psychology of depression from the standpoint of research in the biological sphere.

Dr. Kaufman is an example of a scientist whose research has involved both human subjects and primates, whose background and early training are in psychoanalysis, and who now conducts research as an ecologist and experimental psychologist.

Dr. Schmale, who represents a unique theoretical viewpoint, has been involved in research on depression for some time in association with George Engel. Together they have developed a set of hypotheses about depression which have been highly influential in psychiatric research.

Dr. Spiro is an anthropologist who has had a long association with research on the development of personality in different cultures, and who speaks the language of psychology and psychiatry as well as that of anthropology. Although he has not so far conducted research on depression, our hope is that he will provide us with another perspective on our data, and also that he may be able to contribute some reflections stemming from his own work which will be helpful to us.

Dr. Raskin and Dr. Parloff were asked to think about the problems of translating concepts in the psychology of depression into quantitative terms that can be used to accelerate the research process. This is a continuing and enormous problem for all of psychology, but one which has severely retarded development in the field of depression.

ON TRANSLATING CONCEPTS ACROSS DISCIPLINES

Dr. Jarl Dyrud:

My thinking resembles that of Dr. Beck, with whom I agree that a likely point of attack within the system is the cognitive one. I like the notion that how one appraises matters determines how one feels. The critical elements concern the changes in mental events and, as I mentioned yesterday, I do have some ideas about this field.

I believe that as work in the psychology of depression becomes inter-disciplinary, we must try to avoid syncretism, that is, a premature smoothing out of differences in terms and concepts. If we rapidly try to integrate the thinking of one discipline with that of another, we run the risk of taking terms carefully defined and reliably worked within one context and using them in another where they do not have the same implications. When this occurs the work gets "softer" and "softer." Therefore, I would rather see large areas of terminologic mismatch among the various workers in depression research, at least now, for I believe it is a healthy sign for a young field.

For the last day and a half the notion of "forcing behavior" has been tossed about. As Dr. Beck has pointed out, this is an old concept, described by Adolph Meyer in 1913. He noted that if a depressed patient were given an activity to perform, such as running up and down the stairs, he would be less depressed after he did so. I believe the antidepressant drugs have some of their effect because they increase the tendency to act (by lowering the resistance to motor behavior), which has the feedback effect of enhancing mood. However, none of these maneuvers which are really more short-term in nature addresses the enduring and central problem of cognitive change. This is certainly an area requiring more research and more emphasis.

Throughout this conference we have talked about the supposed "indifference" of the depressed person to his environment. I think it is important to realize that such a concept is an inference at this stage of our knowledge. We could just as easily hypothesize that the depressed person is in reality highly sensitive to certain aspects of his environment—those that confirm his sense of helplessness and hopelessness. They demand autoplastic rather than alloplastic responses. If this were so, then one of the problems of the depressed person would be that he is too tightly linked to environmental control and curiously oblivious to those aspects of the environment that would be plastic in his hands, which is why depressed patients exhibit so little mastery.

Dr. Chodoff: Dr. Dyrud's comments remind me of an anecdote. I recently interviewed a quite depressed man in his late fifties who was neither an insightful person nor the type one could talk to. In essence, he was a simple man who required something to do. His family reported that he had had a depression many years before and was treated by a well-known psychiatrist in Philadelphia who prescribed activity for him. He was ordered to get in his car and drive up Market Street and down Chestnut Street repeatedly. I assume the idea was to force him into some activity, and his family reports that the maneuver was successful. He drove up Market and down Chestnut observing what was going on and trying to pay attention to what he was doing, and in the course of this activity he began to recover. Now of course there is a great deal of suggestion and transference involved, but as a technical maneuver, the enforcement of activity has a long tradition of success.

Dr. Seligman: The success of such a maneuver does not seem so mysterious to me. I believe we can investigate why being forced to engage in behavior affects cognition and mood. It seems to me that if a person drives up Market and down Chestnut or runs up and down the stairs, he observes what he is doing and sees that there are activities he is capable of doing. This is also a very effective way of becoming cognitively convinced about some proposition concerning oneself, for what more powerful way is there to learn that one can do something than by doing it?

Dr. Beck: Two findings from our research bear on the issue of forcing behavior. The first which is important to consider is that depressed patients are actually more sensitive to performance feedback (i.e., feedback from the environment about how they are doing) than are nondepressed psychiatric patients. My second point is that not only are depressed patients more sensitive to these environmental cues, but their reaction to them is stronger than in control patients. For example, after a contrived success experience, a depressed patient will go on to perform better on a particular task than will a nondepressed patient. The chain of events concerns changing cognitions and increased behavior, but the important first step is a minimum degree of forced activity.

Dr. Dyrud: The experience of a friend of mine who was a prisoner in a Japanese POW camp stimulated my thinking about the relationship of the depressed patient to his environment. This particular friend was kept in solitary confinement for a long period and kept himself in shape by keeping track of the days, by feeling master of his environment through other similar techniques, and by not becoming preoccupied with those aspects of the environment over which he had no control. Those prisoners who gave in and became overwhelmed by what they could not control became depressed and died. I have a hunch that in this situation in particular, and perhaps throughout life in general, maintaining one's sense of mastery and hence well-being is the more effective course because it involves discriminating which aspects of the environment are negotiable and which are given.

Dr. Friedman: I believe we have been talking about more severe, perhaps psychotic, depressions in regard to "forcing" activity. I have a hunch that these are the patients for whom this technique will prove most successful. I am also reminded that there are many depressed people who become even more depressed when they encounter success, and believe that these people have a classic "success neurosis" or for other reasons may masochistically need to undermine their own ambitions and successes.

Dr. Chodoff: Depression in the face of success is the same phenomenon that accounts for the negative therapeutic reaction that is a very specific, definite, frequent, and probably the most effective form of resistance to any type of therapeutic intervention. When the patient is confronted with success, he becomes paradoxically more depressed and regresses even further. Freud pointed this out long ago. It is a phenomenon that does apply to depressed patients and one I believe makes some of the behavioral approaches, which stress forced activity for all depressed patients, seem somewhat naive.

Dr. Beck: Experimentally, we do not find that depressed patients react adversely to successful experiences. These research findings are based on work focused on severely depressed patients, but perhaps the success depression occurs more regularly in neurotic depression of a milder degree. I believe, however, that we can resolve our theoretical conflict if we define success more carefully and specifically because success can be a relative thing. For example, I saw a depressed patient recently who was a poet and who became more depressed when he was told that he was a good poet. Well, there are no absolute standards for judging poetry and by his standards he was a failure. When I speak of success, though, I am not talking about success in something with such ambiguous standards as poetry, but in a more concrete sense. For example, card sorting is an activity in which the outcome can be measured and is more certain. If a patient thinks he will not be able to sort 20 cards in 15 seconds, and then goes ahead and tries and actually accomplishes what he thought he could not do, he has succeeded, and in a demonstrable and tangible way. In my experience, patients who experience success of this type respond positively and do not become more depressed.

Dr. Friedman: I think the issue is one of interpretation rather than of precision in defining success. If a patient sorts 20 cards in 15 seconds and is successful even though he predicted he would not be, this is a fact that would be very difficult for him to distort. There is also a certain pressure from the environment and the experimental situation to interpret this as a success. As to his poetry, however, he can discount your statement that it is "good" or "successful" more easily. That doesn't mean though that he is not a successful poet, successful at least by all the usual criteria society has for judging such work.

Card sorting is not a terribly meaningful task for the maintenance of self-esteem, and I would predict that as depressed patients engage in tasks more relevant to their self-esteem, many would become depressed following success. I think the underlying psychodynamics have been explicated rather well in the psychoanalytic literature, where the main problem has been described as a basic fear of assertion of which success is the end product. When such people see themselves as assertive, they become fearful, then helpless, and then depressed. Other investigators have demonstrated to my satisfaction that this often involves murderous thoughts and feelings.

Dr. Tabachnick: This discussion keeps raising the question in my mind of what type of depression we are considering. I am sure most of us have experienced "depression" following successful experiences, or at least a feeling of "let down" at a time when we would ordinarily expect to feel buoyant. I do think that is a state of sadness and "depression," but I believe the underlying problem is a neurotic one. Depression is, of course, associated with it. But I do not think this state is the same as the clinical state of depression which Dr. Klerman has spoken of and which I believe Dr. Beck is referring to in terms of his research. Perhaps Dr. Chodoff's and Dr. Friedman's comments about the paradoxical effects of success pertain more to depressions seen in normal people as well as neurotic individuals, and less to the clinical state of depression that we seem to be reserving for the more serious symptom complexes.

Dr. Kaufman: Aware that I am betraying my bias, I must state that I feel it is a regressive activity for a group of psychiatrists and psychologists to fail to distinguish form from content. I understand and appreciate that Skinner and others really do not value the content and only deal with the form. Nevertheless, I think one of the great gains we have made in psychiatry is our understanding of content and our appreciation of meaning. To imply that a form of behavior such as driving up and down the street or running up and down the stairs is meaningful in and of itself (divorced from what it actually means to the individual) seems to be a regression in our understanding. When a person engages in activity, he will perceive the results of that activity as successful or reinforcing only to the extent that they are meaningful to him. Perhaps the value the doctor places on the activity is meaningful or there are other determinants which the patient brings to bear. In any event, it is the cognitive appraisal of the situation that is most significant for me.

ON THE BIOLOGY OF DEPRESSION

Dr. Frederick Goodwin:

Dr. Katz introduced me as the "resident biologist" but, for reasons I hope to make explicit in my comments today, I would prefer to be called the "resident psychobiologist." I would like to accomplish two goals: first, to comment briefly on the data presented so far, and second, to present a very brief review of where things stand in the "biology" of depression. An "outsider" often feels overwhelmed by the masses of new data generated in this area. Perhaps I can help put this picture in a less awesome perspective, focusing on the limitation of our current knowledge.

I was struck by Dr. Beck's opening comments about the mystery of depression. The paradoxical and often mysterious nature of this disorder has prompted many to think about underlying biological processes. However, most discussions of the biology of depression fail to make it clear which of the several different levels of biological focus is being discussed. This point is illustrated in Figure 1. First, the biological correlates of the *predisposition* to depression in certain individuals represent a "genetic biology." Second are the biological events associated with the triggering of depression in susceptible individuals by stress, certain drugs, or other factors. Third, there is the biology which is "concomitant" with the state of depression. Here we study the biological changes that are the result of the depressed state. Finally, there are those biological changes that accompany (and may account for) the reversal of the depression process, be it by behavioral intervention, a drug, or "spontaneous" remission. It is the last two levels that account for virtually all the current data on the biology of depression. It is hoped that new research efforts will be directed towards understanding the biological correlates of the predisposition to affective illness, with their obvious implications for prevention.

In discussing psychobiology, many pay lip service to the role of biology by saying, "Well, of course, everything that we're thinking or feeling originates in the brain and the brain is an organ and therefore there must be a biology involved." In this context it becomes important to remember the difference between the building and the bricks. That is, it is one thing to describe in chemical terms the nature and properties of the bricks, including the

1. **Biological correlates of the predisposition to affective illness (genetic ?)**
2. **Biological changes associated with depressed or manic state**
3. **Biological alterations produced by anti-depressant or antimanic drugs**

FIG. 1. "Biology" of affective illness.

characterization of defective bricks; it is quite another thing to describe how the bricks are put together. Recently a leading molecular biologist confided to me that it was his enduring conviction that we will never understand the chemistry of thinking, that is it will probably never be possible to define individual thoughts or feelings in specific chemical terms. What biology can approach is the understanding of dysfunction of whole neuronal networks involved in thinking and feeling, and here I refer to the deficiencies in the bricks from which the various buildings are built. My point is that there are some individuals who may have enduring deficiencies in their "machinery" which can be categorized in relation to given illness or symptom groups. Throughout this workshop there has been a tendency to assume that certain conditions are psychologically determined and that others are biologically determined, an either/or dichotomy which assumes that psychology and biology are mutually exclusive.

A number of recent developmental studies in animals demonstrate that behavioral intervention with an animal at a critical developmental period can clearly produce an enduring chemical change in the brain. The reverse is also true, and it has been shown that biological intervention at a critical developmental stage can produce an enduring behavioral change. I believe that during the next decade we will begin to find ways to examine such interactions in the human being. Then when we say that somebody is depressed because he suffered a severe loss in childhood (such as parental separation), it will not be a psychological or a biological statement, but simply a statement with a number of determinants that can be examined in biological and psychological terms. Perhaps the environmental situation prompted the change, but that does not mean we cannot intervene biologically. And, of course, if we find other changes which are biologically rooted, the possibility of intervening on a psychological level is also not excluded.

A very interesting unpublished experiment which amplifies this point was done several years ago at the National Institutes of Health (J. Maas & R. Colburn, unpublished data). It has been known that the beagle puppy has a critical developmental period lasting approximately a week during which it is essential that the puppy remain with its mother and litter. If the dog is separated from its litter during this phase of development, it will never be able to form primary social bonds with other animals. In this experiment, brain norepinephrine was measured, and it was found that during this normal developmental phase this amine increased in the brain. If a dog is separated from its litter during this time, brain norepinephrine does not increase. In the experimental situation, animals were allowed to remain with their mothers and litter, but during this critical phase of development they were given reserpine, which in effect chemically knocked out this elevation in norepinephrine without changing the baseline levels and without overtly altering the behavior of the animals. It was noted that these animals also did not develop primary social bond formation. So, in this instance, *either* a psychological or a biological manipulation accomplished the same thing, i.e., the loss of primary social bond formation. We can turn the process around and state that from a treatment standpoint one can accomplish the same effect using two radically different types of treatment.

Our work at the National Institutes of Health is with severely depressed patients who do not seem to me to be qualitatively the same as patients with the other forms of depression from which many of the data presented at this workshop have been derived. I have heard analogies made between sadness and depression, and also the converse between gladness and euphoria or between euphoria and mania. Such analogies suggest a continuum, with sadness on one end and gladness on the other. This mania-depression continuum does not seem to fit with the clinical data which we have recently been generating, however, and I hope I will have time later to return to this subject.

I would like to turn now to the subject of recent advances in the "biology" of depression. I will be referring to the "NIH neuron," as illustrated in Figure 2. Work in the past 10 years has shown that these critical synapses exist in areas of the brain subserving vegatative and affective functions; that norepinephrine, dopamine, and serotonin are the neurotransmitters regulating the flow of impulses in these circuits; and essentially that the synaptic junction is a chemical transducer which converts electrical energy into chemical energy (presynaptic nerve ending), which is then reconverted into electrical energy (postsynaptic receptors). The complex nature of the processes responsible for synthesis, storage, release, reuptake, and metabolism of the amine neurotransmitters provides many mechanisms for *regulation*, which is of course very important in a complex circuitry such as the brain. Norepinephrine, for example, is a neurotransmitter synthesized from dietary tyrosine and stored in vesicles, as noted in Figure 2. These storage vesicles are in turn affected in a specific way by

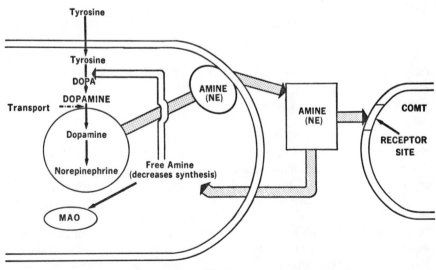

FIG. 2.

the electrical impulses arriving at the nerve ending, resulting in the release of the transmitter substance which is then free to react with the receptor and cause an electrical event to occur at the receptor site. The transmitter is metabolized by one pathway if it is outside the neuron and by a different pathway if inside the neuron. Much of the work in depression has focused on the elucidation of the differences in neurotransmitter metabolism between the inside and the outside of the neuron.

When reserpine was first used in the treatment of hypertension, it was discovered that a significant number of patients were becoming depressed while using this drug (Goodwin & Bunney, 1971). It was at the same time that Brodie's group discovered that reserpine depleted serotonin and norepinephrine from the brain (Shore & Brodie, 1957). These two observations taken together formed the cornerstone of the amine hypothesis of affective disorders, which states that depression is associated with a functional deficit of one or more brain neurotransmitter amines at specific central synapses, and that, conversely, mania is associated with a functional excess of one or more of these amines.

Another serendipitous discovery was that monoamine oxidase (MAO) inhibitors such as iproniazid, when used in the treatment of tubercular patients, produced some mood elevation. About this time it was also discovered that the MAO inhibitors were capable of elevating brain amine levels by inhibiting their destruction, and that in animals, treatment with MAO inhibitors could prevent or reverse reserpine "depression." We thus had a mood-elevating drug which elevated brain amines and a depressant drug which decreased brain amines.

A third piece of evidence was provided by the discovery of the tricyclic antidepressants, originally developed as tranquilizers. Since they did not alter the levels of brain amines in animals, the relevance of the tricyclic antidepressants to the amine hypothesis was initially unclear. The mechanism of action was ultimately found to be the blockade of the reuptake of the amines (Figure 2), so that the amount of amine functionally available *at the synaptic cleft* increased. Thus, the role of the tricyclic antidepressants also fit neatly with the amine hypothesis.

Lithium, a drug with dramatic antimanic properties, also seems to fit the amine hypothesis since animal data suggest a mechanism of action in effect opposite that of the tricyclic antidepressant drugs. Lithium enhances the reuptake of amines at the synapse and effectively lowers the amount of amine in the synaptic cleft. For the sake of simplicity, this is where the amine hypothesis was five years ago, and, with some revision which I will discuss, is where it currently stands.

One of the implications of the catecholamine hypothesis is that mania and depression are at opposite poles of the same continuum. We have gathered evidence that is not consistent with this view. Clinical evidence based on work with manic-depressive patients reveals that manic patients are very often depressed at the same time they are manic. In many cases, mania and depression correlate in a strikingly positive fashion; this may be demonstrated by using rating scales which independently measure mania and depression. Approximately two-thirds of the manic patients we have studied evidence a considerable degree of depression concomitant with their mania. Generally this tends to occur in those patients who evidence full-blown mania, rather than just hypomania, in which case euphoria is the predominant mood. Some clinical examples of this phenomenon are illustrated in Figures 3 and 4.

Before summarizing the current status of the catecholamine hypothesis of affective disorders it is important to review briefly a recent advance in the classification of affective disorders, the concept of the unipolar-bipolar dichotomy. A bipolar patient is defined as a depressed patient with a history of mania or hypomania, whereas the depressive episode is called unipolar when it occurs in a person who is depressed but has no history of mania or hypomania. The unipolar-bipolar classification is summarized in Table 1, and Table 2 summarizes some clinical and biological differences between unipolar and bipolar depressed patients. Differences in the pharmacological responses in the two groups (summarized in Table 3) have recently been uncovered, which further suggests that two separate genetic populations may be involved. This suspicion is corroborated by family history data.

Table 4 summarizes the current status of the catecholamine hypothesis. The major point illustrated here is that three drugs which can increase functional catecholamines in brain (MAO inhibitors, tricyclic antidepressants, and L-DOPA)

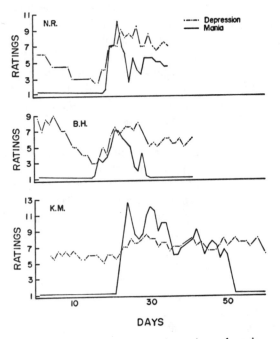

FIG. 3. Relationship between depression and mania.

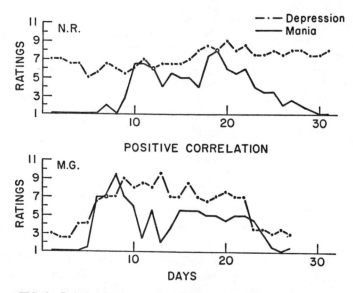

FIG. 4. Relationship between mania and depression no correlation.

can all precipitate mania in susceptible individuals, but three drugs which decrease functional catecholamines in brain (reserpine, lithium, and alpha-methyl-para-tyrosine [AMPT]) all have antimanic properties. The picture of the effects of these drugs in depression is more confused, however, particularly as to bipolar depression. In our experience, tricyclic antidepressants are relatively ineffective in the bipolar group (Table 5). L-DOPA is not an antidepressant in the bipolar patients, and has some antidepressant effects in only 35 percent of

TABLE 1

Unipolar-Bipolar Classification of Affective Disorders

Unipolar	Bipolar
Depression without a prior history of mania or hypomania	Depression with a prior history of mania or hypomania
Problems in classification	
1. Heterogeneity of unipolar group	
2. Consideration of period at risk	
3. Distinction between mania and hypomania	
4. Biased sampling	

TABLE 2

Differential Characteristics of Unipolar and Bipolar Depressed Patients

Item	Unipolar	Bipolar
Clinical features	Agitated or retarded Late age of onset Greater tendency for symptoms of anger, physical complaints, and anxiety	Retarded Early age of onset
Family history	Low incidence of mania "Reducer" on cortical evoked potential Normal or elevated 17OHCS excretion	High incidence of mania "Augmenter" on cortical evoked potential Low 17OHCS excretion
Biological	Plasma Mg^{++} unchanged on lithium Lower CNS dopamine "turnover" Red cell COMT markedly reduced	Increased plasma Mg^{++} on lithium Higher CNS dopamine "turnover" Red cell COMT slightly reduced

TABLE 3

Differential Pharmacological Responses in
Unipolar vs Bipolar Depression

Drug	Unipolar	Bipolar
Lithium	Not an antidepressant	Moderate antidepressant effects
L-dopa	Occasional antidepressant response	Induces hypomania syndrome without decreasing depression
Tricyclic antidepressants	Effective antidepressant	Less effective antidepressant Can precipitate mania

the unipolar patients (Table 6). A finding of major importance has been that when L-dopa is given to bipolar depressed patients, almost all of them experience mania or hypomania without a concomitant decrease in depression (Table 7).

As to drugs that decrease functional catecholamines in brain, reserpine precipitates depression and also has antimanic effects. We have recently had

TABLE 4

Drug-Catecholamine Relationships in Unipolar and Bipolar Affective Illness

Drug	Effect on brain catecholamines	Effects on depression		Effects on mania (bipolar)
		Unipolar	Bipolar	
MAOI	↑ Levels	Antidepressant	?	Can precipitate mania
Tricyclics	↑ (At synaptic cleft)	Antidepressant	Relatively poor antidepressant	Can precipitate mania
L-dopa	↑ Levels	?	Not an antidepressant	Can precipitate mania
Reserpine	↓ Levels	Precipitates depression in some individuals		Antimanic
Lithium	↓ (At synaptic cleft)	No effect	Moderate anti-depressant properties	Antimanic
AMPT	↓ Levels	Increases depression	?	Antimanic

TABLE 5

Efficacy of Tricyclic Antidepressants
in Subgroups of Affective Illness

Item	Unipolar	Bipolar
Response	11	2
No response	2	10
Total	13	12

TABLE 6

Response to L-dopa (or L-dopa and MK485)
in Depressed Patients

Patients	Unipolar	Bipolar
Responders	5	0
Nonresponders	8	10
Total	13	10

TABLE 7

Incidence of Hypomania during L-dopa Administration
in Bipolar (Manic-Depressive) Patients as Compared to
Unipolar (Psychotic Depressive) Patients

Patients	Hypomanic episode	No hypomanic episode
Manic-depressive (bipolar)	8[a]	1
Psychotic depressive (unipolar)	1	12

[a]$x^2 = 11.1$, $p < .001$.

occasion to review the data relevant to the reserpine literature (Engel, 1962) and
have discovered that the proportion of patients on reserpine who experienced
major depressions (analogous to "endogenous" depressions) is approximately 5
percent rather than the generally quoted figure of 15 percent. Furthermore, the
5 percent incidence of depression on reserpine is close to the incidence of
individuals with histories of depression. From these revised data it appears that
reserpine should be considered a precipitant of depression rather than an inducer
of depression, an important distinction. Lithium, another drug that can decrease
functional amines, is clearly antimanic, but also has moderate antidepressant

effects in bipolar patients (Table 8) (Goodwin et al., 1969). aMPT, which decreases catecholamines by specifically inhibiting their synthesis, has antimanic properties and in addition tends to increase depression in some individuals (Brodie et al. 1971).

The original formulation of the catecholamine hypothesis, which stated that depression was related to low catecholamine levels and that mania was related to high catecholamine levels, has been extremely valuable in stimulating research and may still have implications for behavior. However, I believe that as a total and inclusive explanation for all severe depression, the catecholamine hypothesis is not adequate. My guess is that we might find the most consistent correlate of catecholamine function to be the level of psychomotor activity, rather than the presence or absence of depression. Most of the drugs just discussed (Table 4) which increase functional catecholamines in the brain also increase psychomotor activity but do not necessarily have consistent antidepressant activity. A clearer relationship now seems to exist between the onset of mania and brain amine changes than is the case with depression, particularly bipolar depression. We are currently conceptualizing the manic episode as superimposed upon an ongoing depressive process, a process involving biological systems other than just catecholamines.

I have been intrigued by the advances in behavioral models which have been presented at this workshop so far, and I would like to conclude with several comments about their possible application. I believe there are a number of biological studies that should be done as quickly as possible in regard to these new behavioral models. For example, the self-stimulation work of Larry Stein should definitely be applied to the animals that have learned helplessness in Dr. Seligman's laboratory. Finally, I believe the task of trying to find more objective ways to classify patients and to separate those characteristics that are specific to the depressive process from those that are more specific to the character of the

TABLE 8

Differential Antidepressant Response to Lithium in
Unipolar and Bipolar Patients

Response	Patients	
	Unipolar	Bipolar
Unequivocal (complete & partial)	2	12
Probable (complete & partial)	2	21
Total	4	33
None	8	7
Total no. of patients	12	40

person who is depressed would help us immensely in both biological research and in clinical practice.

Dr. Katz: Thank you, Dr. Goodwin, for reminding us of the dynamic interaction of the many systems involved in this problem and also for your excellent summary of the recent trends in biological research. Your comments remind me of the problem we were discussing after Dr. Dyrud's presentation about whether intervening in depression by changing the depressed patient's behavior leads to enduring biologic change. We certainly know from psychopharmacology that we can change behavior and thinking by changing the chemical balance, and we are slowly learning that there are not necessarily one-to-one relationships among the many systems involved.

Dr. Raskin: Dr. Goodwin, when you say there are correlations between mania and depression, do you really mean there is a correlation between manic-like symptoms and depression and that the two seem to occur simultaneously? In other words, do you really mean mania?

Dr. Goodwin: Yes, I do mean mania and not just manic-like symptoms. I do not choose to define mania as absolutely requiring the presence of euphoria (as a pathognomonic sign), then the clinical state I am describing would not be mania. The clinical picture I am talking about could be illustrated by a patient who has a cyclic history of hyperactive behavior and in whose clinical state and history there is no suggestion of schizophrenia, who is observed running around the ward angry, intrusive, hyperverbal, and hyperactive, and showing the characteristic mania thought disorder. I would consider this type of patient manic and, as I stated, we note in many of these patients significant depressive content. In addition to their hyperactivity, they are emitting suicidal messages and the verbal content of their speech is clearly depressive. If you just examined the content of the speech without knowing it was coming from a hyperactive person, you would say the person was depressed. So the psychomotor activity is very "up," and the content of the speech is very "down." Many manic patients recall their manias as quite dysphoric.

Dr. Chodoff: Is this state you are describing perhaps one of agitated depression?

Dr. Goodwin: No, definitely not. As far as I am concerned, agitation and mania are two separate issues. I hope I have made it clear that the behavior is definitely manic.

As aside, an interesting issue exists as to whether mania may represent an agitation equivalent in bipolar patients, since we rarely observe agitation in bipolar patients during depressive phases. At NIH we almost always observe agitation in unipolar patients, but I don't know whether this finding can be generalized beyond our population. We might tentatively say that hypomania or mania is an equivalent of agitation in a population which differs from the one in which agitation usually occurs.

Dr. Klerman: Kraepelin's writings do delineate a category of mixed manic depressives, and there are some patients who in the midst of a manic period will evidence breakthroughs of depressive content and even cry in the middle of motor overactivity. In my experience, however, the number of such patients has been infrequent. I am somewhat surprised at the high incidence of mixed depression and mania that Dr. Goodwin has described.

I am also struck by the comment that the tricyclic antidepressants are not as effective in those patients with a history of mania (bipolar patients). This is a new piece of evidence to me and strengthens some of the doubts I have about the unipolar-bipolar distinction. One of the chronic difficulties with this classification is that different centers throughout the country use different criteria for distinguishing between the groups; for example, the NIH and St. Louis groups differ about how they evaluate the history of mania. It would be helpful if we could have some reliability studies in which the same cases were independently evaluated by representatives of the two groups.

Dr. Goodwin: I think the current state of the unipolar-bipolar distinction is similar to the status of the reactive-endogenous distinction of several years ago. What we need are studies involving cross-evaluation by different centers. Another problem with the bipolar-unipolar concept is that many of the data concerning it are from Europe, particularly Scandinavia and England, where populations and diagnostic practices may well be different.

ON ANIMAL MODELS
Dr. I. Charles Kaufman:

I believe that with his comments Dr. Goodwin has helped to clarify many issues, especially those concerning the relationship between biological and behavioral events. As a final note about biology, I would remind us not to restrict the term to mean biochemistry and perhaps physiology. Some of us who take an evolutionary view of adaptational processes also like to think of ourselves as psychobiologists. In that connection, and despite all the discussion that has proceeded in many divergent directions, it does seem to me that one central theme has emerged from the variety of presentations at this workshop. It is that, underlying all the varieties and complications of depressive and manic-depressive illness, there is a type of *basic organismic state*. Different people here and elsewhere have attributed this basic state to different causes. Some hold it is due to a negative cognitive set, and others contend it is due to a situation in which behavioral contingencies do not mean anything. In any case, what is referred to is a *state of helplessness*—there is nothing the individual can do. Another suggestion that has been advanced is that this organismic state is a response pattern available throughout most of the animal kingdom, and, further, that it has adaptive value. For example, this basic organismic state has been described as a conservation-withdrawal reaction, and the adaptive value has been detailed by Drs. Engel (1962), Schmale (1972), and by me (Kaufman & Rosenblum, 1967).

Incidentally, a principle I learned many years ago seems very useful when we discuss developmental processes. This is that all organisms incorporate past learning experiences, behaviors, and structural apparatuses into their adaptive repertoire for use when they are needed in the future. Perhaps I can illustrate this by commenting briefly on some of the studies with primates that I have done.

As I indicated earlier, I have studied the conservation-withdrawal (anaclitic depression) reaction in monkey infants that have lost their mothers. This reaction is not universal, however, and occasionally an animal that would ordinarily be expected to react with depression after separation from its mother will not do so. My hypothesis is that it does not show this response when it does not need to. For example, the bonnet macaque infants respond to the stress of loss by finding a substitute mother, thereby obviating the conservation-withdrawal reaction.

I cannot state with certainty why bonnet infants get adopted whereas pigtail infants do not and react with depression (conservation-withdrawal). We know that there are genetic differences that doubtless influence the reaction of various species of monkeys to maternal loss. However, we also have been able to demonstrate that the pattern of mothering in the two species we have studied differs remarkably. Pigtail mothers are more protective and restrictive. Thus, bonnet macaque infants grow up with a much greater familiarity with adult animals other than their mother than do the pigtail macaques. The bonnet infants show what operationally might be considered less dependence on their mothers, as evidenced by the fact that they venture farther away and stay away longer; they also show a greater tendency than do the pigtails to play with other animals. Thus, the bonnet infant, by virtue of its freedom and greater familiarity with other animals, is able to foster an adoption when separated from its mother.

We have carried these experiments further and deprived the bonnet infant of the opportunity of finding a substitute mother, and have discovered that it still does not become depressed. I believe the explanation for this finding is that the bonnet, by virtue of its childhood rearing experiences, possesses greater resources and is better able to cope on its own with its social and physical environment. We see then that the bonnet infant has several coping techniques which allow him to deal with the stress of maternal separation. If finding a substitute mother is not feasible, it can fall back on still other adaptive responses. It uses what it has and what it has to. This is another important developmental principle. I hope these examples illustrate my contention that we must examine behavior in a broad context.

I would now like to consider the relationship between mood, behavior, and cognition. Throughout this workshop we have been discussing the question of whether mood leads to behavior, or whether behavior produces mood. In particular, we have been concerned with the state of helplessness in relation to this issue. It seems to me that helplessness has cognitive, affective, and motivational aspects. Helplessness is a perception, an awareness, an appraisal, a feeling state, and, at the same time, it is a tendency to behave in a given way. I view the state of helplessness as a kind of unified psychobiological structure, and I believe that motivational, cognitive, and affective processes are interdependent parts of this structure—not discrete variables which interact with each other to produce such a state.

In distinguishing whether we are dealing with discrete variables or inter-dependent parts, I am reminded of the old argument in psychoanalysis about whether patients change because they develop insight or whether they become insightful after they change. We cannot settle the issue easily, and a great deal of research is needed regarding the relationship of cognition, affect, and motiva-tion, as Dr. Dyrud has also noted. We also need to study the role of attention, which is intimately involved with all three. I am aware that some work done with evoked potentials indicates an increased latency of response and inatten-tiveness, or at least seeming inattentiveness, to external stimuli in depression. We have just scratched the surface, however, and the whole process of attention in depression needs to be studied both psychologically and electrophysiologically.

Throughout this workshop I have been aware of a certain fuzziness when we discuss the issue of hostility. I don't mean to imply that the fuzziness is restricted only to our group, for I have been struck over the years by the imprecision of thought that generally surrounds the relationship among hostility, anger, and aggression. These terms have been used interchangeably in the literature, and I am not certain that they are in fact interchangeable.

When we have talked about hostility-in, many people have commented that self-criticism, self-depreciation, and similar stances do not constitute hostility directed against the self but merely imply a lowered self-image. I would pose this question: If the depressed person who berates himself and calls himself such awful names were to direct this barrage of insults toward another person, would it be considered hostile or not? I don't mean to suggest an absolute answer to this question, for I think we need to clarify our terms more precisely and to begin working on some unresolved problems in this area. For example, we need to separate the causes of behavior from the effects. They are not always identical. Also, similar effects may result from different causes. Consider two situations: in one, a creature kills another creature (usually of the same species) in a power struggle; in the other a predator kills his prey (usually of another species). In both situations a killing occurs, but in one the motivation is aggressive dominance, and in the other it is hunger. We need to know the context in order to understand the behavior. Even so, how we label the behavior will depend on the kind of classification we use. In the examples cited a descriptive classification would likely label both instances as aggressive, but a motivational classification would not.

Dr. Katz: I would like to comment on the interdependence of cognitive, affective, and motivational variables in producing an emotional state. Schachter attempted to create a specific emotional state by artificially producing all of the physiological components of that state. For example, he gave subjects adrenalin and hoped to produce the state of anxiety. He discovered that this was not possible until the subject developed a cognitive set consistent with the emotion being stimulated physiologically by the experimenter. The conclusion that one draws from this work is that a person needs all of the components of the emotion before the whole emotion is actually experienced.

This makes a great deal of sense but when we became involved in some research with LSD and other such drugs I began to question this conceptual scheme. For what we learned was that powerful drugs did in fact appear to create whole emotions in individuals, whether the individual was cognitively ready for the emotional state or not. In response to a drug such as LSD, the individual eventually supplied the emotional content but the drug itself was powerful enough to create the internal chemical changes which produced a whole emotion (Katz, et al. 1968). This finding leads me to reinterpret Schachter's results in the following way. When the inputs from the cognitive, physiological, and motivational areas are relatively low in potency, then all three inputs may be necessary for the production of emotion. However, when the input from any one of these is sufficiently powerful in and of itself, e.g., the physiological effects of a drug of the order of LSD, an emotion can be produced and the input from other processes follows.

Dr. Dyrud: I am concerned about Dr. Kaufman's discussion of form and content. We so often fall into the trap of believing that content and meaning can only be dealt with in a verbal exploratory fashion. We assume that unless we do deal with the content in such a way, there will be no change. And yet there are certainly instances where this is not so. For example, in dance therapy the patient talks little or not at all and moves from small muscle movements to large muscle movements. After such therapy we often find that tremendous changes have occurred in the meaning system of the patient, and we do not know whether it is the encouragement of the dance therapist, the use of muscles (i.e., change in biology), or some other element of the process that has resulted in the change of a whole set of meanings for the patient. But it does happen. The real question is where the optimal point of entry into this system of behavior and meaning is. Does it always have to be on a verbal level? Apparently not!

Dr. Chodoff: Dr. Kaufman asks whether the self-depreciatory statements of the depressives are not really hostile ones. I don't think they really are the same as hostile statements, and I think that anger and issues of self-esteem can be separated. The depressed person may say that he is no good, that he is stupid, etc., and then Dr. Kaufman asks, "If he said such things about others, wouldn't that be hostile?" I'm not sure it would be. I can say to you that I think you are no good or that you are ignorant, etc., and that doesn't necessarily have to be a hostile comment. It may be true, and you may agree with me.

Dr. Kaufman: I would agree with Dr. Chodoff theoretically, but in point of fact we must examine the context in which such statements are made to other people. The statement "you are no good" might very well be true and it might be an objective evaluation, but if I say that to you in the usual social context, it's going to be considered hostile behavior. Finally, I don't think it has to be one way or the other; that is, self-depreciatory statements may sometimes represent hostility directed against the self and at other times the two may be separate. I only meant to raise the question for further consideration and possible research activity.

In summary I would make the following points:

1. Underlying all depressive reactions is a basic organismic state, a state of helplessness.

2. This organismic state is based on a biological response system, present throughout much of the vertebrate order, which is available for dealing with unmanageable stress by favoring survival through the adaptive aspects of the conservation-withdrawal response.

3. The state of helplessness should be viewed as a psychobiological entity in which motivational, cognitive, and affective processes are interdependent variables.

4. If a state of helplessness is the basic phenomenon of depression, we need not postulate a primary role for aggression in depression.

5. The role of aggression in depression is obscured by a conceptual confusion between the causes and effects of behavior and also by a semantic and conceptual confusion involving the relationship among "aggression," "hostility," and "anger."

ON DEVELOPMENT AND THE CONSERVATION–WITHDRAWAL REACTION

Dr. Arthur Schmale:

I think it is important to refer to some of our research carried on at the University of Rochester Medical Center to put my reactions and comments concerning the many interesting presentations and discussions in perspective. Over the past fifteen years I have become increasingly interested in understanding the many manifestations and possible types of depressive behavior. However, much of my time during this period has been spent investigating the psychosocial setting of medical disease onset and the association of this setting with depressive feelings.

In about 80 percent of the subject-patients studied, a consistent psychological setting for the "apparent" onset of medical disease has been found (Schmale 1958). Reference has been made to the significant elements in these settings in various reports as involving "unresolvable object loss," "separation and depression reactions," and "giving up reactions." To be more specific, the setting involves the occurrence of a life event or events which the subject reports as having interpreted as a potential loss of a highly desired form of gratification for which he believes there is no replacement. The life event that may trigger the danger of deprivation may involve actual loss of such gratification, the threat of the loss, or even the symbolic reminder of a past loss. The affective or feeling reaction to such an unresolvable loss is one of depression.

Two different types of depressive feelings have been identified. In one, the feeling of deprivation is attributed to the loss of an external source of gratification. Such gratification is believed to be under the control of someone in the external environment, and it is believed that the only way the loss can be overcome is by a change occurring in the external environment that is not under the individual's control. Thus, either the someone who initiated the deprivation would have to provide the gratification again or it would have to come from some other or new external giving source. This affect is referred to as one of helplessness. The reaction is probably first experienced toward the end of the first year of life.

The second affect of depression is called hopelessness and involves a self-initiated loss for which there is felt to be no resolution. This reaction is first experienced sometime during the third to sixth year of life. The loss involves a failure to achieve a self-set goal or aspiration and at the time the thought occurs, there is an unwillingness to give up the goal or aspiration. Thus, the individual feels he has failed himself and there is no way he or anyone else can overcome his inadequacy.

The psychological reaction that includes the thought of unresolvable loss together with one or the other of the associated affects of depression is what we have come to refer to as the "giving up" reaction (Schmale & Engel, 1967).

It is reasoned that these affects result from different types of early-life deprivations and represent different maturational levels of self and object differentiation.

There are many naturally occurring times in every person's life when it is necessary to give up one concept of the self and important objects for other concepts, goals, or rewards. The timing and setting in which these naturally occurring as well as unexpected losses happen may determine how well an individual can cope, and defend against or accept the feelings of helplessness or hopelessness, and then find new more achievable gratifications, relationships or goals.

It has been our working assumption that during the period when these psychological reactions are experienced, the individual is more vulnerable to whatever somatic predispositions for disease he carries within him or to the ever-present pathogenic influences existing in his external environment. The diseases that may occur involve all diagnostic categories from infectious and degenerative to neoplastic and metabolic. Holmes and Rahe's life-change measurement as a predictor of illness has further served to confirm our results (Rahe, 1968).

Following these studies of individuals who became medically sick, we undertook a study of patients who developed psychiatric illnesses. In about 80 percent of the disease onset periods there was evidence that they had reached an impasse in their lives and felt trapped and unable to cope (Adamson & Schmale 1965). This kind of setting was identified in not only the patients who developed the clinical syndromes of depression but also those found to have an acute schizophrenic reaction, acute brain syndrome, acute situational, or identity crisis reaction.

From this perspective then, what is associated with the feelings of depression or the "giving up" reaction is a part of the setting in which many somatic or psychic syndromes first appear or recur. The experiencing of the feelings of depression in and of itself does not specifically predispose one to the appearance of a clinical syndrome of depression. In this regard, such reactions as an individual's belief that he has no future, there are no objects left to relate to, he has no motivation to find a new solution, or his awareness that the current life situation is similar to a previously experienced event are all a part of the giving-up reaction and are not specific to the clinical syndromes of depression we have heard presented here by Dr. Beck.

This brings us to the differences between the feelings and the syndromes of depression. Our recent concerns and investigations have attempted to delineate the specific characteristics that differentiate the clinical syndromes from the affects of depression. As I have already indicated, a clinical syndrome of depression may have its acute onset in a psychological setting of giving up. Those who go on to experience the clinical syndrome of depression obviously do so because of factors other than those associated with the feelings of depression. Perhaps specific genetic, constitutional, and early experiential factors are important in establishing an individual's predisposition to the clinical syndrome experience of depression. Such predispositions then may become activated at the time the giving-up reaction is experienced.

We have observed from a psychodynamic point of view that adult individuals evaluated as clinically depressed have specific coping mechanisms to help them defend against the feelings of helplessness or hopelessness. Here we find Beck's observations and formulations about cognitive distortions most relevant and important. In fact, in our attempts to understand the differences between the affects and the clinical states of depression, we think the major clue lies in the cognitive distortions that are found in those experiencing the clinical syndromes of depression (Schmale, 1972). In essence, it is as if the feelings of depression are too threatening for these individuals to experience. The conscious idea of giving up and the associated feelings of loss and being immobilized are more than they can tolerate, and from this a neurotic symptom develops. An analogous situation may be seen in the relationship of anxiety to a phobic reaction. The individual who cannot tolerate anxiety feelings may develop a phobic reaction as a means to repress the ideation associated with the previously experienced anxiety. The depressive symptom involves a compromise which allows repression of the ideas and the feelings of depression associated with giving up. As with all neurotic symptoms, there is some gratification as well as some protection provided by the symptom.

In the case of the compromise against the feelings of helplessness, we see a clinical picture involving "the need to prove neglect." Here the distorted cognition, as Beck refers to it, involves the idea that objects are available for gratification but they have been unwilling to provide it. In the case of the compromise against the feeling of hopelessness, we have referred to the symptom formation as one of "the need to prove self-neglect." Here the distorted cognition involves the thought that the individual has the capacity to satisfy all his goals and desires but that he has been unwilling rather than unable to achieve such satisfaction. With this comes the need to suffer not so much out of guilt but out of shame for not having tried harder. More detailed discussions of these concepts and examples can be found elsewhere (Schmale, 1972). Suffice it to say that "the need to prove neglect" is associated with what is usually referred to as exogenous, reactive, or neurotic depression, while "the need to prove self-neglect" is usually related to what is referred to as psychotic depression or melancholia. As with the phobic reaction, by the time the patient is seen by a psychiatrist or is hospitalized the symptom compromise is not completely effective in repressing the loss conflict, and in addition to the symptom of depression, the affects of depression, and the biological anlage of the depressive behavior, the conservation-withdrawal reaction may also be experienced. (More will be said about the conservation-withdrawal reaction later.) It is because of the combination of these three phenomena, which occur when the depressive symptom is not working effectively, that there is so much confusion in the reporting of the behavior of depressed patients who are sick enough to seek help and are available for study.

From this perspective then, I think it can be seen where I take issue with a number of the presentations. For the most part the criteria employed in most of the studies involve an admixture of biological withdrawal and affective and clinical syndrome features. Most of the depression inventories that attempt to measure severity of depression include such a mixture. Frequently, the most psychotically depressed will score low in the self-administration of such inventories while those who are experiencing feelings of depression related to a grief reaction will score high.

Further, I think that when we describe depression in animals, we are probably talking about something more basic and biological than the affects of depression and the clinical states of depression (Schmale, in press). I apologize for mentioning this last when it really deserves first consideration. Dr. Kaufman has likened his observations of monkeys to those of Dr. Engel's about Monica, which Engel has called a conservation-withdrawal reaction. This reaction is thought to be a basic biological adaptive process present in many forms of life and represented at many levels of cellular, organ, and system functioning. It involves a detachment from the external environment when the external environment becomes too stimulating or too depriving. Such inactivity or resting states are seen in hibernation, encystment, and the refractory periods that occur during the cyclical activity of many organs and systems. In man this basic biological mechanism has central nervous system components from which the affects of depression are derived. Again, time does not permit a more complete discussion of this important primary regulatory mechanism, which needs further study (Schmale, in press). It is difficult to consider that the behavior of dogs, monkeys, or any subhuman could function at other than the level of this basic biological mechanism. We do not have to attribute psychic functioning and the related affects of depression or neurotic depressive symptom formations to the behaviors we observe in animals.

Dr. Friedman: Dr. Schmale, if I understand you correctly, you are stating that in a distorted fashion the depressed patient is actually avoiding feelings of helplessness and hopelessness, which constitute the essence of depression. In other words, he is defending against those feeling states much as the phobic defends against anxiety. This seems to agree with the writings of many people, especially those who have contended that the depressed patient actually cannot feel certain affects. Many claim that the depressive is not really hostile or that he does not really feel guilty, and the implication is consistently in line with your thinking, i.e., the depressed patient is avoiding some type of feeling. It would seem to me that depression is adaptive to the extent that it helps a person avoid something he feels would be unmanageable, and it is also clearly nonadaptive because the person is wrong in assuming that he would be unable to cope with the feeling.

Dr. Schmale: Yes, you understood me correctly. The individual's assumptions may be distorted or inappropriate and maladaptive for dealing with his current reality. From a variety of studies we have learned that difficulties in coping with prior loss or deprivations predispose individuals to such maladaptive responses. They are psychically unable to cope consciously with another loss they consider to be unresolvable, as was the one previously experienced. To deal with these changes in role or loss in external gratification, individuals need the capacity to recognize, tolerate, and then master the loss. Dr. Elizabeth Zetzel (1964) has described this as being able to bear the feeling of depression. The inability to bear such feelings of depression is prominent in Dr. Zetzel's concept of the dynamics of the maladaptive state of depression. Obviously, there are some times in life when changes in roles and aspirations are more difficult to tolerate and master than others. Thus, giving up some will be more difficult than others and some individuals will have greater difficulty giving up than others.

Dr. Chodoff: Dr. Schmale, is there really a difference between depression as a signal and anxiety as a signal? As I understand psychoanalytic theory, anxiety is thought to be a signal arising in the ego warning against the recurrence of a traumatic infantile state. The infantile state is one of fear of loss or mutilation, i.e., either separation from the parents or mutilation by the parents. Now this is the same signaling operation that you attribute to depression, and I wonder why we need another signal if the signal of anxiety can warn us against impending loss, separation, or mutilation.

Dr. Schmale: Yes, I think there are differences between signal anxiety and signal depression. Anxiety warns us of a threat of loss or mutilation and something to be avoided, whereas depression as a signal indicates the belief that the threat of loss or mutilation is inevitable and cannot be avoided. Further, these affects and affective signals have different, underlying biological regulatory processes. The feeling of anxiety is related to the adaptive biological processes that prepare for fight or flight activity, and the feelings of depression are related to the mechanisms that prepare for disengagement and conservation-withdrawal inactivity.

Dr. Beck: It has always helped me to remember that anxiety seems to be the reaction to the threat that something will happen, and depression is a reaction to the fact that the traumatic event has already happened.

Dr. Chodoff: Therefore, if one is depressed, that supposedly signals that the traumatic event has already happened, which is not really signaling anything at all because it is a reaction to something that already happened, not a sign that it will happen.

Dr. Dyrud: I too would like to try to explain why I see anxiety and depression as separate signals. We talk about anxiety as if it were a signal and one way to deal with this signal would be to go on and act anxious. That then becomes behavior, an operant which is a way of doing something. Similarly, we must distinguish between hopelessness, helplessness, and the behavior of acting depressed, which is doing something about it. It is an operant. What we see as the "clinical state" in both anxiety and depression is really a response, a way of organizing and doing something about a signal.

Dr. Tabachnick: Is it really necessary for us to specify why we have one signal in one particular situation and another signal under different circumstances? Does everything have to fit into such a neat pattern? After all, people grow up in different ways with different predispositions and it would seem that an individual can react to the threatened recurrence of a traumatic event with either depression or anxiety as a signal. I guess I am in the middle and contend that depression and anxiety can be a signal for the same thing.

Dr. McDevitt: The child development literature supports the concept that anxiety is the signal of some danger which portends the potential loss of the object, loss of the object's love, some threat to one's bodily integrity, or castration anxiety. Signal anxiety comes from one's wishes of a certain type which are spoken of in psychoanalytic writings as libidinal or aggressive wishes, etc. Signal anxiety tells the observer at least that the individual is experiencing a threat or a danger. I think that depression, when we consider it as helplessness and hopelessness, is of a different order. Depression represents either the loss or the threatened loss of an object or the loss of something important to the individual whether it be his goals or his ideals, but clearly it is something that has a bearing on his state of well-being and security. The depressive person, in general, is one who seems to need narcissistic supplies to maintain his sense of well-being and security. I believe these two affects are of a different order, though there is certainly a question of overlap at times. For example, one can be quite anxious about becoming depressed and one can feel depressed about experiencing high levels of anxiety.

Dr. Goodwin: I would like to comment about the sequence of anxiety followed by depression which is observed in the monkey when separated from its mother. As I understand this anxious, restless phase, it may represent an attempt to do something about the stress or loss. This sequence makes some sense from a biological point of view when examined in light of the animal stress literature, which shows that when one stresses an animal chronically without overdoing it, the animal goes through a period in which it increases its synthesis of the neurotransmitters needed for flight or fight. It not only increases the amount of transmitter but also the enzymatic machinery necessary for neurotransmitter synthesis.

However, the animal reaches a point beyond which it cannot tolerate prolonged or increased stress and, if it is pushed beyond this point, one of two things may happen. Either the animal will become exhausted neurochemically (this depletion seems to be a reasonable analogue of the "giving up" phenomenon in that the brain is sort of "giving up," neurochemically speaking), or the feedback control mechanism may become upset so that the animal is left with more enzymatic machinery than it needs (which may be an analogue of the agitated, anxious, or even hypomanic or manic patient). In this instance, the stress on the animal might well change but the animal is "stuck" with a response machinery that is turning over very rapidly and is incapable of shifting its response. Such an analogue is very interesting in the human situation because many of the stresses we endure in a complex psychosocial situation are of this nature.

A paradigm might be the response of hitting another person when we are angry. This response is usually frustrated by considerable social restraint, so that we are not allowed to do what other animals would do naturally in such a situation. It well may be that our biological systems are not as aware of these social restraints as they should be, with the result that they are responding as if we could act spontaneously, even though we are not allowed to do so. Instead this activity has to be expressed in some form of agitation or anxiety, and in some people in the form of hypomania.

Dr. Klerman: Dr. Schmale's comments have been very helpful to me and stimulate some questions I would like to share with you. Although the human infant may be born with the capacity for depression, it does not demonstrate the affects of depression (helplessness and hopelessness) at birth, for they follow a developmental sequence. If Dr. Kaufman's and Dr. Bowlby's work is correct, then depression can only follow the development of social bonds and social attachments. It is only after the loss of such a bond that a person manifests depression. There is thus a timetable, and, as I understand the thrust of Dr. Kaufman's research, the timetable is contingent upon certain environmental inputs. Such a developmental sequence is not to be found with anxiety, however, since fear responses are present at birth or very soon thereafter and seem less dependent on social bond formation.

Dr. Schmale: We may be rushing ahead too fast if we assume that the infant is truly "anxious." To jump ahead and say that anxiety is not tied to social bond formation as is depression may be a mistake, since the distortion may well be in the observer who identifies the infant's cry as anxiety when indeed it may be somatic irritability or hyperactivity. The child who is crying may not perceive the feeling of anxiety. As mentioned previously, we may be dealing with the biological antecedents of such feelings as anxiety or depression. I would suggest that what is called depressive reaction in monkeys, as described by Dr. Kaufman and others, and the learned helplessness which Dr. Seligman describes is more precisely the biological antecedent of the feelings of depression, or as we have referred to it, a conservation-withdrawal reaction.

Dr. Klerman: I think we clearly need developmental studies similar to those Dr. McDevitt has described which will trace not only the evolutionary phylogeny of some of these affects but also their ontogeny in terms of individual development.

Dr. Kaufman: You have to make the distinction between the organismic state and the point at which the "feeling aspect," the internally perceived aspect of the organismic state, comes into being. It does not necessarily follow that the two start simultaneously. Dr. Klerman states that developmentally, anxiety precedes depression. I have stated that the organismic state which underlies depression is the conservation withdrawal response. Let me describe a study that clearly delineates the presence of this response in the human infant. Robert Endy studied the response of newborn infants to circumcision when they were two days old. He found that on the night following circumcision there was an enormous increase in deep sleep compared to the night before. It is possible, as Endy has done, to interpret this increase in deep sleep as a type of conservation-withdrawal from the world.

Dr. Schmale: In summary, then, at least two affective forms and two clinical syndromes of depression have been identified as discrete types of depressive behavior. Further work is necessary to determine more precisely the psycho-dynamics of these and perhaps other forms of depression in order to apply the most appropriate treatment modalities. Such work is also necessary before there can be a meaningful study of the genetic, biochemical, and endocrine characteristics of any or all the various types of depressive behavior.

From a developmental perspective, all forms of depressive feelings in humans probably have their origins in the specific biological regulatory processes called conservation-withdrawal which are manifested by unresponsivity and immobility. Such a reaction, seen at many levels of biological life, is responsible for periodic rest and restitution and entails a disengagement and unresponsiveness to environmental input when the environment becomes unmanageable or unavailable as a source of supplies.

What has been described as depression in animals is probably the behavior associated with conservation-withdrawal. This biological formulation does not require that the animal experience the feeling of depression or the clinical symptoms of the depressive syndrome. Further study of the biological characteristics of the conservation-withdrawal reaction in animals and man should be undertaken.

The feelings of depression initially represent the intrapsychic awareness of the individual's biological responses to loss and deprivation coming from the environment. Memory of these experiences leads to the development of intrapsychic means of avoiding or coping with such experiences.

During periods when the affects of depression are being experienced, individuals appear to be more vulnerable to somatic or psychic dysfunctions which have been traditionally categorized as disease. The intervening links in these psychobiological relationships are yet to be identified. The clinical syndromes of depression involve specific intrapsychic defenses against the experiencing of the feelings of depression. These symptoms are identified by the cognitive distortions that fit the traditional psychoanalytic concept of a neurotic symptom formation. The possibility that early experience, constitution, or genetic factors predispose some individuals to the clinical syndromes of depression requires longitudinal developmental studies for proof.

Dr. Katz: I participated in a recent conference entitled "Depression in the 70's," (Fievre, 1971) which included a section dealing with the problems of classification, description, and epidemiology of depression. Concern was expressed about the differing manifestations of depression seen across varying ethnic groups. Dr. Heinz Lehmann, who wrote the conference's epidemiology paper, tells us that we actually know very little about the influence of culture on depression. Tentative conclusions, such as the idea that the condition we call "depression" may not even exist in some parts of Africa, are rather startling. (Tooth, 1950). I wonder, then, how we can approach the study of a syndrome such as depression without seriously considering the role of culture. Dr. Spiro is an anthropologist and not an expert on depression, but we look to him now to provide a cross-cultural perspective when he comments on the issues we have been discussing for the past day and a half.

ON MEANING AND EXPRESSION IN OTHER CULTURES
Dr. Melford Spiro:

I would like to preface my remarks by stating at the outset that little of my past work has concerned depression and that in a formal sense I know very little about the subject. I have become increasingly interested in depression, however, because my most recent work has been on Buddhism in Burma, where one of the things I found rather interesting and important to my research was that a number of Burmese monks I had met were—to my untrained eye—very depressed and talked in a depressive fashion.

Several omissions occur to me as I review the discussions we have held over the past day and a half. I have been disappointed that so little attention has been given to the antecedents of depression. Other than the separation studies Dr. Kaufman described and the learned helplessness studies that Dr. Seligman reported on, we have heard very little about the life history or social structural antecedents of depression. Another basic area which I believe we have neglected and one I hope we can remedy is that of the psychodynamics of depression. Except for some comments by Dr. Schmale and a brief resume by Dr. Chodoff, we have heard relatively little about psychodynamic constellations in depression.

There are several comments I would like to make based on my own field work. Work I did in Israel relates to some of Dr. Kaufman's findings. He described the reaction of the infant bonnet monkey, which is raised in numerous peer and adult relationships and does not manifest depressive symptoms when separated from its mother. If we look at this phenomenon not only cross-specifically but also cross-culturally, we do see some differences. My work in Israel dealt with kibbutzim, and I was interested in child development in a community where children are reared communally rather than by their parents. Children there do see their parents daily, but are raised primarily in peer groups by professional caretakers. In contrast to the bonnet monkey, one of my striking findings was that when the mother or to a lesser extent the father temporarily left the kibbutz, these children, despite the constancy of their caretaker and peer relationships, manifested symptoms of withdrawal, isolation, crying, night terror, thumb sucking, and what I would call a general depressive syndrome. This constellation of symptoms occurred with such frequency that I felt it had some lasting effect on personality development.

My other comment is drawn from research which I have conducted on Burmese Buddhist monks and from impressions I gathered during a recent trip to Burma. Buddhism has what many people have described as a very pessimistic world view. The basic premise of Buddhism, which all of these people are taught from early childhood, is that life is suffering. The Buddha enunciated four basic Truths. The first is that life is suffering, and these people, at least on the verbal level, believe in its validity. They will say, "Standing is suffering, but sitting is also suffering," "Not eating is suffering, but eating is also suffering," etc. I once heard a psychiatrist tell a (depressed) patient that she was "suffering from suffering." It is of great interest to me that in Buddhist societies such as Burma's there are institutions—primarily the monastic institution—which provide those individuals who take the Truth of suffering very seriously and are depressed with an honorable "charter" for their affective state and an institutionalized means for coping with it. The depressed person who enters a monastery in Burma is confirming the Truth that life is suffering; it is the Buddhist who truly believes that life is suffering who will become a monk and in his life exemplify this Truth. If one really accepts the notion that life is suffering, it is only rational to do those things that enable him to reduce, if not extinguish, suffering—which means, according to Buddhism, to go into a monastery and engage in Buddhist meditation. The primary aim of Buddhist meditation is to overcome suffering, and ultimately to attain Nirvana (the cessation of suffering). The person who in our society might well end up in a psychiatrist's office or a mental institution with the pejorative label of "sick" may in Burma end up in a monastery with an honorific label, "monk" or "meditator."

I would like to make one final comment based on my research in Burma about helplessness and hopelessness. Early travelers characterized the Burmese as a happy-go-lucky people and indeed one writer described them as the "Irish of the East." When I was in Burma in 1961-1962, with the exception of the very depressed monks whom I have mentioned, I rarely encountered anyone who I would characterize as persistently unhappy or to whom I would apply the term "depressed." In 1962 there was a coup and the new military dictatorship began a decade of oppressive rule. When I returned to Burma this past summer I was immediately struck that people whom I had known intimately in the past and who had never shown any symptoms of depression or even talked about unhappiness, now persistently told me how unhappy and depressed they were. The words that came up over and over again—which I find so interesting in the context of our discussion—were "helplessness" and "hopelessness." "Everything is hopeless and we are helpless to do anything about it," they would say. Indeed, they are helpless because they have no available techniques to mobilize resistance to this military regime. They have no guns or other weapons and they face an army in complete control of the country.

In addition to the pervasive depression, I encountered a number of people who, in addition to being depressed and unhappy, had developed ulcers. I have not heard anyone at this conference mention ulcers in connection with depression, and I wonder if anyone has any ideas about this.

The question of guilt and depression, related to certain cognitive sets, has been a recurrent issue of this conference and perhaps some information regarding cognition in a Buddhist society will provide an additional reference point for us. The Buddhist believes that almost everything, whether good or bad, that happens to him in this life is the result of karma. Suffering, then, is the result of bad karma. Since karma is the result of one's own behavior, and since Buddhists believe in rebirth, bad karma may be the result of evil deeds and sins committed in a previous life. In Burma today many people interpret the sufferings caused by the military regime and the failing economy as the result of the bad things they had done in their previous existences. Let me give only one example. One of the first persons I talked with on my last trip to Burma was a woman whom I had known well from my first trip. She was at that time probably the most Westernized woman I had met in Mandalay, and one of the wealthiest persons in that city. She was also very attractive, always beautifully groomed, and a very outgoing person. When I saw her on this trip I hardly recognized her: she had become old, almost slovenly, and practically a recluse, and had not left her house in three years. She was not only very depressed as a result of the loss of her wealth and social status, but in large measure she felt guilty about her situation, as if her own previous actions were responsible for it.

Dr. Katz: Thank you, Dr. Spiro, for your comments, which bring to mind the controversy that raged years back about the guilt-shame theory in the field of depression. The Burmese who carry guilt from generation to generation make our Western guilt seem minimal. They carry it over from one life to the next, from one era of time to another.

Dr. Spiro: Indeed, Buddhist time is measured in eons, and one's life trajectory is not the 70 years one has in this world (what we would call our life span); instead, it literally spans eons and eons, so that an individual believes he can work out his destiny in 40 lives or in 1,000 lives.

Dr. Chodoff: Is there an adaptive value for the individual Buddhist who in an unbellicose way just accepts his suffering? Does such resignation provide any merit in the present or any chance of a better reincarnation?

Dr. Spiro: No, the Buddhist believes that there is little he can do about his present suffering, and that the wisest thing is to engage in those acts which, in Buddhist terms, will bring him merit so that his next rebirth will be a happy one.

Dr. Goodwin: It seems that the Buddhists in Burma are actually unable to resign themselves to their military regime. I would think they would not become depressed and in fact would see their suffering as the logical outcome of their belief system.

Dr. Spiro: I suppose you're theoretically correct. Indeed your comment highlights one of the many paradoxes of Buddhism as it is actually lived, since many of the Buddhist notions are very difficult to accept even for Buddhists. Many inconsistencies therefore exist between what the Buddhist ought to believe, had he really internalized Buddhist notions, and what he actually does believe and how he actually does behave. For him—no more than for us—behavior is a compromise between beliefs inculcated in childhood and other notions and aspirations which reflect later influences.

Dr. Goodwin: Perhaps the people you were seeing were more Westernized and therefore more susceptible to depression.

Dr. Spiro: I gave an example of a woman who was severely depressed and who, incidentally, was highly Westernized. But I would not generalize on the basis of this one case. My offhand impression is that the incidence of depression was equally distributed among Westernized and non-Westernized Burmese.

Dr. Katz: These differences in Western and Asian expressions of the state are reflected somewhat in a study we are conducting among various ethnic groups in Hawaii. The subjects are for the most part psychotic patients in a state hospital, where we have identified several ethnic groups including Hawaii-Japanese, Hawaii-Caucasian, and Hawaii-Filipino. When we analyzed the data for manifestation of depression among these ethnic groups, we found their symptoms to be quite different. The functionally psychotic Japanese patient evidences few or no depressive symptoms, but there are many clearly depressive symptoms among the Caucasians. The differences in depression between the Caucasian and the Japanese may well relate to how these patients describing their distressed state. Indeed, in the Japanese language there are few words for "sad," "lonely," or "blue," although there may be other ways of saying the same thing.

Dr. McDevitt: Dr. Spiro, how old were the children in Israel who reacted so strongly to their parents' absence?

Dr. Spiro: The age range was from 1 to 8 years. I cannot recall the age of those who exhibited this reaction most intensely, although the data are available.

Dr. McDevitt: But it was your impression that such a life experience would be deleterious to their future development. Do you have any outcome information to support this hunch?

Dr. Spiro: We do have outcome information about these children. When we were there in 1950-1951, the oldest among the children born and raised in the kibbutz was 27, and there were only seven others who were over 21. So the personality picture we drew was of the personality of the late teenager. Nevertheless, we discovered that these teenagers were characterized by a noticeable amount of withdrawal. We also felt that though there were a number of inputs that contributed to their ending up withdrawn, their early life experience, which included maternal deprivation, was especially important.

A young clinical psychologist is now working in the kibbutz doing a follow-up study of those individuals we studied 20 years ago. He is using many of the same instruments we did, and our hope is that in the near future we will have further follow-up information.

Dr. Klerman: What is current anthropological thinking about Caruthers' idea that one does not see depression in the Central Africans because they have no structured superego?

Dr. Spiro: As far as I know, we just don't know enough to form an anthropological opinion.

Dr. Katz: Tooth reports that the incidence of depression differs markedly in various parts of Africa and even from tribe to tribe. However, both pieces of work have been criticized from a methodological standpoint.

Dr. Schuyler: Dr. Spiro's description of the Buddhist adaptation to the repressive regime in Burma seems to me to be related to the issue of mastery which we discussed before. Perhaps relating the difficulty in the present to sins and omissions committed in the past is a way of bringing a hopeless situation under control, for then these people can do something about it—they can pray and that may bring some relief from the present situation.

Dr. Spiro: They do not believe anything will bring relief from the present situation, and think that prayer will only help them in future existences.

Dr. Schuyler: I am speaking about the illusion of adaptation. The person who is hopeless sees no way out. These people have a way out. Now in reality they may not really be able to change anything, but I would imagine that if one spoke to a Burmese he would feel he could do something, for he considers the offender to be not the government but himself and therefore he is bringing the situation under partial control—at least conceptually. By this movement to reduce the uncontrollability of the trauma, people also reduce the feelings of hopelessness and depression.

Dr. Spiro: Not really, because from his point of view he really has no control over the present situation. His behavior in previous existences may have been responsible for his present suffering, and his behavior in his present existence can effect the balance of happiness or suffering in a future existence. But he believes he can do little to affect his present situation. Moreover, there is the other side of the coin which I have not mentioned. If the people in some sense "deserve" their suffering because of evil deeds committed in previous lives, so the members of the ruling military regime are believed to "deserve" their good fortune because of good deeds committed in their previous lives. In short, this type of belief system provides religious legitimacy for an admittedly oppressive regime. (The logical and psychological dimensions of this aspect of Buddhist belief are discussed at length in my *Buddhism and Society*, 1970).

Dr. Parloff: I would like to question a point which Dr. Spiro raised earlier concerning the cultural and institutional means for dealing with states such as depression. I wonder if Dr. Spiro would care to comment on the notion that we have arrived at a state of institutionalization of sorts in regard to the counterculture that exists within our society. The kids today, when they drop out, do not have to become depressed and sulk at home, for instead they don certain clothes and join a group of dropouts. They become part of something rather than withdrawing from something.

Dr. Spiro: True. In the past somebody who engaged in the behavior you describe was considered a hobo. But now it has become a group phenomenon and there is almost an honorific label attached with it. I believe this is indeed an institutionalized method of dealing with problems that otherwise could not have been dealt with and might have ended up in the hands of a psychiatrist.

Dr. Beck: I have observed in the counterculture another kind of institutionalization, in which it seems to be a noble endeavor to suffer and be depressed. When these people get together, particularly in sensitivity groups, they tend to honor the person who can talk the most about how miserable he is and, indeed, they seem to make a fetish about being miserable and depressed. They are not depressed about being depressed however, and withdrawal behavior is highly valued.

Dr. Seligman: I have encountered hundreds of undergraduates every day in my duties as a basic psychology teacher and having talked with a number of them over several years, I cannot escape the impression that this is a depressed generation. I see what appears to me to be considerably more depression among college undergraduates than existed when I myself was an undergraduate student. I am also convinced that there are many explanations for this increased incidence of depression. One possibility I would like to emphasize stems from the realization that this generation has grown up with many reinforcers, many good things. The key is that they have received these reinforcers independently of their own efforts to obtain them, i.e., things have been given to them rather than earned by them. That to me is a precondition for depression.

BIBLIOGRAPHY

Adamson, J. D., & Schmale, A. H. Object loss, giving up and the onset of psychiatric disease. *Psychosomatic Medicine*, 1965, 27:557.
Brodie, H. K. H., Murphy, D. L., Goodwin, F. K., & Bunney, W. E., Jr. Catecholamines and mania: the effect of alpha-methyl-para-tyrosine on manic behavior and catecholamine metabolism. *Clinical Pharmacology and Therapeutics*, 1971, 12:218.
Engel, G. L. *Psychological development in health and disease*. Philadelphia: Saunders, 1962.

Fieve, R. R. (Ed.). *Depression in the 70's*. Amsterdam: Excerpta Medica, 1971.

Goodwin, F. K., Murphy, D. L., & Bunney, W. E., Jr. Lithium carbonate treatment in depression and mania: a longitudinal double-blind study. *Archives of General Psychiatry*, 1969, **21**:486.

Goodwin, F. K. & Bunney, W. E., Jr. Depressions following reserpine: a reevaluation. *Seminars in Psychiatry*, 1971, **3**:435.

Katz, M. M. The classification of depression: normal, clinical, and ethnocultural variations. In Fieve, R. R. (Ed.), *Depression in the 70's*. Amsterdam: Excerpta Medica, 1971.

Katz, M. M., Waskow, I. E., & Olsson, J. Characterizing the psychological state produced by LSD. *Journal of Abnormal Psychology*, 1968, **73**:1-14.

Kaufman, I. C. Mother-infant separation in monkeys: an experimental model. In Senay, E., & Scott, J. P. (Eds.), *Separation and depression: clinical and research aspects* in press.

Kaufman, I. C., & Rosenblum, L. A. The reaction to separation in infant monkeys: anaclitic depression and conservation-withdrawal. *Psychosomatic Medicine*, 1967, **29**:648-675.

Rahe, R. H. Life change measurement as a predictor of illness. *Proceedings of the Royal Society of Medicine*, 1968, **61**:1124 (Section of Psychiatry).

Schmale, A. H. Relationship of separation and depression to disease. *Psychosomatic Medicine*, 1958, **20**:259.

Schmale, A. H. Depression as affect, character style and symptom formation. *Psychoanalysis and Contemporary Science*, 1972, **1**:

Schmale, A. H. The adaptive role of depression in health and disease. In *Separation and depression: clinical and research aspects*, American Association for the Advancement of Science, in press.

Schmale, A. H., & Engel, G. L. The giving up-given up complex illustrated on film. *Journal of the American Psychoanalytic Association*, 1967, **15**:344.

Shore, P. A., & Brodie, B. B. Influence of various drugs on serotonin and norepinephrine in the brain. In Garattini, S., & Ghetti, V. (Eds.), *Psychotropic drugs*. Amsterdam: Elsevier, 1957.

Spiro, M. *Kibbutz: venture in utopia*. New York: Schocken Books, 1963.

Spiro, M. *Children of the kibbutz*. New York: Schocken Books, 1965.

Spiro, M. *Buddhism and society*. New York: Harper & Row, 1970.

Tooth, G. *Studies in mental illness in the Gold Coast*. London: H.M.S.O., 1950.

Zetzel, E. R. Depression and the incapacity to bear it. In Schur, M. (Ed.), *Drives, affects and behavior*, vol. 2. New York: International Universities Press, 1964.

SECTION 2
GENERAL DISCUSSION

RESEARCH PERSPECTIVES

Dr. Katz: We have set aside this final portion of the program for an open discussion and also to provide time for reflection about the future. Where do we go next, what types of research are needed, and how do we get there?

Dr. McDevitt: Like Dr. Spiro, I wonder why there has not been more discussion of developmental, dynamic, and structural issues. It may be that they were not the focus of this conference and that they are not of particular interest. It may be because so little is known about such matters, particularly about which pathogenic experiences are specific for the development of depression in later years. Nevertheless, we keep referring back to childhood and particularly to early childhood in our discussions.

I have a hunch I would like to share with you. It seems to me that if one does a study dealing with large samples of cases, he tends out of necessity to stay at the level of the clinical phenomenon that is the surface of immediate interpersonal relationships. In dealing with large numbers of cases it is difficult, if not impossible, to obtain the kind of material that would yield information about the internal structure of the person. Structural components such as the intrapsychic forces (the internal reinforcers), many of which have been acquired early in life and surely have a major bearing on personality and predisposition to depression, are difficult to measure.

If emphasis were placed on intrapsychic processes, I think one would be forced into a more developmental point of view. I believe such an approach is not only important for the understanding of the early precursors of depression, but is also essential for prevention and early intervention.

Dr. Friedman: If we wanted to identify a group of children at high risk for depression, how would we go about it? What would they look like? What would their mothers look like? And how would we study them individually to delineate the determinants of intrapsychic structure and force?

Dr. McDevitt: Dr. Klerman has alerted us to the existence of a potential group for study. I am referring to his description of the children of depressed mothers as being at high risk for the development of depression. Another group worthy of study is those individuals who have experienced parent loss in childhood.

Dr. Seligman: I believe Dr. McDevitt raises an important point. However, the enormous methodological problems involved may preclude the study of these factors in humans. Perhaps there is a way we can capitalize in the future on Dr. Kaufman's research as well as on similar research by Dr. Harlow. Since there are such tremendous difficulties with human predispositional studies, it might be more profitable to study the monkey developmentally. For example, we might want to know how a young monkey that has had certain separation experiences would react as an adult when it encounters marginally depressing experiences or minimal amounts of inescapable shock or small doses of alphamethyl-tyrosine or any other known inducer of depression. Does this seem like a research strategy that might at least begin to reach some of the deeper issues which have been raised?

Dr. Kaufman: We are now beginning a study in which we are going to expose young monkeys to repeated separations about a year or a year and a half apart. We are also doing long-term follow-up studies in infants who have been subjected to separation experiences. The only data which so far bear on the subject come from Robert Hein, who has been studying the rhesus monkey for up to two years after a separation experience. Interestingly, the only variable he has been able to find differentiating the separated infants from unseparated controls is that the infants that have experienced separation several years before show more anxiety when confronted with strange objects, and then only if they are also in a strange environment when confronted with the new objects. There is nothing in these follow-up data which indicates depressive-type phenomena as a result of the early experiences of separation.

Dr. Seligman: That is interesting information. I would suggest as an addition that minimally depressing experiences be presented to such animals as adults to determine whether their depression threshhold has been affected by their previous experiences with separation. Here I think inescapable shock and various types of drugs might be used as stimuli for depression.

Dr. Kaufman: I think that would be a useful next step in this line of research.

Dr. Chodoff: Perhaps Dr. Beck can answer this question. There have been a number of articles about the effect of early parental loss and the role it plays in the development of various syndromes. Is it indeed true that people who become depressed as adults really have a higher incidence of parental loss in childhood or has that notion faded away?

Dr. Beck: The data about this question are sound. There have been about 12 studies relating orphanhood and adult depression. Recently, I reviewed the methodology of these studies, controlling for such things as socioeconomic factors and the mortality rate that can influence death rate of parents. My conclusion is that the best designed studies do show that there is a relationship between orphanhood and adult depression, and that about 30 percent of severely depressed adults have a childhood history of parental loss.

Dr. McDevitt: I don't believe it is sufficient to make such correlations without trying to understand how they came about and why they exist. I would be interested in knowing just what happened to these individuals, and how others who have suffered parental loss manage to overcome it without becoming depressed. In the dog and monkey studies also, I think one would want to look at the phenomenon rather closely to see just how these correlations came about and how and why an early event predisposes to a later attack.

Dr. Beck: I agree with Dr. McDevitt in theory, but reality dictates that we start somewhere. The first step is to notice that a relationship exists between two phenomena, in this case adult depression and a childhood history of parental loss. The second step is to design studies to answer the "how" and "why" of the observed relationship.

We are now ready for step two in depression research and we should begin planning longitudinal studies of a group at high risk for depression. Such research would be similar in design to Norman Garmezy's high-risk schizophrenia studies.

Dr. Klerman: As I have mentioned previously, the children of depressed mothers are a group at high risk. Whether you believe in a genetic transmission or in an environmental transmission, this empirically is a group at high risk for depression. It would be of interest to observe these children and determine how they react to the illness in their mothers.

I mention depressed mothers rather than fathers because the ratio of depression between females and males is 3:1, and also because of an interesting point that Dr. Ekman raised earlier in the discussion. He asked how the children learned to identify affects in the people around them and how they learned to sense from the communications of their mothers such states as guilt, shame, approval, hostility, and joy.

A great deal has been written about the early childhood experiences that predispose to depression—excess dependency, shame, guilt, conditional love, and other constructs of a similar order. Some of these should be observable as we begin to study directly the mothering behavior of depressed women. (A group at New Haven has undertaken studies along this line.) I think one of the more promising techniques I've heard about was that described at this conference by Dr. Lewinsohn, who has been going directly into the homes of depressed people and making direct observations of behavior. I believe that will be very profitable.

Once high-risk children are identified, we might want to look at their cognitive structure. We might want to replicate some of Dr. Beck's work with adults on these children and ask how they are affected by success and failure as they perform a task, and furthermore how their self-esteem is altered by such feedback. In general, I believe the number of studies on both the mothering behavior of depressed women and the behavior of their children is limitless.

Dr. Raskin: In our research we have used one technique we believe shows a great deal of promise, even though it has many pitfalls. We administered the Earl Schaffer Parent Behavior Inventory to our patients and asked them to recall and rate the childrearing attitudes and practices of their parents during their adolescence. We administered the same test and instructions to a control group of "normal" people.

First we tested the validity of the instrument and found the factor structure was the same for the group of normals as it was for the patients, and the factor structure was similar for the youngsters to whom this test had been originally administered and a group of Belgian students used for comparison. Three major factors emerged: "positive involvement," "control through guilt," and "lax discipline."

There were mean differences on ratings on these three factors for the depressed sample as opposed to the normal. Depressed patients rated both their mother and father lower on positive involvement and higher on control-through-guilt, but there was no mean difference between the depressed and normal group on the lax-discipline item. When we further broke down our sample by ethnic groups, we did find a suggestion of a "Jewish mother" factor on the control-through-guilt item. This is an example of possible reconstruction of childhood experiences. True, there is a memory problem when people are asked to recall and record their perceptions of the child training practices of their parents. One encouraging note is that we have found very positive correlations between the scores on these factors and relative's ratings of the parent-child relationship. In other words, the patient's relatives agree with the patient as to the role behavior of the patient's mother and father, which lends an independent validity to the Parent Behavior Inventory.

Dr. Katz: The phenomenology of depression has not been discussed as extensively as I anticipated it would be. We have not seen very many research proposals recently concerning the topic, and I wonder whether anyone is still working in this area.

Dr. Chodoff: We have briefly discussed some of the difficulties involved in this research. As I mentioned previously, I have been working with Dr. Goodwin and Dr. Friedman in trying to develop a research strategy that would tap into some of the psychological predispositions to depression. We have been attempting to design research of a middle range of intensity, that is, not too superficial to miss the phenomena, but not so deep that only one or two cases can be studied. All I can say is that it has been a frustrating endeavor and we almost feel as though we are at a methodological standstill.

Dr. Beck: I think one reason we have not talked about this subject is because our technology has gone about as far as it can. There have been many factor or cluster analytic studies published during the last decade and a multitude of rating instruments have been employed. On reviewing the work, we find that these studies tend to replicate one another and that all seem to reveal the same number and type of factors. I believe we are at a dead end, at least at this superficial level of analysis. If more research time and talent are going to be spent on the phenomenology of depression, then it is going to have to be in the direction Dr. Chodoff is pointing. We need to design research that can give us a grasp of something other than just the manifest behavior.

Dr. Lasky: I would like to second Dr. Beck's comments. The style of research which has been employed in depression work harks back to the early days of the boom in psychopharmacologic research. Then the operational mode was to employ some available measures or rating scales and the clinical paradigm was to use a pair of interviewers who interacted with the patient verbally, paying some attention to the content and making ratings on that basis to form the primary source of data. The nursing personnel would then observe the patient on the ward for periods of time and with varying degrees of reliability. The field has been at this level for a considerable time, all the while improving, refining, and increasing the standardization of the methods—all very necessary and desirable steps but not really true advances. I believe we have reached a plateau of techniques and available measures.

Advances are occurring in some areas, and I believe Dr. Ekman has described one methodological breakthrough. People have been taking motion pictures of patients and children and their interactional events for a long time. In Dr. Ekman's work I see a real possibility for a finer-grained analysis of motoric, nonverbal behavior which would take us considerably beyond what can be observed grossly. The technology is inexpensive, and the opportunity to restudy the phenomena which videotape affords is valuable. What I see as a true step forward now is having the ability to conceptualize categories that can be related to theory, tested, and used as change variables in outcome studies.

Dr. Katz: I tend to agree with Dr. Beck that there is probably a limit to the observational methodology. My background is in psychopharmacology, and whenever we wanted to test the effect of a drug by measuring change in subjective state or mood, we always found it was incredibly difficult to measure even the simplest of subjective states. We were strapped with adjective checklists as perhaps the best measure of mood, but we knew that mood and subjective state had to be described in richer detail for us to understand what was going on inside. I just do not think we have gotten very far at that level of measurement.

Dr. Friedman: Dr. Lasky raises the possibility of collecting large amounts of data on videotape and then analyzing very small units. I think such an approach would end up in a confused and disorganized state because the data would overwhelm the researchers. I can think of a number of ambitious psychoanalytic studies which bogged down because there was either no time or no method available to analyze the huge data stores which had been collected.

Dr. Lasky: You put your finger very much on the problem. What I am proposing would not be an invitation to fill spools of tape with data and then sit down and admire the stack—anyone can turn on a machine and record data. The real challenge is to develop techniques to analyze macropatterns with a real "feel" for what is important. Attention has to be paid to classification and we have to avoid a simple-minded approach.

Dr. Dyrud: I would like to make a brief "anthropological" statement. I disagree with Dr. Lasky to some extent because I am tired of seeing large sums of money spent on the development of data-gathering laboratories from which the output is ultimately minuscule. It is fun and we do it, but what we really need is some further "field" work in depression. That is why I am very encouraged to see Dr. Lewinsohn doing home visits, and I would urge him constantly to improve his observations in the home because that is the "natural setting." The whole issue of reinforcement schedules comes alive when we begin to look at the natural versus the laboratory setting. I like field-work data because they are empirical. Remember, the more experimenter control we have, the more experimenter bias we end up with.

Dr. Seligman: The problem in testing psychodynamic theory is not technological but logical, at least at a simple level. Psychoanalytic theory has proved useful to many of us doing research, but the theory itself seems to me to be untestable. An example would be research concerning the theoretical question of hostility directed inward or outward. One could examine dreams as Dr. Beck did, and let us, for the sake of example, suppose that one found that there was an absence of hostility in the dreams of depressed people, which would refute the original theory. Analysts would say, though, that such a finding really supports the theory since it shows that there are certain defense mechanisms, even in dreams, which prevent the emergence of the true theme. One thus confirms the theory, whether he finds hostility in dreams or not, and thus the theory, in many places at least, is inherently irrefutable and to think about empirically testing it then becomes a logical problem.

Dr. Chodoff: I am reminded of the debates that raged in the Thirties and Forties about psychoanalysis as a science. Though it was decided that in many ways the theory could not be disproved, the "science" of psychoanalysis has lived on. I don't believe the problem is only logical. The issue really is what one can do with psychoanalytic data. If one is trying to come up with imaginative hypotheses which can generate research, then psychoanalytic data are a very rich source. Grinker is a good example of someone who took psychoanalytic hypotheses and devised other ways of testing them.

Dr. Seligman: I agree with Dr. Chodoff. What I was attempting to say is that the necessary work is not technological but logical. That is, one has to operationalize such hypotheses, make them explicit, and then devise means of testing them.

Dr. Klerman: I don't believe the task of validating psychoanalytic theory is that difficult. The research we have been engaged in on hostility is a case in point. Many of the constructs stemming from psychoanalytic theory are easily testable if one conceives of the problem in the proper terms and uses a reasonable type of clinical information.

Another area in need of research is the relationship of personality to clinical subtype of depression; here there are a wealth of hypotheses waiting in the wings. If people don't like the pencil-and-paper questionnaires like the MMPI or the Maudsley or the Murray, then I hope they will accept the challenge of developing new techniques, e.g., field work, for tapping into the same phenomena. In many ways, we have gone as far as we can with our checklists and rating scales and clinical interviews, but I don't think we have exhausted the research possibilities of relative rating scales and certainly not the potential involved in more naturalistic studies.

Dr. Lewinsohn: I would like to comment somewhat tangentially on dynamically-oriented research. An undercurrent of thought implies that unless one looks at the depressed individual in terms of psychoanalytic constructs, he is dealing with the phenomenon in only a superficial way. I believe this is an unfortunate stance because it strongly influences how people approach the subject. I am personally biased in favor of obtaining very careful observational data from which I think we may learn some very unexpected and interesting things about depression.

I think it is also very important to do some basic studies on the cognitive elements which Dr. Beck has been emphasizing to see if they can be manipulated to produce significant change. We also need research on the affect of depression as a motivating force that is similar to much of the work done on anxiety. Whatever the intrinsic merit of the psychoanalytic approach at a clinical level, it has the unfortunate effect at the research level of making people feel that, unless they are employing a psychodynamic research approach, they are not really doing anything important. I do not believe anyone wants such a state of affairs.

Dr. Spiro: I would like to return, whether psychoanalytically or otherwise, to the developmental and genetic approach. Two animal paradigms of depression have been presented here, one the learned helplessness notion, which states that there is something in the experience of the organism that predisposes it to behave in certain ways in the face of trauma, and the other the monkey separation phenomenon, which is obviously derived from the Freudian notion of object loss. If our goal is to foster a developmental understanding of human depression, why can we not take a good sample of detailed case histories which, to be sure, have all the problems involved in reconstructive work, and use them as one primary source of data. Two other sources of data would be the reconstruction by the patient himself and the recall of the relatives. We could then compare the developmental history of a group of depressed patients to a group of normals and developmentally trace the role of learned helplessness and object loss.

This might be a not-too-expensive approach which would not be dependent on intricate technology. We certainly need to know what predisposes people to depression. For example, I am very intrigued by Dr. Beck's notion about the role of negative cognitions in depression, but I think he would certainly agree that a person who views the world and himself as lousy just doesn't wake up one morning seeing things that way. Obviously something happened to him in the past which gives rise to that perception of the world.

Such a reconstructive approach could be undertaken concurrently with the initiation of longitudinal studies. Reconstructive studies would be useful for two reasons: they would give us hints about what to look for in the longitudinal studies and might provide some answers sooner than would lengthier longitudinal endeavors.

Dr. Parloff: Dr. Spiro has posed a very reasonable approach to which I offer one amendment. I urge that other patient categories be included in such studies because I am not sure we have identified the factors that uniquely predispose people to depression. We talk about object loss and learned helplessness, but these same factors have been described as pathognomonic for many different clinical states. If we only compare the depressed person to normals, we may not capture the essence of what makes him choose to handle object loss or learned helplessness or any stress in the particular way he does.

Dr. Klerman: Throughout the meetings we have by and large distinguished between the clinical state of depression and depression as an affective state. Because most of our research considerations have concerned the clinical state, I think we have overlooked the deficit in our knowledge regarding the affect of depression. We do not have a set of study data that delineate the vicissitudes and structural components of the affective state. Research on college students or adolescents might be very helpful in describing the affect of depression because they tend to go through wide fluctuations in moods, are introspective and verbal, and would be able to keep diaries describing mood fluctuations.

Dr. Katz: On that note we must end our discussion. I would like to close with a final vote of thanks to those of you who have prepared papers, to our panelists for their comments, and to everyone for his contribution to this workshop.

PART IV
REFLECTIONS

THE PSYCHOLOGY OF DEPRESSION: AN OVERVIEW

Raymond J. Friedman
National Institute of Mental Health

INTRODUCTION

The preceding chapters bear witness to a resurgence of theoretical and research interest in the psychology of depression. Basic data on variables such as stress, separation, helplessness, cognition, reinforcement patterns, and behavioral characteristics of depressed individuals have stimulated new theoretical formulations, which I am hopeful will in turn generate more sophisticated research.

New data, however, demand integration. The challenging task now before us is to devise a conceptual system that will allow us to order the clinical knowledge and research data in this perplexing area, where "depression" at one and the same time is considered both a normal and a pathological mood; a normal and also an abnormal reaction to loss; an enduring way of life and also a time-limited phenomenon; a state unto itself but also an aspect of other psychopathological conditions ranging from schizophrenia to the identity crisis of adolescence.

Elizabeth Zetzel (1964) has even characterized the depressed person as one who cannot bear the feelings of depression, and Edith Jacobson (1972) has poignantly observed the longing of many depressed patients for the feeling of "sadness," adding that they are often unable to experience "true depression." David Rubinfine (1968) notes that "though we speak loosely of depression as caused by hopelessness, the very basis for depression is hope."

Paradoxes abound: depressed individuals cannot feel depressed, they yearn for sadness, and they are only transparently hopeless. The first goal of this chapter is to present a schematic view of the term "depression" that I have found helpful in unravelling such apparent contradictions. Following the delineation of this approach to classification, areas of research not covered in the preceding sections of this volume will be highlighted. The final goal of this chapter is to present my reflections on the state of the field as well as a series of recommendations concerning future research needs. These comments have been woven into the fabric of the sections that follow rather than being listed separately.

I hope the reader will come away from these pages with a new conceptual scheme, with a broad overview of where depression theory and research stands at the present time, and with an appreciation of the future needs of research and theory on the psychology of depression.

AN APPROACH TO CLASSIFICATION

The reader familiar with the depression literature will undoubtedly have noted the absence of a chapter in this volume devoted to the nosology of depression. This omission reflects a determination to avoid the half-century-old battle between endogenous and reactive depression, neurotic and psychotic depression, unitary and dichotomous points of view, disease and nondisease orientations, as well as a host of other warring neologies.

In reviewing the theoretical quagmire of formal nosology, the temptation is ever present to discard the term "depression" entirely. I believe that such a radical approach would only create more confusion and would merely offer a weak semantic solution to a thorny conceptual problem. Each clinician and researcher must eventually face the issue of how he is going to use this term so that he can order the clinical data he sees and the research literature he reads.

In this section I will outline and then discuss a working framework which I have developed based on my research on the psychology of depression and on my clinical experience in the treatment of depressed patients. This scheme has been useful to me in ordering both research and clinical data, and I have found it helpful in facilitating communication with other investigators.

I propose that the term "depression" be employed in three ways: as an *affect*, as a *clinical state*, and as a *character style*. Consideration of depression in this manner does not represent a new addition to the general literature on the subject, although it has been somewhat neglected until now. Schmale (1972) proposed such a distinction in 1969, and more recently both Klerman (Chapter 5) and Goodwin (Part III) have expressed similar viewpoints. This tripartite division represents a rough, pragmatic, and fluid approach to the problem of conceptualizing an age-old phenomenon. It is not intended to serve as a formal classificatory scheme composed of three categories separated by firm and inflexible boundaries.

The discrete disease orientation of the medical model has fallen into disfavor, and contemporary theorists stress what has been variously referred to as a "psychobiological" or "total systems" approach. This movement away from syndromes and diagnostic entities stresses the "continuum approach" which, when applied to depression theory, hypothesizes that everyday sadness and severe melancholia form poles of a continuum. This mode of thinking stems primarily from the Meyerian influence on American psychiatry which itself was a reaction to the therapeutic nihilism of the Kraepelinian era. So the idea of a continuum has both humanitarian as well as logical appeal, and while it seems to satisfy theoretical rigor, it suffers from one major flaw when applied to depression theory and research—it defies common sense. To assume that sadness differs only quantitatively from severe depression blurs meaningful psychodynamic, psychobiological, and adaptational considerations. An expanding body of clinical and research data mitigates against the continuum hypothesis and supports the necessity of differentiating the affect from the clinical state of depression.

The Affect of Depression

I use the term, "affect of depression," to refer to a basic feeling of sadness which is part of the fabric of life and which is noted in states of grief and periods of disappointment, and which has even been described as the "malady of our times" (Buchwald, *Washington Post*).

Depression and anxiety are ubiquitous human affects. I propose that we begin to think of the affect of depression in a manner similar to our approach to the affect of anxiety. Anxiety is freely used to refer to a basic feeling of uneasiness which periodically occurs in everyone, yet it also refers to a clinical state, for example, "anxiety neurosis." Likewise, depression can refer to both a basic feeling as well as a more defined clinical state.

At this juncture the reader may well ask why I stress the necessity for distinguishing the basic affect from the clinical state of depression, especially if it is just a matter of common sense. The answer, I believe, is simple. There is a paucity of research concerning depression as a human affect, and unless we conceptualize it as such, we can never study it.

The history of the affect of depression is an intriguing one because for many years the affect was considered a "second-class citizen," the step-child of anxiety. Freud concentrated on anxiety, making it the pivotal affect not only of the psychoneuroses but of all psychic symptomatology. Depression was regarded as merely a defense against anxiety, and this theoretical prejudice remains influential on the contemporary scene. The 1952 American Psychiatric Association *Diagnostic and Statistical Manual of Mental Disorders* (DSM 1) stated that "anxiety is allayed and hence partially relieved by depression and self-depreciation." Malerstein (1968) concludes from this that in effect depression is regarded as nothing more than a defense against anxiety.

Bibring (1953), Greenson (1959), Bowlby (1960, 1961), Engel & Reischman (1956), Schmale (1964, 1971), Malerstein (1968), Sandler and Joffe (1965), and now Klerman 1972 (Chapter 5) are among the researchers and theoreticians who have envisioned a central role for the affect of depression. Perhaps none has had a more profound effect upon contemporary depression theory than Bibring, who hypothesized that depression was an affect in its own right and that it represented the affective component of the individual's recognition of a state of helplessness. Malerstein goes a step further, arguing that not only should depression be considered on an equal basis with anxiety, but that it should be assigned the "pivotal" role in our considerations of psychic functioning.

What then has been the theoretical and research thrust concerning the affect of depression? We really have few laboratory studies concerning depression, and this is surprising when we consider that anxiety has been studied as an emotion in everyone from psychiatrists interviewing patients to astronauts functioning in outer space Schachter and Singer (1962) have contributed significantly to our understanding of emotional states, but both their work and that of Valins (1966) have tended to focus primarily on the affect of anxiety. Innovative laboratory studies such as these are certainly in order for the affect of depression.

One pioneer in the clinical study of depression as a basic affect has been George Engel (1956, 1962), whose extensive observations on the infant Monica led to the hypothesis that the central nervous system is organized to mediate two opposite patterns of response to a mounting need. He commented:

> One of these is an active pattern in which the infant through crying and motor activity in effect achieves gratification of his needs through the need-fulfilling (though to him yet unknown) external object. The other pattern is essentially a conservative one in which the infant reduces activity, heightens the barrier against stimulation and conserves energy, as, for example, does a hibernating animal. Indeed, this may be considered a property of all living tissue and not of the central nervous system alone.

Engel thus hypothesizes that there are two basic biologically-rooted reaction patterns to stress: a state of mobilization for action, and a conservation-withdrawal reaction. The implication is that the former is the anlage of anxiety, while the latter forms the bedrock of what will subsequently become the affect of depression.

Based on his observations, Engel proposes that the affect of depression is adaptive. Klerman elaborates on the adaptive significance of the affect of depression by identifying four adaptive functions of all affects, including depression. These are: (1) social communication, (2) physiological arousal, (3) subjective awareness, and (4) psychodynamic-defensive.

The Clinical Depressive State

I employ the term "clinical depressive state" to refer to a complex of symptoms, including the affect of depression, but also other affects such as anxiety, guilt, hostility, as well as motivational, vegetative, and cognitive disturbances. I do not consider this state to be just the severe pole of a sadness continuum, but rather I see it as qualitatively different. Klerman (Chapter 5) proposes that the clinical depressive state is phenomenologically distinct from the basic affect of depression. Goodwin (Part III) notes that it has a distinct psychobiology, and Schmale (1970, 1971) provides the most dramatic illustration of the difference between the affect and the clinical state. He studied a group of women whose husbands were dying of cancer and observed that while all of these women exhibited the affect of depression (they were all sad), only a small percentage developed a "clinical state of depression" (consisting of retardation, extreme hopelessness, suicidal ideation, etc.) requiring psychiatric treatment. In other words, most of the women were sad and unhappy, but only a few developed a state that most psychiatrists would describe with a diagnostic label. We can thus distinguish a clinical depressive state from just the presence of the affect of depression on the basis of at least two criteria, one being severity and the other the presence of a symptom complex.

A third and persuasive argument that the clinical depressive state is qualitatively different from simple states of sadness stems from the work of many psychoanalysts who have pointed to the defensive nature of the symptom of depression in the clinical state. Zetzel (1964) has referred to the clinical state of depression in terms of symptom formations resulting from an "incapacity" to bear the feelings of depression and, as noted in the Introduction, Jacobson (1972) highlights the depressed person's inability to experience sadness. Thus, many investigators have concluded that the clinical depressive state represents a symptom complex that serves to aid the individual in avoiding the experience of the basic affect of depression. Such reasoning makes it most difficult to retain a continuum point of view and also touches on the question we considered previously of the adaptive significance of depression. Such psychodynamic considerations have led me to conclude that the clinical depressive state represents a maladaptive attempt to cope with the affect of sadness (and the underlying issues of loss and helplessness). In the previous section the research evidence supporting the adaptive role of the basic affect of depression was reviewed. We are drawn to the conclusion that the basic affect is adaptive whereas the clinical state is maladaptive, a contrast that constitutes a fourth distinguishing feature between the two.

Having defined the "clinical depressive state," I now wish to consider the research effort concerning classification. A contemporary debate regarding the classification of depressive disorders has its roots in the Kraepelinian era; suffice it to say that the debate continues unabated. The distinction between endogenous and exogenous depression, autonomous and reactive disorders, and psychotic and neurotic depression has been summarized elsewhere and needs no repetition at this point (Beck [1967], Klerman [1971], Chapter 3). The latest attempts at classification are the bipolar-unipolar distinction first proposed by Leonhard (1962) and the primary-secondary classification advanced by Robins, et al. (1972). Both await research verification, and both share the potential of eventually being validated on a biological level, which would represent a breakthrough in the classification of depression.

A host of research efforts designed to verify certain classificatory ideas as well as to investigate various symptomatic pictures exist and are exemplified by the works of Kiloh and Garside (1963), and most recently by Mendels and Cochrane

(1968). Yet another approach to classification is the factor analytic method. The work of Grinker (1961), Overall (1962), Friedman, et al. (1963), and McNair and Lorr (1964) exemplifies this.

In my opinion, this line of inquiry has often represented a circular and at times obsessive attempt to understand the phenomenon of depression. I agree with Beck's (Chapter 3) statement that this line of inquiry is at a "dead end." Such studies offer the appeal and reassurance of statistical precision but sacrifice depth and cogency.

The Depressive Character Style

There currently exists a robust literature (Adler [1961], Arieti [1959], Arieti [1963], Berliner [1966], Bibring [1953], Bonime [1960], Bonime [1966], Chodoff [1970], Jacobson [1953], Schmale [1971], & Zetzel [1966]) describing the lifestyle and ongoing "personality constellation" of depressed people. This term has become a frequent topic of discussion, has attained the status of an "entity" in the research literature, and I believe merits inclusion as a third use of the term "depression."

In pursuing the concept of the "depressive character" we enter the muddy waters of an area of investigation which seems not to fit with the discussions of the clinical depressive state nor with the more basic studies of the affect of depression. When Bonime (1966) states that "depression is a way of living—a sick way," one can only wonder whether he is referring to (1) a person who continuously gravitates within a clinical state of depression, (2) the lifestyle of someone who is predisposed to depression, (3) a specific and ongoing character constellation, or (4) some combination of chronic depression, predisposing characteristics to depression, and character style.

Schmale (1972) is more specific in his delineation of the "depressive character style." A general theory developed by Schmale and Engel and their team of investigators at Rochester stresses, as I have throughout this chapter, that depression refers to both a basic organismic state (the basic affect) and to a symptom complex appearing in individuals who must defend against the "normal" affects of helplessness and hopelessness (the clinical depressive state). However, Schmale notes that many individuals who would ordinarily be predisposed to repeated clinical depressive states develop "personality features which provide some protection against the frequent re-experiencing of either the feelings of helplessness or hopelessness."

Schmale then proceeds to define two characteristic defensive patterns, one designed to defend against a high helplessness predisposition and the other against a high hopelessness predisposition. The former, he contends, is observed in individuals who relate to few other people but who depend on those people for their narcissistic identification. They are described as "sticky," "demanding," and "pessimistic." Schmale notes that these individuals are often labeled "orally aggressive," "orally dependent," or "narcisstic" characters. Those defending against a high hopelessness predisposition utilize what Anna Freud (1946) has described as the mode of "altruistic surrender" as a character defense. They are zealous in their assumption of responsibility and believe that "selfless persistence in working toward a goal provides satisfaction irrespective of whether the goal is reached" (Schmale, 1972). Schmale concludes by noting that individuals in this subgroup are frequently called "masochistic," "pseudo-independent," or "obsessive." Individuals who have been described as "wrecked by success" (Freud, S., 1957) are included in this category of character formation.

In a recent paper entitled, "New Views on the Psychodynamics of the Depressive Character," Bemporad (1971) emphasizes four psychodynamic aspects of the depressive character: (1) dependency on a dominant other, (2) fear of autonomous gratification, (3) the establishment of bargain relationships in which the individual "denies himself autonomous satisfaction in return for nurturance from the dominant other," and (4) an inability to alter the environment.

It appears to me that both Schmale and Bemporad, as well as others (Adler [1961], Arieti [1959], Arieti [1963], Berliner [1966], Bibring [1953], Bonime [1960], Bonime [1966], Chodoff [1970], Jacobson [1954], & Zetzel [1966]), are describing the basic premorbid personality that predisposes individuals to clinical depressive episodes. They are focusing, however, on an intermediate stage during which the individual is in a state of dynamic equilibrium. When these characterological defensive patterns are disrupted, the individual becomes clinically depressed.

Why then should the "depressive character" be distinguished psychodynamically as a group separate from those who develop clinical depressive states? Some possible reasons are as follows:

1. Many authors have hypothesized that these individuals are clinically different from those who develop clearcut depressive states, and thus for research purposes it becomes necessary to differentiate these two groups.

2. As Chodoff (Chapter 3) notes, many of these authors remain unclear about the type of depression they are describing. I strongly suspect that the descriptions of these character patterns refer to individuals predisposed to milder or "neurotic" depressive episodes and may not be applicable to those who will later develop more serious clinical states.

3. Separation of symptomatic states from characterological states has a long tradition in psychoanalytic writings and possesses therapeutic utility.

4. This category may represent the expression of a natural clinical inclination toward delineating a "borderline" state when describing any type of psychopathology. Klerman (Chapter 5), in describing these individuals, notes that "depression has come to dominate their existence, and has been molded into a persistent life style. These people often fluctuate on the borderline between normality and mild chronic depressions, and they represent a condition

analogous to the borderline state of schizophrenia. Thus, the depressive character is to clinical depression as the borderline state is to schizophrenia."

5. The delineation and separation of a "depressive character" permits investigators to study this subgroup of individuals in relation to the depressive constellation without feeling that they must unearth these characteristics in all individuals who experience depression. Thus, future systematic research on individuals possessing this character structure may aid the search for a meaningful categorization of depressive states.

ETIOLOGICAL CONSIDERATIONS

In section I, consideration was given to the "what" of depression, and I now wish to turn to the question of "why." If depression is a basic affect, a clinical state, and a character style, the logical question remains, "How do they come about?" Since I have hypothesized that the affect of depression is a biologically rooted response to stress, my comments in this section will focus primarily on the clinical depressive state and the depressive character style. I will also focus on etiological factors of a "psychological" nature, but I remind the reader of the extensive and fascinating biological research endeavor concerning depression. Reviews of this body of work abound (Coppen [1967], Klerman [1972], Secunda [1971], Williams [1970] & Williams [1972]).

Personality and Psychodynamic Aspects

The literature in this area is voluminous, and clinical research concerning personality and psychodynamic variables falls into two rough categories. Most authors, especially psychoanalysts, advance theoretical considerations based on their clinical experience. As Chodoff (Chapter 3) has noted, they often fail to delineate the sample from which their conclusions have been drawn; but for the most part such psychodynamic considerations evolve from the study of the manic-depressive or psychotic-depressive individual. A second order of research data emanates from those clinical studies in which an attempt at systematization occurs. A group of depressed individuals is selected and systematically studied, and those personality variables believed to be etiologically significant are described. The second line of inquiry differs from the first primarily in its research sophistication.

A review of the psychoanalytic contributions (and current controversies) to depression research is beyond the scope of this chapter. The reader is referred to a thorough investigation conducted by Herbert Rosenfeld (1959), who, in his review of the psychoanalytic literature on depression, reaches the conclusion that there appears to be scant disagreement concerning constitutional factors, the role of aggression, the importance of the first year of life, and the essential contribution of narcissism. He points out that controversies abound concerning the role of and development of superego factors in depression, but he notes that there is consistent agreement concerning the role of aggressive impulses in regard to superego formation as well as in the genesis of depression. While the etiological role of the first years of life are stressed by most psychoanalysts, there remain broad differences of opinion regarding the details of early infantile development in this regard. Rosenfeld concludes that "it would appear from this survey that much interesting research is being done, and remains still to be done, on the whole problem of depression, the main growing points at the moment apparently being along the lines of increasing our knowledge of the very early infantile phases predisposing to later depressive breakdown; the details and nature of the mechanisms and identifications found in depression; and the understanding of schizophrenic features in depression."

Paul Chodoff (Chapter 3) has summarized the wide-ranging literature on the premorbid personality of people who are at high risk for depression. He hypothesizes that "depression-prone people are inordinately and almost exclusively dependent on narcissistic supplies derived directly or indirectly from other people for the maintenance of their self-esteem, their frustration tolerance is low, and they employ various techniques—submissive, manipulative, coercive, piteous, demanding, placating—to maintain those desperately needed but essentially ambivalent relationships with the external or internalized objects of their demands." Chodoff also notes that it is quite possible that personality may only "color" the depression and may not be a primary determinant.

One area of research that has been neglected to date concerns the intermorbid functioning of people who develop clinical depressive states. Psychoanalytic writers tend to view such individuals as having disturbed psychological functioning even when they are not clinically depressed, whereas many psychiatric observers have emphasized the supposed "normalcy" of such individuals during intermorbid periods. Such a split in opinion further highlights the need for systematic research on the intermorbid functioning of depressed individuals.

While it is important to evaluate the internal psychic state of individuals prone to clinical depressive episodes, there is also a pressing need to develop research that will help us describe and understand the behavior of such individuals. The work of Lewinsohn (1969, 1971, Chapter 6) is an example of research that is attempting to describe how depressed individuals respond to significant others and how they interact in groups. Similar research needs to be conducted on these individuals following their depressive episode, so that we can garner more knowledge regarding the intermorbid period.

Stress and Precipitating Events

Following in the Meyerian tradition of considering mental disorders as reactive patterns to life stress, an extensive literature concerning the relationship of depression to environmental precipitating events has flourished. However, Paykel (1970), in a recent review, noted that, in spite of this extensive literature, there existed only six studies concerning depression and environmental events that evidenced any systematic control or the use of comparison groups.

Klerman (Chapter 5) presents a study utilizing a modified version of the Holmes-Rahe Schedule (1967) (an instrument that quantifies the stress of environmental events). He concludes that "we are forced into the situation in which: (1) loss and separation are not universal in all depressions, (2) not all individuals who experience loss and separation will develop depressions, and (3) loss and depression are not specific to clinical depression, but rather may serve as precipitating events for a wide variety of clinical conditions that are not only psychiatric but also general medical (Holmes & Rahe 1967)." These considerations lead Klerman to the conclusion that the clinical state of depression represents a failure at adaptation.

Grief is generally regarded as a paradigm of acute stress, a precipitating event that is followed by a clearcut depressive episode. Indeed, grief was the entrée utilized by Freud (1959) in his studies of depression. The animal model work of Kaufman and Harlow has followed the theoretical lines set forth by Freud and others and rests on the assumption that depression follows object loss. The critical question for research purposes, though, concerns the relationship of the process of normal mourning to what we have come to call the clinical state of depression. Grief is considered to be a separate syndrome by Lindemann (1944), a disease state by Engel (1961), and a form of mild reactive depression which usually does not come to psychiatric attention by Clayton (1968), et al., who followed a group of 80 patients after the loss of a spouse and discovered that over 50 percent developed symptoms of depressed mood, sleep disturbance, and crying.

Clayton and collaborators note that in their population only 2 percent sought psychiatric treatment, which led them to conclude that normal grieving is a form of reactive depression which differs from the misguided states of grieving that usually do come to psychiatric attention and form the basis of many psychodynamic explanatory models of depression. They, as well as others (Yamamoto [1969], Yamamoto [1970]) advance a strong argument in favor of separating the process of normal mourning from the clinical state of depression. It thus follows that there exists a valid niche for the study of normal grieving, which may well represent an area of research distinct from the study of pathological grieving.

As noted previously in this chapter, numerous investigators have hypothesized that the clinical depressive state represents a symptom compromise designed to defend against the conscious awareness of the affect of depression (Bonime [1960], Bonime [1966], Jacobson [1953], Jacobson [1954], Schmale [1958], Schmale [1971], Zetzel [1960], & Zetzel [1964]). Benton (1972) quotes Proust (1941), who wrote: "We are healed of a suffering only by experiencing it to the full. Happiness is beneficial for the body, but it is grief that develops the powers of the mind." Benton then hypothesizes in a similar vein that "in clinical depression . . . the stress is not felt as a loss in the ordinary way because of defenses against that impact. Stress disturbs those defenses and has an indirect depressive impact." Benton goes on to hypothesize that when the loss of an object results in depression, the stress of the loss has not had a "normal impact" but has resulted in a depression or other dysfunction because the patient did not value "what he has lost for itself, but rather for the psychological compensations it supplied."

Bowlby (1960, 1961) has also linked the development of "depressive illness" with the inability to accomplish the normal task of grieving, which includes the toleration of the pain of loss. He differentiates three stages of normal mourning. The first is an anxious phase in which the individual's attachment to his loved object remains intact and cannot be terminated. During this stage the bereaved person may experience separation anxiety but not true grief. Reflecting on the development of pathological mourning, Bowlby notes: "So long as the response systems are focused on the lost object, there are strenuous and often angry efforts to recover it; these efforts may continue despite their fruitlessness being painfully evident to others and sometimes also to the bereaved himself. *In this phase are sown, I believe, the seeds of much psychopathology*." He then goes on to describe the normal process of mourning, which includes a second phase of personality disorganization accompanied by pain and despair, and a third phase of reorganization which allows the individual to form new object relationships and which completes the work of mourning.

Such empirical clinical hypotheses deserve careful research interest and point to the following conclusions:

1. Hypotheses advanced by Benton and Bowlby may be operationalized and researched. We need to learn what factors cause some people to become trapped in the first stage of mourning and, conversely, what those strengths are that allow most people to advance in a more adaptive manner. This line of investigation approaches one of the critical questions in depression research, i.e., given similar stresses, why do certain people become depressed whereas others do not?

2. "Normal grief" deserves to be studied in its own right as a separate syndrome which, while it may resemble depression, seems to differ from the clinical state of depression which reaches psychiatric attention so frequently. Such research seems most likely to add to our fund of knowledge concerning depression as a basic human affect. Similarly, we also await a "biology of grieving."

Communication Patterns

Paul Ekman (Chapter 8) has presented a résumé of his work concerning nonverbal behavior and its potential application to psychopathology research. Ekman's technological breakthrough in the measurement of nonverbal behavior may usher in an era of research on subtle communication of affect and may allow us to begin to approach questions concerning the nonverbal interaction between people. One exciting area of research which emerges is the study of the depressed mother and her child. My hope would be that we could determine how depression is communicated from mother to child, and when it is, how it is responded to by the child.

The measurement of nonverbal behavior also introduces a new parameter to clinical studies. The variables Ekman describes may prove to be sensitive indicators of change in the clinical course of depressive states. Studies are required that will attempt to quantify the amount and type of nonverbal behavior present at the onset, during, and at the conclusion of a depressive episode. Such research may allow more precise recording of the clinical course, and I believe may suggest new items for inclusion in the usual rating scales we have employed in depression research.

Longitudinal Studies

In the preceding paragraphs I have discussed hypotheses regarding personality and psychodynamics, the possible role of stress, and the importance of communication patterns between mother and child. I wish to draw the reader's attention to the fact that this discussion has, of necessity, focused on knowledge gained by way of retrospective studies.

Longitudinal studies offer the possibility of approaching the questions raised above with greater power and precision. I believe there is an urgent need, as in the area of schizophrenia, for the development of long-term follow-up studies of children thought to be at high risk for depression. We have some indication that there are two groups of high-risk children, one composed of those who have suffered an object loss early in childhood or infancy and the second composed of the children of clinically depressed mothers. Once such a group is selected, many of our questions concerning communication, personality factors, the role of stress, formation of psychodynamic constellations, and ultimately the issue of etiology will come into sharper focus.

Animal Models

The search for an animal model of depression represents a new and exciting approach. While it is my personal belief that we stand to learn more about biological variables from animal work, I wish to review two types of animal models in the psychology of depression.

The loss-separation model. In 1945, Spitz (1945, 1946) described a syndrome occurring in hospitalized infants who had been denied maternal contact. He noted that many of these infants failed to thrive, that their mortality was high, and that they were withdrawn and unresponsive and appeared to be depressed. He chose the name "anaclitic depression" for this condition.

In the mid-1950's, Bowlby (1960), in his studies of the mother-child relationship, confirmed Spitz's findings. Bowlby advanced the hypothesis that anaclitic depression was the result of the separation of the infant from its mother, and he further contended that the depression represented a true state of mourning in the child. Bowlby also described an initial stage of "protest" consisting of agitated (anxious) behavior, soon followed by withdrawal and retardation (depression). In addition to stressing the similarity between anaclitic depression in the infant and mourning in the adult, Bowlby also hypothesized that the loss in childhood of a loved object significantly predisposed the individual to the later development of pathological mourning.

While there is now considerable disagreement about whether the syndrome described by Spitz and Bowlby is truly analogous to the clinical state of depression in the adult, we can with some certainty state that their findings stimulated a considerable research effort, which is currently exemplified by the work of Harlow and his associates at the University of Wisconsin (Harlow [1955], Harlow [1971], McKinney [1969], McKinney [1971], & Senay [1966]) and Kaufman and his colleagues at the University of Colorado (1967).

We have learned that primates develop a state that looks like and empathically feels like depression in human beings. This model offers a means of testing a theory of etiology (object loss) and also has the potential of determining what other variables, both within the affected primate and within the social field, influence the development and the subsequent course of depression. The work of Kaufman in this regard has been highlighted elsewhere in this volume (Part III).

The helplessness model. Edward Bibring (1953) significantly advanced the psychoanalytic theory of depression in 1953 by proposing that the basic mechanism of depression was the "ego's shocking awareness" of its helplessness in regard to its aspirations. Relating to issues of self-esteem, he defined it as "the emotional expression (indication) of a state of helplessness and powerlessness of the ego, irrespective of what may have caused the breakdown of the mechanisms which established the self-esteem."

Gaylin (1968) amends Bibring's hypothesis by noting that the crisis in self-esteem which Bibring emphasizes is really a crisis in self-confidence. For our purposes, it is important to note that both Bibring and Gaylin are saying that the depressed individual is one who has lost his belief in his ability to cope with stress, i.e., to solve problems.

The theory of depression advanced by Bibring differs significantly from earlier analytic hypotheses (Spitz and Bowlby) which stressed the significance of object loss. Primate research provided a ready means for testing the object loss hypothesis, but until the present we have not possessed an experimental paradigm which would permit a test of the helplessness theory. A partial resolution of this impasse has been afforded by the work of Dr. Martin Seligman, which is presented in Chapter 4 of this volume.

Dr. Seligman advances the thesis that the state of "learned helplessness" in animals is analogous on several dimensions to the state of clinical depression in man. He hypothesizes that animals develop learned helplessness (depression) when they are unable to control trauma, and he adds that it is not the trauma itself that produces the state of depression, but rather that the depression arises when the animal is in a situation in which what it does has no bearing on what happens to it. Seligman's model is the first experimental paradigm of Bibring's hypothesis, and Seligman's own formulation closely approximates Gaylin's amended version of Bibring's depression mechanism.

Perhaps the limitation of all animal models, and certainly the learned helplessness model, is the inability to capture, in an animal situation, anything similar to the intrapsychic phenomena noted in depressed humans. From a strictly behavioral viewpoint, however, similarities between the behaviors noted in the learned helplessness situation and in human depressions are striking.

REFERENCES

Abraham, K. Notes on the psychoanalytic investigation and treatment of manic-depressive insanity and allied conditions. *Selected Papers on Psychoanalysis*, New York: Basic Books, 1953.

Abraham, K. A short study of the development of the libido, viewed in the light of mental disorders. *Selected Papers on Psychoanalysis*, New York: Basic Books, 1953.

Adler, K. Depression in the light of individual psychology. *Journal of Individual Psychology*, 1961, 17, 56.

American Psychiatric Association. *Diagnostic and statistical manual of mental disorders* (DSM I), 1952.

Arieti, S. Manic-depressive psychosis. In Arieti, S. (Ed.), *American handbook of psychiatry*. New York: Basic Books, 1959.

Arieti, S. Studies of thought processes in contemporary psychiatry. *American Journal of Psychiatry*, 1963, 120, 58–64.

Beck, A. T. Thinking and depression. 1. Ideosyncratic content and cognitive distortions. *Archives of General Psychiatry*, 1963, 9, 324.

Beck, A. T. Thinking and depression. 2. Theory and therapy. *Archives of General Psychiatry*, 1964, 10, 561.

Beck, A. T. *Depression*. New York: Hoeber, 1967.

Beck, A. T. Cognitive therapy: Nature and relation to behavior therapy. *Behavior Therapy*, Vol. 1, 1970.

Beck, A. T. Cognition, affect, and psychopathology. *Archives of General Psychiatry*, 1971, 24, 495.

Bellak, L. *Manic-depressive psychosis and allied conditions*. New York: Grune & Stratton, 1952.

Bemporad, J. New views on the psychodynamics of the depressive character. Vol. 1, *World Biennial of Psychiatry and Psychotherapy*, 1971.

Benton, R. F. The structure of the depressive response to stress. *American Journal of Psychiatry*, 1972, 128, 10.

Berliner, B. Psychodynamics of the depressive character. *The Psychoanalytic Forum*, 1966, 1, 244.

Bibring, E. Mechanisms of depression. In Greenacre, P. (Ed.) *Affective disorders: Psychoanalytic contributions to their study*. New York: International Universities Press, 1953.

Bonime, W. Depression as a practice: Dynamic and therapeutic considerations. *Comprehensive Psychiatry*, 1960, 1, 194.

Bonime, W. The psychodynamics of neurotic depression. In Arieti, S. (Ed.), *The American handbook of psychiatry*, Vol. 3. New York and London: Basic Books, 1966.

Bowlby, J. Grief and mourning in infancy and early childhood. *Psychoanalytic Study of the Child*, 1960, 15, 9.

Bowlby, J. Process of mourning. *International Journal of Psychoanalysis*, 1961, XL, 2, 317.

Buchwald, A. Article in *Washington Post*.

Carney, M. W. P., Roth, M., & Garside, R. F. The diagnosis of depressive syndromes and the prediction of ECT response. *British Journal of Psychiatry*, 1965, 3, 659.

Chodoff, P. The core problem in depression: Interpersonal aspects. In *Science and Psychoanalysis*, Vol. XXVII, New York: Grune and Stratton, Inc., 1970.

Clayton, P. J., Desmarais, L., & Winokur, G.: A Study of Normal Bereavement. *American Journal of Psychiatry*, 1968, 125, 168.

Coppen, A. The biochemistry of affective disorders. *British Journal of Psychiatry*, 1967, 113, 1237-1264.

Engel, G. L. & Reichsman, F. Spontaneous and experimentally induced depression in an infant with gastric fistulae: A contribution to the problem of depression. *Journal of the American Psychoanalytic Association*, 1956, 4, 428.

Engel, G. L. Is grief a disease? *Psychosomatic Medicine*, 1961, 23, 18.

Engel, G. L. Anxiety and depression—Withdrawal: The primary affects of unpleasure. *International Journal of Psychoanalysis*, 1962, 43, 89.

Engel, G. L. *Psychological development in health and disease*. Philadelphia: W. B. Saunders, 1962.

Fenichel, O. *The psychoanalytic theory of neurosis*. New York: W. W. Norton, 1945.

Ferster, C. B. Animal behavior and mental illness. *Psychological Record*, 1966, 16, 345.

Freud, A. *The ego and the mechanisms of defense*. New York: International Universities Press, 1946.

Freud, S. Some character types met with in psychoanalytic work. *Standard Edition*, 1957, 14, 311, London: Hogarth Press.

Freud, S. Mourning and melancholia. In *Collected Papers*. Vol. 4, New York: Basic Books, 1959.

Friedman, A. S., Cowitz, B., Cohen, H. W., & Granick, S. Syndromes and themes of psychotic depression: A factor analysis. *Archives of General Psychiatry*, 1963, 9, 504.

Gaylin, W. *The meaning of despair*. New York: Science House, 1968.

Gero, G. Construction of depression. *International Journal of Psychoanalysis*, 1936, 17, 423.

Gillespie, R. D. Clinical differentiation of types of depression. *Hospital Report*, 1929, 79, 306.

Greenson, R. R. Phobia, anxiety, and depression. *Journal of the American Psychoanalytic Association*, 1959, 7, 633.

Grinker, R. R., Sr., Miller, J., Sabshin, M., Nunn, R. J., & Nunnally, J. C. *Phenomenon of depression*. New York: Hoeber, 1961.

Hamilton, M. & White, J. M. Clinical syndromes of depressive states. *Journal of Mental Science*, 1959, 105, 985.

Harlow, H. F., Dodsworth, R. O., & Harlow, M. K. Total social isolation in monkeys. *Proceeding of the National Academy of Science*, 1955, 54, 90.

Harlow, H. F., Harlow, M. K., & Suomi, S. J. From thought to therapy: Lessons from a primate laboratory. *American Scientist*, 1971, 59, 538.

Hill, D. Depression: Disease reaction or posture. *American Journal of Psychiatry*, 1968, 125, 445-457.

Hoch, P. H. & Zubin, J. *Depression*. New York: Grune and Stratton, 1954.

Holmes, T. H., & Rahe, R. H. The social readjustment rating scale. *Journal of Psychosomatic Research*, 1967, 11, 213.

Jacobson, E. Contribution to the metapsychology of cyclothymic depression. In Greenacre, P. (Ed.), *Affective disorders*, New York: International Universities Press, 1953.

Jacobson, E. Transference problems in the psychoanalytic treatment of severely depressed patients. *Journal of the American Psychiatric Association*, 1954, 2, 595.

Jacobson, E. The self and the object world: Vicissitudes of their infantile cathexes and their influences on ideational and affective development. *Psychoanalytic Study of the Child*, Vol. 9. New York: International Universities Press, 1954.

Jacobson, E. *Depression*. New York: International Universities Press, 1972.

Katz, M. M. The classification of depression: Normal, clinical and ethnocultural variations. In Fieve, R. R. (Ed.), *Depression in the 70's*. London: Excerpta Medica, 1971.

Kaufman, I. C., & Rosenblum, L. A. The reaction to separation in infant monkeys: Anaclitic depression and conservation-withdrawal. *Psychosomatic Medicine*, 1967, **29**, 648.

Kaufman, I. C., & Rosenblum, L. A. Depression in infant monkeys separated from their mothers. *Science*, 1967, **155**, 1030.

Kiloh, L. G., & Garside, R. F. The independence of neurotic depression and endogenous depression. *British Journal of Psychiatry*, 1963, **109**, 451.

Klein, M. Mourning and its relationship to manic-depressive states. In: *Contributions to Psychoanalysis, 1921-1945*. London: Hogarth Press, 1948.

Klerman, G. L. Clinical research in depression. *Archives of General Psychiatry*, 1971, **24**, 305.

Klerman, G. L. Clinical phenomenology of depression: Implications for research strategy in the psychobiology of the affective disorders. In Williams, T. A. & Katz, M. M. (Eds.), *Recent advances in the psychobiology of the depressive illnesses*. Washington, D.C.: U.S. Government Printing Office, 1972.

Kraepelin, E. Manic-depressive insanity and paranoia. In *Textbook of psychiatry*, (Translated by Barclay, R. M.) Edinburgh: Livingstone, 1913.

Leonhard, K., Korff, I., & Shulz, H. Die temperamente in den familien der monopolaren un bipolaren phasischen psychosen, *Psychiatrie, Neurologie, und Medizinische Psychologie* 1962, **143**, 416.

Lewinsohn, P. M., Weinstein, M. S., & Shaw, D. A. Depression: A clinical-research approach. In Rubin, R. D. & Frank, C. M. (Eds.), *Advances in behavior therapy*. New York: Academic Press, 1969.

Lewinsohn, P. M., & Shaffer, M. The use of home observations as an integral part of the treatment of depression: Preliminary report in case studies. *Journal of Consulting and Clinical Psychology*, 1971, **37**, 87.

Lewinsohn, P. M., & Libet, J. Pleasant events, activity schedules, and depression. *Journal of Abnormal Psychology* (in press).

Lewis, A. J. Melancholia: Clinical survey of depressive states. *Journal of Mental Science*, 1934, **80**, 277.

Lindemann, E. Symptomatology and management of acute grief. *American Journal of Psychiatry*, 1944, **101**, 141.

McKinney, W. T., & Bunney, W. E., Jr. Animal model of depression. Review of evidence: Implications for research. *Archives of General Psychiatry*, 1969, **21**, 240.

McKinney, W. T., Suomi, S. J., & Harlow, H. F. Depression in primates. *American Journal of Psychiatry*, 1971, **127**, 10.

McNair, D. M., & Lorr, M. An analysis of mood in neurotics. *Journal of Abnormal Social Psychology*, 1964, **69**, 620.

Malerstein, A. J. Depression as a pivotal affect. *American Journal of Psychotherapy*, 1968, **22**, 202.

Mendels, J., & Cochrane, C. The nosology of depression: The endogenous-reactive concept. *American Journal of Psychiatry*, 1968 Suppl., **124**, 11.

Mendelson, M. *Psychoanalytic concepts of depression*. Springfield, Ill.: Charles C. Thomas, 1960.

Meyer, A. In Leif, A. (Ed.), *The commonsense psychiatry of Dr. Adolf Meyer*. New York: McGraw-Hill, 1948.

Overall, J. E. Dimensions of manifest depression. *Journal of Psychiatric Research*, 1962, **1**, 239.

Paykel, E. S. Life events and acute depression. American Association for the Advancement of Science Meeting, December, 1970, Chicago.

Proust, M. *Remembrance of Things Past*. (translated by Moncrieff, C. K.). London: Chatto & Windus, 1941.

Rado, S. Psychodynamics of depression from the etiological point of view. In Gaylin, W. (Ed.), *The meaning of despair*, New York: Science House, 1968.

Rappaport, D. Edward Bibring's theory of depression. In Gill, M. (Ed.), *Collected Papers of David Rappaport*. New York: Basic Books, 1967.

Robins, E. & Guze, S. B. Classification of affective disorders: The primary-secondary, the endogenous-reactive, and the neurotic-psychotic concepts. In Williams, T. A. & Katz, M. M. (Eds.), *Recent Advances in the Psychobiology of the Depressive Illnesses*. Washington, D.C.: U.S. Government Printing Office, 1972.

Rosenfeld, H. An investigation into the psychoanalytic theory of depression. *International Journal of Psychoanalysis*, 1959, 40, 105.

Rosenthal, S. H., & Gudeman, J. E. The endogenous depressive pattern: An empirical investigation. *Archives of General Psychiatry*, 1967, 16, 241.

Rubinfine, D. L. Notes on a theory of depression. *The Psychoanalytic Quarterly*, 1968, 37, 400.

Sandler, J., & Joffe, W. G. Notes on childhood depression. *International Journal of Psychoanalysis*, 1965, 46, 88.

Schachter, S., & Singer, J. E. Cognitive, social, and psychological determinants of emotional state. *Psychological Review*, 1962, 69, 379.

Schmale, A. H. Relationship of separation and depression to disease. I. A report on a hospitalized population. *Psychosomatic Medicine*, 1958, 20, 259.

Schmale, A. H. A genetic view of affects: With special reference to the genesis of helplessness and hopelessness. *The Psychoanalytic Study of the Child*, 1964, 19, 287.

Schmale, A. H. *The role of depression in health and disease*. Presented at the American Association for the Advancement of Science Meeting, December, 1970, Chicago. To be published in the proceedings of a symposium.

Schmale, A. H. The psychic trauma of death of husband. *International Psychiatric Clinic*, 1970, in press.

Schmale, A. H. Depression as affect, character style and symptom formation. In *Psychoanalysis and contemporary science*. Vol. 1, 1972.

Secunda, S. K., & Friedman, R. J. *Special report: The depressive illnesses*. U.S. Department of Health, Education and Welfare, National Institute of Mental Health, December, 1971.

Seligman, M. E. P., Maier, S. F., & Greer, J. Alleviation of learned helplessness in the dog. *Journal of Abnormal Social Psychology*, 1968, 73, 256.

Senay, E. C. Toward an animal model of depression: A study of separation behavior in animals. *Journal of Psychiatric Research*, 1966, 4, 65.

Spitz, R. A. Hospitalism. *The Psychoanalytic Study of the Child*, 1945, 1, 53.

Spitz, R. A. Anaclitic depression: An inquiry into the genesis of psychiatric conditions in early childhood. *The Psychoanalytic Study of the Child*, 1946, 2, 313.

Sullivan, H. S. *Clinical studies in psychiatry*. New York: Norton, 1956.

Valins, S. Cognitive effects of false heart-rate feedback. *Journal of Personality and Social Psychology*, 1966, 11, 400.

Weissman, M. M., Klerman, G. L., & Paykel, E. S. Clinical assessment of hostility in depression. *American Journal of Psychiatry*, 1971, 128, 261.

Williams, T. A., Friedman, R. J., & Secunda, S. K. *Special report: The depressive illnesses*. U.S. Department of Health, Education and Welfare, National Institute of Mental Health, 1970.

Williams, T. A., Katz, M. M., Shield, J. A., Jr., (Eds.), *Recent advances in the psychobiology of the depressive illnesses*. Washington, D.C., U.S. Government Printing Office, 1972.

Yamamoto, J., Geigo, O., Tetsuya, I., & Saburo, Y. Mourning in Japan. *American Journal of Psychiatry*, 1969, 125, 12.

Yamamoto, J., & Imahara, J. America and Japan—two ways of mourning. A paper read at the 126th Annual Meeting of the American Psychiatric Association, San Francisco, California, May 13, 1970.

Zetzel, E. R. Depressive illness. *International Journal of Psychoanalysis*, 1960, 41, 476.
Zetzel, E. R. Depression and the incapacity to bear it. In Schur, M. (Ed.), *Drives, affects, and behavior*. Vol. 2, New York: International Universities Press, 1964.
Zetzel, E. R. The predisposition to depression. *Canadian Psychiatric Association Journal*, 1966, 11, 5235.

EPILOGUE: ON FUTURE DIRECTIONS

Martin M. Katz
National Institute of Mental Health

In reflecting on the content of the conference papers, one is struck by the sheer diversity of psychological points of view currently brought to bear on the concept of human depression.

In a field that appeared to be static, on a plateau, we note a vigorous new style and a decided shift in emphasis. The current emphasis as regards theory and research on the psychology of depression has moved from the more traditional, introspective, phenomenologic study with its heavy reliance on psychodynamic theory, to a harder "behavioral" framework of thinking. Psychologists are currently less interested in what the patient says and thinks, more in how he behaves and how the environment works to reinforce or to negate this behavior. Ferster discusses the theory in some depth and Lewinsohn's research program is exemplary of the model. It reflects a new "naturalistic" style in the approach to investigating the patient's psychological, experiential state, i.e., there is more intense study of the patient's social behavior outside the clinic—his manner of relating in everyday behavior; research efforts are aimed at identifying the personal and the environmental factors that initiate and reinforce the "depressed" state. Even the work of Ekman on the roots of emotional expression focuses on behavior, in this case, nonverbal expression, as the basis for understanding the experiential state, again avoiding verbal content and the introspective world of depression.

This style, direction in thinking, is in accord with the strong behavioristic trend in psychology generally, influenced primarily by the teachings of Thorndike through Skinner. But, also, from the learning field, Harlow's "behavioral" learning approach brings with it the notion that we might be able to reproduce in animals the circumstances and the emotions we wish to study in humans. Thus, we see in the related comparative work described by Kaufman a similar model of depression in the infant monkey brought about by early separation from the mother, but a phenomenon that turns out not to be universal, occurring in only one of the two species studied. Seligman introduces a quite different model, one based on an enduring state of "learned helplessness," a condition produced in the animal by the early experiences of persistent, uncontrollable trauma.

As regards the "animal model," it is useful to note that it is certainly possible that animals experience depressive-like affect, which thus provides the possibility of developing an animal model for a specific clinical state. A number of scholars feel that the development of pathology of mood states occurred earlier than cognitive pathology in the evolutionary process and that although it is extremely unlikely that one could ever develop an animal model for as complex a thinking disorder as schizophrenia, it is possible for the affective state of depression. The separation of infant monkeys from their mothers and the depletion of catecholamines with pharmacological tools have been tried by scientists with success. The pioneer workers in this field include Drs. Harlow, Kaufman, McKinney, Maas, and Redmond. It is possible to produce animals that seem uninterested in their environment and show behavior that could be interpreted as depressed. It remains, however, a model, a simulated state, one that bears resemblance to, but cannot as yet be validly extrapolated to depressive mood in a human being.

To clarify and assess the progress of traditional psychodynamic approaches to the understanding of these phenomena, Chodoff's review of research on the premorbid personality in depression, provides a highly thoughtful analysis of the best research of the psychoanalytic era. In selecting the most significant research studies on the characteristics of depression-prone people, he notes the lack of adequate technology and argues for the importance of finding a middle ground. In order to attack the really important clinical research problems in this sphere, psychological methods must be developed which are capable of capturing the complexity of the experiential state, yet which still meet basic scientific requirements. The analysis keeps us in contact with the important advances and continuing controversies in that highly complex approach to understanding human behavior. Schmale, also, brings psychodynamic thinking to bear on the concepts of "helplessness and hopelessness," the antecedents of depression, but more from the standpoint of traditional clinical medicine. These are concepts that he and George Engel have contributed and that have had such a marked impact over the years on clinical research, generally, particularly in the fields of depression and psychosomatic medicine. Klerman summarizes various fragments of work which are more eclectic in their theoretical orientation. He reviews, for example, recent work on refining the systems of classification, research contrasting the more recent systems—bipolar-unipolar, primary-secondary (Robins), and new typologies with traditional schemes; explores new insights into the relations between personality structure and specific manifestations of depression, and examines the new investigational and measurement emphasis on the impact of "life events" on the depression-prone person.

Finally, as regards theory and research, Beck provides a broad view of his notions about the power of cognition, the "negative set" in assuming command of the depressed human organism. By proposing that the cognitive disorder *precedes* rather than follows the depressed state, he contributes alternative ways of thinking about etiology and approaches to therapy.

It is important to call attention to that final discussion in the volume in which a substantial set of recommendations is presented about possible directions of research, a list the breadth of which would probably not have been developed 10 years earlier. They reflect new areas of research activity and identify critical issues. Such issues that appear reasonably open to attack now consist of the following:

1. Distinguishing between "normal" and clinical depression, between depression as an affect and as a clinical syndrome. Recent work indicates that it is not the intensity of mood that distinguishes patients from normals but rather how severely the behavior and social performance are impaired—how capable patients are of continuing to function adequately in everyday activities.

2. Identifying characteristics of child and adult populations at high risk for developing clinical depression in later life.

3. Characterizing the "depression-prone" personality.

4. Investigating the influence of culture on the etiology and nature of depression.

5. Extending the notion of animal models beyond the "infantile separation" model to others to permit the testing of concepts like "learned helplessness."

6. Experiments which will test the comparative validity of various assertions from the new behavior and cognitive theories.

The newer behavioral methods described in detail by Lewinsohn, treatment techniques that grow directly out of the Beck cognitive set theory, the renewed emphasis on characterizing and quantifying the impact of "life events," and the proposed animal models all help set out new guidelines for the future.

Against a background, then, of what appeared to be an area of serious neglect in the field of clinical research, we now find a more diverse set of theories developing and a new style of experimental attack in unraveling the nature of this enigmatic human state.

Success in resolving the complex interrelationship of biology and psychology, and solving the major issues of etiology and treatment, is still a long way off. But if we can project from the results of this recent conference, there is now more reason to be optimistic about its attainment.

AUTHOR INDEX

Numbers in italics refer to the pages on which the complete references are listed.

SUBJECT INDEX

A

Adult character:
  manic depressive, 63
Adverse events, 9
Affect of depression, 283–284
Affective depression, 190, 197
Affective disorders, 244
Affective expression, 103
Age, 150–151
  and social skill, 176
Aged, the:
  and disengagement, 175
  feelings of rejection, 176
  loss of interest, 176
  motivation, 176
  potentially reinforcing events, 176
  psychophysiological symptoms, 175
  response-contingent-positive
      reinforcement, 176
  self-esteem, 176
  and suicide, 189, 193, 195–196, 199
  turning inward, 176
Aggression (see Hostility; Anger)
Aggressive acts, 42–44
Aggressive drives, 137
Aging, 175–176
  disengagement, 175
  rate of behavior, 175
Agitation, 250

Amine hypothesis, 243
Amines, 248
AMPT, 247, 249
Anaclitic depression, 115, 292
Anal elements, 61
Anger, 42–44
Animal model, 132–134, 241, 261, 262,
      292–294
  anaclitic depression, 252
  escape-avoidance behavior, 86
  immunization from hopelessness, 121
  learned helplessness, 83, 85–88, 114,
      117–120, 262, 293
  loss and separation, 115–117, 132, 133,
      292–293
  norepinephrine, 241
  reinforcement, 29
  Reserpine, 241
  social communication, 132
Anorexia, 181
Antidepressant drugs, 133, 236
  (See also drugs by name)
Anxiety, 92–93, 99, 135, 153, 259–262,
      283
Appetite, 190
Arousal of defenses, 134–135
Assertive training, 104
Autonomic reactivity, 165, 167
Autonomous course, 140
Availability of reinforcement in the envi-
      ronment (AvaiRe), 158, 160